Law and Society Today

LAW AND
SOCIETY TODAY

Riaz Tejani

UNIVERSITY OF CALIFORNIA PRESS

University of California Press, one of the most distinguished university presses in the United States, enriches lives around the world by advancing scholarship in the humanities, social sciences, and natural sciences. Its activities are supported by the UC Press Foundation and by philanthropic contributions from individuals and institutions. For more information, visit www.ucpress.edu.

University of California Press
Oakland, California

Library of Congress Cataloging-in-Publication Data

Names: Tejani, Riaz, 1977- author.
Title: Law and society today / Riaz Tejani.
Description: Oakland, California : University of California Press, [2019] | Includes bibliographical references and index. |
Identifiers: LCCN 2019011918 (print) | LCCN 2019017017 (ebook) | ISBN 9780520968400 (ebook) | ISBN 9780520295742 (pbk. : alk. paper)
Subjects: LCSH: Sociological jurisprudence—History. | Sociological jurisprudence—United States—History.
Classification: LCC K370 (ebook) | LCC K370 .T45 2019 (print) | DDC 340/.115—dc23
LC record available at https://lccn.loc.gov/2019011918

Manufactured in the United States of America

28 27 26 25 24 23 22 21 20 19
10 9 8 7 6 5 4 3 2 1

For Aina and Milo

Contents

Preface

Welcome to *Law and Society Today*. This book is the culmination of twenty years of reading, talking, writing, and teaching about pathways between legal norms and institutions on one hand and society and culture on the other. At the start of those twenty years I was, like many of you, a student getting my feet wet in the subject.

Sociolegal studies—as the "law and society" field is often called—was surprisingly mysterious to me. It had to be more than just alternating looks at law and social processes. It had to be its own thing. But in those years experts weren't sure what that was exactly. Was it the "sociology of law"? Kind of, but sociology was far from the only approach; it also needed the input of anthropologists, political scientists, historians, and so forth. Was it going to help prelaw students with a glimpse of law school, or law practice? Again, kind of, but it had to be neither of those two things, since it was a college course about law *in* society. I distinctly recall my professors eschewing any core textbooks. They didn't even use "readers" or essay collections. In those days there weren't any. They gathered their own favorite articles and released them to us—with all the proper copyright permissions, I am quite sure.

Fifteen years later, given the chance to teach a law and society course in the University of Illinois system, I jumped at it. By that time, there were numerous dedicated textbooks, readers, and collections. Yet I found most—even the best ones—lacking in important ways. By that time, I also had a law degree of my own (plus a gently used membership in the California Bar), as well as a PhD in sociocultural anthropology with an emphasis in law and politics. I found the available books overly formal and institutional in their presentation, heavily weighted toward criminal justice as colleges and universities had grown to emphasize that major as a vocational value-add, or dominated by the theory and methods of sociology—where much of the early law and society research had taken place. Above all, most were written by nonlawyers who paid little attention to what lawyers actually did as engaged members of the society they affected.

I wanted a body of material I could proudly offer my students that was lively in its presentation and interested in *both* civil and criminal justice systems (after all, the number of civil cases filed in federal court in 2017 outnumbers the number of criminal cases by about four to one).[1] I wanted a text that drew from all of the relevant law and society disciplines, including anthropology, history, public policy, economics, and law. And I wanted something that spoke about the inner workings of law—about doctrine and procedure, for example—as only lawyers might know it. My students, I felt, deserved such a text. But there was none out there.

So I decided to assemble my own. I began by collecting raw articles, book chapters, and mixed media the way my own professors had more than a decade earlier. I then put together dozens of lesson plans, Power Point slide decks, question-and-answer sessions, quizzes, and writing assessments around these materials. I taught from these resources for several years to high student satisfaction—including feedback from former pupils that they were now using some of this stuff in their first-year law school days. Finally, in late 2016, I was speaking with Maura Roessner from UC Press and she told me they were looking for a fresh approach to law and society for a new course text. I said I thought I had one and explained it. She agreed, and it became this book.

Law and Society Today is the lively, comprehensive, interdisciplinary book I wished I had had when I began teaching the subject. It draws from the major fields that make up sociolegal studies while inviting you, the reader, to evaluate the contributions each has made. It presents key theories that law and society has long held dear—like critical race theory, historical materialism, disciplinary power, and more—but it always checks these against current and recent examples from the worlds of civil and criminal justice. In its final pages, it looks to the future, to new developments like genetics, climate change, and social media, to ask how far our current understandings will reach in explaining the worlds of tomorrow.

In bringing together these disparate sources and influences, this book covers a lot of ground. It understands that this course is taught in a wide array of academic settings and departments, course levels, and degree programs. It remains versatile in its language, abstraction, and theoretical suppositions. Instructors can easily skip sections here or there or take them out of order if that suits local needs better. Factual examples chosen are interesting and current, but there are always more happening every day. Students should feel welcome to bring their own experience to supplement all that this book claims to offer. In that sense, the book really is about law and society *today*. *Today* means the issues are pressing, and the book tries to earn your attention for them in a way that most others take for granted. *Today* means the issues are all around you, in the technologies you use to be a good student or in the stories that connect you with your peers. *Today* means the book combines ideas in ways that might surprise an older generation of students. And *today* implies a yesterday to build upon and a tomorrow worth working hard for.

Acknowledgments

Many things happened as this book came into being. Some were just life being lived, others the very opposite. I lost my dear wife Elina to complications from leukemia in November 2017. She had supported this project from the moment I discussed it with her in her hospital bed in St. Louis. She would have been proud to see it completed, and reaching its audience. She taught me so much in our ten years together. An exemplary human being, she was a quiet but firm voice for justice of all varieties. The sections on human genetics especially bear her traces: Elina was a geneticist by vocation and a biochemist by training. She was one of the smartest and most gifted people I ever met, and I miss her tremendously. But she left me with two bright, kind, and curious children named Aina and Milo. They have her best qualities. Throughout our journey, they held me close as much as I did them. For their unbridled intellect and innate sense of right and wrong, both of which influence my thinking, I thank them deeply.

Most of the book was written in Springfield, Illinois, where I was on faculty at the local University of Illinois campus. There, in the months after Elina's death, the children and I were taken in by a local family whose sense of adventure, intellectual curiosity, and creative expression gave us energy to continue. For this, I thank the wonderful Gwen Griffen and her own junior support crew—Flossie, Sophia, and Ivan. The energy that went into completing this project at such a difficult time could not have been mustered without the fortuitous partnership between our families.

Similarly my collegial family at the University of Illinois–Springfield helped considerably. They hired me to be the "law and society" guy in the first place, and then when family crisis hit they relieved me of extraneous obligations. They checked in on me relentlessly and offered assistance every time. Without that support, I could not have finished this book. For this I have to thank Eugene McCarthy, Gwen Jordan, Deborah Anthony, Richard Gilman-Opalsky, Brandon Derman, John Transue, Mark and Ellie Buxton, and Tih-Fen Ting. Other supporters in the community deserving mention are Sara Phillips, John and Sharon Kwedar, Peggy and Richard Fix, Jesse and Nina Harris, Kitsy and Jackie Armhein, and the Suess, Rothfus, and Price families.

Prior to completion of this book I moved to the University of Redlands. There, I benefited from the collegiality and support of new colleagues, including Carlo Carrascoso, Denise MacNeil, Allison Fraiburg, Neena Gopalan, and Johannes Moenius. I also thank Kathy Ogren, Thomas Horan, and Keith Roberts for generally supporting projects of this nature.

Finally, at UC Press, Maura Roessner was a superb editor; she remained both gracious toward my situation and demanding in her expectations of the material. Editorial assistants Sabrina Robleh and Madison Wetzell were a pleasure to work with, as was ace copy editor Elisabeth Magnus. Finally, I'd like to thank the reviewers who provided voluminous feedback on the chapters included here. Thanks especially to Shane A. Gleason, Benjamin Kassow, John Sloan, and Mihaela Serban.

INTRODUCTION

*L*aw and Society Today is the first-ever problem-oriented survey of sociolegal studies that smoothly integrates important theories with easily understood real-world examples. It offers the reader a broad overview of law and society *after* the significant economic and political changes of the 2000s and 2010s, including, among other things, the rise of *neoliberalism* and the large influence of law and economics in law teaching, policy debates, and judicial decision making. In Unit 1, the reader learns about the unique and important orientation behind this fresh approach. The Introduction explains why a new approach is important today and situates the book amid existing survey books and readers in the law and society community. Chapter 2, "Where Law Meets Society," explores some of the key issues that arise as law and society both change quickly and struggle to keep pace with one another. Chapter 3, "Comparative Legal Communities," then broadens these horizons by placing North American law and society in its broader, global context of parent legal families and the diverse nations of the world around us.

Introduction: Legal and Social Change

1

Gene splicing, presidential tweets, superstorms, and kids with three parents. What do these all have in common? They are all new, and they all combine the powerful changing forces of law and society. Some might have sounded like fiction a generation ago, but today they are almost commonplace. These advances in technology, new norms about freedom of speech, accumulated effects of air and water pollution, and redefinitions of the family all sit at the boundary between what is legally and socially permissible.

The field of law and society, or sociolegal studies, has always been about this interplay of legal and social change. Experts in the field long studied cases where reasonable people were trying to make sense of innovations in law by living them in the real world, or innovations in culture by interpreting them for the law. But over the years, the core books about law and society became relatively fixed even as law and social change seemed to have accelerated. Some emphasized the theories that had been developed without checking these against real-world examples, while others proceeded topically through institutions almost like science books, walking the reader through the various "systems" of law and society as though these could be understood like systems of the body or the physical world. The truth is that legal and social practices are complex because people are complex. And law and society change because people are constantly changing.

Law and Society Today takes change seriously by offering a new approach to this fascinating field. It adopts an *integrated* approach to theory and evidence, and it incorporates the latest thinking about how communities determine right and wrong by prioritizing legal and social norms. By integrating theory and evidence, the book chooses not to present these in wholly separate sections of text. Rather, it maintains attention to both simultaneously, making abstract concepts and ideas more readily memorable to the reader and taking seriously the "grounded theory" approach of some social science fields. To put it more simply, theory and evidence "flow" together more smoothly in ways not present in other existing treatments. Isn't that closer to how the real world operates?

Additionally, this book adopts a *constructivist* approach to the topic that many will find novel. The idea is not to suggest that there is no "real" world but rather to posit that our understandings of it come to us from working with the building blocks of knowledge—things like language, symbols, practices, and beliefs. Experts in fields like anthropology, sociology, literature, and cultural studies have been looking at things this way for a while, so it was time to incorporate their advancements into discussions about law and society. This doesn't mean we must take for granted that law is socially constructed, or society legally constructed, but it does suggest that we consider those claims as we evaluate the phenomena captured in the chapters below.

Finally, *Law and Society Today* will strike readers as "new" for taking on the role of economic thought in Western life today. Most in the social sciences and humanities have been calling this prominent role "neoliberalism." This technical-sounding word simply stands for "market fundamentalism"—the notion that many of our big social problems can be fixed by giving people more freedom, letting them compete to gain greater wealth, and then allowing them to spend that wealth as they see fit. Social security, Medicare, welfare, food stamps, public housing—all of these are considered counterproductive under neoliberalism because ultimate faith lies in the individual person or family to take care of itself. When this breaks down—as it sometimes does—nongovernmental actors are better at handling the solutions. Law and governments should stay clear, because they don't operate efficiently and don't encourage returning to individual autonomy. So the thinking goes.

The influence of this thought on law and society in real-world settings has been enormous. In the core study of law, a relatively recent school of thought called law and economics has made substantial inroads in legal education globally so that new lawyers cannot finish their training without exposure, if not conversion, to the supposed wisdom of markets. In social policy, the exact government programs listed above—ones relied upon by millions in the United States and abroad—have experienced deep cutbacks for lack of public support. What I mean is this: faith in markets as the solution to social problems may or may not be well founded, but we should at least agree that it has become deeply influential. It is that deep influence that this new law and society book is able to capture.

Yet this book is not altogether new. Like its predecessors, it maintains an abiding interest in the social justice questions and concepts that have driven law and society conversations for so many years. How does the sovereign power of the state circulate so far out from state institutions? What does it mean that those we imprison for crime are so disproportionately racialized, gendered, and poor? How are categories like race, gender, and poverty themselves created through legal measures against crime? All of these questions run though much of this book; it is therefore faithful to the classic law and society subfields such as critical race theory, prison studies, law and poverty, and civil and human rights. Experienced readers will therefore recognize familiar topics like gender intersectionality woven into the existing chapter on identity, or criminology in the chapter comparing criminal and civil justice systems. The point was not to lose the baby with the bathwater, but to hold the baby in new and enriching ways perhaps more suited to the new future it faces.

When I came to teach law and society to a new crop of undergraduates several years ago, it was clear to me that a reboot for the subject was very much in order. A lot had changed since I was a student. Explaining why, this introductory chapter is divided into two remaining sections. In the first, it maps out in greater detail key sites for *sociolegal change.* There it describes changes to daily life that challenge existing social and legal norms. It then moves to discuss broader cultural change brought on by an increasingly "diverse" or *multicultural citizenry.* Next, it describes new developments in *technology* that push the boundaries of accepted behavior in both law and social life. Building on this, the section looks then at the phenomenon we now call *globalization* as a fourth major change agent placing stress on existing rules and processes. Finally, following from globalization is a new problem described below as *legal pluralism*—the idea that multiple legal systems might have to coexist under one single jurisdiction, government, or geographic area. Together, I hope it becomes clear, these changes offer important justification for the ongoing study of law and society, as well as for a revised approach that tries to view it today as a process of "mutual constitution." As I will reiterate throughout, the book's general claim is that the "social" role of law is being gradually but increasingly construed as *economic*—about the maximization of wealth more than the search for what is morally "right."

As seen below, the many changes confronting us today—for instance, multiculturalism and globalization—have seemed to encourage this shift. The moral basis of law becomes harder to pursue or justify when there are numerous historical, religious, and cultural traditions to choose from. In a diverse society, in other words, *who* should get to decide right from wrong? The move to economic definitions of "right" appears to escape this problem. There seems to be no

Figure 1.1 George Albert Harris, *Banking and Law*, mural on Coit Tower, San Francisco, CA, 1934.

"who" required when valuations of right and wrong come down to a basic, mathematical formula about money. Legal decisions favoring the greatest wealth-creating activity, or party, want to appeal to a supposedly universal, human drive toward greater prosperity, comfort, and security. And yet, the clear problem is how to assess prosperity, comfort, and security. For the financially literate today it might mean numbers on the page of a bank or investment account statement. For an older generation perhaps it meant cash money under a mattress. For today's young people, the comfort brought by greater financial reward may pale in comparison to the discomfort brought by rampant inequality, or global environmental degradation. What benefit are new industrial jobs when the factories they support spew harmful emissions? What is an extra million dollars when the future of human habitation on earth is now in question?

These questions were already being posed by indigenous cultures in Asia, North America, Australia, and the South Pacific when they were first contacted by European settlers centuries ago. Yet economic determinism—the notion that the natural world exists for human wealth exploitation—spread through the ages of discovery, colonization, industrialization, and now globalization. Today, it may be the predominant lens through which Western law and policy makers view the world. *Law and Society Today* invites you to reflect upon this progression, its implications, and its alternatives.

SOCIAL CHANGE

Books such as this often begin with an inventory of "social change." They remind the reader that the world is constantly shifting and that law must continue to adapt. This adaptation impulse is meant to justify the investment of time and energy in courses on law and society. More often than not, authors of these books are social scientists, most commonly sociologists. For them, "social change" is very low-lying fruit: it is the very same phenomenon that justifies, perhaps more than any other field, sociology in the first place. For this reason, our first response may be to ask why this is uniquely important to law and society. The answer would almost certainly be that "social change" causes an ongoing *gap* between society and the law meant to govern it.[1]

Law and Society Today does not begrudge studies of this gap. But it hopes to add more nuances to its discussion. Any chasm between what law means to accomplish and its actual effect on social practices, relations, and structures—we must recognize—is a product of changes not just in society but also *in law itself*. If I were a sociologist I might find this statement vexing: Without legal training how would I know what law *is*, let alone what it *was*, so that I could observe changes? How could I get inside the minds of legislators, judges, and attorneys, the parties most responsible for bringing about change in the legal system? And why would sociologists give up the notion that society reigns supreme even over legal authority when doing so might mean surrendering the terrain on which sociological expertise is based?

This book's approach, therefore, is not to discard sociological approaches but to temper those with veritable legal knowledge. Its author is a trained lawyer and social anthropologist offering the reader unique access to some of the fascinating, technical aspects of law that make it non-negotiable even in social spaces, as well as access to the "culture" of expertise itself that makes the tension between legal and social knowledge so fraught, and so interesting. The competition between the trained lawyer and the trained social scientist, I suggest, in other words, is itself a key dimension of law and society and forms an important part of any thorough survey of this exciting field.

There can be little doubt that social practice changes fast, and this is at least a part of why we study law and society. A list of such recent changes is easy to generate. Over the past thirty years, for example, we have witnessed a near revolution in the structure of family relations in the Western world. Fewer adult couples are getting married, most do so at a later age, and many who choose to marry wind up in divorce proceedings and settlements. As a result, single families are now spread across two or more households, and arrangements that once were determined privately (e.g., school tuition, parental time) are now determined by courts or dispute settlement officers.

At the same time, the processes by which we make families have expanded. Many traditional couples seek out clinical services for in vitro fertilization

(IVF), allowing two parents to have children despite signs of infertility, advanced age, or even in some cases the death of one of the genetic parents. The same technology now permits same-sex couples to bear a child and allows surrogate mothers to carry fertilized eggs to term in cases where the genetic mother is unable or unwilling to undergo the experience. IVF and surrogacy are both governed by private contracts between parents and service providers, and except in rare circumstances the courts are unlikely to intervene against validly formed agreements in these markets.

Another key area of changing social practice has been the public role of religion in the West. Whereas Catholicism and Protestantism were once the dominant faiths of people in England, France, and the United States, today they are but some among many belief systems and institutions espoused by communities in each of these metropolitan countries. **Public law** tends not to favor one religion over another, and indeed the doctrine of "separation between church and state" has been institutionalized in France and the United States with different nuances in each. But apart from this **separation doctrine,** social practice in these Western countries has increasingly deemphasized religion as a decisive form of belonging and community. The once-common practice of shuttering stores on Sunday has given way to remaining open seven days a week, ostensibly on the realization that opportunities for profit do not stop in the name of tradition. The once-popular phrase "Merry Christmas" has given way to "Happy Holidays," acknowledging in part the decline of Christianity's social dominance and the rise of greater diversity of belief and practice. Both of these examples, it should be observed, have been met with anxiety and frustration among groups who view them as indicators of spiritual abandonment or merely "political correctness." In any event, the religious underpinning of civic rules about official holidays, commerce, and public observance appears to be on the wane.

Meanwhile, in criminal law, one of the most important new developments in the United States has been the complete or partial legalization of marijuana in many states. While marijuana remains a "Schedule I" controlled substance according to federal law, its usage for medicinal and recreational purposes has grown significantly among the "millennial" generation—those born just before and after the year 2000. States wanting to reduce their prison population or gain tax revenue from this growing economy have, incrementally over the past few decades, reduced law enforcement, moved to legalize prescribed medical use, and finally decriminalized entirely this widespread substance.

These are but a few examples where changing social practice has had immediate and overt implications for law and law enforcement in recent years. They remind us that legal norms are often an extension of social norms and that evolution in some of the basic ways we live our lives leads to adjustments in law and adjudication. But beyond everyday practice Western societies have changed in more profound, long-term ways that deserve emphasis.

MULTICULTURALISM

The first of these is sociocultural diversity. *Diversity* refers here to the plenitude of difference in the human environment. We call this "sociocultural" because the differences we recognize are both social (dealing with the way people relate to one another) and cultural (dealing with the way people communicate with and interpret one another).

Take for example the midsized American city of Long Beach, California. If you lived in that city in 1970 and were "white," that is to say of European or Caucasian descent, you would reside in an area where some 85 percent of your neighbors were also "white."[2] Under those conditions, ability to read and understand English, interest in attending a Christian church, and enthusiasm to celebrate Christmas and Easter would have been so widespread as to be taken for granted. The municipal laws of Long Beach in those days may or may not have been effective in maintaining complete order (recall that 1970 came just after the urban unrest of the late 1960s), but they would at least be considered reflective of the values of most residents.

Fast-forward to the year 2010. In that year Long Beach was one of the most socioculturally diverse cities in all of the United States (see figure 1.2). Its white-only (i.e., non-mixed-race) population was 30 percent,[3] and much of the remaining 70 percent of the now larger population hailed from a vast array of countries that included Vietnam, Cambodia, the Philippines, India, China, Korea, Mexico, El Salvador, and Guatemala among many others. With them on arrival to the city came distinct social structures (e.g., family relations) as well as cultural practices (e.g., food preparation, worship, and community celebrations). Now one must ask whether everyone in the city can read English sufficiently to understand municipal laws and signage. If not, what languages should law appear in? How will courts operate when managing disputes among and between these groups? And how do they adjudicate cases in which state law conflicts with ethnic or community values?

Even more starkly, the law of immigration itself has shaped whether and how "new" arrivals have even come to settle in the West. In the case of legal immigration, the United States long observed "preferences" in national origin (i.e., "what country you come from"). This meant that those leaving from some countries were legally more welcomed to immigrate than those leaving others.[4]

Meanwhile, undocumented immigration remains a highly sensitive issue. Some have embraced the factually erroneous idea that clandestine immigration to the United States is largely responsible for extant criminality and for economic stagnation among select segments of the society. During the Obama administration, periodic waves of undocumented youth migration from Central America proved especially troublesome as leaders struggled to balance compassion and sanctuary with fiscal responsibility and public backlash. More recently, the Trump administration presided over the longest government shutdown in

Figure 1.2 Cambodian traditional dancers performing *La légende de l'Apsara Méra*. Photo by Jean-Pierre Dalbera, 2010 (Creative Commons). The ethnic Cambodian population of Long Beach, California, is one of the largest outside of Southeast Asia.

United States history over financing for a border wall premised on unfounded beliefs about the threats posed by Central American migrants and asylum seekers. In reality, the undocumented immigration issue has been a recurring part of domestic US politics since at least the Second World War, and it often follows cycles of economic boom and bust in the American working class.

An important reason to reflect on this involves refugee and asylum policy. Traditionally, the United States and western Europe have acted as havens for the destitute and endangered populations of the Global South. Refugees and asylees have been welcomed and allowed to normalize their status in the new host country on the primary basis that, were they to return home (though "home" often no longer exists), they would face grave danger. Drawing on a **liberal tradition** that values compassion for humanity and deemphasizes ethnic divisions, Western nations have prided themselves on welcoming such people. In many cases, this pride is also mixed with a sense of duty: countries like the United States, England, and France have been complicit in destabilizing refugee-sending countries through postwar colonialism, military interventions, and forced economic reforms.[5] Unfortunately, these feelings of pride and duty are increasingly absent. The contemporary situation in Syria, with its concomitant exodus of refugees, is one such example. There, a dictatorial regime that presided over the past several decades lost control of much of the country to Daesh ("Islamic State"), which gained momentum in the wake of the Iraq War and brutalized the civilian population struggling to escape. Willingness to accept these escapees, who are bystanders to a global conflict that has drawn in the United States and Russia, has been waning in both Europe and the United States, with many Americans voting in 2016 on the fear that "their" country was being overrun by people who claimed to be refugees but were actually terrorists readying to strike.

Multiculturalism, in short, brings challenges for domestic law, and therefore law and society studies. While on one hand legal institutions and rules must adapt to better handle new arrivals, their doing so poses some adjustments to the circumstances of host communities. At the same time, a sound reading of law and society in the chapters below teaches that law is *always* working to manage difference and belonging among communities. Under modern multiculturalism, the forms of difference may be new, but the struggles are not.

TECHNOLOGY

A second key agent of change has been technology. This has brought revolutions in social interaction, which, in turn, pose challenges for legal rights, redress, and remedies.

One example comes from the sheer quantum leap in computer processing speed and data transmission. Whereas it was once cutting edge to operate entire government agencies on the power of wall-to-wall computer mainframes, today the power of those units has been condensed down into pocket watches, handheld devices, and even children's toys. On the larger end of the spectrum, buildings full of computer servers (computers that store and transmit data rather than merely process for personal use) are able to channel, collect, and sort all of human knowledge in a matter of days or even hours. This has brought about the "**big data**" revolution where information collected from online activity, credit card transactions, vehicle registration, ATM withdrawals, and telephone conversations is collected on every participating member of society. Using the supercomputing strength mentioned above, companies and state agencies are able to compose a profile of behavior that can in turn be used for law enforcement, product marketing, and political analysis.

The success of "big data" has depended upon several other developments in technological hardware and software. Smartphones now connect roughly 70 percent of Americans to one another.[6] This increased connectivity seems to have resulted in greater detachment from real-world activity, causing more personal injuries from distraction in auto and pedestrian accidents, and in rare but notable cases death from "selfie" photographs in precarious positions (e.g., near cliffs). It has also boosted the proliferation of "fake news" and conspiracy theories through fast-spreading "memes" and unverified information sources.

Obsessions with handheld devices and smartphones, as well as with the "selfie," are themselves outgrowths of new "social media." Unlike traditional media, sometimes called the Fourth Estate as an additional check on government powers, **social media** comprises the general population communicating en masse in direct, distributed fashion. Facebook, Twitter, and Snapchat are only the latest commercial incarnations of a revolution that began years ago with platforms such as Six Degrees, Friendster, and MySpace. Common to all of these has been a capacity for individuals to create a "profile"—essentially an online home base or personal space to which can be appended biographical information, photographs, interests, and so forth. Also common have been easy, push-button interactions such as "poke" or "like" that in a single click tell friends (and "big data" collectors) one's preferences, tastes, and whereabouts.

Social media have introduced a whole new host of challenges for law. If one of law's real-world functions has been to exercise social control—to keep people behaving in useful ways—this function was initially absent in the early days of social media. Today, legislators and law enforcement, not to mention media platforms themselves, are coming to terms with how best to police virtual interaction to prevent injury and criminality. In the months before and after the 2016 election, for example, hate speech exploded on Facebook and Twitter in a manner that clearly expressed real social pathologies, but also in a manner that was often not actionable on the part of law enforcement, even if one particular agency held jurisdiction. Well before this, courts were already hard pressed to find liability in cases of online defamation—reputational harm caused by online speech—because the companies hosting such information, for example Facebook, Google, and Twitter, and Snapchat, had been granted immunity to prevent overcensorship in this developing medium.

GLOBALIZATION

Increased connectivity through social media transcends erstwhile national borders and is therefore itself part of the larger evolution we call "**globalization.**" But globalization is more than just the advent of better connectivity. It is also the advent of a new global space in which previously separated groups and institutions act upon and against one another. More than ever, what globalization means is that policy action taken in one locale, say inside the US state of California, can have direct impact on experience and life chances in once remote places such as the rainforest of El Salvador. Internal approaches to food labeling in France, meanwhile, may immediately affect the livelihood of West African plantation workers. The connectivity relevant to understanding globalization is therefore not simply the social connectivity described above; it must also include connections through information, finance, migration, and trade.

Similarly and paradoxically, globalization has heightened transnational connections but diminished local connections for many. When labor migration brings foreign workers to small-town America, for example, locals have a harder time settling disputes among themselves and must instead submit in greater numbers to the sovereign power of the courthouse. In this way, many feel, "community" is lost to global linkages that favor high-level commercial gain while ignoring local culture, custom, and control. With this loss of community may also come a loss of common values. Long-standing ideas of "right" and "wrong"—even ones that differed in their local flavor from broader national ideas—may become challenged by the arrival of new residents bringing their own traditions, lifeways, and worldviews. Sometimes, as in the case where a local community *fears* outsiders as different or inferior, this can be a good challenge. Other times, such as where small towns have been able to settle conflicts peaceably among themselves, this challenge can be destructive and costly.

Scholars in the fields of international relations (IR) and cultural anthropology have long studied these developments. IR has evolved through several key phases, beginning initially with the tradition known as *liberalism.* There, humanity is understood as essentially good and productive, and international policies between nations are framed with this in mind. Countries should, accordingly, treat each other with respect and support to foster economic integration and growth, and the philosophical tenets of freedom, equality, and private property ownership should all be cultivated through international dealings. Against these assumptions, the tradition of *realism* emerged in the Cold War era to describe the new world order of international risk, threat, and deterrence. If liberal thinkers believed people and the countries they represented were inherently good, realists believed these actors were in fact, deep down, bent on conquest and expansion. The realist experts believed that the world was a dangerous place and that countries should be prepared at all times for national defense at almost any cost.

Toward the end of the twentieth century, Western nations became increasingly involved in **development** around the world. Countries that had been left impoverished after decolonization, and therefore susceptible to the realist expansionism described previously, could benefit from direct investment and nongovernmental (e.g., charities) support on the ground. Under this regime, international relations began to forge themselves not through state-level action but rather between and among members of international "civil society." Describing this new order, *constructivism* entered as the third main school of international relations. IR constructivists borrowed heavily from the neighboring field of cultural anthropology, in which international fieldworkers spent great amounts of time in the developing world learning about lifeways, infrastructure, religion, and family ties—just some of the many "everyday" ways in which societies are built and maintained. By studying these aspects of social and economic life in their daily context, researchers gained a picture of how people in faraway places constructed and viewed the world around them. Realizing that these same people, through the rise of international migration and trade, maintained connections with family and friends far across national borders, researchers came to view them as increasingly responsible for what has come to be called "globalization." Much like the constructivists of IR, this book looks for the *human* building blocks of law and society.

LEGAL PLURALISM

Finally, *pluralism* refers to the condition of having many objects or ideas under one heading. For example, America is religiously "pluralist" insofar as it contains at least six different major religions. Though one may be sociologically dominant, the presence of the others in strong numbers causes shifts to the overall culture such that "Merry Christmas" in companies' commercial marketing has mutated to "Happy Holidays" with the aim of not excluding any one religious group from their market. **Legal pluralism**, then, must refer to the presence of multiple legal regimes under one geopolitical unit. A geopolitical unit might be a country, or it might be a continent. If it is legally pluralistic, it has two or more legal systems that apply to its people for different reasons. In some instances members of different religious communities may be best governed by the laws of their own religion, even though they reside in a place with other religions. Israel, a country with Christians, Jews, and Muslims in large numbers, is one such place. India, with Hindus and Muslims along with Buddhists, Sikhs, and Jains, is another.

It surprises many to learn that the United States observes similar legal pluralism on religious grounds. Here, state law governs matters of marriage and the family, but marriage contracts can specify arbitration in the case of conflicts before a religious cleric. Orthodox Jews are one community that avails itself of these services, in which rabbis can rightfully serve as adjudicators among American Jews. Use of the same practice by American Muslims has attracted considerable attention and fear in recent decades as lawmakers and activists have railed against an "invasion" of Islamic sharia law into the United States. Beneath this alarmism, however, actual use of Islamic law by formal American legal institutions is nearly negligible, and reactions against it may serve more of a political function than anything else.

But the domestic reaction to sharia in the United States points to the very real development of diversity in culture and values within single American jurisdictions. Whereas a county or a state used to be characterized as having a singular "cultural background" from which laws could be derived—for instance German in Pennsylvania or Dutch in New York—today even small towns in the rural Midwest are home to a wider variety of people and their national origins. Court systems must be more willing to offer non-English translations and interpreters, and attorneys must be better able to communicate with clients from backgrounds different from their own.

Beyond the presence of differing legal cultures under one legal "system," we are also witnesses to the growth of multisystemic jurisdictions where single sovereign territories might be composed of multiple subsidiary legal systems. On the one hand this is not new; it has existed for centuries in the governing form known as federalism. **Federalism** describes the coexistence of two levels of sovereignty in a nation-state. The United States, from its foundation, has been a key exemplar of federalism. For most of its history, a large portion of legislation and policy—the portion that most directly affects people's lives—is created and administered at the state level. California, Idaho, Georgia, and Massachusetts all, for example, administer their own webs of property, family, criminal, and accident law. On top of these webs is overlaid a second layer of "federal law" created by national legislation, federal court rulings, and administrative agencies like the Environmental Protection Agency or the Department of Education. This "dualist" system has existed from the days of US independence, but it has also evolved considerably over time, so that constitutional lawyers and historians today spend decades mastering the distinctions and interconnections of state and federal authority. Importantly, federalism is by no means unique to the United States and has thrived for nearly as long in places like Switzerland, Germany, Nigeria, and India—all of which have some form of national and local power sharing.

On the other hand, legal pluralism has grown in the last fifty or so years, with more complex, larger, and more technical forms. This trend is often described as **regional integration,** where *regional* refers to the larger continents to which countries belong—Finland in Europe, for example—and *integration* the development of stronger relationships between those. The European Union remains the prime example of regional integration today. During World War II, the nations of Europe joined by the United States engaged in a bloody, costly military battle with their neighbors. The "Axis Powers" (Germany, Italy, and Japan) were aiming to control most of Europe and Southeast Asia to subjugate many of its people, and the "Allied Powers" (United States, Russia, England, Free France), were seeking to restrain the Axis bloc and liberate themselves and their neighbors. The result was a six-year conflict that nearly destroyed, physically and emotionally, much of the European region, including several key cities.

In the wake of this destruction, European leaders were faced with the difficult task of not only healing the wounds of war among neighbors but also rebuilding their metaphorical neighborhood. In a concerted effort to accomplish both, statesmen from France and Germany initially formed an "economic community," agreeing to import and export deals for the supply of coal and steel to help rebuild western European railways, bridges, roads, and buildings. Formalized in the Treaty of Paris of 1951, the European Coal and Steel

Community created the first modern international organization aimed at unifying former warring countries on the basis of a "common market" in raw materials. From there, upon realization that increased economic transactions required greater political unification, the economic community grew into a governing system with regional legislators (European Parliament), a supreme court (Court of Justice), and a president. With economic and political integration have indeed come greater peace and stability, as well as a stronger presence in global trade. However, today many have grown disillusioned with "Europeanization," as they feel the promises of prosperity it meant to bring have been fulfilled only for the regional elite. The 2016 "Brexit" vote in England was the culmination of this disillusionment and raised, for the first time since its inception, the specter of European disintegration.

Meanwhile, other continents have tried to emulate the EU model, if only in simpler forms. The Southeast Asia region is home to Association of Southeast Asian Nations (ASEAN), South America is home to the Mercado Común del Sur (MERCOSUR), and West Africa is home to the Economic Community of West African States (ECOWAS). And of course, the United States has for twenty years been—with various successes and failures—a party to the North American Free Trade Agreement (NAFTA). The goal in each of these has been to integrate a region of nations for heightened trade, security, and global presence in the way Europe has been so successful since the 1950s.

Regional integration, along with federalism before it, is an example of how legal pluralism has become a fixture of our modern world. Legal pluralism, meanwhile, is but one reason, along with social change, globalization, technology, and multiculturalism, why a closer look at law and society is so critical today. Students and practitioners of business, finance, social sciences, humanities, and law will all engage with these concepts and problems in the real world. For that reason, this text is written for nonspecialists, and it invites readers of all backgrounds to join in its journey through the key issues in *Law and Society Today*.

CHAPTER 1 REVIEW

Key Terms

- Public law
- Separation doctrine
- Liberal tradition
- Big data
- Social media
- Globalization
- Development
- Legal pluralism
- Federalism
- Regional integration

Further Discussion

1. Why is a new approach to the study of law and society warranted today?
2. Does law drive social change, or does legal change drive society?

Where Law Meets Society

Imagine a cold, rainy morning. You slept badly, your alarm didn't ring, you woke up late, and now you're late for school or work. As you walk, bike, or drive, your heart is pounding and you're worried you'll miss a test, or get fired. It's already a bad day. Now suddenly a police siren blurts into the air behind you and you leap in surprise. An officer asks you to "stop" and walks up to you. At that point you may feel nervous, angry, or even puzzled about what—if anything—you've just done wrong. The officer explains that you broke a law and must show your identification. As you reach for your ID, you're faced with a simple choice: tell the officer about the kind of day you are having in an attempt to talk your way out of trouble, or quietly hand over your documents and accept your fate before the law.

What do you do?

Law and Society Today is about the questions raised in this encounter. Why were you walking versus driving? Why were you going to work rather than school? Why did the officer stop you? Why did you feel nervous, angry, or puzzled? What rule did you actually break? Why must you have shown ID? And above all else, should you have remained silent or raised your voice to the law? The book is also about *who* gets to answer those questions. Should it be the lawyer, the judge, or the jury—empowered by institutional knowledge? Should it be the citizen, the police

Figure 2.1 Motorist stopped for moving violation in the state of Florida. Photo by Einar Jørgen Haraldseid, 2009 (Creative Commons).

officer, or the lawmaker—tuned in to what's good for "the community"? Or should it be the social scientist—trained in the study of human behavior? In most cases, we prefer to give certain questions to certain groups. Questions about transportation and work go to the social scientists. Questions about law enforcement are left for police, while questions about rules and documentation go to lawyers, judges, and lawmakers. But the last question, whether to speak or stay silent, is something no single group can answer by itself.

That is because the very meaning of law, what it's supposed to do, is actually something of a mystery. Is law a set of *formal* rules to be applied to everyone across space and time, or is it just a starting point to guide behavior while remaining *realistic* about human differences, disadvantages, and limitations in compliance? These two approaches, "formalism" and "realism," organize much of how legal thinkers approach the world. **Formalism** tells us that rules and institutions are autonomous, acting separately from social influences like politics, economy, culture, or class. **Realism** says that law can or should be serving these influences, usually to improve life for people. Over roughly the last one hundred years in American legal history, these two positions have engaged in a steady tug-of-war, with each appearing to win out in some periods but lose in others. A professor teaching law and society from the formalist perspective would emphasize the long list of legal institutions such as courts, juries, police, and prisons. A professor teaching from the realist position would emphasize the "social"—the impact and experience of these institutions upon flesh-and-blood people as viewed through sociology, psychology, and anthropology, among other things.

This book engages both views of the world and seeks a compromise. What if law is neither wholly independent of social life nor wholly subservient to it? What if, instead, law and social life, through their ongoing push and pull, actually help construct one another? This question comes from a way of thinking known as **constructivism**.

Constructivism describes the view that the objects of human thought and emotion—what we would consider "reality"—are actually made up of smaller units, the way a building or a bridge might be. Unlike true building blocks, these smaller units are simply other, taken-for-granted ideas like words, symbols, values, and so forth. The human world around us, accordingly, is not natural, or given, but something that has emerged through centuries of individual action, large-scale events, exercises of power and force, and acceptance of institutions and practices.

Our reality, in other words, is made of what the French sociologist Emile Durkheim called "social facts." A **social fact** is a truth accepted, not because it exists *outside* or *before* human thought, but because enough people have come to accept it as fact. Social facts can be disorienting, reminding us that the world is of our own making. But they can also be liberating: if facts are social, then the bad ones—ones like racism and inequality—are ones that we can improve upon. If we embrace constructivism, then we can believe we have the power to change the world for the better. This is especially hopeful for those who suffer at the hands of others, or from inequalities structured into the environment.

By embracing a constructivist approach, this book approaches law and society from outside the formalist-realist divide. Law's reality, it holds, does not fully reside in the written codes or casebooks, or in the experience of average people. It lives instead in the space between, where formal rules and practices meet and interact with the people they affect. This book assumes, in short, that law and society help construct one another.

This is not to say, by any stretch, that they are one and the same. For years, law and society teachers tried to explain the "legal" as just one small part of social life. Law, they said, was simply a form of social practice. But if this were true, then the "gap" we see between morality and law would be a mistake. Our morality tells us it is "good" to rescue a drowning stranger, but our law—at least in the English and American traditions—remains quiet about this. This gap between moral and legal norms is but one example where law does not appear as a mere subset or follower of society and instead appears to be doing something a little different. In many cases, rather than follow, law acts as a leader. This is in part due to its role as an expert community, vocation, and language. Lawyers are "learned professionals," and society still looks to them for solutions to widespread problems of injustice, inequality, and inefficiency. Law takes in new information, determines how to improve social behavior, and then implements those improvements through case decisions or new statutes—and their enforcement. In these instances, the law seeks to further social progress.

Over the past forty years, "progress" has been defined more and more in economic terms. Whereas law and society teachers could once say that moral philosophies about "right" and "wrong" were most important to the delivery of justice in society, for some today this would not be true. Today, economic theories are some of the more influential ideas about justice among high-level judges. This change has been a long time coming; high-level judges have been applying economic theories to tort law—the area of law covering all civil wrongs not arising out of contract. Writing on US accident law in 1972, Judge Richard Posner concluded that

> when the cost of accidents is less than the cost of prevention, a rational profit-maximizing enterprise will pay tort judgments to the accident victims rather than incur the larger cost of avoiding liability. Furthermore, overall economic value or welfare would be diminished rather than increased by incurring a higher accident-prevention cost in order to avoid a lower accident cost. If, on the other hand, the benefits in accident avoidance exceed the costs of prevention, society is better off if those costs are incurred and the accident averted, and so in this case the enterprise is made liable, in the expectation that self-interest will lead it to adopt the precautions in order to avoid a greater cost in tort judgments.[1]

Rather than proposing a new or revolutionary idea of accident law, Posner was in fact describing the way in which he and others felt US courts had long been treating it. For these thinkers, **negligence,** the nucleus of a **common-law** accident suit, was an economic concept, not a moral one. The list of cases influenced by this type of thinking is too long to print here. Nevertheless, it is important to note that not *all* judges base their reasoning in the principles of economics, and a strong humanist and social justice current remains among law and society professors.

But unlike almost every other law and society text, this book takes very seriously the newfound influence of law and economics. Where does it leave social explanations? Whose economic well-being does it most benefit? How does it influence law teaching, or professional ethics? And maybe most importantly, how does it affect the way we govern ourselves?

But if previous visions of law and society are dated, why even study this broad subject? *Law and Society Today* captures the new relationships between legal and social change in our contemporary world. That world now includes genetic modification, real-time video conferencing and streaming, rapid global cultural exchange, and split-second financial transactions from one side of the world to the other. A good law and society book must find a meaningful way to make sense of these changes.

In the past, scholars believed that society changed and law simply followed. Numerous examples across our legal environment could once support this position. The rise of the railroads brought an explosion in tort (e.g., personal injury) doctrine, the advent of birth control inspired Supreme Court privacy jurisprudence, and the growth of combustible petrochemicals saw changes in "strict liability" rules. But something is different today. Now the legal system itself is rapidly changing and social practices are forced to keep pace. Plea agreements and binding arbitration clauses keep a larger share of cases away from juries. Big corporate law firms have downsized. Large legal tasks such as document review are outsourced to staffing agencies. Some law jobs are even sent offshore to India and Africa at lower cost. And new software is permitting artificial intelligence machines to serve the role of legal researcher. Meanwhile, law schools graduate more legal experts with fewer open attorney jobs to gainfully employ them. Even as this all occurs, the ability for average, everyday people to access an attorney to settle problems appears to be decreasing. So the story of law "keeping up with society" may no longer hold true, and a new law and society approach must comprehend both the legal and the social spheres as capable of extreme changes in their own right.

WHAT IS LAW?

The term *law* has been given many definitions throughout the course of human history. Illustrating an approach now known as **natural law,** Aristotle called it "an embodiment of Reason, whether in the individual or the community." The British legal philosopher known for **legal positivism** called it simply "a system of rules." The American jurist Oliver Wendell Holmes, known for **legal realism**, said it was "the prophecies of what the courts will do." Although each definition is compelling, none seems broad enough from a law and society perspective.

The story that opened this chapter presented you with a choice whether to accept the officer's determination that you broke a law or whether to try to talk your way out of it on the basis of your special circumstances. If you preferred the second, should you really be able to explain yourself in this way? If you were a lawmaker, what factors would you consider before allowing this kind of spontaneous appeal to law enforcement? Several factors should come to mind. First, there is a formal process and people must respect it. **Process** is a key aspect of modern law seeking to ensure uniform application of the rules—though it often falls short of doing this. While it often takes time, it is there to protect the legitimacy of the system, as well as the rights of the individual. Allowing people to bargain with officers to explain their conduct may flout formal processes established with good reason. Second, process is intended to ensure **equal protection** of the law. Without it, two individuals charged with the same conduct could be treated very differently and wind up with differing outcomes. Not only would this lack of uniformity be unfair, but it would make changing one's behavior to comply with the law difficult or unnecessary. This leads in turn to the third issue: there are important policies behind our laws, and allowing exceptions may fly in the face of those. Most traffic laws are designed to protect innocent drivers going about their business and, for that reason, do not excuse "accidental" law breaking. If they did, they would excuse the wayward driver—perhaps an elderly person who turns without looking—even after he or she injures someone. One major policy behind traffic laws is to ensure predictable safety and maintain the smooth flow of traffic. In a world where your liability depends on your individual age and capacity, other drivers might lack the predictability that makes roadways reasonably safe and therefore usable. Finally, if individual lawbreakers could appeal directly to officers for excuses from liability, each individual officer would possess the discretion currently afforded judges and juries. Although officers already exercise a choice whether to administer a "ticket" or written citation, they do so on the basis of observed conduct. Ideally at least, they "judge" us on the basis of what we appeared to do in front of them. Taking into account a person's individual history, circumstances, or capacities forces officers to make more complex decisions about things they cannot see, in ways they are not equipped to carry out in the field. Moreover, it brings us around full circle to the idea that there is *already* a process for making appeals built into the legal system. So for at least these reasons we lean away from allowing people to talk their way out of legal citations.

But there is another side to this. Letting officers hear a person's on-the-spot plea for mercy may actually be a good thing. It may promote some of the goals of our legal system. The first is fairness. With civil and criminal justice we *can* and do exercise control in how we administer justice. Allowing a police officer to hear a person's circumstances before issuing a citation may make for a more fair system. It may exonerate those who act without intention, or who otherwise do no wrong, while focusing valuable resources on those who make the *choice* to do wrong.

The second is efficiency. In **civil court,** every time a plaintiff sues a defendant, regardless of the strength of the claim, the defendant is entitled to a "day in court." Often, a judge is able to dismiss the case before it goes to trial, but even the process up to that point requires time, money, and energy on the part of attorneys, clerks, judges, and others. In **criminal court,** the plaintiff is the state, but the procedure is otherwise similar. Moreover, because of the very detailed criminal codes of most jurisdictions, low-level criminal violations such as drug possession are extremely common and lead to a great many defendants being called before a judge. The arrival of each new criminal defendant into the justice system represents significant new expenditures of time, money, and energy. A system that allows law enforcement officers to excuse certain low-level infractions may therefore increase judicial efficiency and maximize judicial resources by ensuring that only serious cases enter the system.

The third reason for allowing such discretion is the most sociological or anthropological one: people are different and their social circumstances vary.

The reasons for causing a car accident may be completely different for a thirty-five-year-old professional bachelor in a sports car than for an eighty-five-year-old grandmother with impaired vision. The circumstances that lead to drug crime for a seventeen-year-old youth in South Los Angeles and a thirty-four-year-old investment banker on Wall Street may be vastly different. Should the pair in each example be treated the same way under the same law? Before answering, we must consider the many social conditions that are involved in each situation. When we impose civil or criminal sanctions on any of these individuals, we are also affecting their relationships with other people in their communities, families, the economy, and so forth. Do any of them have dependents, children, or elderly people who depend on them for care? Do any of them operate a business whose failure would affect employment for others? And does the violation committed by any of them involve a larger web of regrettable conduct (e.g., trafficking, money laundering)? None of us exists in a social vacuum; we are all connected through formal and informal networks to family, communities, cities, and beyond. Allowing law enforcement to consider these connections as they impose a sanction may allow them to distinguish between the violations and injuries that cause the most harm to the society as a whole.

The entire debate about whether we should be allowed to "talk our way out" of a legal infraction is, at bottom, a debate about what law should be. On the one hand, some of us—those who prefer not to allow this kind of immediate mercy—would like the law to remain autonomous. Autonomy of law means that the world of legal rules and processes operates separately and apart from social circumstances. Today, this idea seems hard to swallow. But in the not-too-distant past, lawyers, judges, and professors believed strongly in the free-standing nature of legal knowledge, truth, and reasoning. Like algebra or theoretical physics, those thinkers felt, the law has an underlying logic that remains untouched and unchanged by the messy, emotionally charged circumstances of everyday life. Legal formalism and positivism each, in their respective ways, maintained this line of thinking. This was felt to be one of law's key strengths. It meant the application of law to solve problems could be evenhanded to ensure fairness. It could be "blind" to guarantee equal treatment. It could have a formal structure that was readily discovered and replicated from case to case. And it meant individuals—the subjects of legal ordering—could act consistently, knowing that the law would respond in predictable ways.

Those who feel one should be able to bargain with law enforcement to explain individual circumstances seem to feel that law is not autonomous but rather socially embedded. Though it may operate in ways that are often formally distinct—such as by having a separate expert legal profession or a judge who abstains from political questions—law should in fact be just one part of the larger social structure of a modern society. This allows it to be understanding of differences, humane in its treatment of the poor or the weak, practical in its solution to human problems, efficient in its use of community resources, just (rather than merely expedient) in arriving at conclusions, and moral in its encouragement that we pursue "the good" in human nature and organization.

One of the great legal minds of the twentieth century, Roscoe Pound, spent considerable time thinking on these issues. The *Journal of Legal Studies* recognizes Pound today as one of the most cited legal scholars of all time.[2] There are several reasons for his sweeping influence. One of these is that he reflected deeply on the nature of law itself at a time when the Western world underwent substantial questioning of its basic values. In 1942, Pound published the important essay "What Is Law?" in which he compared his own moment with key moments in Western history long before him.[3] He first described the "Classical Age," a period leading up to the start of Christianity and during which the Roman Empire reigned over Europe. During that time, rulers seemed little interested in discovering and upholding the "truth." Influenced by the contemporary philosophies of *skepticism*—the embrace of doubt over any certain knowledge—and *epicureanism*—the embrace of human pleasures as the only form of certain experience—the Classical Age of which Pound wrote was one where faith in the human ability to discern truth was at a historic low.

Nearly 1,500 years later, following the European Renaissance, Western philosophers occupied themselves widely with the pursuit of universal knowledge through refinement of the **scientific method.** This new mind-set embraced a "faith in human reason" over and above all the mysteries that moral philosophy, religion, and naturalism had said were unknowable. In other words, the human mind, through rigorous study and application, could master the world around it. This period brought both the scientific revolution and the European "Age of Discovery."[4] The scientific revolution resulted in a great leap in new knowledge about natural processes relating to weather, geology, the human body, the animal kingdom, and even outer space, thanks in large part to the invention and refinement of new research tools such as microscopes, thermometers, and magnetic compasses. The European Age of Discovery meant that humans could travel greater distances more safely and in greater numbers, allowing European powers to sponsor exploration in regions of the world previously unknown to them. Finally, new exploration yielded a wealth of new natural resources, from gold and silver to agricultural crops and animal products, that, in turn, further enriched Europe and allowed its leaders to expand their power. Altogether, this period following the Renaissance was, in Pound's eyes, opposite to the Classical Age: it represented the triumph of human reason over moral doubt.

Finally, the mid-twentieth century, the period just following the Second World War, during which millions of soldiers returned from the battlefields to homes in England, France, the United States, and elsewhere, was marked as "a new era of disillusionment" by the observing Roscoe Pound. And how could it *not* be? Returning soldiers and their families had witnessed the horrors of modern war, including chemical warfare, weapons of mass destruction, and scientifically organized human extermination camps. All of these were

BOX 2.1   Dean Roscoe Pound

Roscoe Pound was born in 1870 in Lincoln, Nebraska, the son of a pioneer law-yer, judge, and state senator. Although one might imagine him to have been des-tined for a distinguished legal career, Pound came very close to taking other paths in life. He entered college at the University of Nebraska, where he studied botany, the field of plant science especially important to the agricultural mid-western United States. On graduation Pound did enter Harvard Law School, but he soon dropped out, never to receive a formal law degree from the program. Young Roscoe then returned to Nebraska and earned a PhD in botany, again from the state university. After some years teaching he became director of the state botanical survey and discovered a rare lichen that still bears his name: *Roscoepoundia*.[1] During this time, Pound maintained his interest in law by first passing the Nebraska state bar—at the time not requiring a formal law degree—and becoming commissioner of appeals for the state supreme court. Finally, Pound began teaching law, first at Nebraska, then at Northwestern and Chicago, and finally at Harvard Law School, where he became dean and presided for sev-eral decades until retirement in 1947.[2] This story is important to students of law and society because it reminds us to pursue our interests and go where life takes us in the search for problems and their solutions. The legal academy and profes-sion have each benefited from this unusual Renaissance man, whose thinking was likely shaped by living "outside the box."

---

1. Mark R. Ellis, "Roscoe Pound (1870–1964)," in *Encyclopedia of the Great Plains,* ed. David A. Wisehart (Lincoln: University of Nebraska Press, 2011), http://plainshumanities.unl.edu/encyclopedia/doc/egp.law.043.
2. Ibid.

promulgated at one time or another under the auspices of Western "civiliza-tion." The questions raised by all of this, as well as by new research into the cultures and values of non-Europeans that were fast disappearing under colo-nialism and postcolonial industrialization, led in turn to new relationships with the truth. The first result was a **moral relativism** that prevented Western-ers from judging right from wrong on a global scale the way they had learned to do during the European Enlightenment. Once the world became smaller and different value systems were on more equal footing, how could any *one* system be charged with deciding right from wrong? The second was the related rise of a new **rights discourse** in which new members of Western societies, freed slaves, immigrants, the disabled, and victims of sex and gender discrimination, among others, could claim "equal protection" of the laws and seek redress when the truth of their experience was denied. As minority groups become more enfranchised, they could couch their claims for legal redress in terms of civil rights. His era, Pound said in short, was a new period of uncertainty and doubt concerning the existence of absolute truths.

An important focus for this doubt in Pound's day was the very meaning of the word *law*. What lawyers actually cite are, for Pound, *rules, principles, conceptions,* and *standards*. A rule, he writes, is a statement of law attaching consequences to a definite set of facts.[5] Facts in this sense often include a type of action. Rules, by this definition, often take the form of "If . . . then . . ." statements, such as the hypothetical "If a person refuses to pay taxes then he or she shall be subject to a penalty of not less than six months in federal prison."

A *principle,* meanwhile, is a form of precept where no set of facts is referred to or known.[6] Consider the example that "a person who negligently injures another shall be liable to compensate the other for his or her loss." Here, the determination that someone has been negligent can come only after a long, protracted investigation, but the weight of the principle remains strong even in its vagueness.

Conceptions, then, are the principles that work as catch-alls—boxes into which entire cases can be placed to trigger application of a line of subsidiary rules.[7] One example Pound himself gives is that of the "sale." A sale of something is a form of transaction that, when present, triggers a set of subsidiary requirements and expectations. If someone tells you that they just made a "sale," for instance, but say they have not given up anything of value and do not plan to, you can safely conclude they may have violated a precept that sales always involve an exchange of one item for another.

For Roscoe Pound, *standards* were the last important category of legal precepts that jurists might think of when you ask them to define the word *law*. In the study of law and society, I would further suggest, standards are plausibly the most important form of precept. They are, as Pound says, the "measure of conduct prescribed by law from which one departs at his peril of answering for resulting damage or of legal invalidity of what he does."[8] Our civil justice system is filled with "standards." Perhaps the most famous is the "standard of reasonable care" in our accident law. You may already be asking yourself, "What is reasonable, and who decides?" Exactly. *Reasonable care* is essentially a placeholder for the civil jury. That body, made up of nine or twelve "average reasonable people," is asked to decide whether the conduct of the responsible party met or fell below the "reasonable care standard."

Visualizing this in a car accident case, for instance, we might find that the court has easily and verifiably learned that one driver crashed into another. The court has also learned that the crash caused no personal injury but "totaled" (in other words, destroyed) the second driver's car, requiring a full replacement worth $20,000 to be equivalent. The defendant, the driver who may be wrongful, readily admits "causing" the crash and having had a "duty" not to cause the crash by driving reasonably; the defendant also admits that the result was a $20,000 property bill that will have to be paid by someone. The *only* remaining question, and the one on which both sides disagree, is whether driver 1's speed was reasonable that day. Driver 1's lawyer argues that unexpected fog at the time of the crash intervened to make even the most reasonable care unhelpful at the time, and that the client was immersed in it too quickly to adjust speed. Driver 2's lawyer argues that the fog was easily visible from a distance and thus should have factored into driver 1's speed on the road that day. Would a "reasonable person" have slowed down in time?

As this illustrates nicely, a major feature of our accident law is a type of precept—a standard—whose specific content often remains unknown until long after the harmful action it was meant to prevent. I have elsewhere referred to this kind of standard and the jury process on which it relies as a legal "black box"—a mystery that has survived tucked into our rules for centuries.[9] But why tolerate or even embrace black boxes of this kind? To law and society thinkers, the answer will be easy: *law* is not *society*. Law cannot substitute its own wisdom for the wisdom of society. If reasonable members of a society could disagree—about the proper speed on a suddenly foggy highway, for example—then they should be protected in doing so even at the heart of our civil justice procedures. Hence, we embrace standards in the law.

Despite all this flexibility to deal with changing circumstances, certain features of law's very nature work to limit its effectiveness. This is something of a "glass half full" kind of problem. On the one hand, law does so much to keep modern societies together and working smoothly. On the other hand, those who know it well can point to numerous limitations on law's ability to help solve problems. One of these is its ability to determine the facts.[10] This may seem odd to the first-time reader; surely if something is a "fact" then it is known to be true by two or more people. Many basic facts, such as "December is a month that comes after November," or "A heavy object thrown into the air will eventually fall back to the ground," are so obvious and accepted that they never need to be proven in a court of law and judges can simply acknowledge them. Experts call this taking "judicial notice." But in our case-based court system the more detailed facts of any particular controversy are often the subject of great dispute. Was the defendant swerving before the accident, or looking downward at a smartphone? Did the defendant have controlled substances in his or her system? One of the basic limits of law's efficacy is its ability to discern all of these facts. Often the parties disagree and offer their own competing versions of the harm-causing event. At that point, it is up to the judge or the jury to evaluate which account is most credible. The ascertainment of facts can therefore become a "beauty contest" between two different accounts of the same series of events.

Another limitation on law's efficacy is its difficulty enforcing duties. A duty is the underlying obligation that says you or I "should" do something. The obligation to drive on the highway with "reasonable care" is a duty. The obligation to fulfill the terms of a contract is a duty. The obligation that trustees of a deceased celebrity's estate should administer the estate faithfully is another

BOX 2.2   Law and Equity

The United States used to observe a distinction between *law* and *equity*, inherited from its mother country England. Principles of law were formal rules observed by the king's courts and settled into common-law decision making. Principles of equity were more informal rules derived from moral philosophy. They were, in other words, principles rooted in fairness. To bring a claim in a court of law, the concerned party would need to frame their case in terms of pre-existing theories for legal recovery—for example, "trespass." Because many cases fell outside these formal boxes, parties had the option to bring their case to a court of equity (or chancery in some jurisdictions). In such cases, the court would decide the outcome on the basis of more general notions of right and wrong rather than particular legal rules and remedies. England abolished the distinction between law and equity in the 1880s, whereas the United States did not formally merge these two at the federal level until its adoption of the Federal Rules of Civil Procedure in 1938. At the level of state law, only a few jurisdictions maintain the distinction today.

important duty. All of these examples are legal duties: they are, in theory, enforceable in court. Yet people often have a very difficult time enforcing duties on one another. A stranger driving recklessly next to you on the highway may swerve and nearly kill you, and in doing so has breached a duty owed to you. But unless they actually collide with your car and then can be identified for having done so, the duty breached will never be enforced. Many times, the agreements people make under contract describe certain obligations that cannot be specifically enforced. If a prizewinning painter agrees to paint a beautiful family portrait for $10,000 and then produces a horrible finished product, the family probably cannot enforce the duty created under the contract—though they might be able to recover the money spent in securing it plus "general damages" for the hassle created. Would cash money in this instance be a good substitute for a high-quality family painting?

That question leads to one final limitation on law's efficacy according to Dean Pound: legal remedies are often unsuited to *righting* certain *wrongs*. Although the law allows plaintiffs to request **equitable remedies** such as an apology, or an injunction not to act on something, by far the most common remedy at law in the United States is monetary damages—basic money.

If you are held responsible for a car accident, your ultimate obligation to the injured person will likely be to pay a sum of money at once or over time. This may seem appropriate after a car accident. The money may allow a victim to pay medical bills and buy a new car.

DEFAMATION AND THE LIMITS OF LEGAL REMEDY

But what about the many other kinds of legal harm to which law must be applied? As with the family painting above, the breach of contract with the brilliant artist may result in an award of money damages, and this money may allow the family to hire a new artist to do the job. But this will never procure the unique, prizewinning services of the original artist. It will always, therefore, be inadequate.

The problem is particularly evident when a person suffers harm to their reputation thanks to something another person has said—otherwise known as **defamation.** Most countries have some variation of this, but each defines it slightly differently. Here, we view it in some detail to give one clear picture of the struggles faced when law addresses harm to intangible interests like reputation. As you continue reading, keep in mind that similar problems arise in related areas such as emotional distress, invasions of privacy, and even trademark law.

Defamation is injury against one's reputation by spoken or written speech. It is defined legally as "the publication of defamatory matter of or concerning the plaintiff to at least one individual" other than the plaintiff (victim) or the defendant (speaker). Notice that the only "harm" created in an act of defamation is reputational: it amounts to some form of lost prestige or status among the victim's peer group. If someone accused you in front of your friends of cheating in school—assuming your friends are an honest bunch—this would likely diminish your reputation in front of them. If this statement could be shown to be false, you would likely have an actionable claim for defamation. You might feel temporarily vindicated by bringing this claim and going before a judge. But, once this reaches a court, the question would immediately become *how much* you were harmed by the accusation. The court would try to ascertain whether the perceived violation of your school's academic integrity policy might have injured your ability to earn an income. Perhaps it would cause suspicion among professors. Maybe then you would have a hard time securing letters of recommendation. Potentially then you would not be able to apply to law school, succeed, pass a bar exam, and practice at a top law firm.

Taking all this information into account, the court would have to estimate the amount of income you had lost and the likelihood that all the parts of this story would have come true otherwise. On the basis of all that, the court would still only award you money. Would this make you feel better? Would money substitute well for your reputation? For your future career? If the answer is "no" or "not entirely," you are not alone. Roscoe Pound wrote that "we try to hide the difficulty by treating the individual [*sic*] honor, dignity, character, and reputation, for purposes of the law of defamation, as assets. . . . But it is not so obvious what else the law may do."[11]

So the reputational harm that defamation imperfectly attempts to remedy illustrates the limitations of law and the dependency of law on society. Defamation has evolved in the United States from what was once just a common-law wrong by one individual against another to a more complex legal claim inflected by Supreme Court decisions, often involving large media organizations and implicating freedom of speech—perhaps one of the founding principles of the American Revolution.

To have a strong case for defamation, a plaintiff must show some form of actual harm. This is most easily proven in cases where victims have suffered financially from the harm to their reputation. The victims most likely to suffer financial harm from wrongful speech about them are those who have the most invested in their own name or image: celebrities. Celebrities may include famous actors and musicians, but they now increasingly include those serving in government, those running for office, and even certain people who become famous simply for being famous. In all of these cases, the individual's fame is an important source of their income or credibility, so statements making them look bad often cause direct, actual harm. But such celebrities currently have a very difficult time winning defamation actions against the media. Why?

To understand this we must briefly trace the history of defamation law in the United States. Once upon a time, defamation was an assertion by one individual that another had said something false about him or her that had harmed the latter's reputation. This meant that a victim had to show three things. The first was "publication," a term that here meant only communication to at least one other person. This was the most simple of the elements, since it required only a witness or a piece of writing attesting to the communication. The second was "defamatory matter," meaning that the content of the communication was of such a nature that it would cause harm. And the third was "of and concerning" the victim; this meant the statement had to be specific and therefore not about a broad group of people. The second and third requirements are keys to the social importance of defamation in thinking about law and society.

"Defamatory matter" is by its very essence a *social* category. To one person words may sound offensive, derogatory, or indicative of immoral action, but to another they may also sound perfectly harmless. Moreover, the question is really not whether the alleged victim feels them to be harmful but whether the victim's peers—friends, neighbors, family, professional community, religious community—feel them so. The individual's reputation exists only among those groups and can be harmed, therefore, only among them. So the victim would be invited to produce evidence of what his or her community thought about the words, and then the judge, if considering it to be a difficult call, would send the question of "defamatory matter" to the jury. The jury in the American system is supposed to be a group of lay citizens called upon at random to serve on cases to represent the voice of "average reasonable people." They are, in other words, the voice of "society."

In many cases the question whether the words were defamatory is easy but the question whether they were *about* the victim is not. Here again, the jury serves an important social function. It answers whether average reasonable people within the victim's peer group would understand the statement to be about, that is to say "of and concerning," this victim. The most important point to realize is that, under this traditional law of defamation, and still today, the words do not have to mention the victim by name or point to him or her directly to be construed as being about that individual, and thus actionable. Everything so far describes the "common law" of defamation—how things were done based on centuries of case law in England and the United States.

But over the course of the twentieth century, ideas and words became increasingly distributed not by individuals but by large media organizations. First, radio, newspaper, and magazine publishers established themselves as the primary vehicle for citizens to learn about current events, as well as new and life-altering consumer products. Then television took on this role, remaining the king of media until recently, when the Internet replaced it as the primary means by which most Americans obtained news of the world. In all these formats, ideas were researched and composed into words by writers, journalists, production teams, and the like, but they were published by large organizations to very large audiences spanning the entire nation. If these organizations got something wrong, their potential to do serious harm to someone's reputation was vastly larger than among individuals in prior eras of human history. On the other hand, in a growing nation where population was concentrated more and more in large cities, and where the vast distances between communities had to be bridged by the free flow of information, media organizations had to be protected in their ability to investigate, report, and occasionally make mistakes.

All of this came to a head in 1964. As far as US history goes, it was a very eventful year. The rock 'n' roll band the Beatles arrived and began a music revolution in America. Congress enacted the Civil Rights Act, the most robust federal legislation outlawing discrimination in public accommodations and employment on the basis of race, religion, sex, or national origin. And the US Supreme Court decided the landmark case *New York Times v. Sullivan.* Chapter 4 of this book offers a more detailed picture of *Sullivan* in the context of historical arguments made in US case law. For now, it suffices to say that this case introduced a new layer to the common-law doctrine of defamation. Recall that up to this time a plaintiff needed only to show "publication of defamatory matter of and concerning" him- or herself. In a complex case involving the widely circulated daily newspaper the *New York Times,* the Supreme Court confronted the problem that penalizing the *Times* for a mistake could "chill" free speech in the United States.

Newspapers, the court reasoned, are hardworking professional organizations with increasingly well-trained journalist-investigators. But they can make mistakes. Relying upon sources in a community, for instance, they might obtain inaccurate information and, after reasonable efforts to fact-check, they might publish their findings before discovering the information was wrong. Given the likelihood that this would happen at some point, and given the great damage this might cause, would you as a newspaper owner at the time have been willing to report on controversial stories and events? Such events in the early 1960s were likely to include the rapid political and social changes taking place at the heart of American society. The states and the federal government continued to struggle over racial integration—in particular the sovereign authority to resist or implement it.[12] Related conflicts took place on college campuses—especially the University of California, Berkeley—where students demanded the right to speak and write freely on campus but were rebuked by university administrators.[13] Reporting on these kinds of events often meant commenting on the actions of public officers and government leaders, any of whom could suffer substantial actual harm from the resulting reputational damage. If you were a newspaper owner, you would probably steer clear.

For the Warren court in *New York Times v. Sullivan* this was a terrible thing. Remember that the common-law defamation standard required that the defendant show his or her statement to be substantially *true.* If you were a journalist being sued, this would be costly and time consuming if it could be done at all. The financial and time burdens for defending oneself from a defamation claim would discourage journalists from reporting on facts that could even be *possibly* untrue. The standard would force newspapers to comment only on the most obvious events and stories—precisely the kinds of information the public least needed. Something had to be done.

Writing for a majority of the nine justices, William Brennan offered a solution to fix the problem. From now on, victims of defamation who were "public officials," that is to say government or state agents acting in their official capacities—could not simply assert the three elements of defamation against a media organization. They now had to meet two additional requirements: falsity and fault. *Falsity* meant the victim now had the burden to show that the information was substantially false rather than simply making its claim and waiting for the defendant to show the opposite. *Fault* meant that the victim had to also show that the media defendant published the information when *it should have known better.* This translated into a showing of either "knowledge" of the correct information or "reckless disregard" for the possibility of correct information.

Altogether, this new rule was called the **actual malice** standard. Since 1964, the actual malice standard has protected journalistic speech about important, often controversial matters and has allowed information to come into public view before it could be "proven" true. Benefits of this approach might be seen in the clarity achieved after dubious government scandals ranging from My Lai and Watergate to Iran-Contra and the Monica Lewinsky affair.

In the years after *Sullivan,* the Supreme Court further expanded actual malice doctrine to cover media speech about nongovernment actors whom it called "public figures." This expansion was long predicted in Roscoe Pound's discussion of legal precepts. As he described it, a *conception* was a type of precept that allowed entire cases to be categorized together to permit the application of common rules to decide their outcome. In this line of thought, modern-day celebrities might also fit within a conception that treated them the way the Warren court treated public officials. Remember that newspapers in the 1960s needed extra free speech protections to allow them to comment on difficult and slippery issues of their day—issues that the general public would consider "newsworthy." Over the ensuing decades, the rise of film, television, and fashion celebrities meant that nongovernment individuals—people famous not for making or enforcing public policy—exercised greater and greater influence on public life. Even before it became popular for celebrities like Angelina Jolie or George Clooney to take up social causes, famous figures like actor Fred Astaire and talk show host Johnny Carson were considered newsworthy to many. Their actions and statements were already, in themselves, important events. The courts decided in the decades after *Sullivan* that the greater protection afforded by the actual malice standard would, in effect, apply to certain celebrities, as they were "public figures."

All of this played out dramatically for the actor Tom Cruise. Star of classic and blockbuster films like *The Outsiders, Risky Business, Top Gun, The Last Samurai,* and the *Mission Impossible* franchise, Cruise has had a storied career as an actor and producer. He has also gone through several public divorces that the news and tabloid press have found irresistible to their readers. In 2012, Cruise was divorcing from his then-wife actress Katie Holmes. The two had given birth to a daughter who was six years old at the time and of considerable interest to the public as a child of "Hollywood royalty." That year, two popular magazines *Life & Style* and *In Touch* published stories claiming that Cruise had "abandoned" his young daughter through the divorce. Quickly, Tom Cruise filed suit for defamation on the belief that this accusation would tend to harm his otherwise clean, heroic image in the public eye.[14] Given everything just said about the evolution of defamation law and the Poundian "conception" that certain public figures belonged to the same class of plaintiffs that the public officials of *Times v. Sullivan* spoke of, how would you imagine this played out?

As you might have guessed, Cruise did not take kindly to being accused of child abandonment. Although the actor had featured in several PG-13 and R-rated films, he had maintained a relatively clean image for a Hollywood male actor working since his teenage years. Indeed, Cruise's most controversial quality was his high-profile membership in the Church of Scientology—what some might consider a religious cult. Therefore, in late 2012 Cruise filed suit in a California federal court asserting *defamation*. To do this he had to assert that the magazines were published, which they undoubtedly were. He had to show that the story was "of and concerning" him, which by naming him directly they undoubtedly were. And he had to assert that the information contained—particularly the charge of abandonment—was "defamatory" or that it would tend to cause harm to his reputation. This last element was made easy by Cruise's public "good guy" image. Moreover because Cruise had by this time become a film producer—someone who initiates business deals to get movies made—harm to his reputation could be doubly damaging: not only might others not wish to hire him as an actor, but they might avoid doing lucrative movies with him as a producer. All told, Cruise claimed damages in the amount of $50 million for harm to his reputation.

If this seems like an easy case, it was not. That is because in addition to all of the above, thanks to *New York Times v. Sullivan* and subsequent defamation jurisprudence, Cruise had to also show that the magazines defamed him with *actual malice,* that is to say with "knowledge or reckless disregard" as to the falsity of their claims of abandonment. In other words, did they or did they not know better? Proving that they did would be very difficult. It often is, and for this reason celebrity lawsuits even against "gossip" papers and magazines in print or online are very seldom successful.[15] So in the end Cruise settled with the German publisher of *Life & Style* and *In Touch* for an "undisclosed" amount.[16]

CONCLUSION

We study law and society today because the relationship between these two large concepts has changed dramatically. Whereas it was once plausible to say that society changes and the law struggles to keep pace, today it is clear that law has become an important tool for driving social change itself. Not only that, but in the practice of law in courts and conference rooms, economic calculations have become a predominant means by which to translate harm into remedies. Drawing upon key law and society influences such as Dean Pound, we are able to recognize some of the many ways in which this translation can be inaccurate or inadequate.

Defamation offers a fitting example of why and how Pound viewed "social control through law" as imperfect. Whereas some might still believe law reigns supreme *over* society, they are best able to make this claim when reading law as a set of formal rules. From a *realist* perspective, looking at law in action the way Pound did, we see that legal precepts are often highly limited in their ability to rectify social wrongs. In defamation, a person's reputation has been injured by another person saying or writing something critical, inaccurate, or misrepresentational. By the law we have inherited a plaintiff can only translate this injury into money and can recover no more than that amount. In today's world, increasingly influenced by economic approaches to law, faith in the translational value of money maybe at an all-time high. Large corporations factor damage settlements into their operating budgets, while commerce and trade increasingly serve as a bargaining chip in international diplomacy. These developments are all part of the neoliberal approach to law highlighted critically in this book.

Still, in defamation, no amount of money can fully repair a person's social standing among his or her peers. The relationships people develop, often over decades of work and building, are in that sense "priceless." Law struggles to make sense of all of this because it is, by most accounts, the best we can do. This struggle need not be viewed as failure. In some ways it is a roaring success. In a world where life changes fast and relationships can be more important than money, human beings have devised creative, philosophically rich ways to resolve problems and to repair those relationships as best as they know how. And it is in this act of creative applied philosophy that law meets society.

CHAPTER 2 REVIEW

Key Terms

- Formalism
- Realism
- Constructivism
- Social fact
- Negligence
- Natural law
- Legal positivism
- Legal realism
- Process
- Equal protection
- Civil court
- Criminal court
- Scientific method
- Moral relativism
- Rights discourse
- Equitable remedies
- Defamation
- Common law
- Actual malice

Further Discussion

1. Should individuals be allowed to "talk their way out" of a traffic ticket? Why or why not?

2. Why should we study law and society today? In doing so, what recent changes should be taken into account?
3. Who was Roscoe Pound, and why was he so influential?
4. What is defamation, and what balance has defamation law attempted to strike since the 1960s?

Further Reading

Cohen, Andrew. "Today Is the 50th Anniversary of the (Re-)Birth of the First Amendment." *Atlantic*, March 9, 2014.

Molloy, Antonia. "Tom Cruise Settles $50 Million Defamation Case over Claims He Abandoned Daughter Suri." *Independent*, December 23, 2014. www.independent.co.uk/arts-entertainment/films/news/tom-cruise-settles-50million-defamation-case-over-claims-he-abandoned-daughter-suri-9022484.html.

Pound, Roscoe. "What Is Law?" In *Justice According to Law*, 35–62. New Brunswick, NJ: Transaction, 1997.

Zara, Christopher. "Tom Cruise vs. the Gossip Rags: How Hard Is It to Win a Defamation Case?" *International Business Times*, October 25, 2012.

Comparative Legal Communities

3

In 1993 Christopher Simmons recruited a friend to help him with a plan. The pair broke into a mobile home on the outskirts of St. Louis, Missouri. There, they found a forty-six-old female truck driver by the name of Shirley Crooks, whom they tied up, blindfolded, and kidnapped. After robbing her home, the pair drove Mrs. Crooks in her own vehicle to a bridge, where they threw her, still alive, into the cold waters below. Shirley Crooks was found in the river, lifeless, the following day.

Believing all the facts above, most people might agree that Christopher Simmons and his associate were guilty of several crimes—the most serious of which was murder. Many would also say that the pair, or at least Simmons for having masterminded the plot, should have received the maximum punishment—the death penalty—for this heinous crime.[1] But there was one problem: Simmons was just seventeen when he did all of this. This meant that he was a "juvenile" under the law, a characteristic that raised questions about his ability to truly understand right from wrong, and one that made his potential execution a matter of great controversy.[2] The trial prosecutor did succeed in obtaining the death penalty. This decision was later appealed by Simmons's lawyers at the Supreme Court of the State of Missouri. There they argued that the application of a death sentence to a juvenile was a violation of the

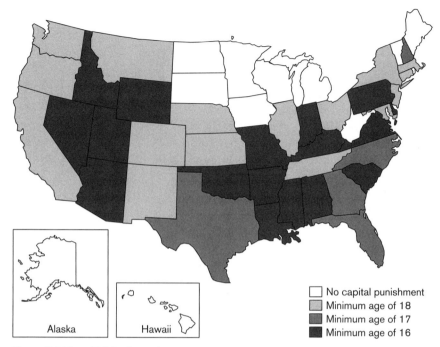

Figure 3.1 Map of US death penalty states in 1993.

US Constitution—specifically its Eighth Amendment prohibition on "cruel and unusual punishment."[3]

The Missouri Supreme Court agreed with this argument. As figure 3.1 shows, Missouri had been one of seventeen US states with a minimum age of sixteen for criminal execution. Another five states had a minimum age of seventeen, while sixteen kept their minimum at eighteen. The remaining twelve states had outlawed executions entirely.

In other words, the various states of the United States were sharply divided on the question of when exactly a convicted criminal should be eligible to receive capital punishment. In situations such as this, the US Supreme Court—interpreter of the "supreme" law of the land—has often been more likely to hear a case. But if it was to decide what the Constitution "said" about this issue, and if it was the highest court in the land, where should it look for guidance about the rightfulness of a "juvenile death penalty"?

Lawyers for Simmons argued that the court should look outward, beyond US national law, to examples in the global community. And that is what the court did. In a five-to-four majority opinion, the Supreme Court upheld Missouri's finding that the death penalty as applied to any juvenile was "cruel and unusual" and thus unconstitutional. Most importantly, it did this largely on the basis of a consultation of *foreign* and *international* sources of law. Said Justice Kennedy, writing for the majority: "It is proper that we acknowledge the overwhelming weight of international opinion against the juvenile death penalty, resting in large part on the understanding that the instability and emotional imbalance of young people may often be a factor in the crime. . . . The opinion of the world community, while not controlling our outcome, does provide respected and significant confirmation for our own conclusions."[4] This reliance on non-US law did not sit well with the four justices who disagreed. In a thought-provoking dissent, Justice Sandra Day O'Connor conceded that the role of foreign and international consensus could be influential in US constitutional law, but she said that this role should be only "confirmatory"—that it should be relevant only when it confirms opinions already popular among the US states. In this case, O'Connor said, because no clear agreement had yet emerged around whether juveniles could be executed in at least some instances, foreign and international consensus could not be confirmatory and was thus not relevant. The conservative firebrand Justice Antonin Scalia went even further. In a separate dissent, he argued that non-US law should play *no* role in US constitutional decision making. Citing the United States' history of opting out of international treaties and conventions on human rights, Scalia wrote that "the basic premise of the Court's argument—that American law should conform to the laws of the rest of the world—ought to be rejected out of hand."[5]

Although *Roper v. Simmons* may appear to show the court disagreeing over whether a kid should receive a death sentence prior to his eighteenth birthday, the combined opinions reveal a much larger debate: Should foreign and international law *even matter* in American law? The majority said it should, at least in matters of fundamental rights like protection against cruel and unusual punishment.

But what about everything else? If the global legal community is important enough to consult on the death penalty, what is its value for US law and society more generally? The study and comparison of domestic law in relation to foreign and international norms is known as comparative law. Not the study of a single "area" of law the way criminal or tort law is, comparative law is a method of legal research and interpretation that draws on examples and explanations from all over the world. While challenging at times, this approach is extremely beneficial for several reasons. Under globalization it is increasingly important to know what one's neighbors are doing to resolve certain legal disputes—ones that might soon involve some of our own citizens. As countries come together in larger treaty and trade organizations, it is fundamental to understand "where they are coming from" in their approaches to law and legal reasoning. This is especially important in our neoliberal age, when it is tempting to consider "free-trade" law as culturally neutral and open to all players. As lawyers take on more and more foreign and international clients, they are well served by knowing the reference points of systems those clients may emerge from. Finally, in attempting to solve complex problems arising from new social arrangements and technological advances, lawyers, legislators, and judges need not "reinvent the wheel" if they can study how the same problems have been resolved by their counterparts around the globe. Just as Western researchers study ancient and folk medicines in the Amazon, central Africa, India, and China to find "new" remedies for familiar ailments, so too might lawyers collect and apply legal innovations from far corners of the globe.

This chapter lays the foundation for those efforts because a basic understanding of law in comparative global context is now essential for understanding US law and society. Where do we fit in? How much do we have in common? Do we share a past? Can our lawyers practice somewhere else? Are we moving farther apart or coming closer together? What happens when traditional laws disappear? These are a few of the questions addressed in the pages below. The first part describes the key categories that make up comparative law and then delves into the main "legal families" of the world. The second part examines key topics in comparative law studied across those families, including *legal transplants, common core, harmonization,* and *legal pluralism.* As it compares what "we" do with what "they" do, this chapter encourages you throughout to think on whether and how foreign and international examples might be used to improve our own approaches to law and society. By exploring how different countries deal with justice, it also invites you to consider how varying approaches to law, morality, and economics shed light upon our own assumptions about these seemingly fixed ideas.

LAW IN THE WORLD

Any discussion of law and society in the United States must take account of where American legal institutions and culture sit within the larger history and structure of world legal systems. This effort resembles the work of geography, anthropology, and perhaps even zoology. It is geographic in the sense that it forces us to study national borders and jurisdictions and their evolution over time. Spain was once part of the Islamic Empire. Turkey was once part of Christian Europe. Finland has been part of Sweden, Germany, and Russia at different times. And almost all of Africa was once under the "legal" authority of various European powers. Contemporary law and society in these places is shaped by these geographical shifts, and this means that we often have more in common with foreign legal systems than most would think. Similarly, comparative law is much like anthropology. This is because it forces us to look not only at what formal legal authorities say "in books" but also at what experts and subjects do with law "in action." This emphasis on practices is a key characteristic of legal anthropology, a discipline that studies legal communities through long-term fieldwork and in comparative perspective. Finally, looking at world legal

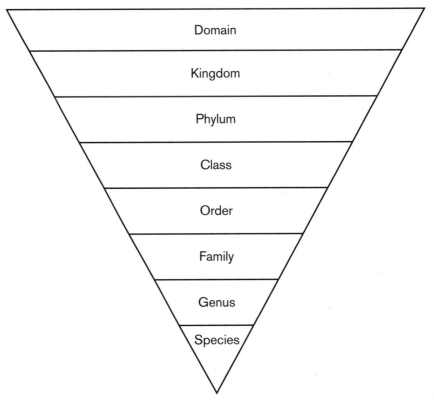

Figure 3.2 Standard scientific taxonomic categories.

systems is a bit like zoology—the field in which scientists spend a lot of time understanding the characteristics of animals, developing classifications for them, and then placing all known animals into these various boxes. Zoology, you may recall from high school, labels all organisms by kingdom, phylum, class, order, family, genus, and species (see figure 3.2).

Experts on comparative legal communities have also spent substantial time classifying the legal institutions and practices of the world. Needless to say, their chart looks different. From biggest to smallest categories, it comprises *legal tradition, legal culture, legal system,* and *legal family.* To define these here, we will use the term *jurisdiction,* meaning an area over which a set of courts and rules has authority. A **legal tradition,** therefore, is a historically rooted way of doing things in any particular jurisdiction. A **legal culture** is a contemporary snapshot of practices, assumptions, and values that underpin approaches to law in a community. A **legal system,** in turn, is the network of institutions, procedures, and professionals that make up the "nuts and bolts" of a given jurisdiction. And a **legal family** is an umbrella category that groups together common legal systems—often because of shared history, practices, or institutions.

If these definitions sound like jargon, some examples may be helpful. In the terms laid out above, how might you classify the following legal object?

> The late justice Antonin Scalia's position that the Constitution should be interpreted according to original intent of the Framers.

While more than one of these labels above might apply, I would hope that you at least saw this object as part of a *legal tradition.* That tradition has been called "originalism" in the United States. It refers to a long-standing approach—though with differing levels of popularity over time—of interpreting the US Constitution according to what some experts believe to be the original meaning intended by the drafters of the document. In fact, because originalism makes a claim about the origins of American constitutional thought, we might even describe it as a legal *meta*-tradition; it is a traditional approach to the idea of legal tradition! But, it is important to note, originalism, like other legal traditions, can, within a single jurisdiction, coexist alongside others. Next to originalism in American constitutional theory, for example, lies *living constitutionalism.* This approach, which by the way also makes claims about the "Framers' intent," says that the Founding Fathers wanted their document to be updated and reviewed in light of contemporary social and political currents in each era. To illustrate the other categories, the Supreme Court itself could be classed as part of a *legal system,* and American constitutionalism, including its popular language of civil rights and civil liberties (as in "I know my rights!"), might be considered *legal culture.* But what about *legal family?*

Legal family describes the broader geographic and historical network in which the American legal system developed. Taking into account several different expert theories on this, we can proceed in this chapter on the belief that there are at least five main legal families (figure 3.3).

Common Law

The legal family just described, to which the United States belongs, is known as English common law or simply **common law.** A fuller list of common-law countries includes—besides the United States—Canada, Ireland, Nigeria, South Africa, India, Pakistan, Malaysia, Singapore, Australia, and New Zealand among others. The vast geographic breadth of the common law is a testament to the onetime power of the British Navy. Once the greatest military organization in the world, it allowed English explorer and merchant ships to penetrate the far corners of the world's oceans and secure trade routes that made new British settler-colonialism a lucrative enterprise. Through colonization by settlement and military conquest, the relatively tiny territory of Great Britain spread its legal system and traditions to nearly every continent of the world.

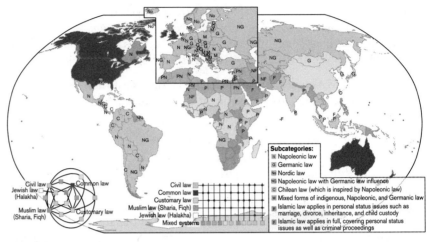

Figure 3.3 Map depicting legal families around the world.

Several key features characterize English common law. The most important may be reliance on **case law** for legal authority. In this type of system, individual parties bring a dispute before a neutral judge in hopes that he or she will decide favorably for their side. As you already know, the United States broke off from England roughly 250 years ago. However, its original colonies spent the 150 years before independence under English authority, and therefore English law. Dozens of other countries dispersed across the globe all share a similar experience. Independent today, most of these chose to retain English legal institutions and practices long after the British left—even where they once had rich legal traditions of their own. As a result, the systems of all these countries share an adversarial approach where two opposing parties bring evidence-based claims before a neutral judge, and they rely on past cases as the primary source of legal authority.

But the effect of any one decision is to create a "rule" that must be followed in all similar cases that arise subsequently. This rulemaking feature of case law is the result of another key feature labeled ***stare decisis***—a Latin phrase meaning simply to "stand by things decided." This one principle explains much of common-law decision making.

Suppose a case arises in which a college student uses the Internet to make threatening comments toward his chemistry professor. The comments are posted on a university discussion forum—for example, about housing and dining services on campus. The threat is significant enough to cause fellow students to report it to campus police, who in turn alert the professor, who in turn cancels class that afternoon. Campus police post a security detail in front of the faculty member's office until the matter is investigated and declared resolved. Referred to local prosecutors as a violation of a law against criminal threats, the case comes before a judge. Although the judge has never seen a case quite like this one before, colleagues on the bench have recently decided one case involving a student who posted similar threats on a bathroom wall, and another case in which a former student left a threatening voice mail for a professor using the campus phone system. The former resulted in no finding of guilt, while the latter resulted in guilt plus a six-month jail term. In our case involving the chemistry professor today, the judge cannot simply ignore those prior decisions. Under stare decisis, he or she must, reviewing the best arguments on both sides, make a decision as to whether using the university's Internet chat room is more like posting on a bathroom wall or more like leaving a directed voice mail. Although different jurisdictions may reach different conclusions on this question, each must remain consistent in its application of its reasoning to all subsequent Internet threat cases. This is just one of several reasons why published court opinions in our system are peppered with dozens and dozens of references to earlier cases.

Since the United States and other countries declared their independence from England, many years and many historical events have left their mark on the various common-law systems of the world. With these have come alterations, innovations, and divergences in the way common-law reasoning is applied and organized in its many different cultural and natural environments. Nevertheless, and perhaps because of rather than in spite of globalization, common-law systems of the world all generally still share the same foundational characteristics: reliance on case law, adversarial justice, and stare decisis.

Civil Law

The next major legal family in our world is known as **civil law.** Scholars are quick to point out that the term *civil* here can be misleading to English speakers for a few different reasons. In the United States, we use that word alongside *criminal* to describe our two main branches of procedural rules, and two separate court systems (see below, chapter 10). Our threatening student in the example just mentioned would likely be brought into "criminal court," while a different student hit by a car walking to class would likely bring suit in "civil court."

Civil law in this context, however, refers to the legal systems of the world that trace their lineage back to Roman and Germanic law on the European continent. While there has indeed been historical mixing of this tradition with English common law at certain moments, most countries remained faithful to one tradition more than the other. Today, civil law countries include most of continental Europe, with France and Germany as the usual exemplars. But it also includes most of Latin America and much of Africa. In addition, important countries in the Middle East and East Asia have taken key features of civil law and "overlaid" them onto Islamic or Chinese law foundations (discussed below). What, then, are some of these key features?

If common law relies primarily upon the use of case law, civil law differs in this major respect. Civil law countries, drawing heavily on their Roman influence, instead rely upon **codes,** extensive and elaborate compilations of definitions, principles, rules, and sometimes instructions for interpreting these. The use of codes was not unique to the Roman Empire. The ancient Babylonian king Hammurabi inscribed his laws onto a large decorative stone around the year 1754 BC in what is now the territory of Iran. Needless to say, however, language, culture, and history play an important part in why the legal codes of the Romans became the template for European law. The Roman Empire existed for roughly 1,500 years,[6] starting in 27 BC, and it stretched from the British Isles in the northwest to North Africa in the southwest, and from Egypt in the southeast to Armenia in the northeast—though its territory contracted and expanded multiple times over its long history. Across this vast territory and expanse of time, at least nine different emperors ruled from a seat of power that moved from Rome to Ravenna in modern-day Italy and then to Istanbul in modern-day Turkey.

This complex history is important to us for one major reason: Roman law in its heyday had to cover many different cultures, climates, economic activities, and political institutions. Its rules tended to be very general, and in the early years cases were adjudicated by private citizens registered to participate as a judge at the election of the disputing parties. Later, the empire created a system of bureaucratic judges to serve this purpose. The law itself was divided into several main subject areas, including the law of citizens, pertaining to individuals; public law, pertaining to state institutions; and natural law, pertaining to all people universally. Interestingly, several of these distinctions and categories remain in place in civil law today. This is in large part because one of the last Roman emperors, Justinian, spent considerable effort consolidating the complex and sometimes conflicting legal systems of the empire into a series of singular, definitive texts in the sixth century AD. These texts came to be known as the Justinian Codes, and it was only through their collection and eventual rediscovery by Italian legal academics that the bulk of Roman law survived and influenced much of the world. Once rediscovered, the codes became the centerpiece of legal education at the University of Bologna, Europe's oldest university and the exclusive site at which aspiring lawyers once had to study before returning to their home territories to practice law in the Middle Ages. Between the development of unified codes and the prominence of law teaching in Bologna, Europe became the distinct and unified center of civil law before the Age of Discovery. With the discovery, exploration, and colonization of other continents, European powers, notably France and Spain, would spread the civil law system of legal reasoning as far and wide as England spread its common law.

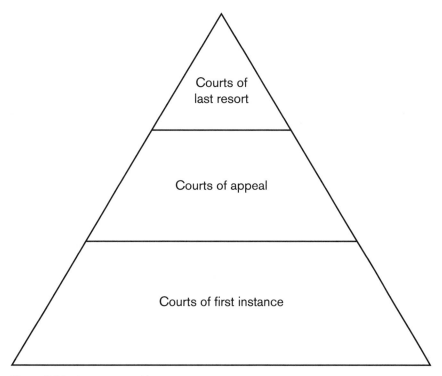

Figure 3.4 Basic court pyramid structure.

Apart from its wide geographic distribution, the civil law legal family shares with the common law a few important features reminding us that both families have been influenced by common history and philosophical foundations. The first similarity is that each classifies, teaches, and learns its law according to separate subject areas. How these areas are divided is somewhat different, but the fact of their division is the same. **Private law** subjects like contracts and torts are distinct from **public law** subjects like criminal, constitutional, or administrative law. Whereas the terms *private law* and *public law* do not typically appear in American law schools, they feature prominently in France. Still, US common-law books may omit this distinction but adhere strictly to the separation of their underlying subject areas.

Second and relatedly, these separations give rise to separate court pyramids (figure 3.4). A court pyramid is a structure that calls for different court institutions to hear different types of cases depending on their substance. An accident case in tort law would not be allowed in the criminal court, and a murder case would not be heard in civil court. Once again, how these distinctions are drawn may vary, but the fact of their importance is common to both families.

Furthermore, these are "pyramids" by virtue of the next common feature: the existence of multiple levels of review. Procedural rules require most cases to be initially brought to a **court of first instance,** the lowest-level court authority in any particular pyramid hearing any case for the first time. In the United States, these are generally known as "trial courts," but in France they are called *tribunals d'instance* (civil) or *tribunals de police* (criminal). But when one party definitively loses at this first level, they are generally able to bring their case to a **court of appeal.** Whereas courts of appeal in the United States must take all trial facts as given and review only interpretations of law, second-level courts in civil law countries like France can often reopen the facts and ask for more. Finally, the top of any court pyramid consists of a **court of last resort.** In the United States and now England we call this the Supreme Court (of each state or of the nation itself), but the specific names in France do not refer to the finality of their judgments. The highest court in France is either the *Cour de Cassation* for private law cases or *Conseil d'Etat* for public law. The existence of *two* courts of last resort in France is a result of there being actually *two* court pyramids, one for private and one for public law. As in climbing a real pyramid or mountain, the one you start with determines the one you finish with. In the United States and England, separate subject matter pyramids appear at the lower levels (for instance, civil versus criminal court), but these all tend to conclude at the top with a single court of last resort: the Supreme Court of the state or the nation.

Finally, both civil and common-law families share two key threshold features: a separation of powers and judicial review. **Separation of powers** means that by design, usually in a constitutional document, the courts are made solely responsible for interpreting and applying all law, the legislators are responsible for designing and adopting it, and the executive is responsible for implementing and enforcing it. In practice, countries vary in their strictness toward these separations, but as a general matter these separations are found in most countries of the two main families. This gives rise, in turn, to the last key feature, that of **judicial review.** This is the power for the courts to independently review the validity—usually measured in relation to a constitution—of all new "law" including legislation as well as executive-issued orders, regulations, and directives. This feature, it is often suggested, is the most reliable "check" on abuses of power by any of the other branches of government. Some feel it may give too much power to judges, but this criticism must admit that judges exercise no real power without support of the executive enforcement or the democratic source for legislative authority among "the people." Moreover, as the framers of the US Constitution envisioned it, this "check" was often the only protection for minorities in a country where "the majority rules."

Having listed these similarities, we should highlight four major differences between the two families. One is a difference in the primary source for legal norms in each family. Recall that common-law systems rely primarily upon cases as their source of authority. Arguments about what the law says are generally then arguments about how any one case or "line" of cases applies to a new case. The study of law in those systems is thus also primarily a study of cases. But in civil law countries, cases are secondary to codes. *Codes* in this sense refers to compilations of explicit legal rules organized usually by subject matter. These compilations are not simply identifiable; they are officially *adopted* by the states of civil law countries and then published as the official source of law there.[7] Students studying law in those countries are expected to memorize and apply the law from these collections, and judges apply the language of any given code section anew to cases that come before them, rather than applying previous interpretations of those from previous cases. In France, for example, the majority of law is compiled in the *cinque codes* (five codes) drafted under Napoleon: a Civil Code, a Criminal Code, a Commercial Code, a Code of Civil Procedure, and a Code of Criminal Procedure. A separate "modern" code adds an array of administrative laws to this foundation.

A second difference will be the main source of legal expertise in each family. In common-law systems the highest-level experts are usually judges. In the United States, for instance, judges are trained lawyers and ongoing members of their state bar organizations. Judges are considered the most learned professionals and the most reliable authorities for interpretation of what the law "says." Needless to say, the highest court judges are the highest valued in this regard. In civil law countries, meanwhile, judges are often a separate professional group from lawyers, and they refer heavily to another group for guidance on applying the codes. Notice that they do not envision themselves "interpreting" the law—to do so would appear arbitrary or inconsistent from the larger "spirit" of the codes. Rather, civil law judges see themselves as "applying" the law. In doing so, they rely considerably on law professors for interpretations. Professors in civil law countries are trained specifically in high-level scholarly thought, have advanced legal degrees (beyond the professional credential that is deemed sufficient in the United States), and have experience in advanced research into legal history, legal rhetoric, or law and society subjects. In short, the highest level of legal expertise as a general rule in civil law countries is law scholars rather than the sitting judiciary.[8]

The third feature distinguishing common- and civil law families is the underlying purpose of their legal procedures. In the common-law tradition, lawyers for each side are partisans for their client. They are barred from knowingly offering false information to the court, but they are given substantial freedom to mobilize evidence for the explicit benefit of their own client to the detriment of the other party. Judges, meanwhile, are considered neutral adjudicators looking to be persuaded by the lawyers' evidence, reasoning, and interpretation of prior case law to the case at hand. From the perspective of the legal system, this is, effectively, a competition between two adverse visions of justice and the facts and law it should be based upon. This is therefore called an

adversarial system. Civil law courtrooms, on the other hand, operate quite differently. There the judge or judges function more like investigators seeking to discover the one true account of events. They are often assisted in this regard by a state attorney sitting in on the proceedings, as well as by the attorneys for each party to a dispute. Partly because the court conducts the factual investigation into things, the process of **discovery** in the civil law systems is considerably cheaper for the parties than the process in common-law countries like the United States.[9] This investigatory role played by courts in Europe and Europe-influenced regions is labeled an **inquisitorial system.**

The fourth difference between common and civil law is the philosophical structure of the two systems. We already saw that reasoning under the common law emanates from individual judges applying case law norms to new disputes. Through this ongoing application of old to new, law appears to evolve smoothly in those systems—though not necessarily slowly, since new cases can displace old ones rather quickly. But legal change, we must therefore recognize, is driven by individuals bringing disputes before judges rather than judges simply "acting" upon the changing social world. Law and society under the common law is thus, at bottom, fine-tuned by regular people like you and me. Between this party-driven foundation and the relative autonomy of the court adjudicator, the common law may be described as structurally individualistic. Note that this comports somewhat with legal culture generally in the United States, as well as in England, Australia, and other old commonwealth countries, where individual rights, private property, and citizenship have been viewed in terms of freedom *from* the collective.

Conversely, the legal systems of the civil law family are, from a distance, the opposite. To begin with, in several systems judges sit, even at the court of first instance, on three-judge panels to hear basic disputes. This means there may be three times as many trained judges. Further, because lawyers are not just partisans of their client but also advisers to the court in its investigation, their training and profession are more standardized and regulated by the state. The structure of the civil law legal system is generally less individualistic and rather more **bureaucratic.** Operating as a bureaucracy, it is held together and adapts to change not by individuals pursuing their self-interest but by the legal profession and judiciary working as a whole toward accepted social values.

So much for the main similarities and differences between common-law and civil law systems. The picture has been painted here with large brushstrokes, so individual examination of specific countries would likely find variations from the averages described here. As discussed later in this chapter, the variations that have arisen in the modern era are actually showing increasing **convergence** of the two families: common-law nations are using more and more codes, while civil law countries are relying more and more on cases.[10] Nevertheless, the underlying spirit of the two families, with common law

BOX 3.1   "Law and Society" or "Law and Economics"?

Individualism appears to be a running theme in both English common law and English political economy. The economic theorist Adam Smith famously wrote, "Give me that which I want, and you shall have this which you want, is the meaning of every such offer; and it is in this manner that we obtain from one another the far greater part of those good offices which we stand in need of. It is not from the benevolence of the butcher, the brewer, or the baker that we expect our dinner, but from their regard to their own interest. We address ourselves, not to their humanity but to their self-love, and never talk to them of our own necessities but of their advantages. Nobody but a beggar chooses to depend chiefly upon the benevolence of his fellow-citizens."[1] As you read this book, consider how this affinity between law and economics lends itself to contemporary views of society as, at bottom, a web of economic relationships.

_____

1. Adam Smith, *An Inquiry into the Nature and Causes of the Wealth of Nations*, book 1, chap. 2, "Of the Principle Which Gives Occasion to the Division of Labour," para. 2 (Indianapolis, IN: Liberty Classics, 1981).

remaining highly fact driven by reliance on cases and civil law remaining more interested in abstract public policy by virtue of the codes, remains.

Socialist Law

Until recently, the two preceding families were rivaled by a third major legal family that covered a sizable portion of the world map. Though relatively young compared to the others, **socialist law** was able to develop into a robust tradition in a fairly short time thanks in part to great centralization and bureaucracy, as well as an apparent ideological uniformity. That is to say, while combining the use of case law and codification, the socialist legal family was characterized most of all by its general vision of justice as that which serves the interests of the socialist or communist party. What were those interests?

Briefly, a recap of socialist doctrine may be necessary to an understanding of what socialist law sought to accomplish differently from the other two major families. Although it shared with those many of the same institutions, for instance, state-run courts with formal procedural rules and different court pyramids, it appeared to diverge from them in its ideological unity. In general, socialist doctrine held that the capitalist economies of Western nations like England and the United States had come to enslave men and women within their purview.

Taking, for example, the industrial manufacturing plant of the late nineteenth century in either of those two countries—such as a shoe factory—socialist theory viewed the central feature of the economy as human labor. Each day, workers left their homes to travel by foot or public transport to arrive at the factory, clock in, and begin their day's work. Industrial studies had already begun to divide those workers up according to their specific tasks, so that some specialized in building the foot soles, others the heel, others the leather covering, and still others full assembly. The shoes produced would be priced at a certain amount—let's say sixty dollars in today's currency. At the time, capitalist economists said that this price was a function of what consumers were willing to pay and that the labor that went into producing the shoes should be valued according to this as one of many overhead expenses. Socialist doctrine developed by the key communist theorists Karl Marx and Friedrich Engels took issue, arguing instead that the price of the shoes should be objectively valued according to the labor it took to produce it. This labor, meanwhile, should be valued by the basic needs of the laboring class to live, survive, and reproduce through the generations. Without this, they said, labor would effectively burn itself out over time.

Under the socialist view, what capitalists were doing was asking the laborers to work a certain number of extra hours in the day to produce the shoes, but instead of paying them the full value of their creation paying them only a fraction of that. A worker would have generated enough value to earn his own pay by, say, 2 p.m., but the company required him or her to continue producing value until 6 p.m. The final four hours of value were effectively taken from the worker for the (ahem) sole benefit of the company itself.

Socialism as a political-economic ideology therefore sought to fix this problem. It viewed capitalism—in which the self-interest of the ownership class would drive it to invest in materials, tools, and building facilities—as simply a primitive stage in a historical evolution toward socialist economy. Once that economy was achieved, Marx and Engels said, ownership would be transferred to the collective society and laborers would be paid for their labor's full value. Laborers could then better afford to buy the commodities they were producing, and the system would support itself. To arrive at this new stage of human history, a socialist party was necessary to organize workers, mobilize their political power, and ensure the transition from the previous stage.

The interests underpinning the socialist legal family of the world, therefore, were the interests of this socialist party. On one level this meant passing new laws to place factories and land under "collective" ownership through the national state, and therefore settling private and public law disputes in a manner that reinforced the legitimacy of that ownership. But on another level, this meant reimagining justice—normally a deep reflection on what is "right" or "wrong"—as that which was "right" for the society or its putative representative, the party.

So far, I have spoken of socialism or the socialist party as one thing. There were in fact at one time dozens of socialist countries around the world.[11] One reason for this was the onetime dominance of the Soviet Union—modern-day Russia—over international affairs. Today the only avowedly socialist countries are China, Cuba, Laos, and Vietnam. At one point or another in modern history, this list was joined by Afghanistan, Albania, Angola, Benin, Bulgaria, Cambodia, Congo, Czechoslovakia, Ethiopia, East Germany, Grenada, Hungary, North Korea, Mongolia, Mozambique, Poland, Romania, Somalia, Russia, Yemen, and Yugoslavia.

These observations of the socialist law family beg two important questions. First, why did it eventually fail in most places? Second, if socialist law is driven by ideology, are nonsocialist families like common and civil law *free* from it? As to the first question, there are numerous competing answers. Some scholars have said that wherever it was implemented as state socialism it was always implemented incorrectly.[12] They point to the fact that in most systems that experimented with socialist governance, the party leadership often abused their power to quietly seize undue control over an unauthorized amount of resources such as land or wealth. This meant the workers were effectively still alienated in their labor, but instead of helping to enrich nonstate capitalist owners they were supporting the covert enrichment of public officials. In some cases this form of alienation was *even worse* than that seen in the most capitalist economies, leading to food shortages, long lines for government support, and no opportunities for creative escape through small business ownership.

As to the second question, the short answer must be a resounding "No." Although Western comparative law scholars often describe socialist law as primarily in the service of a reigning ideology of collective ownership and party control, they rarely take the time to compare this to their own legal family and the economic conditions it supports. Our system too supports ideology. Historical evidence in the common law is easily found in the writings of John Locke, one of the greatest influences on European political philosophy and therefore one of the foundations of modern law. Locke wrote that civilized man realized at some point that if he worked extra hard, or extra intelligently, he could accumulate more resources than his average neighbors. We might illustrate this by imagining an ancient farmer plowing his earth long before the common era (BCE). One day, the farmer learns that if he feeds his ox wild grass blended with a special sand found only on his farm, the ox will digest more quickly, gain more energy from eating, and plow the earth 50 percent faster. The farmer then begins using this process to yield 50 percent more crops than his neighbors. Some of this surplus he stores away underground; the rest he is able to trade for other goods. Eventually, the neighbors begin noticing all of this; they realize the special sand is unique to this one farm and that they will never be as productive as their lucky neighbor. Locke said that in just such an instance man realized the important need to protect his own private property from jealous neighbors and the need to invest his powers of self-protection in a government to create rules about ownership and enforce them in case of conflicts. This surrendering of individual or household power to the government would be to benefit the farmers individually, and it would be premised upon the protection of distinct, private rights to property separate and apart from collective property. So while the farmer's special technique for producing more food *could* be taken away and used to benefit all his neighbors, political man, according to Locke, decided from this moment it was wiser and fairer to secure each individual in his right to unequal property ownership.

Importantly, it does not really matter whether Locke was factually accurate in his speculative view of ancient political history. All that matters is that Locke's followers accepted his ideas as if this were all true. His thinking influenced rationalist philosophy in Locke's own England.[13] It overtly influenced many of the Founding Fathers of the American Constitutional Convention.[14] And it influenced the great philosophers of the French Revolution shortly thereafter.[15]

In contemporary Western law, both common-law and civil law systems, we in turn see clear traces of this influence. Property law in England and the United States is a robust, complicated, and factually fine-tuned subject area with specialized subdivisions like "real property," "personal property," and "intellectual property." In each of these, the fundamental feature of ownership is title—the verifiable proof that an individual, family, or corporate entity owns the land, object, or trademark, for example. With title secured, anyone can then sell or lease out certain "rights" in that land, object, or trademark, thereby turning it from a thing of value into a thing capable of creating new value through divisibility and trade. Beyond title, therefore, common-law property also looks to proof of usage rights. Although different in the evidence and formalities required for ownership or usage, most civil law countries have similar respect and protections for private property holding and exploitation. The suggestion then that socialist law was ideologically driven while common and civil law were not, confronted by just this one example of property law, must be questioned. To the extent that it reveals Western legal families partaking in their own ideological projects, and to the extent that those projects favor private property, freedom of contract, and exchange value, the ideology of common- and civil law countries appears increasingly to be one of market fundamentalism.

With the three largest legal families in part explained, we turn now to the remainder of the world. Apart from being separate from common, civil, and socialist law, they indeed have little in common except maybe the fact of being often synthesized with one of these previous main families. The remaining legal families include Islamic, Chinese, Hindu, Hebrew, and indigenous tribal law. But wherever these still exist, they are typically combined with a layer of common, civil, or socialist law.

Islamic Law

Egypt is a case in point for this dualism. It is an Islamic country with very deep historical attachments to Arab culture and language. Given its history, it is unsurprising that Egypt follows Islamic law. This is usually called **sharia,** though it is very important to distinguish various uses of this term in the English language. For scholars of Islamic law, *sharia* simply describes the body of religious doctrine arising out of the Muslim holy text, the Qur'an, that governs the moral and social behavior of members of that faith. One analogy might be the canon law (religious Christian law) that coexisted with Roman law in Europe during the Middle Ages. Sharia consists solely of specific precepts from the Qur'an, legendary norms observed by founders of the Muslim religion, and expert scholarly interpretations of the former in contemporary society. The resulting body of norms is both deeply personal (e.g., governing how to wash before prayer) *and* immanently public (e.g., dealing with commercial transactions). Most importantly, it says nothing about causing harm to non-Muslims or antagonism to sociocultural strangers. On the contrary, a devout Muslim is obliged to show kindness, generosity, and respect to strangers or foreigners. Use of the term *sharia* among Western countries like the United States, England, and France in recent years often misses this depth. Taking acts of terrorist violence committed by a few dozen individuals, it then imputes this behavior to the entire belief system those actors lay claim to and extrapolates their intentions to all people confessing that belief. It is important therefore, in a course on law and society, to specify what one means by the term *sharia.*

In many Arab countries, traditional Islamic law coexists with common- or civil law institutions. In Egypt, for example, sharia governs personal morality and family law; it also influences commercial and contract norms, as well as related areas like finance and social welfare. However, for basic civil, criminal, and administrative matters, Egypt since 1949 has used a well-developed code system that was originally modeled on the French Civil Code. Egypt's Civil Code was developed and drafted by the local legal scholar Abd El-Razzak El-Sanhuri. But because of Egypt's important role at the forefront of Arab culture in the twentieth Century, other neighboring countries closely followed its example. The result is that Syria, Iraq, Libya, Kuwait, and to some extent Jordan are all influenced by the Egyptian and therefore the French Civil Code.

As for the legal culture of Islamic law, generalizations must be qualified in the same way they would be for the legal families described above. England and the United States may share language, moral philosophy, and similar institutions, but on close inspection they differ considerably—on the use of the death penalty, for example. On that subject, the United States is actually closer to Islamic countries. Similarly, Islamic law countries share an underlying foundation in sharia, but they vary in their specific applications of its rules.[16] Nevertheless, qualitative researchers have generally described Islamic law as being

or refuting tribal autonomy over things like religious exercise, gambling, alcohol, property, and fishing and hunting rights. As a broad conclusion, it may be fair to say that indigenous and tribal law the world over is increasingly respected, but the bar may have been very low to begin with, and native sovereignty remains subject to recognition by Western legal institutions.

ISSUES IN COMPARATIVE LAW

The map of world legal systems and traditions may be fascinating in its own right, but scholars engaged with this kind of research go beyond legal geography. What they are interested in frequently are the ways in which law can be borrowed from one system to solve problems in another. Some have tried to find fundamental features that *all* legal systems share—as if to seek a kind of "universal grammar" of law. Others have used these insights to develop plans to harmonize or bring different national legal systems into unity with one another. Finally, under widening globalization leading some to argue that the "world is flat," many now study the importance of different and multilayered legal approaches within single jurisdictions.

The first of these interests has been called **legal transplants**.[22] As far back as the Greek city-states, legal scholars studied the law of foreign cities to garner solutions for their own legal dilemmas.[23] A transplant is literally a living thing taken from one location and implanted in another. Unlike organ tissue or plant organisms, legal transplants don't need to be "taken" in the sense that an absence is created; they only need to be copied. One great example of this is the concept of "community property" now fixed in the jurisdictions of several southwestern US states. *Community property* refers to the practice of treating all property acquired during a marriage as jointly owned by the husband and wife unless otherwise specified separately by contract. Entirely foreign to English common law, community property instead comes from the Spanish-speaking legal tradition of that region and its erstwhile rulers. In some senses more of a "holdover," community property has also been transposed into the common-law jurisprudence of those states.

The second interest is known as the **common core** approach. This method for studying law comparatively seeks to find institutions, ideas, and underlying policies that diverse legal jurisdictions *already* hold in common. "In nearly all fields of law," write Ugo Mattei, Teemu Ruskola, and Antonio Gidi, "even in the absence of organized unification efforts, there appears to exist a *common core* of legal concepts and precepts shared by some or even most of the world's legal systems."[24] The common core approach looks below surface rules to find functional similarities between legal systems. Reaching a high point in the 1950s and '60s at Cornell Law School, common core became a hopeful methodology for seeking international peace and stability just decades after Europe and much of the East were destroyed by the Second World War.

One of the possibilities this raised was for multiple national legal systems to join together in larger regional or global law systems. This effort, also called **harmonization,** was an extension of the peace and cooperation motive behind the common core approach to comparative law. But whereas common core looked for deep, preexisting similarities, harmonization looked to create a common set of rules and institutions. The military powers of the world, especially France and Germany, which had pulverized each other twice in thirty years, could not renew hostilities if they cooperated in the rebuilding of Europe. Out of this idea the European Coal and Steel Community was born, giving rise to new regional trade rules and setting the course for what would become the legally robust European Union.

The fourth key interest for comparativists has been in some senses a counterpoint to harmonization. Once regions of the world unite in legal ordering, what becomes of the different legal traditions that evolved over centuries? What happens to the deep local and national wisdom of those traditions for solving specific conflicts within bounded legal cultures? Some researchers have come to suggest that we should embrace different legal traditions even within the same single jurisdiction because—as in the examples of Egypt, India, or Israel above—this is the only way to ensure that ethnic diversity remains honored and protected. This **legal pluralism** can result in dualist systems like that of the United States, where fifty state legal cultures coexists with a single federal one, or it can result in highly diverse legal systems like the one on the island nation of Mauritius in the Indian Ocean, where immigrants from India, Africa, China, and France all coexist under their own distinct traditions, unified by a common public law and interest to maintain peaceful living in a small space.

CONCLUSION

Legal transplants, common core, harmonization, and legal pluralism are just some of the key features of contemporary comparative legal analysis. Each takes the diversity of world legal systems and gleans from it a different set of lessons, but all are aimed at achieving a level of social order through finely tuned norms and dispute resolution. Importantly, all four are deeply tied to human history: they index wide cultural interchange, human migration, conflict and cooperation, and globalization, all the while seeking the best solutions for coping with the changes these bring. But if humans stayed home all the time, none would be possible or necessary. Comparative law and society is therefore a study of the human condition—a restlessness and curiosity about the world that motivates us to go farther.

CHAPTER 3 REVIEW

Key Terms

- Legal tradition
- Legal culture
- Legal system
- Legal family
- Common law
- Case law
- Stare decisis
- Civil law
- Codes
- Private law
- Public law
- Court of first instance
- Court of appeal
- Court of last resort
- Separation of powers
- Judicial review
- Adversarial system
- Discovery
- Inquisitorial system
- Bureaucratic
- Convergence
- Socialist law
- Sharia
- Legal transplants
- Common core
- Harmonization
- Legal pluralism

Further Discussion

1. What is the difference between a legal tradition and a legal family?
2. What role does stare decisis play in the common-law and civil law families?
3. Do all systems formally observe the separation of public law and private law?
4. Explain the difference between convergence, common core, and harmonization. Give examples when possible.

Further Reading

De Cruz, Peter. *Comparative Law in a Changing World*. London: Routledge Cavendish, 2008.

Mattei, Ugo, Teemu Ruskola, and Antonio Gidi. *Schlesinger's Comparative Law: Cases, Text, Materials*. New York: Foundation Press, 2009.

Watson, Alan. *Legal Transplants: An Approach to Comparative Law*. Athens: University of Georgia Press, 1974.

LEGAL CONSTRUCTIONS OF SOCIETY

I n the previous three chapters we learned generally about the changing relationship between law and society as new technologies and forms of communication bring about new social interaction and the potential for different kinds of harm. Close readings of those chapters should support the constructivist approach that informs the remainder of this book. Unit 2 examines "Legal Constructions of Society"—the numerous ways in which law shapes the building blocks of which communities, states, and even nations are made. Chapter 4 delves into US legal history in the double sense of "law as history" and "law's use of history"; both suggest that law plays a vital role in nation building. Chapter 5 examines how our ideas of *family*—the smallest indivisible social unit—are shaped by legal rules and institutions. In chapter 6, the reader learns about the subtle but sometimes large-scale ways in which our personal attachments to physical space often come from law and policy. Chapter 7 then turns to spiritual belief and practice to explore how, particularly through rules about "free exercise" and "establishment," the law shapes this important building block. Finally, in chapter 8, the unit turns to class, race, and gender as key features of identity formation on which law has exerted considerable influence—particularly in American society.

History

This chapter is the first in a series on the fundamental "building blocks" of social life as shaped by law and legal institutions. If Unit 2 suggests that law helps to construct society, each of these chapters answers the question, "Out of what?" In this chapter, the answer happens to be "Out of history." That is to say, a group of people cannot understand itself as a "society" unless it subscribes to some shared story about its past, its creation, or its survival. The chapter first introduces several key concepts useful to unpacking the meaning of "history," the most important of which is *nationhood.* Next it revisits a familiar legal case to highlight the use it makes of historical ideas. And the last portion of the chapter challenges that use by revisiting, in some detail, the early history of law in the American colonies to challenge much of what, we are sometimes told in high-level legal opinions, makes up "our" shared past.

Since the advent of written language, humans have attempted to document their experiences emphasizing certain interpretations of events over others. According to some key thinkers, humans possess an innate sense of themselves as embedded in a larger story.[1] Others say we are not simply embedded, but are rather the drivers of history.[2] Either way, writing ensures the importance of this in social life. Writing allows us to broadly share ideas that were once only our own, or shared by only a few. Whereas spoken language can convey ideas to small groups, before recording technology it could do so only in front of relatively small audiences. Long before the invention of the bullhorn, microphones, amplification, or magnetic tape recording, written text was the only means by which to convey ideas widely and ensure their preservation in time.

Our sense of common participation in a larger story, and the need to share experiences through writing, suggest something very important about the relationship between history and society. Without the documented shared past, there might be collective groups, or families, but that sense of belonging to the larger story would be absent. Even further, as this chapter suggests, law plays a vital role in shaping both historical events and our memory of them. In the pages that follow, you will see some of the ways in which law *becomes* history when it finds itself at the center of key battles, events, and victories, and the ways in which law *uses* history to legitimize itself as "official." Through its influence on and through history, law helps to define society itself.

In saying all of this, it is important to clarify what is not meant here. Even the most successful students of high school history may be surprised by the approach of this chapter. History, it says, is not just "what happened, and when." It is a combination of things that happened, things that still are happening, and all the work that must go into choosing what to officially accept as "historical." This work entails memory, interpretation, and framing.

Like the term *history*, memory is a deceptively simple concept. At first blush it seems to be simply that which we recall in the short, medium, and long terms. But as recent writers interested in these nuances have said, it is actually much more. Memory is a process; it entails experience, perception, meaning making, and organizing. This last step is especially important; when historians choose to write something down as a significant historical event, they are also choosing *not* to write down other things as insignificant. The remembering that goes into writing history is thus also a forgetting.

Interpretation is a related process. Historians make not only choices about what to include and exclude as noteworthy but also decisions about noteworthiness that are ultimately matters of interpretation—of reading meaning from events as if they themselves were kind of like texts. Was the Boston Tea Party really important? Was it more so than other events that took place on that day in Massachusetts? Historians have long said yes, not because Americans find tea so relatable (we prefer coffee now), but because the event *meant* the colonists were utterly fed up with England's taxation of American import goods. But notice how this reading may not be obvious from the overt facts of the event: a group of several dozen white male colonists disguised as (what they believed were) Mohawk Indians boarded several ships late at night and dumped their cargo overboard. Like any act of political disobedience, it could have been interpreted as mere criminality. But it wasn't, at least not in a national-historical perspective. That is in part because of another important sociological process known as **framing** (see box 4.1).

Framing, according to the sociologist Erving Goffman, is an interpretive position-
ing of an event or experience such that it is imbued with meaning from a particular perspective.[1] Whereas multiple interpretations might be possible, framing
ensures that the interpretation of one group of viewers becomes the dominant
one. Framing can make an event that appears criminal in one epoch appear
heroic in another. And it can make acceptance of that interpretation a requirement for membership in the society.

1. Erving Goffman, *Frame Analysis: An Essay on the Organization of Experience* (Boston: Northeastern
University Press, 1986).

Framing is an especially important feature of the neoliberal approach to law
addressed in this book. That approach fundamentally views law as a protector of
individual, private interests in the name of economic exchange. It discourages
uses of law that would build a strong social safety net for the poor, or the disen-
franchised. This might sound cruel or callous to some. But its proponents have
succeeded in framing the debate differently. They see it as being not about "equality" but rather about "freedom," and consider social benefits provided by the public to those in need as encouraging laziness, and limiting collective freedom.

HISTORY AND NATION BUILDING

Framing of events through the writing of history has two other important side
effects. One is that it shapes the relationship between sociocultural **difference**
and **belonging,** or sameness. Traditionally, human societies were bound
together through deep connections of ancestry, blood, spiritual belief, and military necessity. As population grew and we evolved into complex, urban communities, the primordial connections just described became less important. In
large global cities, people came to live among others of different language, culture, and religious faith. Under these conditions, social cohesion was needed
but it would have to come about through something new: a sense of shared history developed through literacy and education. In the modern era, scholars
have suggested, the mass social solidarity of multicultural nations like the
United States, England, or France is the result of a shared view of history. Goffman's framing, therefore, becomes more than just a way of seeing important
events. It also becomes a way of belonging to a society.

History in this way has been an essential feature of nation building. A
nation is a collection of people larger than neighborhood or community that

believes in a shared past or shared future and that often lays claim to territorial sovereignty. This last feature of claimed territory is actually of declining importance in the age of the Internet, where instant communications transcend territorial space and make living together less important to members of some nations. History, as you might imagine, is critical because it offers nations the sense of a shared past or shared destiny. Also, because history is not just "what happened" but also a particular reconstruction of that, national leaders are able to commission their own version of history and offer this to the population for maximum effect. Examples of this abound through time, and some are more sinister than others. In prewar Germany, the Nazi Party carefully crafted a "history" of the German people as a singular "race" with a glorious past that had been spoiled by the supposed influx of foreigners (Jews, gypsies, etc.). With this history accepted, they were able to convince their population that the future depended on removing foreigners. Similar uses of the "glorious past" narrative have unfolded in Turkey, Uganda, Rwanda, the former Yugoslavia, and most recently the United States. The framing of the past through the writing of history is an important element of nation building and, as these examples suggest, can often lead to brutality in the present. But it often does not. In many cases shared history and nation building can have a constructive, peacekeeping function.

Two key theories help to explain how this works. The first comes from the British historian Eric Hobsbawm, who offered the idea of **invented tradition.** "Traditions which appear to be old," he wrote, "are often quite recent in origin and sometimes invented."[3] The key to an invented tradition is not its newness but, on the contrary, its ability to imply a "continuity with the past."[4] Examples of invented tradition are common in a relatively new nation like the United States. One happens to be the fall holiday of Thanksgiving. Although the annual holiday commemorates the first harvest of English Pilgrims in the new colonies in 1621, Thanksgiving did not become an annual event until the mid-nineteenth century and was not formalized until 1863, when President Lincoln sought to unify the country amid the Civil War. Perhaps most importantly, the culinary dishes eaten on America's Thanksgiving, dishes such as turkey, sweet potatoes, green beans, and cranberries, were not available in the early years celebrated by the holiday.[5] Much about this holiday, annually connecting US families of all religious, linguistic, and cultural backgrounds with their Pilgrim ancestors, is a more recent invention. But this makes it no less significant. On the contrary, it shows how the meaning of a new practice—in this case cooking and feasting—becomes imputed backward through time and then shapes the future by creating a common culture for contemporary citizens.

This new shared culture is the subject of a second important theory of history and nation building. The same year Hobsbawm issued the invented-tradition thesis, another English scholar named Benedict Anderson released a small but important book called *Imagined Communities.* Anderson's basic idea was

Figure 4.1 Jean Leon Gerome Ferris, *The First Thanksgiving*, ca. 1912.

that along with the rise of modern nation-states came an important cultural technology in the West. Large print media like newspapers and magazines were made possible by new printing machines and ink, as well as the commercial demand for advertising channels that would reach the growing middle classes in Europe, England and the United States. By reading the same newspapers and consuming the same advertised products, millions of strangers in these countries—separated by hundreds or thousands of miles from each other—now participate in a common culture making them, in effect, one shared community. But, Anderson points out, the true site for this sense of commonality lies largely in the imagination of individuals. For Anderson, the parallel appearance of nations and print media was not mere coincidence; he defined modern nations in terms of this imagined community: "I propose the following definition of the nation: it is an imagined political community—and imagined as both inherently limited and sovereign. It is imagined because the members of even the smallest nation will never know most of their fellow-members, meet them, or even hear of them, yet in the minds of each lives the image of their communion."[6] What, you may be asking, does this history lesson have to do with law and society? I suggested at the beginning of this chapter that law both becomes an important part of history and makes use of it. If so, then can it be said that law contributes to invented traditions or imagined communities? Can law, in other words, serve the function of nation building by influencing these important processes?

DEFAMATION REVISITED: HISTORY IN *TIMES V. SULLIVAN*

In the defamation case of *New York Times v. Sullivan* (see chapter 2), the Supreme Court weighed competing legal rights. To recap, the case was filed by an Alabama police commissioner named L. B. Sullivan who was in charge when police arrested Dr. Martin Luther King Jr. for perjury and suppressed student protests on university campuses. *The New York Times* printed an advertisement soliciting donations for Dr. King's legal defense fund, and in it the text asserted, among other things, that the police had targeted King deliberately and had locked protesters in their school cafeteria. Sullivan argued that these statements of fact were false and that his reputation had been badly damaged by the advertisement.

Recall that to win under the common law—that is to say independent of any statute or constitutional rule—Sullivan would have had to prove that the statements about him were more likely than not false, that they were seen by at least one other person, that they would tend to harm the reputation of someone in the minds of reasonable people, and that they were reasonably interpreted to be about him in particular. Here the newspaper admitted early on that the statements might have been inaccurate, and no one disputed that a high-circulation paper like the *Times* was "publication" in the technical sense meant by defamation law. The last two questions—"defamatory matter" and "of and concerning" the victim—were somewhat more tricky. But Sullivan ultimately won at the trial court level, and the lengthy appeals process began thereafter.

The Supreme Court of the United States typically only hears about 5 percent of cases that come before it every year; for the rest that are denied, the appellate decision becomes the final outcome. In deciding whether to hear the case the Court looks for "special and important" reasons. Often this includes unifying different states or regions of the United States on matters of important controversy. With this in mind, researchers have said, it is no coincidence that *Times v. Sullivan,* apparently a case about defamation law, was immanently about free speech in the **civil rights era.** On matters of race and racial equality, the United States was more divided than at any other time since the Civil War. Some wondered if new civil unrest would erupt as a result. Northern states like New York saw themselves as the vanguard of racial justice, while southern states like Alabama viewed themselves as protectors not of racism or injustice but rather of "states' rights," the freedom for state governments to determine locally appropriate rules for their communities. In this environment, other values were coming increasingly under fire. For example, the freedom to think and speak out publicly and collectively about political problems and leaders was becoming constrained by local agencies charged with maintaining "law and order."

In this climate, the two competing rights of *Times v. Sullivan* were some of the most consequential in American law. These were the right to be free from

Figure 4.2 Martin Luther King Jr. Photo by Marion Trikosko, 1964.

reputational harm protected under the common law and the fundamental right to free speech "guaranteed" under the First Amendment of the US Constitution.[7] If journalists wanted to report meaningfully on the social upheavals and political leadership of the day, they fell in the middle of these two rights. Prior to this case, the right to freedom from reputational harm for public leaders like police commissioner L. B. Sullivan was no different than for anyone else. Even though a police commissioner was in charge of enforcing law and

BOX 4.2   The Changing Idea of "Rights"

"Rights" are frequently understood as absolutes—as things that we must respect, or things that people owe us no matter what. For this reason they are sometimes called "fundamental," "basic," "civil," or "natural." But the reality borne out by history is that the meaning of "rights" changes considerably over time. Nowhere is this more apparent than in the American Constitution's very own Bill of Rights. Over centuries of Supreme Court jurisprudence, they were extended from free white men to racial minorities and to women. Often, despite their apparently "natural" quality, these rights were not generously given but had to be actively claimed through civil disobedience and protest. In law and society today, rights pose a conundrum to scholars trying to determine where one person's rights end and another's begin. From affirmative action in college admissions, to religious discrimination at food establishments, to refusal of lifesaving medical care, the struggle over competing rights continues.

making local policy, he or she could be criticized no more freely than a private citizen who skipped church or drank too much whiskey. Clearly, this rule had flaws.

So *Times v. Sullivan* was ultimately a case about the right to criticize public officials—ranging from the president of the United States down to local police chiefs—at a time in the nation's history when public speech seemed more valuable than ever. As described in chapter 2, the end result was a new rule that recognized the constitutional right to free speech and balanced it carefully against reputational protection. That rule, the "actual malice" standard, was later extended to cover not only government officials but also public figures like many celebrities, and it remains the rule applied today.

In coming up with this useful compromise, the Supreme Court could simply have relied on existing legal authorities. Obviously, the Constitution was an important one. But the Court also had at its disposal the law of certain states—many of which already applied an actual malice standard with great effect at the state level. Yet instead of stopping there, Justice William Brennan writing for the majority of the court cited US history. He did this in two important senses. The first was in the sense of **law as history.** In a common-law country like the United States, anytime a court makes a decision it must cite previous cases. But at the Supreme Court, the highest in the land, these references are also citations to big historical events. Prior court cases themselves have become history, and through their appearance in contemporary ones they continue to live on. Law, in this sense, *is* history.

In making a case for the need for national unity on the right to freedom of speech, Brennan cited a previous important case called *Whitney v. California* about a man who had violated a state criminal act by "inciting" undesirable political activity. The court in *Whitney* held that even this type of speech had to be protected to foster healthy competition among ideas in the United States.[8] Brennan quoted his predecessor Louis Brandeis as saying that this was part of a historically rooted "culture of free expression" that predated even the Constitution.

> Those who won our independence believed that public discussion is a political duty; and that this should be a fundamental principle of the American government. They recognized the risks to which all human institutions are subject. But they knew that order cannot be secured merely through fear of punishment for its infraction; that it is hazardous to discourage thought, hope and imagination; that fear breeds repression; that repression breeds hate; that hate menaces stable government; that the path of safety lies in the opportunity to discuss freely supposed grievances and proposed remedies; and that the fitting remedy for evil counsels is good ones. Believing in the power of reason as applied through public discussion, they eschewed silence coerced by law—the argument of force in its worst form. Recognizing the occasional tyrannies of governing majorities, they amended the Constitution so that free speech and assembly should be guaranteed.[9]

It is important to remember that this eloquent passage from one of our most influential jurists serves no authoritative function in the *Sullivan* opinion. Offering some of the historical tradition in which the *Whitney* decision was grounded, it reproduces that view of history anew in *Sullivan.* In this way, the Supreme Court's own prior reasoning becomes evidence for the shared history that it claims underlies the creation of a national actual malice standard in 1964. This practice arises time and again in Supreme Court reasoning, and it is one we might call *law as history.*

But also, Brennan showed us a second related phenomenon: **law's use of history.** Midway into the opinion, he is describing the importance of political dissent and criticism. He wants to illustrate a time when the nation's founders flirted with the repression of political speech, and then sharply rebuked this. Brennan's example, the Sedition Act of 1798, is a great one. Under that rule, it became a federal crime "if any person shall write, print, utter or publish any false, scandalous and malicious writing or writings against the government of the United States, or either house of the Congress, or the President, with intent to defame or to bring them, or either of them, into contempt or disrepute; or to excite against them, or either or any of them, the hatred of the good people of the United States."[10]

This rule seems quaint or even authoritarian in contemporary perspective. Today criticism of the president and legislators is so common it has given rise to new genres of television and print media programming. Moreover, although most of us don't agree with all the criticisms, and even though some of them prove to be based on false information, we protect the right of media outlets to carry on their criticism because it has something valuable to offer democratic society at large. But remember that this perspective has come from centuries of discussion and debate about free speech. At the time of the Sedition Act, early in the nation's history, it was not clear how this would all play out. The United States was the first country of its kind; would it fall apart if people were permitted to openly question their authorities in government? In the years after the act was passed, people realized it was better to risk finding out than to suppress speech. The new Americans had, after all, fought a war with England to free themselves from these same kinds of rules under the king. Ultimately, the Sedition Act was repealed—not invalidated by the Supreme Court but dismantled by the same legislative body representing the American people. As Brennan said in *Sullivan*, this dismantlement was itself the strongest historical evidence for the value of public political dissent in the minds of most Americans. "Although the Sedition Act was never tested in this Court, the attack upon its validity has carried the day in the court of history. Fines levied in its prosecution were repaid by Act of Congress on the ground that it was unconstitutional."[11] So Brennan's invocation of the Sedition Act is striking for two connected reasons. The first is that the act itself—a piece of federal legislation that would have been supreme over all law except the Constitution—was long since expired. Whereas federal statutes can be and often are the basis for the legal rule in Supreme Court opinions, in this case the act is not at all that. Second and relatedly, the appearance of the Sedition Act in *Sullivan* is purely decorative; it illustrates by historical example what *not* to do when making decisions about people's right to criticize their government—or speak falsely in doing so. The act is for these reasons an example of the law's *use* of history to explicate its underlying policy.

In *Sullivan*, both the law as history and law's use of history approaches are employed to reinforce the idea of national unity. Torn asunder by the civil rights struggles of the late 1950s and early 1960s, American society needed to be unified in its approaches to equal protection for fundamental rights. *Sullivan* was but one example from the period, but this was an era of numerous landmark decisions aimed at addressing racial and socioeconomic inequality and divisions. Yet in moving in this direction, the Court had to repeatedly assert that the values of freedom and equality had always been the shared values of the American nation. In this regard, the opinions of the period made reference to a shared past dating back to the Framers in which "all men [were] created equal." The legal institution of the Supreme Court, we must therefore recognize, was *itself* participating in a rewriting of American history. To understand why, a closer look at that history is in order.

CHALLENGES TO THE NATIONAL MYTH

Brennan's opinion utilized the technique for constitutional interpretation known as originalism. Forced to decide on the constitutionality of federal or state laws coming out of legislatures and courts, the Supreme Court must effectively ask whether the constitution "says" the rule in question is legal. But of course, the Constitution is a written document so, by itself, it doesn't say anything. Faced with a reader, however, it lends itself to interpretation and applications: in that encounter between the text and the reader it does say something. But what it says depends on much. For many judges, the Constitution says only what its original drafters thought it said. For others, it is a "living" document whose meaning can change over time. The first view, orginalism, is an immanently historicist position. It requires figuring out how people thought, spoke, and wrote during the eighteenth century and then searching through period-correct records for debates and opinions present at the time. One such source has been *The Federalist Papers*, a series of newsletters issued anonymously by several partisans of a strong central government in the years leading up to 1789. Not reliant upon *The Federalist Papers* for clues about original intent, Brennan's opinion in *Sullivan* did invoke the passage and quick reversal of the Sedition Act. Presenting this, Brennan wrote that a culture of free expression was a popular ideal among the colonists before the Revolution, as well as among the first Americans long after. But is this really true?

The freedom to criticize public officials defended in *Sullivan* was said to be a shared value in American history. However, several key legal historians have pointed to the many, many people who were not free in the days of the early republic. Three main groups fall into this category. The first is women; in the early colonies as well as after the Revolution, women were not permitted to vote in public matters, nor were they commonly allowed to hold property in their own name.[12] A woman's property was in fact subject to male ownership, so women were wards of their parents until marriage, and of their husbands thereafter. For this reason, marriage itself was critically important, and divorce was almost unthinkable.[13] The traditional rule making a woman's belongings property of her husband was known as **coverture,** and it was not until the middle nineteenth century that individual states began passing laws to undo this oppressive regime. Until that time, the public fear was that property ownership would erode women's attachments to the husband and the household, and would thus undermine the unity of the family. This meant that for roughly the first seventy-five years of American independence—a victory won largely for the purpose of better securing property interests in the New World—women were excluded from one of the core freedoms. But that was not the only one: women also were barred from electoral voting for an even longer period. Although the right to vote was extended to nonwhites and former slaves with the Fifteenth Amendment to the Constitution in 1870, women continued to be excluded from elections until the Nineteenth Amendment in 1920. Though arguably not about "expression" in the sense that Brennan, Brandeis, and others touted in *Whitney* and *Sullivan,* the legal marginalization of women during the founding period of the nation gives us pause about accepting the originalist narrative of freedom and equality espoused by those justices.

Two other groups were equally if not more excluded in those early days. Although the Declaration of Independence proclaimed human equality as "self-evident," we know for a fact that it was not treated that way. Black Africans kidnapped from tribes on the west coast of Africa were forced into ships and brought to the colonies as slaves. Some estimates put the total number of slaves reaching the United States at roughly four hundred thousand. As forced labor, they were "unequal" not only by definition—for instance, in their freedom to control their destiny—but also in being treated with violence, brutality, and cruelty. And not only were they not free to express themselves with respect to civic life, they were not even free to speak about domestic matters in the households, farms, and plantations where they resided. Another group treated similarly were the native Indian tribes that existed at the time of European settlement. Upon Columbus's arrival in the West Indies, it is estimated, there were between two and seven million natives inhabiting the territories of North America. Early contacts between the Indians and settlers of New England were mixed with periods of cooperation and mutuality (as in the first Thanksgiving) interspersed with periods of deceptive land bargaining, broken treaties, and intense military conflict. Although the Indian tribes of the Great Plains and Southwest remained "free" for several more decades, the tribes of the Atlantic Seaboard were largely decimated by violence, disease, or displacement by the time the Constitution came into being in 1789. As if these histories were not already evidence enough, the Constitution itself enshrined the exclusion and inequality that these two groups would experience. There, at article 1, section 2, the drafters explained how representatives of Congress would be apportioned to states of varying populations. States in the North had the greatest number of white Europeans, but states in the South had greater absolute populations if the many slaves that had been imported to work southern plantations were taken into account. Congressional representatives were supposed to be apportioned according to population size. So depending on who counted in the population, one side would get more representatives and therefore more power in the legislative branch of government. The architects of the new democratic republic came to a "compromise" that said, "Representatives and direct Taxes shall be apportioned among the several States which may be included within this Union, according to their respective Numbers, which shall be determined by adding to the whole Number of free Persons, including those bound to Service for a Term of Years, and excluding Indians not taxed, three fifths of all other Persons."[14] The so-called "three-fifths" compromise was that Indians would not count and "all other persons," meaning African slaves, would count at a fraction of their presence. Some have said this was merely an administrative formula, but others argue that, in rather plain English, it determines Indians and slaves to be less than whole persons. This distinction is overly academic; the reality was that Indians and slaves (and their descendants) were not to be represented in government at an equal rate to whites. Their participation in civic life was discounted, and their freedom to express dissent was not even considered. Brennan's "culture of free expression" supposedly common to the nation since its inception was therefore far from universal. Not only that, but its limitation to a fraction of the population was meant to secure that fraction over and above those mentioned here. The mention of this common history in *Sullivan* is meant to serve an important nation-building function at a time of deep national strife, but it is necessary to separate the unifying value from the truth value of its claims about a shared past. Brennan's opinion, in other words, mobilized an invented tradition in the service of what he and others hoped would be a stronger imagined community.

LAW, LANGUAGE, AND IDEOLOGY

This use of an important case opinion for nation building described so far is not unique. Cases may be the fundamental feature of English common law but statutes—legislative acts—are increasingly important too. In civil law countries, the balance is inverted with codes predominating and cases supplementing the remainder of law. In all cases, law is deeply rooted in the capabilities and limitations of language. Originalism is a significant result of this: the meaning of the Constitution must be constantly rediscovered through its association with other texts. Brennan's use of historical events and historic legal precedents in *Sullivan* supports a story about the birth of the nation that is intended in turn to support the outcome in that case itself. The language of the opinion therefore reflects an ideology that is at the center of American national identity. **Ideology,** for our purposes, is a taken-for-granted worldview that reconciles apparent contradictions in the social environment. The enslavement of Africans by white Americans, for example, was a contradiction given the pronouncements of the Declaration and Preamble to the Constitution. But this contradiction could be reconciled by a worldview of race in which dark skin was a permanent mark of moral and intellectual primitivism. Slavery, by this token, was not only acceptable but favorable because it "domesticated Black Africans in a new land of opportunity."

Law and society scholars have long studied the relationship between language, law and ideology. Elizabeth Mertz describes how statutes regarding American Indians in the United States and blacks in South Africa both deploy language in ways that depict their respective nations as generous in allocating land use to their nonwhite populations.[15] Both nations use language in a way that conveys an ideology reconciling the contradictions of minority sovereignty and dependency in each country. The writers Austin Sarat and William Felstiner have studied the use of language among family law attorneys in New England to document the ways divorce lawyers utilized certain words to separate the past, present, and future of dissolving marriages.[16] Those attorneys mobilize "distancing words" to avoid entanglements in a spouse's emotional past, while reframing the ongoing divorce as a battle of strategy over the household resources.[17] In both examples, language in law betrays its ideological function of reconciling contradictions that would otherwise make legal solutions difficult or unappealing.

A similar linguistic move is made by Brennan. His *Sullivan* opinion describes the need for an actual malice standard in terms of the great value of free expression in a democratic society. Slavery and racism, in this telling, are evils resulting from a poor market of ideas. Protection of free speech, Brennan seems to suggest, helps encourage debate and therefore a rooting out of bad ideas like slavery and racial segregation. In one of many instances of this, he quotes the famous Justice Learned Hand saying that the First Amendment "presupposes that right conclusions are more likely to be gathered out of a multitude of tongues, than through any kind of authoritative selection. To many this is, and always will be, folly; but we have staked upon it our all."[18] Simply put, the linguistic move of using "we," "us," and "ours" in describing the culture of free expression is a large part of this ideological twist. Since its foundation, women and minorities in the United States had been excluded from civic life. To be now included (in the 1960s), they had to envision themselves as part of an imagined community. That community imagined itself as fundamentally "free" as to speech and the press—among many other things. Therefore, to gain their freedom, new groups had to imagine themselves part of a group that had always been free. The ideology of a perennial "we" in American law reconciles the contradictions of American nationhood itself.

OUT OF MANY, ONE: REREADING LEGAL HISTORY

Law and society in the United States were once extremely diverse, but out of that local diversity had to come national unity. If *Sullivan* imagined a shared past committed to free expression, and if many had long been excluded from that past, how did law actually function in early US history? More importantly, to the extent that *Sullivan* and other cases have helped construct the United States as a singular nation, how necessary was this, and what would we look like if it had never happened?

Any summary of early colonial law must begin with the caveat that the English were *not* the first to settle North America, and that there were millions of native people already living across the continent in varying states of social and political organization. With their organization came robust systems of tribal law, in many cases tied to native religion or spiritual belief. In talking about US legal history we begin with the first English settlements because they were the earliest form of the sociolegal systems we see around us today. The first such settlement was the Roanoke Colony in what is now North Carolina. Unlike the later religious exiles of the Plymouth Colony, the English settlers of Roanoke were commissioned by the British crown under Sir Walter Raleigh, who sent an envoy of roughly one hundred men, women, and children led by a man named John White. The group landed in North Carolina in 1587 and began the long process of establishing primitive infrastructure. White left the settlement, including his own family behind, to return to England for more supplies. But on return in 1590, he and his men found every last colonist missing without a trace. This first experiment in settlement became known as the "Lost Colony" of Roanoke, and historians and archaeologists continue to investigate the mystery of its disappearance. The story of Roanoke is significant to law and society for one very important reason. It reflects clearly the great fragility of English society as it attempted to gain a foothold in the New World. Diseases like malaria, extreme weather such as Atlantic hurricanes, and potentially unsympathetic neighbors like the Indians could all be challenges in their own right. Combined, these factors made life, let alone social organization, precarious. For this reason, law in the new colonies was especially important for maintaining order and ensuring the future.

After the failed settlement of Roanoke, the Jamestown colony of Virginia was established in 1607 amid the territory of the Paspahegh Indian tribe. Within three years nearly 80 percent of the new colonists had died from disease. In 1608, a resupply envoy brought the first Polish and German as well as the first female settlers to the New World, and in 1619 the first African slaves were brought over. Early law in this period was, as one would expect, primitive. Disputes or criminal complaints were adjudicated by a single, undifferentiated tribunal consisting of non-legal experts. Early government lacked the "separation of powers" that was later a hallmark of American democracy. And legal precepts in this new territory had to adapt to differences in local conditions. Perhaps most importantly, the settlers initially did not want to import English common law exactly as it had existed in the mother country. There, the king remained the supreme adjudicator, and much of the legal order was in place to protect the interests of the landed elite in a world of scarce resources. Similarly, the early colonists mistrusted the legal profession as both defenders and beneficiaries of this system, and few trained attorneys were willing to give up steady law practice in England to take up building tools in the new settlement.[19] Early colonial lawyers were thus "attorneys in fact"— lawyers without any special training in school or a law office.

After Jamestown numerous other settlements emerged on the Atlantic coast of North America. From the wintry cold of Massachusetts in the North down to the subtropical heat of Georgia in the South, the geographic and climactic diversity of the region alone may have been cause for political and legal innovations and experimentation. Each colony specialized in its own agricultural and artisan production—rice, indigo, and tobacco in Virginia versus fishing and shipbuilding in Massachusetts. Adding to this, the colonies had been organized by several vastly different political structures. Some were under royal charter; others were for-profit corporations complete with shareholders back in England. If all this wasn't enough, there were at least five major religious groups present, as well as various European cultures and languages including Dutch, German, and Spanish. The influential legal historian Lawrence Friedman therefore writes that early colonial law was in a constant tension between uniformity and diversity—differences emerging from the various local conditions, charters, and cultures present.[20] Even though initial opinions toward English law and legal profession were sour, the colonists realized that they could not simply reinvent the wheel. The years after settlement were thus marked by an *increasing* openness toward English legal influences. Illustrating this evolution were colonial approaches to land law, criminal law, and commercial law.

Perhaps the most uniformly different was the relative abundance of land. In England all land was under private or royal ownership, and title to land was based on an elaborate system of tenure—or use rights. The various benefits of access to land were separated from ownership itself so that rights to water or minerals, as well as recreation and farming could be bought and sold independently from the ownership title itself. Indeed, few people were actually permitted to own land absolutely. Those who did were of high social status, so land holding and socioeconomic class went hand in hand. England also observed a rule of **primogeniture** according to which land title by law passed to the first-born son of a family's next generation. All of this was meant to control ownership and disposal of rights in a context of scarcity.

In criminal law, the colonies evolved from the primitive to the refined. Initially, criminal complaints were adjudicated by a layperson sitting as judge without formal training in law or penal justice. Lacking in long-term common-law memory, early colonial criminal law relied heavily on the Bible for precepts about right and wrong, and sometimes **moral panics**—fears about illicit activity taking place en masse—resulted in waves of repression and criminalization, as in the Salem Witch Trials of 1692 and 1693. As colonial law matured, however, criminal law was written down and disseminated in codes. These codes still bore the influence of Puritan Christianity, and many of their biblical traces remain on the books to this day.[21]

Commercial law, finally, was similarly mixed between customary and modern forms. The Law Merchant or *lex mercatario,* an existing international regime of commercial law dating back to the medieval period in Europe, was still influential. It held that commercial transactions should be governed by freedom of contract, with conflicts resolved in favor of honoring agreements, and with state intervention kept to a minimum. The new colonies also honored a system of **commercial paper,** a system of unsecured promissory notes that probably aided in economic development in a land of greater speculation where credit mattered more.

The presence of forced labor was one final important addition to commercial law in the colonies. One form was **indentured servitude:** individuals could contract with another party to sell in advance their labor for a fixed period of years, and they were then bound by that agreement despite future wishes to rescind. This arrangement would have been relatively more common in the colonies than in England, because poor English and European immigrants would contract with families or private companies for the costs of ocean passage to be paid through future years of compulsory servitude. This arrangement was widespread in the seventeenth century, but it declined over the next century thanks in part to the "cheap" availability of labor from slaves. Slavery, therefore, was the last major feature of colonial commercial law. Slaves were chattel property of white owners, and their escape and return were juridically treated like the loss and return of any other movable property—an approach that had to be upheld by courts throughout the period.

Finally, although early colonists were hostile to lawyers and made use of attorneys in fact, the century before the Revolution saw increasing English influence over an increasingly formal legal profession. As in England before the colonies, the legal profession grew into an upper-class society. Many "read law" under the supervision of older attorneys, but some also made the long journey back to London where they studied at the Inns of Court and apprenticed to become full **barristers** in the English dualist tradition. The pre-Revolution period also saw the publication and dissemination of key English law treatises such as Sir William Blackstone's *Commentaries on the Laws of England* and Sir Edward Coke's *Institutes of the Lawes of England.* These texts, some of the only English-language law texts in wide circulation in the colonies, would have a large influence on the framers of the Constitution. After the outbreak of hostilities during the Revolution, intercourse with England ceased, as did the growing practice of studying law at the Inns of Court. American aspiring jurists would have to study at one of the brand-new law schools, such as William and Mary or Litchfield in Virginia and Connecticut respectively, or they would have to "read law" under a practicing attorney. In all cases, Blackstone and Coke grew in influence before American jurists like Joseph Story and James Kent produced their own native treatises and these began to supplant the influence of England on the American common law.

Throughout this history, US law underwent rapid change from a condition of improvisation and lay practice toward increasing organization and expertise. With that, the diverse innovative practices in the various colonies shifted toward greater uniformity and predictability. Out of many different legal practices there came into being one single legal system without which the nation itself might have remained fragmented.

CONCLUSION

This chapter has suggested that history is a fundamental building block of modern societies, and that law plays a critical role in the formation of historical accounts of the past. A building block is an essential part of the whole, but it becomes functional only in relation to other parts like itself. History, we will see, works in concert with the subjects of each of the following chapters to bind people together and keep them cooperating smoothly—sometimes through moments of great conflict and crisis.

The American nation has endured several such moments. The period surrounding the case of *Times v. Sullivan* is a prime example of this. Against a backdrop of racial segregation and urban unrest, the defendant in the case—the *New York Times*—published an advertisement calling for support of Dr. Martin Luther King in hopes that northern elites would contribute financially to defend King from what the ad's authors considered malicious prosecution. Criticizing southern public officials for their involvement, the publisher was sued by one of these officials for reputational harm, forcing the Supreme Court of the United States to weigh private interests in reputational protection against public interests in freedom of speech. Hoping to secure a nationwide standard for reaching this balance, Justice Brennan's opinion articulated a revised rule supported, he argued, by a long tradition of free expression in the United States.

A brief look at the several groups excluded from full participation in the early U.S. colonies suggests that this long tradition may be, in large part, a construct. Prevented from holding property rights and from voting for that same period, women were not "full" members of the society and therefore were not entitled to full freedom to express themselves publicly. American Indians and African slaves were also very present in colonial society, yet they too were discounted from citizenship, and later from full representation in the new American experiment with democracy.

Brennan's effort to recount the history of unified interest in free expression was thus an exercise in two key uses of history for nation building in the tumultuous 1960s. On one hand, it sought to develop a culture of free expression as something that had *always* been with the nation. The result of developing something new and then reading backwards into the past, free expression was something of an *invented tradition*. But also Brennan saw this culture as belonging to the entire national population of the United States—from California to Massachusetts. He spoke to this national audience in his opinion and asked them to imagine themselves as a unified whole—an *imagined community*.

This chapter's look at the great diversity of the early colonies underscored the substantial work that went into forging this community over time. What had once been a group of many state political structures, languages, cultures, and legal systems, was fused over time, through numerous small acts of nation building, into a single society under a federal government. History, in this way, is constructive of the key groups it speaks of. Above all else, as we have seen, it is far more than just "what happened, and when."

CHAPTER 4 REVIEW

Key Terms

- Framing
- Difference
- Belonging
- Nation
- Invented tradition
- Imagined community
- Civil rights era
- Law as history
- Law's use of history
- Coverture
- Ideology
- Primogeniture
- Moral panics
- Commercial paper
- Indentured servitude
- Barristers

Further Discussion

1. After reading this chapter, how would you explain the idea of "history"?

2. In what ways was Brennan's opinion in *Sullivan* contributing to invented tradition or imagined community?

3. What factors made law in the early U.S. colonies different from law in England at the time?

4. Describe the relationship between law, history, and ideology.

Further Reading

Friedman, Lawrence. "American Law in the Colonial Period." In *A History of American Law*, 29–90. New York: Simon and Schuster, 1973.

Irons, Peter. "Morally Sinful by the Word of God." In *A People's History of the Supreme Court*, 3–16. New York: Viking Press, 1999.

Mertz, Elizabeth. "The Uses of History: Language, Ideology, and Law in the United States and South Africa." In *The Law and Society Reader*, edited by Richard Abel, 361–80. New York: NYU Press, 1995.

New York Times v. Sullivan, 376 U.S. 254, 1964.

Zinn, Howard. *A People's History of the United States*. New York: Harper Collins, 2005.

Family

In the last chapter we saw one of the many ways that law contributes to a society's sense of itself. By commemorating past events, legal court opinions give them an official meaning that gets conveyed to future generations—not just of lawyers but of lay citizens affected by the decision. In addition, important legal rules themselves make history by changing the course of public behavior and future events. History, in short, one of the key building blocks giving a society its sense of collective "self," is intimately tied to law. But this is only a beginning.

Society is composed of webs of relationships in a community, town, city, state, or nation; it is therefore made up of individuals in direct relation to one another. So, forgetting momentarily about large collectives, any argument that law and society are linked must grapple with how basic interpersonal relations are imbued with legal significance. When we are together with loved ones, we tend to think of ourselves as "in private," out of reach of the strong arm of the government. Does law really have a say in those relations?

Perhaps you have a brother or a sister. Maybe you have several. For as long as you can remember, you have probably known your brother or sister as a member of your family or as a friend. But have you ever stopped to consider why you are connected *more* to that blood relative than to nearly every other person you will meet in a lifetime? Even if you no longer speak, your brother or sister can never really be divorced, or erased from your family history. Why is that? It turns out that the law has much to say in defining the relationships you have with other people—even before you meet them. In this chapter we examine in brief just what it says, and why. The general question throughout is simple: What should be the role of law in determining the basic parameters of the family? In trying to answer this question, this chapter argues that law oscillates over time between trying to strengthen the family **structure** and trying to support its **functions**.

To make this claim, the chapter first explores the Western notion of "family" as a form of kinship relation that social researchers have been fascinated by for many years. **Kinship,** readers will soon see, is the study of strong social relationships. It is almost literally the glue that binds societies together both in terms of creating discrete family units and in terms of binding multiple families together into larger tribes, clans, communities, and so forth. Even political theorists have, at times, identified family kinship as the basic indivisible unit of political society.[1]

Second, the chapter delves into a discussion of the two primary areas of legal intervention into family relations. The first of these is **parentage,** or the manner in which parent-child relationships are established and maintained. The second is **succession,** or the way a household's wealth is distributed upon the death of all parents. These two themes, parentage and succession, are two of the most important ways that law intervenes to define what a family is, or can be. Using these subsections to discuss legal constructions of the family, this chapter highlights how family relations can be fluid and how their specification in law gives them their appearance as natural and timeless.

Whether the institution of the family *should* ever be changing is another important question. If the primary goal of the family is to ensure survival of the next generation, can it do so best by remaining firm as social context evolves? Or can it better ensure survival by adapting to changing social circumstances? For example, could the rise of same-sex marriage partnerships offer a new kind of nuclear family stability in a world of dissolving male-female marriages? These questions are directly related to law and society: legal institutions are responsible for fixing the categories of family amid changing circumstances, but they are often moved to allow new family dynamics to emerge.

KINSHIP

The study of family relationships has occupied a central place in what was once called the study of "Man." Today, more cognizant about the politics of equating all people with only one gender, experts would rather call this the study of humans or human cultures. They are referring of course to the field of **anthropology,** although in the decades since its inception the study of family relationships has spread into numerous other fields such as sociology, politics, economics, and law. That is because, precisely, the family is a complicated institution whose role spans many of these other important ways of studying the world.

Traditionally, anthropologists referred to the study of family relations as kinship studies. This term was more "scientific" because the concept of "the family" was truly only a Western and modern one. Whereas European households made up of blood relatives might have understood themselves as families—the word *family* (or *la famille* in French) being derived from the root *familiar*—non-Western social units would often stretch this category. In many cases, the most important figure of the so-called family was not a parent or grandparent. For example, among the Iatmul tribe of Melanesia's Papua New Guinea (near Australia), studied by the famous anthropologist Gregory Bateson in the 1920s, the most important figure was the uncle—specifically the mother's brother. This maternal uncle, or *wau*, carried a critical dispute-resolution function in the tribe by performing a dramatic, spontaneous ceremony known as the *naven* whenever an individual accomplished something of value in a manner that could upset or offend the pride of his or her own elders.[2] Bateson gives an example of a young boy who builds his first canoe as one possible moment where the *naven* ceremony played a key role in maintaining tribal stability. The maternal uncle, for this reason, held broad social significance in a way not paralleled in Western societies. Studies of this encompassed more than simply the study of family ties; they were about the basic structure and function of relationships holding the society together. So although this chapter is about law's construction of society at the site of family relations, it is also in the spirit of kinship studies about much more than just that. It is also a way of understanding the role family relations play in binding us into larger communities.

Two key features of the family are its structure and its function. Both bind people together, though for different reasons. The structural role puts each person in his or her "proper place" in the web of personal relationships he or she takes part in. In this respect the family can be defined in terms of the hierarchy and connections between its people: brothers and sisters occupy one level, mother and father one level higher, and maternal and paternal grandparents still one level higher than that (see figure 5.1).

Visualizing the family in this fashion can be very helpful; it allows us to see where any individual sits in relation to his or her "generation," and those that preceded and follow it. But notice that "time" is nowhere captured in this chart. The family depicted is, once all children are born, unchanging in its relations. That is important because this structural quality of family relations is an inherently *stabilizing* force. Once relationships are created through birth, they are never destroyed—not even in death. The French sociologist Pierre Bourdieu criticized kinship anthropologists for these models because, he said, they left out the all-important role of time. Without that key feature, does the model below really tell us how a family "works"?

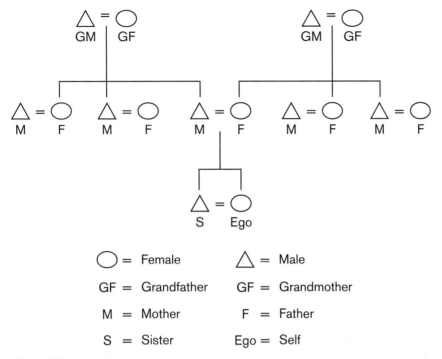

Figure 5.1 Basic kinship chart.

In response, other researchers preferred not simply to model family relation-ships but instead to study family practices. They wanted to know how living in a family unit helped human beings survive in their natural or social environ-ments. The functional role allows the family to survive from one generation to the next. As a thought experiment, imagine for a moment a world without fam-ily organization. Children could still be born of two biological parents, but sup-pose that after birth newborn babies were handed over to the entire community, or perhaps a committee representing it. Children would then be raised by this committee without the bonds of parents and siblings, and they would be ush-ered into adulthood with only the community as their master. Now suppose, in mid-childhood, one such child falls gravely sick with a high fever. The commu-nity elders know there is nothing they can do, but they know of a "doctor" in another village many miles away across a dangerous expanse of land or water. Who, at this point, would travel that distance, perhaps carrying the child, or perhaps bringing the doctor back to examine her? In the natural environment humans once occupied—where infection and disease took the life of half the children born—each one's survival was important for the survival of the entire community, and for the human species more generally. But without the bonds of what we might call family "love," few individual members might feel motivated to risk their lives to save the young. Rewinding this thought experiment and playing it back with family attachment reinserted in the story, we can imagine that the child's parent or perhaps brave older sibling would take on the challenge of a treacherous journey because the loss of one individual would inflict emotional pain on those around her. This is but one example of the "functionalist" approach to family found in early social science. It explains "love" in terms of risk taking and selflessness of a kind that ensures the success of younger generations. Other examples could just as easily refer to food, clothing, shelter, and even education as similar "goods" bestowed upon the young by virtue of their membership in a caring family. All of these have definite functional benefits to individuals, communities, and the wider human species.

Historically, social researchers fought among themselves about which of these—structure or function—was most important. Without clearly defined structure, there would be no sense of duty to take care of another person; for instance, I might love all children, but I would not be duty bound to care for those outside my family in part because we would not be connected in a clear family structure. And without functional benefits, there might be no evolutionary point to observing or respecting family structure; when doing so *costs* more in resources or human lives over time, people have tended to alter family structures to better suit their survival needs. Coming up in the sections below are examples of both structuralist and functionalist assumptions within family law as it tries to resolve delicate problems in human households. What matters most is how legal approaches to defining family have actually swung between structural and functional definitions. Those swings help explain what appear to be drastic changes in approaches to the family over time.

PARENTAGE

Who counts as a person's mother and father, and why? Most of us never stop to ponder this question because the answer seems so obvious. In fact, it is frequently these most taken-for-granted facts about our world that, upon closer inspection, reveal the most about how that world comes together. A person's mother and father are the two people who *made* them; but notice that *made* in this case can have either biological or social meanings. In most cases, it is still true that exactly two people provided the genetic material to make any living person. But what about cases when one or both of them do not *raise* their offspring? What about cases when one or both biological parents are no longer living? What about when a new pair of adults have legally adopted another's child? What about "surrogacy," where the embryo of two parents has been carried in the womb by yet a third person? What about new cases when three or more adults have contributed genetic material to making a new human?

Those questions reflect some of the new biomedical advances that make parentage more complicated today. But there are also social changes. Beginning in the early 1970s, US same-sex couples began formally seeking the right to marry. This was followed by several decades of piecemeal, state rulings both for and against the right of same-sex marriage. By the 2000s this had led to a patchwork of US state laws protecting and prohibiting this right until the Supreme Court finally reheard the matter in 2015 and ruled 5 to 4 that same-sex marriage would be legal in all fifty states.[3] In the debates surrounding this case, proponents of same-sex marriage frequently highlighted the close parallels between *Obergefell* and another earlier case, *Loving v. Virginia*.[4] Taken for granted as a right by 2015, *Loving*'s innovation was that, as of 1967, interracial couples would finally be allowed to legally marry. The legalization of interracial and then same-sex marriage represented changing attitudes and possibilities in family arrangements that would go on to make the parentage question at once more complex and more open than before.

Another historical change has been a shift in the Western world from extended to nuclear families. In the not-too-distant past, before the rise of modern air travel and high-speed communications, human beings tended to live together in **extended families** known for their large size, multigenerational makeup, stronger *social* bonds, and sharing of household duties. They were large because couples tended to have more children to ensure some survivals in a time when infant and childhood mortality rates were higher. Families were also larger because children were often put to work on farms or in industries to help support their household. Finally, extended families were large because they combined different generations under one roof: grandparents, parents, siblings, cousins, uncles and aunts, and nieces and nephews. This last feature meant that elderly members were cared for by younger relatives, and babies could be left in the presence of grandparents. In these ways, home care or **affective labor** was not yet a service to outsource from the household and certainly was not constitutive of entire, lucrative industries. Making use of the "care" given by different generations, the extended family was characterized by complex social relations. Children felt responsibility to their elders, grandparents maintained positions of authority and dispute resolution, and uncles and aunts could help socialize young people—training them in the burdens and privileges of social membership—into adulthood. Further, as already suggested, the conventional duties we think of such as parents raising children, or children respecting parents, were spread across wider groups in the days of the extended family. Young people depended on all elders of a household, not just parents; and multiple adults beyond one's birth parents shared the burden of feeding, bathing, clothing, and caring for the youth of the family.

For many today, these realities about life in an extended family seem pretty remote from daily experience. But many still grow up in families with these qualities. In some communities, for example, it is not uncommon for siblings of

Figure 5.2 Extended family of Hermann A. Wideman. Photo taken in Hawaii ca. 1888.

the same generation to buy homes and raise children on the same street or neighborhood. Among US immigrant families from Asia and Latin America, a sense of duty toward one's parents well into their old age is instilled from birth. And for many who cannot afford expensive child care, continued reliance upon grandparents to care for infants and toddlers during the workday is the only way to put food on the table. Features of the extended family remain with us.

But it is also safe to say the situation has changed for a great majority of those living in the United States and western Europe today. Instead of sharing a household in the ways just described, most children now live with only their parents and siblings. We call this arrangement the **nuclear family.** By comparison to extended families, nuclear families are smaller (see figures 5.2 and 5.3), consisting of only two generations, socially less complex, and, on the surface, more self-reliant. Of all these features, the last is most controversial and interesting.

The nuclear family, consisting of only two parents and one or more children, has become the basic household unit in the United States and western Europe. If grandparents are nearby, they are usually in a separate household of their own or in assisted living communities. This means that intergenerational care is less direct than in the extended family household. In cases of "assisted" living, care for the elderly is literally outsourced to private companies that run large apartment and condominium dwellings with onsite nurses, catering, and housekeeping—all forms of labor once carried out by families themselves. These businesses now make up a multi-billion-dollar-a-year industry. For law,

Figure 5.3 American nuclear family, including mother, father, sister, and brother. Photograph by Staff Sgt. Natasha Stannard, 2017.

they have introduced a whole host of new issues requiring solutions. Are such facilities to be regulated like hospitals and clinics? Should proprietors be liable for illnesses or death among their aging clientele? And can these facilities be housed in ordinary residential neighborhoods?

Equally significant about this outsourcing of elderly care is the diminished role of older generations in the day-to-day lives of children. While in many cases grandparents in good health remain intimately involved with their grandchildren, more and more seniors spend their last decades farther removed from their own children and grandchildren. On a social level, this means that young people are increasingly less exposed to the experiences of aging and that physical and mental ailments that come with age are viewed as "sickness" and segregated from the wider society. Young people may also be more ignorant of physiological changes that are a normal part of the life course. The wider society in turn becomes more preoccupied with youth, as seniority becomes viewed in itself as a kind of living afterlife.

On a practical level, the absence of the elderly from the lives of the young removes an entire supply of affective labor that could assist with child care. This compels parents to place their children in child care facilities—day cares and preschools—nearly from birth in order to keep the daily work hours required in the conventional labor force. Like assisted living, child care is now a multi-billion-dollar industry. It too has spawned a large regulatory and legal regime that attempts to ensure the safety and well-being of kids placed with professional caregivers acting **in loco parentis,** or legally in the place of the parents. And perhaps most importantly, this whole arrangement, in which seniors and children are cared for by nonfamily experts while parents must work long hours to afford such services, has created a total economic system that separates caring labor from the family and turns industrial labor into the best available means to "provide" for a family.

The effect, as you might imagine, is to weaken the social bonds that once tied families together. Whereas parents once depended on the grandparents for help, and grandparents depended on parents for care, the advent of caring industries has weakened the bonds making up this mutual relationship. Today, therefore, young families may live thousands of miles from the previous generation, and some children grow up never knowing their living grandparents—or any elderly persons, for that matter. These are, undeniably, social changes with enormous implications in human history. But what do they have to do with law? In other words, what role does the *state* play in all of this?

By *state*, we do not mean regional jurisdictions like California or New York—although they too play a role at their own scale. *The state* refers to the full apparatus of government institutions, officials, bureaucrats, and even outsourced government functions carried out by private companies funded by public money. While the state in this sense does include the president or the courts, it also can include public utilities, emergency first responders, or parks and recreation custodians. More to the point, it includes the regulatory agencies, public financing programs, and compliance trainers and inspectors who ensure safe management of caring industries such as senior care and child care facilities. Without the support of the state for these industries, in other words, they could not reliably substitute for the care once provided within and among families themselves.

In other words, the modern reliance upon outsourced care industries that has been crucial to the development of the modern nuclear family—separated in its social relations from extended family members—has depended heavily on enlarged state oversight and financing. This has often been referred to as the modern "welfare state." But it does not always result in "welfare" or direct monetary subsidies for households. Rather, it is a modern form of governance that provides for citizen welfare because this helps to support a growing economy. Although it does not provide for *all* needs, the welfare state, through financial and legal support, has helped to drastically alter family relations in the West. If this is challenging to take in, one way to better understand this is to examine it cross-culturally. Take, for example, three countries: Mexico, Sweden, and China. All three have undergone key shifts in their standard family structure, and all three shifts are attributable to the financial and legal provisions by the national state of each.

Mexico is a Catholic country whose largest demographic group consists of people of mixed Spanish and indigenous ancestry. For students and researchers in the United States, Mexico is particularly interesting in that it borders the United States directly to the south, and Mexican Americans (both US and foreign born) are one of the fastest-growing minority populations. Starting from approximately nine million people in 1980, this community now makes up more than thirty-five million people in the United States today.[5] For this reason, Mexican kinship relations may have a special influence on life in the United States. This has been especially true with Mexican American working-class families. Although the strongest kinship ties in Mexico are among nuclear family relations, rural poverty in the country has prompted many families to reside in overlapping households that pool income to ensure subsistence through mutual aid. Where extended family members may have migrated to the United States, many send money (known as remittances) "home" to support a family unit far larger than just the immediate kin group. For immigrant extended families in the United States, many of whom are unable to access government assistance because of their undocumented status, economic cooperation beyond the nuclear family has been equally significant. In short, the absence of social welfare for the rural poor in Mexico and for Mexican American working-class immigrants has prompted greater reliance on the extended kinship group for the most prominent reason of economic stability. The relative absence of the state, for these communities, has encouraged more extended family relations.

Sweden, meanwhile, is a far more economically prosperous country. There, adjusted average income per person sits at approximately $47,000. Compare this, for example, to Mexico's figure of about $17,000.[6] Sweden is considered a democratic socialist country: it is a representative democracy but taxes its citizens heavily in order to provide very extensive social welfare benefits to everyone. One key example is Sweden's national parental leave and child care policies. For new parents, the state provides for 480 days of paid parental leave anytime a child is born or adopted. For decades the Swedish government has offered a monthly stipend for each child roughly equivalent to the costs of monthly day care expenses. The combined results of these family-friendly policies have been multiple. New parents have relied less and less on the affective labor of extended family members such as grandparents, and new parents, especially mothers, have been more eager to rejoin the workforce after giving birth compared to other countries. In the 1990s, Sweden had 86 percent of new mothers in the workforce. State benefits also extend to domestic partners, correlating in turn to a falling marriage rate and a growing cohabitation rate. Together these facts lead to one primary conclusion: the robust social welfare state of Sweden not only has contributed to the growth of nuclear families but has actually shifted the nuclear family into a more "modern" form where children's well-being is virtually guaranteed but the institution of marriage has grown increasingly obsolete.

China offers a third comparative case study on the connection between state policy and household affairs. Once upon a time, the people residing in modern China lived among large family clans or *tsu*, which provided mutual support among one another through moneylending, dispute settlement, education, property protections, and so forth. Note that these are all activities we commonly associate with governments today. In a tradition dating from this early period, Chinese families tended to reside together in multigenerational households, with the grandparents and grandchildren caring for one another out of a strong sense of duty.

China has since undergone several dramatic political shifts, including the adoption of communism, which sought to replace family self-reliance with common ownership and state control, and more recently "state capitalism," which maintains a communist centralized economy but sees the government acting in many ways "for profit." As the Chinese population reached high density in the 1980s, the state introduced its famous "one-child policy," in which new parents were permitted only one offspring before substantial penalties were applied. This policy succeeded in controlling population growth, but what do you think its effects might have been on the household structure as a generation of "only-child" families came of age? The result was a small young adult population but a large aging population. Nowadays, it is not uncommon for a married couple—each spouse the only child of his or her generation—to take care of four grandparents. The Chinese norm is toward extended families, but notice how, thanks to deliberate family planning laws, these look quite different from the extended families of historic North America.

All told, the comparative look at Mexico, Sweden, and China offers valuable perspective on the relation between law and the family. We tend to think of household arrangements such as whether to live as extended or nuclear families—or what the precise makeup of these arrangements might be—as "private" matters. In the United States, the Supreme Court has even interpreted the first ten amendments of the Constitution to imply a *right* to make such decisions privately or unfettered by state meddling. But the reality instead appears to be that family arrangements are dramatically affected by how the state decides to provide care for its people, or to solve (or not solve) social problems like wealth inequality and overpopulation.

State welfare policies have an important influence on family structure because they alter the way family members rely on each other over time. Yet an even more direct influence is family law itself. Family law governs marriage (including same-sex unions), adoption, surrogacy, child abuse and endangerment, and most matters arising from family dissolution, including divorce, divisions of property, and child and spousal support. Family law also controls the all-important issue of paternity. While *paternity* describes the status of the male parent toward the child, *parentage* describes the more general question of "who the parents are"—male or female. It just so happens that there are typically few cases—outside of adoption—where the mother's identity is ever in doubt.

Legal approaches to parentage are often broken down into "traditional" and "modern" forms. Traditionally, when the identity of the father was in doubt, common-law courts of England and the United States tended to apply what was called a **marital presumption.** Presumptions are an important technical feature of the law that warrant some explanation. A presumption is a fact whose presence remains uncertain but is likely enough that courts are willing to assume it to be true unless they are told otherwise. In negligence law, for instance, there once was a rule that said minors between the ages of seven and fourteen years were *presumed* incapable of negligent (e.g., unreasonable) acts. Minors between fourteen and twenty-one were meanwhile *presumed* perfectly capable of committing such acts. Because negligence turned on the question of reasonableness, and because kids tend not to exercise consistent "reason," the presumption in both age groups allowed for great flexibility. That is because a presumption is really just a starting point: the court will assume it to be true unless the opposing party in a lawsuit proves otherwise. For accidents commit-ted by those under fourteen, one can imagine, the victim would try to argue that the child was very mature in other aspects of his or her life such as school-work and household chores. For accidents committed by those over fourteen, arguably, the teenager's own lawyer would be wise to offer evidence that the teen was unusually immature in daily activities. Known as the "rule of sevens" for the age brackets it created, this rule shows that presumptions are merely refutable starting points for factual assumptions.

The marital presumption in family law's approach to parentage was quite similar: it said that anytime a child was born to a married woman, the courts would presume the husband to be the infant's biological father unless proven otherwise. But babies are precious and cute; why might a man wish to avoid being tied to one? The answer, as in many places, relates to money. Biological fathers were, and indeed still are, expected to provide for the material well-being of their offspring. This was particularly true before the rise of the mod-ern welfare state, and it has become increasingly true again now that govern-ments in the Western world have lessened economic aid to families in favor of more market-based approaches. This expectation of financial support placed an incentive on men to **rebut** the marital presumption when possible, thereby severing the "procreative tie" to the new child. What sorts of evidence might this require?

The most obvious would be direct evidence of the identity of the true bio-logical father. As one might expect, this was often difficult to procure. Alterna-tively, husbands were allowed to show evidence that the child was conceived at a time when they were not engaging in sexual relations with their wife. Most commonly, this argument was accepted from merchant or military sailors in the days when trade and commerce required sea voyages lasting months or even years. In such cases, would-be fathers argued that they were "beyond the seven seas" in the period surrounding the child's conception. In this regard, the proof was not direct evidence of the true father but rather direct evidence of the impossibility of the marital presumption.

A second key feature of the traditional approach to parentage was a legal preoccupation with **legitimacy.** *Legitimacy* refers to the family status of a child; an orphan child without married parents would be considered illegitimate, and therefore not entitled to the inheritance benefits normally attaching to offspring. If, for example, three adult children were fighting over their father's financial estate after his death, two siblings might argue that the father of the third sibling was in doubt, and that therefore their brother or sister was ineligible to receive his or her inheritance. The estate might then be divided into halves rather than thirds. Inheritance was not the only right attached to legitimacy. In early US states—borrowing from England, no doubt—public office could not be held by illegitimate offspring.

There were, therefore, two ways of establishing legitimacy in this "traditional" period. The first and more obvious I have already discussed: the biological tie. The second, adoption, was of nearly equal strength in the eyes of the law. While the formal process of adoption may have varied over time, the fundamental premise that adopted children were legally as legitimate as biological children has been surprisingly constant. There has been one important exception to this, however. In the area of intestate succession—or inheritance absent a valid will document—adoptive status is sometimes a distinguishing feature, though not as you might think. The difficult questions have been whether and when children given up for adoption should still inherit from their original biological parents and whether biological parents can continue to inherit from children under the same conditions.

The answer has been "It depends"; different states have created different solutions to this. Alaska, Idaho, Illinois, and Maine, for instance, have mandated that all inheritance rights can continue after children are given up for adoption. Kansas, Louisiana, Rhode Island, Texas, and Wyoming, meanwhile, limit postadoption inheritance rights to children only.[7] The point of this survey is to show the substantial variation between jurisdictions on the question above. Adoption has long been a recognized pathway to legitimacy, and legitimacy was once central to certain legal rights under the common law. But the precise implications of adoption have varied and, like all of family law, have been largely dependent upon the law of each state.

In contrast to these traditional common-law approaches, "modern" approaches exhibit two key features. First, they rely more on statutes. The chief example of this is the Uniform Parentage Act (UPA) of 1973 and its successor statutes. The UPA was developed by the National Conference of Commissioners of Uniform State Laws. This body was one of several charged with developing standardized legal codes in various areas of American law so that they could then be adopted, one by one, in the many state jurisdictions. The goal was to create uniformity among the states in important and increasingly interconnected fields. Similar uniform laws have been adopted in the areas of criminal law, commercial law, and torts. Needless to say, with increasing movement of people across state lines—particularly for employment purposes—uniformity in parentage law became essential by the 1970s. One of the UPA's key innovations was to eliminate the legal significance of "legitimacy." The 1973 act prohibited discrimination in all matters of public life on the basis of not having legitimate parents.

A second important feature of "modern" parentage law was the increased reliance on biomedical science. Use of biological testing, specifically blood tests, to verify parentage has been around since the 1920s. In those days, testing for blood "type" matches between children and parents was helpful, but it could only exclude about 30 percent of the male population from paternity. A decade later, scientists discovered they could test for specific proteins in blood serum— the clear fluid that carries blood cells around the body—and that children's serum possessed only those proteins present in their parents. This resulted in a 40 percent exclusion rate: better but not nearly up to legal standards. After the discovery and development of DNA testing, scientists discovered that they could "fingerprint" white blood cells in children and parents to determine paternity with the ability to exclude 80 percent of the male population. Finally, in the 1990s, a new form of genetic testing emerged that could exclude 99.99 percent of men to determine paternity with near-flawless accuracy.

Courts began to admit blood test evidence already in the 1930s, but it wasn't until the 1973 UPA that use of such testing was codified into law. The UPA said, in effect, that blood test evidence could uniformly be introduced to rebut the marital presumption in paternity cases. It did not say what weight should be given to this evidence in relation to all the many other facts of a case. With the increasing accuracy described above, however, it appears that the weight of this evidence increased over time. In 2000, the UPA was amended to limit the time in which a father could present this evidence, but the general admissibility without reference to weight was left intact. Further amendments in 2002 stated more clearly that genetic testing could be ordered by courts without paternity action being filed against a father but that refusal of such testing could initiate paternity proceedings against a suspected father. The 2002 act also set baseline standards for establishing the validity of genetic testing, presumably to avoid the possibility that DNA evidence might have been contaminated or deteriorated.

All of this interest in DNA for determining parentage leads to a striking conclusion. Parentage law had started out prior to modern medicine with considerable faith in biological science. It *presumed* that the social bonds of marriage were stronger than any other relationships and treated married men as the likely fathers of their wife's children. This presumption sought to establish an all-important procreative tie between parents and infants. The marital presumption was, in other words, shorthand to establish a biological connection. For that reason, under the traditional common law, legitimacy was fundamental to a child's initiation into "civilized" society, and without it one might have been excluded from participation in civic life. Legal adoption, meanwhile, could potentially substitute in cases where the procreative tie was lost, but as scholars point out, adoption as a basis for legitimacy really sought to *imitate* biology more than replace it. As evidence of this, writers cite the conspicuous fact that adoption agencies generally paired orphaned children with parents they felt looked the "same."[8] They also point out that adopting parents preferred, and continue to prefer, infants over more grown children in need of homes. This, it was believed, could allow children to at least "pass" as the biological offspring of their parents. Adoption, often treated as a potential shame, was therefore not something discussed openly in order to preserve the public presumption that a biological tie rather than legal documentation legitimated a child.

In the early modern period of family law, particularly as nontraditional families with single parents, same-sex parents, and interracial parents grew more common, biology came to matter less. Instead, courts focused more and more on the "best interests of the child"—a legal standard in family law that emphasized children's needs over social perceptions. The marital presumption became less a matter of establishing a procreative tie than a matter of establishing child support responsibilities. If an adult man, even one not married to the mother, began treating the infant "as if" it were his own—for instance by caring for, supporting, and representing to others this was his child—courts were more likely to establish parentage irrespective of the marital status, or biological tie. This meant, in many cases, that even after a biological father came forward after some time, he could be excluded—for better or worse—from parental rights if another man had "held out" this child as his own. Some have described these developments as a move in the legal community away from biology and toward a more social conception of parentage.

But pendulums swing in both directions. The rise of genetic testing through DNA analysis has created what some call a return to biology—this time at the level of molecular biology dealing with human characteristics at the microscopic scale of the living cell. There, inside each of us, our molecules contain strands of information that, when analyzed closely, can tie us irrefutably to our closest and most distant kin. Courts have enthusiastically embraced this technology in parentage cases for two main reasons. First, judges have long struggled with certainty in the courtroom, and they are impressed with this level of reliability.[9] But second, as mentioned above, judges are also motivated by a wider trend toward outsourcing longtime state functions. For instance, as part of its broader welfare benefits program, the US federal government long provided Aid to Families with Dependent Children (AFDC). Provision of welfare money to families with dependent children below a certain income level began in 1935 and continues into the present, though under a different name. But as

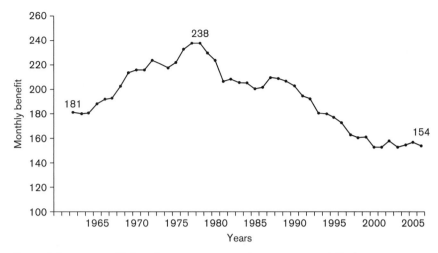

Figure 5.4 AFDC monthly benefit amounts over time (in constant 2006 dollars). Source: US Department of Health and Human Services, "Indicators of Welfare Dependence: Annual Report to Congress, 2008," December 20, 2008, figure TANF 2, https://aspe.hhs.gov/report/indicators-welfare-dependence-annual-report-congress-2008#ftanf2.

figure 5.4 shows above, benefits provided through this program peaked in the late 1970s and have declined sharply ever since. Why might that be?

It could simply be due to the fact that AFDC-type family households have fewer children than before. But this is barely true. In 1978, when the average benefit was at its highest, families had on average 2.1 children. In 2006, they have 1.8.[10]

A major shift in the years between 1979 and 2006 was the rise of neoliberalism—a new policy movement away from social assistance from governments that required higher taxes and toward greater emphasis on personal responsibility and thus lower taxation rates. The election and popularity of President Ronald Reagan and Prime Minister Margaret Thatcher in the 1980s in the United States and England were a strong indication of public support for these moves. In some ways a reaction against the "rights revolution" of the 1960s, so-called silent majorities in both countries felt that they were being forced to pay for aid to poor and unemployed families who contributed little to society. Worse, many of these older, rural and suburban voters believed poverty and unemployment were the hallmarks of ethnic and racial minority communities who, they believed, lacked a strong work ethic and family values. Further, with suburbanization or the exodus of white middle-class households from the cities to nearby suburbs, many taxpayers never even had to see the families depending on social assistance to survive. Why, some felt, should *they* have to pay taxes to support people in *those* communities?

This sentiment has been expressed in the reasoning of court decisions on parentage. On one hand, such decisions represent an *expansion* of parental rights. A key example was the 1996 Personal Responsibility and Work Opportunity Reconciliation Act. Authored by Republican congressman Clay Shaw and signed into law by President Bill Clinton, the act framed AFDC benefits as "temporary" and required that recipients reenter the job market. For this reason it was labeled "workfare" by many. The act also mandated that states work harder to establish paternity and enforce stricter child support rules, and it made paternity testing a requirement for new benefits recipients. In effect, further revealing the ties between government support policy and family structures, the act mandated a return to biology in order to shift the burden of support back onto traditional parentage and away from public welfare systems. Recalling our comparative examples, this would be the opposite of what countries like Sweden have done in trying to increase family social welfare over time.

Everything said so far deals primarily with parentage—the establishment of parent-child relations for both functional and structural reasons that ultimately help preserve the stability of human societies. But what about *after* parentage has been created? What about the moments when parentage ties are near their end? This question is about the end-of-life moments when decisions must be made regarding the disposition of property acquired during life. By what rules must a person's estate upon death be divided, and for whose benefit? These questions are all about the law of succession.

SUCCESSION

As the term implies, succession is about who succeeds a person as owner of his or her **estate.** An estate is all the property a person owns at the time of his or her death. Your estate, if you are a college student, is probably smaller than that of someone approaching eighty years old—the approximate life expectancy of a US adult. By that age, a person has probably worked in the labor force for decades, earned a steady income, possibly put away retirement savings or earned an employer pension, and seen the benefit of years of interest earned on regular lifetime savings. This might describe the average senior, but there are of course large variations due to personal spending habits, medical expenses, or great financial or business success. Regardless, there are two primary ways that the law can distribute the estate of a person who has died.

Probate, the first way, is a court process that takes place when a person has established a valid "last will and testament" or "will." The first few steps of probate procedure are to simply establish the validity of such a document, and there are specific rules in each state about how to do that. Most states have, for example, strict rules requiring the number of witnesses that must sign off on a will. They also say that wills drafted with pen and paper—rather than typed or word-processed—don't require such witnesses. These and other rules are generally meant to confirm that the document is authentic, that it expresses the true wishes of the person who has died, and that it is the "last" version of itself and therefore final. Young people of college age may not be intimately familiar with this process, or may not imagine the panoply of conflicts that can arise surrounding it. Such problems may stem from remarriage of the deceased parent so that children and the new spouse disagree about the decedent's wishes. They may stem from the deteriorating mental condition of the parent just prior to his or her death so that named heirs disagree about terms of the will drafted in that period. Or they may stem from heirs simply finding out that the estate, or their individual share of it, was much bigger or smaller than they had thought it would be. Typically, every person has full autonomy over how they wish to dispose of their estate upon death, and barring instructions that involve crime or moral turpitude, they can do what they wish with property so long as this is stated clearly in a will. But what about people who do not draft a will, or who died before they had the opportunity?

The law considers this situation **intestacy**, and here it employs a variety of default rules inscribed under state law for dividing up the estate. Such rules of succession often require that the estate pass first to the surviving spouse, then to the children in equal shares, and then to the grandchildren in shares divided from that of their parents if no longer present. In cases where no heirs can be located, the property of an estate **escheats** or defaults to the state government itself. And in nine US states primarily along the West Coast and southwest border, **community property** rules allocating all property earned during marriage to both spouses equally also apply.

Other complicating factual scenarios, more common each year, include children from adoption, from previous marriages, or with half-relations to siblings through one but not both parents. As we saw in the discussion above, different states offer different solutions to dealing with these growing complexities. Suffice it to say, however, that family law across the various US states is trending toward greater equality among children of the same generation in one family despite slight differences in parentage. But, as I suggested earlier, sometimes children are not the ones fighting over an estate.

In the social world of celebrities, children are often very well provided for in the form of a will. The "rich and famous" tend to plan carefully for old age and death, and they possess deep resources to pay attorneys to help organize their affairs. They are frequently detached from their extended families, who remain part of the normal world of regular people, or whom they "fall out with" earlier in life for a variety of interpersonal reasons. So, in planning their estates, celebrities may tend to focus less on family structure and more on function: How will my spouse and children survive when I am gone? Meanwhile, extended family members like uncles, aunts, and grandparents—among those who supported the actor or musician earlier in life—may take issue: without them there would be no family fortune, and now that there is, the larger family structure should be preserved into the future. These observations might describe a number of Hollywood celebrity estate histories, but few could be more colorful than that of the late singer Michael Jackson.

Jackson captured the world's attention from a very early age. He was initially the "lead singer" of his family's musical group, the Jackson Five. Devout Jehovah's Witnesses, the family from Gary, Indiana, led by parents Joe and Katherine, had nine brothers and sisters. Exposing his children to music from an early age, Joe Jackson formed his sons Jackie, Jermaine, Tito, Marlon, and Michael into a pop group starting from about 1964. By 1967 the boys were consummate professionals involved with touring, recording, television appearances, and merchandising. Throughout this time, several of the boys played backing instruments, and all sang. But it was Michael, the youngest and highest voice of the Five, who showed the clearest stage presence, dance skills, and vocal range. The Jackson Five grew in popularity through the 1970s, eventually adding their littlest brother Randy and dropping the "Five" from their name.

Michael had already begun recording albums by himself in 1972, but it was not until 1979's record *Off the Wall* that he established himself as, alone, more popular than the Jacksons. That album, produced by the virtuoso Quincy Jones, included collaborations with other greats like Paul McCartney and Stevie Wonder and produced five hit singles, setting the stage for Michael's consistent recording success for the next thirty years. His 1982 album *Thriller* is considered the top-selling album of all time; it more than doubled the sales of the Beatles' best record. Of Jackson's next four albums, three exceeded sales of twenty million copies. That success would bring vast sums of money into Michael's estate, and it would allow him to purchase other important artists' publishing rights—the ownership rights to license songs for TV and movies at substantial profit—over the ensuing decades. One such artist Jackson "bought" was the Beatles—their entire catalog.

Now may be a good time to pause. Given everything said so far in this chapter, where do you think this is all going?

In 2009, Michael Jackson died from a heart attack caused by a toxic combination of prescription drugs found in his system. He was only fifty years old, and because of his reclusive, eccentric lifestyle the death was a great shock and mystery to the public, spawning numerous conspiracy theories and an outpouring of grief among fans. In the fifteen or so years prior, Jackson had fathered three children, all with his second wife. By most opinions, Jackson's fortune would go to these three teenagers. There was just one problem.

By 2009, the millions and millions of dollars Michael Jackson had accumulated from decades of album sales and music licensing were substantially depleted. Living a lavish lifestyle, Michael had also given generously to his family and friends, as well as complete strangers—particularly children. A potent symbol of this lavish spending was Jackson's infamous three-thousand-acre

"Neverland Ranch" compound in Santa Barbara, California, just north of Los Angeles. The property was built to resemble Disneyland, and had fifty amusement park rides including one roller coaster, exotic animals, and ornate landscaping. Following Michael's death, his estate maintained ownership of the property, committing considerable resources into restoring it for sale. In 2017, the restored property was valued between $65 and $100 million.

Neverland was just one of the major sources of debt Jackson had incurred. In conjunction with his legal expenses and lavish lifestyle and gifts, at the time of his death his estate was in debt for approximately $400 million. But several developments would soon change this. First, the death of Jackson himself sparked renewed interest in his life's work: music, music videos, and movies. This sales boom brought in millions. Second, the publishing catalogs Jackson owned were placed as part of his estate in the hands of **executors,** two attorney friends of Jackson who had helped him during his life. How do we know these two attorneys were given control? It says so in Jackson's last will and testament. What is more, these attorneys were promised a fee of 10 percent of the estate itself. If you were one of them, and if you were in control of Jackson's eclectic but vast real, personal, and intellectual properties after his death, what would you do? If you were his family, would you worry about this control, or about this seemingly large fee percentage? Would you be upset that control went to friends rather than family? Keep in mind that a related **trust** was also established by the will providing for the well-being of the three children. But what about Jackson's parents and siblings? At the time of probate, when the estate was in debt and when the will was officialized, Michael's siblings, even his closest ones like sister Janet, said very little.

That was probably wise. It turns out that the fee gave the lawyers a *personal* investment in the financial success of the estate, and that their control of his properties gave them a substantial opportunity to turn his business affairs around. The two attorneys, considered **fiduciaries** in their role as executors, ceased lavish allowances paid to family members, reinvested publishing income, and maximized the value of the Jackson brand over the ensuing years. By 2017, the Michael Jackson Trust was estimated to be worth approximately $1 billion.[11]

Enter the Jackson family once more. With the flow of steady allowance money capped by the executors, and with the new realization that the estate was turning a vast profit from Jackson's longtime holdings, the siblings came forward in 2012 arguing that the last will and testament was in fact invalid. They argued that the executors had been "despised" by their brother, that the fee they were receiving was abnormally high, and that their mother Katherine Jackson—custodian of the three children and in some senses provided for in the will—was being tricked. In one incident the siblings barged into Katherine's home where the children lived, leading to a brawl between extended family members of two generations. In another, they removed Katherine from the home, taking her to a "spa" across state lines and keeping her out of cell phone contact. Michael's own children appeared to have grown estranged from their uncles and aunts. "Although I am happy my grandma was returned," his son Prince wrote, "after speaking with her I realized how misguided and how badly she was lied to. I'm really angry and hurt."[12]

This extended foray into the Jackson clan, while dramatic and perhaps unexpected, raises important questions about family, law, and society. Could the Jackson family be considered a nuclear or extended one? Clearly this depends on whose perspective we adopt, but even then the answer is not clear. As his will suggests, Michael felt a strong bond with his children and wanted them to be provided for. But he entirely eliminated their mother from its terms. For whatever reason, Michael appeared to want the children kept independent from his adult siblings. But he also wanted the three kids to be raised by his own mother Katherine (the singer Diana Ross was named as a backup guardian). The children would, in effect, be reared by neither parent, but they were to be kept in a "nuclear" type household—perhaps to remain free from the dramas of a large family that Michael had himself grown up with.

Second, what function did Michael envision for his relationship with his children? By providing for them extensively in the will, and by isolating them from their uncles and aunts, he appeared to embrace his role as provider to ensure their survival—which in this case might include survival of their comfortable lifestyle. This embrace is further visible in Michael's lifetime support for several of his adult siblings. If taking care of family financially was so important to the singer, he must have recognized that family has a duty to ensure the survival of its members.

Third, we might ask, what was the underlying cause of the family dispute after Jackson's death? From one perspective it was all about the money; the Jackson siblings—some successful in their own right but most not—might have been very upset that their main source of stable income after many years had been placed in the hands of outsiders and then cut off. Commentators online at the time asserted competing theories about this, saying that the siblings had given Michael his start in music, backing him up in the Jackson Five and beyond. Some referred back to the legal trouble Michael had experienced, pointing out that several of the siblings had remained by his side throughout the painful and emotionally taxing court trial. For these commentators, the siblings were perhaps justified in claiming a kind of "right" to income from the vast estate.

But those on the other side pointed out that Michael had probably undergone considerable trauma growing up in a show business family and that the siblings had contributed to that. They also highlighted the fact that claims from the siblings came only *after* the executors had turned the family fortunes around dramatically. Finally, those suspicious about the family's motives saw their behavior toward Michael's children and their grandmother as tantamount to blackmail.

Also, one could ask, what about the role of the attorneys in all of this? They were in fact named as executors in the Jackson will, and they were in fact lifetime associates of the singer, counseling him through some of the more difficult financial ventures he had engaged in. But could they really have faked the will, or pressured Michael at a time when he was ill the way the siblings asserted? Or, if not these things, could they be accused of misconduct for drawing 10 percent from the proceeds of their management success? These questions all related directly to the code of professional ethics—specific to each state—that all attorneys, even client "friends," must abide by. In the years after the siblings came forward, no evidence was put forth suggesting the attorneys had violated this code. On the contrary, by generating such a vast profit from the estate and paying off its debts, most would say, they had fulfilled their fiduciary duties toward Michael and his **beneficiaries**—the children—beyond expectation. Note that their duties under trusts and estates law, taken on when they agreed to serve as executors—flowed to those individuals and not to the extended family. The idea of the extended family structure held together for functional purposes was, in other words, counter to the intentions inscribed in the will, and therefore not within the purview of Michael's attorneys.

CONCLUSION

The dramatic life and death of the singer Michael Jackson is a memorable summary of the themes broached in this chapter. Born of a large nuclear family, Michael broke free as a youth to define his own life and earn his own fortune. Along the way, even as he endured intense scrutiny from fans and the media, he married twice and eventually started his own family. Meanwhile, he observed and respected the bonds of extended family, agreeing to "take care of" his adult siblings who had not achieved nearly the same success. No law required him to do this, but social ties and, perhaps, belief in the functional purpose of family to provide for one another motivated his generosity during life.

Death was clearly another matter. Michael's last will and testament showed that he clearly wanted to provide for his children first and foremost and left the siblings out entirely. Indeed, he even left out his children's natural birth mother, instead providing for their grandmother and ensuring that the kids could stay with her. By entrusting the management of his affairs to nonfamilial entertainment lawyers, Michael also made a statement that business and friends were more trustworthy than family. The laws of succession and parentage defined what the family would look like more than blood ties themselves. Should we be surprised that family chaos ensued? Would we want it any other way?

The social institution of the family has changed considerably from traditional to modern times. From a standard practice in the West of two parents of separate genders giving birth to several children and living among extended relatives, the family has evolved to now comprise a wide variety of configurations, differences in lifestyle, and household arrangements. In general, the modern welfare state—wherever in the world it has developed—has tended to "free" families from extended relations, making the nuclear family increasingly successful and increasingly the norm. But with the modern rollback of public budgets and social safety nets, families are increasingly forced to fend for themselves and may again begin turning toward the support of extended relatives.

We tend to think of the family as an independent institution, separate and apart from law and politics. If "blood is thicker than water," we like to also believe it is stricter and more resilient than even law. Parents care for children out of love, not obligation. But the topics in this chapter remind us to question this assumption. Family norms sit somewhere between law and society, and they can very much be shaped by changes in both arenas. But the influence runs both ways, and new family needs as to both structure and function, brought on by wider environmental factors, also have a way of pulling law and society in new directions.

CHAPTER 5 REVIEW

Key Terms

- Structure
- Function
- Kinship
- Parentage
- Succession
- Anthropology
- Extended family
- Affective labor
- Nuclear family
- In loco parentis
- Marital presumption
- Rebut
- Legitimacy
- Estate
- Probate
- Intestacy
- Escheat
- Community property
- Executor
- Trust
- Fiduciary
- Beneficiary

Further Discussion

1. Explain the difference between structure and function. How does this distinction apply in talking about family?
2. What is the marital presumption, and why was it necessary for so long in Western family law?
3. What technological changes have reshaped the structure of families today, and how has the law responded?
4. Is the discussion of trusts and estate law relevant to discussions of family? Why or why not?

Further Reading

Cohen, Phillip N. *The Family: Diversity, Inequality, and Social Change.* New York: Norton, 2014.

Meyer, David. "Parenthood in a Time of Transition: Tensions between Legal, Biological, and Social Conceptions of Parenthood." *American Journal of Comparative Law* 55 (2006): 2106–7.

Myers, John, and Henry Krause. *Family Law in a Nutshell.* 6th ed. West Academic Publishers, 2016.

Place   6

Where are you right now? If I gave you five seconds to answer this question, maybe the response would describe the room or the building you are in. Maybe it would describe the campus or the city where this chapter finds you. Or it could just as easily describe the relationship you have to those locations: "home" or "work" for instance. The point is that *where* one is may seem simple, but it can be defined in many different ways. This chapter explains law's frequent role in those definitions.

In the last chapter we saw key ways in which law affects notions of the family, and in which changes in family norms can exert pull on family law. We spoke of family as an institution; while it may refer to one single small group of people, it is also an idea that transcends that singularity to mean the concept of family as it applies to entire communities. This brought us to considering family in Sweden, in Mexico, and in China. But what makes those countries distinct to begin with?

To be on the ground in either of those countries is to experience a rich assortment of sights, smells, tastes, and sounds, many of which are unique to their corner of the world. Even as we speak increasingly of the "global" world in which all are connected, we encounter more and more the vast differences between communities. Whereas early globalization scholars predicted those differences would disappear in short order—through international flows of culture, data, and money, among other things—what we have really seen is the opposite: many communities now increasingly separate and distinguish themselves from neighbors out of a combination of pride, fear, and loyalty to the past. Along with the other themes in this book, this chapter considers community, the basis for these feelings, to be partially constructed by and with law.

All communities are bound together by common attributes. The most basic of these has traditionally been a sense of **place.** As with the question I asked you above, place, where you are, can never be as simple as a room or a building. It must also somehow include your *experience* of those. So for any individual, place can be understood as a combination of two distinct things: a physical location *and* the meaning we attach to it. The same is also true of large groups of people: my community is not simply my neighborhood or district in a city or town; it is that physical location plus the meanings the people living there get from it.

Communities often express their sense of place through law. Legal norms tell people at a physical location what they can and cannot do within that space, and these restrictions and permissions go a long way in securing the meaning of space to the people who experience it. Consider, for example, a wildlife preserve area protected by law near a large city. The area has been set aside by lawmakers for public recreational uses including hiking, biking, fishing, and kayaking. The legislature, after extensive research, determined that the area would serve a vital function for children and adults from the poorer inner-city neighborhoods of the city. In those neighborhoods, families could not afford to take time off work, purchase train or plane tickets, or pay for extensive stays in hotels near national parks like Yosemite or Yellowstone. Lawmakers, persuaded that people need to experience nature in order to recognize its value and support its protection, set aside this wildlife area as a local teaching resource so that urban citizens could enjoy the same communion with nature that wealthier residents in the suburbs long enjoyed. The lawmakers who set aside this area are told that the preserve has an overabundance of deer and could benefit from licensing deer hunting six months out of the year to local hunters. The permitting process could be an added source of revenue. But once hunting is allowed in the area, it poses a danger to hikers, bikers, fishermen, and kayakers, so public recreation will have to be suspended. What should these lawmakers do? Their decision will do more than establish use rights within the nature preserve. It will express the kind of *place* the community wants this wildlife area to become. In that way, lawmakers will play a direct role in attaching meaning to the location they have been given responsibility for. But they will also decide the kind of *users* they wish to occupy its spaces. If hikers are favored, hunters will be excluded and treated as outsiders; if the hunters are favored, the hikers will be considered outsiders. This defining of outsiders and insiders is one of the key means by which law operates to attach meaning to space.

But notice that lawmakers need not ever say their policies are creating meaning. Usually, these laws are about other things. Who gets to come in, what goods and services are allowed there, and what recreational or artistic acts are permitted all come down to what the law says, and all are determined by modern legal rules. Laws made about these three domains—migration, trade, and culture respectively—form a large portion of what legislatures and attorneys fight over every day in our legal system. Therefore, even though few if any laws describe themselves as being about our sense of "place" in the world, many are engaged with this work on a routine basis.

This chapter is about the ways in which law shapes our notions of "place." It moves from the large to the small scale. The first section below examines the making of place through the definition of insiders and outsiders. It deals with law and policy over migration. The next section explores the making of place through rules about the movement of goods and services, or trade law. The chapter then turns to legality, culture, and urban space. There, it examines the fraught battle for meaning among inner-city communities through the unique forms of cultural expression innovated in conditions of poverty, precarity, and repression. Here, hip-hop culture serves as a paradigmatic example of the struggle over meaning in urban spaces. Importantly, this chapter is not *about* migration, trade, and urban culture. Rather, it mobilizes these three things to comment on a larger issue: the legal construction of place in contemporary society. It would be tempting in a chapter such as this to focus on a flood of current events. We resist that temptation here in favor of examples about which we now have the wisdom of time and reflection. Therefore, this chapter draws on historical as well as recent examples, and it spans a wide range of topics—ones not obvious to some—to underscore the effect of law in shaping our notions of "place" in society.

MIGRATION

Population movements across vast global space seem like a new phenomenon. One of the world's busiest "ports of entry" for immigration, for example, has become Los Angeles International Airport, an institution in air travel of relatively recent vintage. But this is the exception more than the rule. As of this writing, hundreds of thousands of people have migrated from the war-torn Middle East toward eastern Europe, and they have done so largely *on foot.* The nations of that region have made headlines trying to resist the "new" flood of people. Still more recently, thousands of Central American refugees have arrived at the US southern border on foot, seeking asylum from brutal violence and crime in countries like Guatemala, Honduras, and El Salvador. As of summer 2018, many of those migrants have been detained and criminally prosecuted, and their prosecution has allowed them to be separated from any children they may have traveled with.

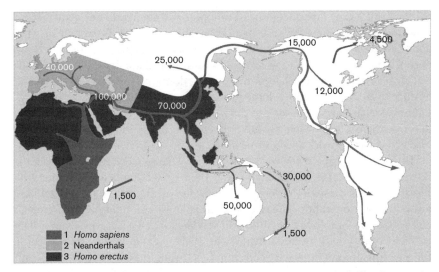

Figure 6.1 Map showing North American human migration and settlement. Originally created by Magasjukur2, 2010 (Creative Commons).

But humans have migrated on foot for most of their history. The earliest humans arrived in North America, for example, not by boat but by literally walking across the land bridge that once spanned the Bering Strait between Siberia and Alaska (see figure 6.1).

So while the underlying causes of migration, from the Middle East but also elsewhere, may be new, the mode of transportation, and indeed migration itself, are ancient. We might use this opportunity to recall, also, that the borders humans have erected to prevent mass migrations in the intervening years are the result of nation-state political organization—a recent development in the span of human history.

For most people today, two kinds of human migration may be of direct interest. The first is **rural** to **urban** migration. *Rural* describes areas of land sparsely populated by human beings and often reliant upon agriculture, petroleum, or mining industries. *Urban* designates geographic areas around large cities where population densities are highest and where building constructions are largest and close together. Whereas rural economies tend to depend on the use of large tracts of land, urban economies tend to depend on chains of rapid commercial transactions and therefore closer proximity of people to one another—in other words, less space separating individuals and organizations. As a result of this basic underlying difference, several more comparisons can be made. Rural communities often depend on one or a few industries or even corporations to employ their people, to provide social welfare benefits like medical insurance, and to invest in infrastructure such as roads or rail transport. Urban communities are economically more diversified and therefore see the involvement of *many* different firms or organizations. Rural communities are often far from the centers of decision making in finance, law, and policy, while urban areas, with greater access to travel, money, and education, are usually the centers of power. Finally, rural areas have historically been less diverse—that is, home to fewer kinds of people with racial, ethnic, and linguistic differences. Urban centers, as you might guess, are often the most diverse in these ways. There can be great exceptions to these general bird's-eye observations, and indeed, much of this chapter deals with the creation of those exceptions through law and policy.

During the industrial age, when human ingenuity saw the advent of factories and efficient manufacturing techniques best represented in the legacy of Henry Ford, populations in both the United States and Europe migrated from rural communities to urban centers. **Fordism** brought the concept of "assembly line" labor so that product manufacturing was broken down from beginning-to-end craftsmanship into multiple specialized steps. For this efficiency to churn out vastly more products, vastly more laborers would be needed; people moved to big cities knowing that they could give up farm life—in which daily life was governed by natural processes like the sun rising and setting, or seasonal rain and shine—in favor of the more predictable, indoor factory life. In the United States in particular, peak industrialism coincided roughly with the emancipation of African slaves who had been forcibly brought to the country over several hundred years prior and then suddenly "freed" to work for landowners in precarious conditions as tenant farmers; their rights to actually own land were slower to arrive. When the prospect of steady income from factory work arose in the late nineteenth and early twentieth centuries, six million African Americans took this opportunity to make a fresh start. Great urban centers like Los Angeles, St. Louis, Chicago, and New York—along with the rich urban cultures of music, dance, literature, and art they produced—were the products of this African American "Great Migration."[1]

While this was, on the one hand, a migration driven by economic need, it was also one driven by a demand for social justice. African Americans emancipated from plantation and domestic work in the US Deep South were "freed" into communities that greatly feared them. Former slaves, who for a century had been beaten, sometimes raped, and treated as human "**chattels**" were now expected to live peacefully alongside former slave owners. In many cases, these white landowners were vastly outnumbered and feared becoming the targets of retaliation. Groups like the Ku Klux Klan arose in part to "protect" whites from this perceived threat and many times took the law into their own hands by retaliating or preemptively striking against feared threats. Stories from that postemancipation period, a time known as "Jim Crow" after the new laws passed to keep African Americans in check, abound with instances of unprosecuted lynching, arson, and beatings for such "offenses" as talking to a white person. Under these conditions, African American urban migration was driven by economic **pull factors** and civil justice **push factors**, both of which helped to recast rural and urban spaces as unsafe and safe "places" for nonwhites in the country.

If these were historically the bases for domestic migration within the United States, similar forces have since become pull and push factors for transnational migration. Many people reading this find themselves in diverse, multicultural environments—places where immigrants from many different countries have settled and established new lives. But our environments were not always multicultural. What transformed them was a complex history of global migration with its own push and pull factors. In the United States, for example, many Irish immigrants arrived in cities like Boston and New York after fleeing the Great Famine of 1845–52. In this period, in which potatoes—Ireland's staple food crop—rotted in their fields, the sheer threat of starvation *pushed* hundreds of thousands out of Ireland. In the New World, growing industrialization created a demand for unskilled labor as miners, construction workers, and servants, which *pulled* many to fulfill those roles. This story, in which economic need acts as the driving force in migration, is perhaps the most common. But in numerous other cases war and violence can be even more motivating. Millions of European immigrants arrived in response to the First and Second World Wars, and more recent waves of political **asylum** seekers have fled to North America from East Asia, the Middle East, and Latin America.

The United States' relationship with Latin America has been especially complicated and deserves more attention here. Today, voices calling for a "border wall" immigration restriction say that Central American and Mexican immigrants pose a significant risk to US citizens, especially in border states. But, for decades, the United States welcomed migration from these regions as a fundamental component of its agricultural economy. Shortly after World War II, these needs reached an all-time high as population and economic growth raised demand for food production. As Americans moved toward the cities, labor needed to cultivate food crops was in short supply. But immigration controls on Mexican immigration had been restricted. The federal government had passed the 1924 Immigration Act capping the number of non-European immigrants at a very low level, but it soon learned that European arrivals preferred industrial and service work over agriculture. So agricultural businesses and farmers lobbied the US government to allow more Mexican immigrants to come work in the fields. The result was the Mexican Farm Labor Agreement of 1942, which permitted Mexican men to cross the border to serve as temporary migrant labor; this shortly became known as the **Bracero Program.** The program provided for basic living conditions and a minimum wage in exchange for *braceros*, or manual laborers, who were "welcomed" to work seasonally but were then forced to return to Mexico. The agreement said that these workers could not be used as "strikebreakers," and they could not themselves unionize or demand better conditions. Over its twenty-two-year operation the program employed nearly five million people across twenty-four US states.[2]

The Bracero Program was finally terminated in 1964. This was a very eventful year in American history; it marked the arrival of the Beatles into US pop culture, and it saw a large escalation in American involvement in the Vietnam conflict. But 1964's termination of the Bracero Program did not, by any means, end Mexican labor migration. In 1965 the United States passed the Immigration and Nationality Act technically ending the quota preferences for European immigrants. Suddenly, new immigrants from Asia and Africa were permitted to apply for work visas and arrived in the United States to fulfill specialized labor needs. Dating from this period, for example, the US medical profession has seen a large number of medical doctors hailing from the Indian subcontinent and East and West Africa. But it also permitted increased legal migration from Mexico and Latin America. In the twenty years after 1970, Latin American immigrants made up nearly 50 percent of all immigration, and Mexico alone accounted for roughly half of that.

For a variety of reasons, however, along with increased and diversified legal immigration came large numbers of undocumented migrants. Many of these were simply temporary workers who had overstayed their visas and blended into the active service and agricultural economies of the American Southwest. With rising Spanish-speaking populations, US citizens began to react against the "browning of America" through immigration. Policy makers wanted a solution that would allow the millions of existing undocumented people to regularize their status, while at the same time shutting the door—at least partially—to further clandestine migration. The result was the 1986 Immigration Reform and Control Act or IRCA.

IRCA was developed with the explicit purpose of addressing the growing undocumented problem. It set in place a penalty system for employers using undocumented labor, and it relegalized seasonal labor by implementing a registration system for migrant workers during periods of high demand. It also allowed for "amnesty" for those lacking proper immigration status, setting forth requirements to show evidence of long-term, stable residence in the country, as well as a clear criminal history. Notably, regularization for those who met these requirements came with an exclusion from welfare benefits for a period of five years. As described in the last chapter, this was the 1980s, a period of return to liberal political economy, which considered social welfare not just a burden on modern governments but also a long-term burden on the human spirit.

In this period, three legal anthropologists set out to understand the effects of immigration, and the underlying pull factor of industrialization, on small-town rural America. In *Law and Community in Three American Towns*, Carol Greenhouse, Barbara Yngvesson, and David Engel each conducted **fieldwork** in three separate communities. These communities were distributed between the Midwest, New England, and the South and were given pseudonyms so as not to jeopardize the participants in their study. *Law and Community* was written in the early 1990s, just after the Reagan and Bush years, which saw the return of conservative political and economic values after the tumultuous years of the 1960s and '70s. By the time these authors conducted their research, effects from the 1965 Immigration Act could be seen in the increased presence of nonwhite immigrants around the country. Thus Greenhouse, Yngvesson, and Engel document shifting ideas about "insiders" and "outsiders" in small-town America at a time when people were faced increasingly with human differences like race, class, language, religion, and moral values.

Most interestingly, the authors found that both insiders and outsiders stood in close relationship to the law and the courts. Insiders, for example longtime white residents of Engel's "Sander County, Illinois," believed that interpersonal disputes in areas like contract or personal injury should still be settled between neighbors directly and not through formal legal process. One example might be an accident case in which a worker was injured by heavy machinery on the job. Insiders, locals said, would band together and support the family of the injured worker. Membership in the community alone was enough to merit fair treatment, and it also meant that individuals injured would not take advantage of their fate to extract a windfall settlement in monetary damages from the business owner. But for new residents in the area, "membership" was of little help. Many of them nonwhite, they were already perceived as outsiders, and they were hardly part of the social networks that tied individual and families into larger collectives. Several even chose to live on the outskirts of town, making their ability to settle disputes with "neighbors" even more unlikely.[3] So what did they do?

So-called outsiders in Engel's Sander County turned to the courthouse itself for dispute resolution. Whereas this is not unusual to most of us in cities today, in small-town America at the time—as Engel documented—it was often perceived as an act of desperation, hostility, and self-aggrandizement. It meant that the injured party wanted a big payout and was willing to tear apart the community for his or her own benefit.

What does all of this have to do with this chapter's main theme of "place"? Sander County, like Hopewell and Riverside—the other towns portrayed in the book—depicted itself as a place where formal law stepped in as only a last resort. The social mores and traditions of "community" were enough law for insider residents to feel comfortable and, more importantly, protected. Thus anyone who departed from this was circumscribing him- or herself as an "outsider." The very concept of place—in other words, of inside versus outside—was cast through one's relationship to the law. The "right" thing to do when injured was not to seek formal justice. This belief, the authors say, erected a moral boundary that could be far more effective in delineating "place" than any physical boundary was.

Engel's research participants confirmed this. They said there were a lot more African Americans and Mexicans living in their town because a new canning plant had opened nearby. Whereas local leaders had planned for new industry to "revitalize" the local economy as small farming gave way to agribusiness, residents had not counted on new residents arriving permanently with different cultural practices and attitudes.[4]

The arrival of new migrants in Sander County, Illinois, locals felt, altered the legal culture that had made their community—and probably many like it in rural America—so livable. In chapter 4 of this book, we saw how modernization brought groups into larger and larger collectives that came to be called "nations." We also saw historical storytelling or invented tradition, such as the case of *Times v. Sullivan,* as an important feature of the nation-building or imagined-community formation process. The story of Sander County, Illinois, reflects the opposite; when new groups enter an existing community, they may bring different values with respect to injury, conflict, and dispute settlement. But because they were outsiders, Engel's participants *had* to rely upon formal law much more than their neighbors. Since they did this, locals viewed them more obviously as "outsiders." In circumscribing newcomers as outsiders, locals in turn practiced and repeated, again and again, their own notions of what Sander County meant to them. It meant a site where people knew one another and settled differences without the law. Matching the location of the county with this meaning of traditional, nonlitigious community, they constructed Sander County as the "place" they said it was, without reflecting deeply on their own role in this construction.

Recent debates over immigration reflect a similar protectionism. Since 2016, US federal authorities have planned a southern border wall, erected a ban on immigration from primarily Muslim countries, and enforced new criminal penalties against asylum seekers. The fragility of constructions of place becomes clear only under stresses brought about by social change. In this case, early forces of globalization made a new manufacturing plant "a good idea" to community leaders who needed to revitalize their economy. These forces came from a particularly economic form of globalization that came with easier shipment of goods and technologies in the late industrial period. It was, in short, a period of increasing ease and interest in global trade.

TRADE

Writings on "globalization" have enjoyed considerable popularity in the last two decades, in part by emphasizing the newness of the term and the idea it represents. Chapter 3 of this book described some of the genuinely new legal implications of increased global exchange. But the newness of this phenomenon remains open for some debate. Humans have engaged in trade across cultural, linguistic, and geographic borders for many thousands of years. Ancient artifacts from Scandinavia have been found among Native American archaeological sites. Early Greeks and Romans traded with partners in India. The "Silk Road" connected ancient China and India. Dutch explorers established the earliest European bases in Southeast and South Asia. And the Atlantic slave trade systems saw Spanish, Portuguese, and later English traders forcibly acquiring peoples from West Africa and transporting them to the New World. Their ships then returned to Europe with commodities such as sugar and tobacco. These were processed and exported throughout Europe, as well as back to Africa, completing what has become called the "Triangular Trade" of the Atlantic slave system.

Europe in the Ages of Discovery and Exploration was still the "Old" continent; it had consumed much of its own natural resources, its living conditions for most were squalid (before public sanitation techniques had become widespread), its people were recovering from a devastating plague, and its commodity markets were relatively plain and undiversified. With the easing of travel between continents thanks to new technological advances in shipping and navigation, interest in non-European commodities drove the great explorers most of us read about in school. That means that even in its earliest form global intercourse was greatly driven by economic motivations. People comfortable in their European cities were willing to cross oceans and mountains to meet new people because, at a basic level, the voyage promised to bring riches. Largely on the basis of wealth from this exploration and expansion, the great nation-states of Europe came into being as economically powerful "places" where politics and economics were closely united.

The importance of trade to political and legal stability in contemporary Europe cannot be overstated. Trade, in other words, was at the center of Europe as a "place" in the sense we know it today. By the mid-twentieth century, Europe had just ended the Second World War, which had nearly destroyed its basic infrastructure, not to mention its economic stability. German military bombers had gutted factories and key buildings in England before the Allies routed them from France, forcing them to destroy bridges, tunnels, and railways in retreat. By the time Germany surrendered, the European continent was in shambles. If any attempt was to be made to rebuild, considerable resources would be needed, and not all countries had all resources.

Realizing this, and with considerable support from the Americans under the Marshall Plan to help rebuild the continent, European powers, foremost France and Germany, founded the European Coal and Steel Community (ECSC). The ECSC was formally established in 1951 and would come to include Belgium, Italy, and the Netherlands. Formalized under the Treaty of Paris, it served as a central authority for the distribution and trade in natural resources necessary for building roads, bridges, tunnels, and a rail network that would connect most of western Europe at the time; eastern Europe remained largely under Soviet (modern-day Russian) influence. The ECSC was the first formal international organization modeling the principle of **supranational** governance, that is to say a kind of political authority that sits over and above any national differences. Its architects believed that in addition to help rebuilding Europe by pooling comparative advantages in coal, steel, and other commodities, economic cooperation of this kind would help avert new international conflicts on the continent. If people "belonged" to a supranational entity, their national differences could never cause the same conflicts just seen in two world wars.

This kind of political and legal agreement among neighboring countries has been labeled **regional integration.** Regional integration is immensely important for law and society today because it challenges the association between law and the nation-state that we have all come to take for granted over the past several centuries. As chapter 4 above explained, written and unwritten law became a major form by which specific values—free speech, for example—became installed as "national" values. In court opinions citing legal traditions as authority, the highest court in the United States was able to superimpose these values on all states within the Union in times like the tumultuous 1960s, when the North and the South, not unlike during the Civil War, seemed to hold deep-seated differences with regard to racial and ethnic differences. To the extent that the Warren Court of the 1960s handed down numerous decisions inspiring a new wave of liberal toleration—decisions covering racial integration, the right to contraception, and the right to an attorney for the poor—these were ultimately national decisions.

Regional integration is the partial or complete legal integration of larger multinational regions. Europe, including nearly thirty "member states," is one example. North America, including Canada, the United States, *and* Mexico, is another. Can leaders in each of these regional units really agree on legal norms that could bind all states and their citizens equally? If so, what might be the likely problems in this?

Several regions have already made considerable headway toward legal integration at the regional level. Just as with the ECSC, however, this new multinational cooperation arrived on the back of economic development. It maximizes national comparative advantages in industry, natural resources, and human labor. At least four different models for regional integration have come into being since the 1950s. **Economic unions** are the first form. They eliminate internal import taxes on goods and services, enable the free flow of labor and capital, implement a common external tax on all imports, and develop unified economic policies, including, in the case of Europe, a common currency. A second example is the Economic Community of West African States, or ECOWAS (figure 6.2). Headquartered in Abuja, Nigeria, ECOWAS was developed by treaty with the explicit purpose of bringing the neighboring countries, some extremely poor with agricultural economies and others rich with oil and gas deposits, into complementary relation for the mutual benefit of economic

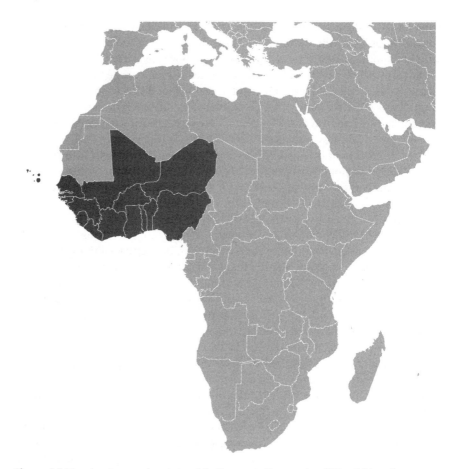

Figure 6.2 Map showing member states of the Economic Community of West African States (ECOWAS).

development. This being said, political and legal integration through ECOWAS has remained secondary.

The second form of regional integration is a customs union. **Customs unions** are looser than economic unions; they erase import taxes normally placed on goods and services across internal borders. They also then implement a common import tax on nonmember states. The purpose is to increase the internal flow of goods and therefore increase demand for products in broader scope. Customs unions are a form of legal integration in the sense that the laws on import trade must be standardized across a region, but the integration is limited to only this area of socioeconomic life. No unified economic development policies govern, and most nontrade matters are untouched:

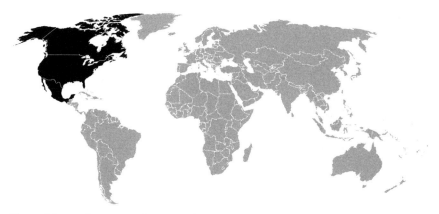

Figure 6.3 Map showing member states of the North American Free Trade Agreement (NAFTA) as of 2018.

individuals still need travel documentation, monetary policies remain separate, and social and human rights continue to be national in scope.

Free-trade agreements (FTAs) are the last major form of regional integration. The loosest in form, FTAs reduce taxes on trade between member states but allow each country to set its own policies with respect to the rest of the world. The most high-profile FTA for Americans is the North American Free Trade Agreement or NAFTA (figure 6.3).

In the United States, NAFTA was signed into law in 1994 by President Bill Clinton. Its passage brought considerable debate about the effects of closer trade relations with Canada, and especially Mexico. Would the reduced taxes on Mexican imports cause these imports to flood US markets and put American workers out of their jobs? Would US factories move across the border to take advantage of cheaper labor in Mexico? And would the new law encourage or discourage international migration between these countries? Advocates for the agreement argued that NAFTA would in fact reduce undocumented immigration to the United States. This was because, they said, lower trade barriers would mean higher demand for Mexican commodities—especially agriculture. This would in turn increase the value of Mexican labor, boost wages, and finally raise the quality of life among the working poor in the country. Once this occurred, Mexicans would have less reason to make the dangerous journey across the border illegally. Proponents of NAFTA said, in other words, that increased trade would mean decreased migration. This appealed to many Americans, who feared that they were being "overrun" by undocumented immigrants speaking Spanish—particularly in the border states of California, Arizona, New Mexico, and Texas.

The benefits from NAFTA were quickly realized. It increased exports across the three member countries in North America, in turn boosting worker productivity and urban wages, and therefore consumer activity. It also sparked a new wave of **foreign direct investment** (FDI) in Mexico, the country most in need of economic development. But at the same time, two of the key benefits hoped for went unrealized.

Rural poverty, rampant in much of Mexico because of limited infrastructure and investments outside the cities, had been one of the leading causes of undocumented migration to the North. Although NAFTA benefited many in the manufacturing centers of Mexico's larger cities and therefore boosted the size of the country's modest middle class, the rural poor saw very limited benefit. On the contrary, because it forced a policy of "free trade" on Mexican farmers, the agreement allowed heavily subsidized American agricultural products like corn to be sold across the border, in effect competing with local producers and driving many out of business. The public policies driving "free trade" led to a groundswell of support in rural Mexico for a new communist-inspired resistance movement known as the Zapatistas after the Mexican revolutionary war hero Emiliano Zapata. The Zapatistas declared their movement public on January 1, 1994—the day NAFTA took effect.

Much like the Immigration Reform and Control Act of 1986 before it, NAFTA architects miscalculated the effect their policy would have on push and pull factors of migration to the United States. The increase in rural poverty drove greater numbers of undocumented migrants to seek better fortunes north of the border; it also increased trafficking in illicit drugs and persons. Gaining partial control of this traffic was a new, dangerous criminal organization, MS-13.

MS-13 stood for Mara Salvatrucha, a Salvadoran street gang from 1980s Los Angeles. In the early '80s, thousands of refugees from the Central American nation of El Salvador arrived on US soil seeking to escape a bloody civil war that had opened up between the country's military government and a coalition of rebel groups. Over the course of the twelve-year war, roughly seventy-five thousand people would be killed in the small nation. Many believe that the United States, by supplying the Salvadoran regime with weapons, indirectly exacerbated the conflict. From its early years, civilians began fleeing the country, often by land across Central America and southern Mexico. The migration routes were thus well established by the mid-1980s.

Meanwhile, the Mara Salvatrucha in Los Angeles evolved into a complex criminal organization expanding into drug and human smuggling. It set up trafficking hubs in Mexico, which served the group well as a way station between the South and the US border. As MS-13 grew into organized crime, police crackdowns in Southern California placed many of its members behind prison bars. Under the 1986 IRCA, then, hundreds of these MS-13 prisoners were deported back to Mexico and Central America. There they maintained strong ties with the organization and effectively expanded its scope from an urban street gang in to an international crime syndicate spanning several countries.

We should pause here to point out an important comparison. The nation-states of Canada, the United States, and Mexico had under NAFTA agreed to "give up" a modicum of state sovereignty in the name of "free trade." Much like Europe in the same period, they viewed economic globalization as a more important priority than hardening borders and their enforcement. An increase in transborder migration further added to the apparent dissolution of national autonomy. But, as this was happening, the nonstate actor of MS-13 was growing in organizational strength, financial power, and control over what the German sociologist Max Weber called "the legitimate use of physical force."[5] MS-13, in other words, offers a stark example of how new alignments under economic globalization may have dramatically shifted the balance of power from the nation-state to nonstate actors. A concurrent growth in **private military companies** (PMCs) in the ensuing period offers yet another.

By the 2010s, MS-13 was one of the most powerful forces in Central America, and its violent action toward the populations of Honduras, Guatemala, and El Salvador could not be controlled by those nations' governments. In El Salvador, a country with only six million inhabitants, it was not unusual to see six hundred murders per month. Newspapers celebrated in early 2017 when finally, after several years, the country saw a day with no homicides.[6] Imagine that you had a young family with school-age children living under these dangerous and frightening conditions. What would you do?

Beginning around 2014, entire families, as well as many unaccompanied children, began arriving at the southern US border as undocumented migrants. In that year the number from Central America totaled roughly 250,000.[7] The next year it fell slightly. And by 2016 it was approximately 220,000.[8] US president Barack Obama declared the situation a "humanitarian crisis." The children and families could not be absorbed into the United States overnight, but they also could not be sent back to their country without high risk of death or torture. In summer 2018, the crisis resurfaced after the Trump administration chose to criminalize asylum seekers for arriving illegally. This step meant separation of children from parents and a new cottage industry of nonprofits housing undocumented children. Although the administration reversed its separation policy under criticism, it has been slow to reunite those children already ripped from their families in the interim.

Perhaps even more importantly, the Central American refugee crisis, as it came to be known, revealed much about the status of the United States as a "place." For many, especially along the border in cities like San Diego, Tucson, or El Paso, the vast numbers of Spanish-speaking undocumented migrants felt like a major threat to American geography, law and order, and culture. To them, it compromised the integrity of US borders, it threatened local law enforcement with higher crime, and it forced longtime Americans to have to understand a "foreign" language. For these people, the United States meant a place neatly defined on the map, tightly governed by state and federal policy, and universally navigable through the English language. Even though most of the new migrants were mere children, locals felt that *their* place was being destroyed to make room for "outsiders." Much like the local natives of the Sander County study, they claimed not to "hate" anyone or any group but felt that their way of life was being threatened and that law and legal culture were a critical component of that.

On the other side of this debate were those with a very different sense of America as a place. For them, the United States was "a nation of immigrants," a country of humanitarian generosity, and a land of opportunity for people in need. Most importantly, perhaps, it was a place of pluralism, where no single culture, language, or set of values ruled the others. These feelings echoed the notion of political liberalism articulated further below in chapter 7 with respect to religious freedom protected by the government itself. For these people, the legal culture of the United States itself held the capacity and the commitment to help people in need across social and cultural differences.

Which of these positions is the right one? Which do you agree with? For purposes of this chapter the answer is not essential. Indeed, as you reflect on this, consider above all else how you would talk about this with classmates and colleagues on the other side. Whereas for many people the legal culture of the United States requires that they embrace one or another of these positions in a very complex debate (one that connects many complicated institutions and social developments), we might consider instead that it is much more than that. It could well be that the ingenuity of legal culture in the country is that it protects the right to hold either opinion, the right to express that, and the right to associate with others who feel similarly. It also encourages us to put ourselves out there and to debate peacefully and civilly with others who may have something new to say that our positions do not already comprehend.

But above all else, the point in the above discussion has been to illustrate the ways in which "place" is intimately connected to feelings about insiders and outsiders, and therefore to the legal constructs like immigration law and international trade agreements that define those. The definitions offered by objects like IRCA and NAFTA, both salient behind the story of change in small-town America as told by writers like David Engel, operate from the national to the local level. Both laws had emerged at the highest levels of the federal government. IRCA emerged from the US Congress as authorized under its **plenary power** over "naturalization" of new citizens.[9] NAFTA emerged as a treaty negotiated by the presidents as authorized under article 2 of the Constitution.[10] But by setting forth definitions of who could legally stay in the country and how, or by redrafting trade rules expressly to curb migration from one country, these national-level laws reestablished the meaning of belonging in the United States from the moment of their adoption. They said, effectively, that persons of Mexican origin (and indeed most Latinos and Latinas in the United States) could be presumptive outsiders.

At the same time, even though all of these new rules actually increased undocumented migration from Mexico and further south, they also suggested that the presence of more outsiders might have to be tolerated as a by-product of economic globalization. Indeed, the strength of the US economy since the Second World War could arguably have been based upon both the Baby Boom rise in population and the influx of millions of hardworking new immigrants from non-European countries after 1965.

This emphasis on macroeconomic priorities over and above social and cultural ones seems to have clear causes and effects. On the one side, growing commitment to the "global economy" ahead of respect for national differences seems to have emerged out of the **Washington Consensus** of the late twentieth century. This term, coined by English economist John Williamson, describes a set of ten principles espoused by key Washington policy institutions during the 1970s and 1980s on the topic of Latin American development. Responding to the rise of Marxist rebel movements made popular in the region because of brutal dictator governments, policy think tanks and intergovernmental organizations like the World Bank and International Monetary Fund (IMF) advocated a series of key principles on which all US foreign aid should be premised. These principles included now-common ideas like moderate taxation rates, trade liberalization, privatization of state-run industries, and secure enforcement of private property rights.[11] All of these became part of the growing political-economic movement now known as neoliberalism. Spelled out by Williamson in 1989, they were also deeply at the heart of most of NAFTA. In other words, the developers of the agreement had hoped to use market economy (in its 1980s formulation) as a magic bullet to solve problems with uncontrollable undocumented migration—a widely perceived threat to America's sense of itself as a "place."

But instead, this fundamental push for a regional market economy had largely the opposite effect. It brought poverty to certain regions of Mexico and Central America, driving rural residents north to find their fortunes in American factories and agriculture. This is in turn encouraged industries to use immigrant labor as a cheaper alternative to American workers. The new policies also drove many US factories south to make use of cheaper materials and labor on the Mexican side of the border. And it sparked new antiglobalization revolts like the 1994 Zapatista uprising in southern Mexico—which many Latino and Latina Americans, not to mention antiglobalization protesters generally, took inspiration from. As in other chapters of this book, the effect of market economy on "place" through reorientations of national immigration and trade policy shows the mutual construction always unfolding between American law and society.

LEGALITY, CULTURE, AND URBAN SPACE

In Engel's Sander County, we saw some of the ways in which white American "insiders" perceived migrant and immigrant "outsiders" through their different relationship toward law and the courts. We called this a difference with respect to *legal* culture. But what about other forms of culture in that community or in others? For anyone reading this section today, whether in big cities or in small towns, perhaps you have already seen the many ways "outsiders" appear in and reshape the cultural landscape. Why might they do this?

Years ago, when I was a young boy growing up in Southern California, it was not "cool" to be different. This was precisely the time of the Washington Consensus, and of IRCA and NAFTA. In those years, young people from other countries mostly wanted to blend in with our surroundings. But for many this was not an option.

So that period, the 1970s through the 1990s, saw a revolution in American popular culture where "outsider" kids invented and perfected new art forms that would be a source of pride and accomplishment, reclaiming the spaces around them as *their* own places. Ultimately their creations became lucrative businesses on which large fortunes would be made. While many examples of this pop culture revolution abound, none is more potent than the world of hip-hop.

Hip-hop is many things to many people. First, it is a style of music that includes what used to be called "rap" but is more expansive than that early art form; it now includes a variety of related styles, subject matter, and compositional elements. Musically, it is founded upon heavy beats, sharp, clearly descriptive lyrics, and a vocal delivery that emphasizes rhythm and percussion way beyond melody and harmony. As some might summarize, it is a kind of spoken word poetry set to a beat. But hip-hop is also much more than music. As early as the 1980s, groups like Run-DMC documented in music the ways in which hip-hop was an entire lifestyle, or culture. They spoke of clothing, shoes, jewelry, electronic audio equipment, and more. But what does all of this have to do with "place"?

What many people, even die-hard fans, may not realize is that hip-hop engaged in the attachment of meanings to physical spaces through negotiations and renegotiations of law. First, the form itself was the product of large-scale immigration. After the Immigration Act of 1965, the United States began receiving workers and families from many regions of the "Third World," including the Caribbean. This region of islands between North and South America had long been, thanks to the trans-Atlantic slave trade, a hub for African forced immigrants and servant labor from many different tribal cultures in Africa. The different African cultures combined with local Arawak indigenous culture, as well as Asian-Indian and white-European elements, to form a unique "creole" admixture in music, food, language, and in some cases religious practices. Following the 1965 law, many from the region—notably from Jamaica,

Haiti, Dominican Republic, and Puerto Rico—began arriving in eastern cities like New York and settling in the housing projects and low-income neighborhoods of places like the Bronx, Queens, and Brooklyn. Migrants to these areas brought with them an important form of entertainment known as the "sound system," in which DJs sporting high-power audio equipment and large collections of vinyl records would travel around the community and set up planned or improvised dance parties in the street, warehouses, parks, community centers, and abandoned buildings.

This was significant because it reclaimed those spaces as places of community life, fun, and enjoyment. The United States had, by about 1975, reached the end of its postwar economic boom and saw a crippling recession followed by high inflation. Many were forced to live off public assistance because they could not find stable employment. Under those conditions, the DJ sound system was sometimes the only form of affordable, social entertainment individuals could afford. Furthermore, it brought people out of their homes and apartments to mingle and dance in the **public square.** But immediately these impromptu dance parties sparked reactions from law enforcement. Hip-hop became associated with the new street art of graffiti, local gangs began to control and fight over money and "turf" carved out from the public space, and the music itself seemed to take over urban inner-city neighborhoods, where sound ricocheted off concrete buildings stacked closely together to accommodate the high population density. Around this time, modern narcotics like crack cocaine made their way into these spaces, furthering gang traffic, struggles for control, and violence.

From the early 1980s, the music itself began to reflect this urban decay. "The Message," recorded by Grandmaster Flash and the Furious Five in 1982, made stunning observations of the squalid conditions in New York's inner city neighborhoods like Harlem. The jump from DJ dance music to social commentary had happened quickly. At parties throughout the late 1970s DJs began using partners to talk and rhyme over the music to get crowds energized. They became known as MCs, and their performances were direct descendants of the Jamaican dancehall "toasting" form that immigrants had brought with them en route to the United States. Hip-hop's emergence there coincided with the decline of the inner city: factories closed or moved, middle-class whites sold their property to buy homes in the suburbs, banks refused to offer home and business loans in the abandoned areas, schools declined with the loss of property tax revenues, illicit drugs became the most reliable source of income for young people coming of age in this world, gangs rose to prominence, and urban police were forced to adopt increasingly militarized practices to combat rising violence. Hip-hop proved an ideal form in which to document and comment on these changes. Few groups illustrated this more than the Los Angeles artists N.W.A., whose music openly challenged the Los Angeles Police Department (figure 6.4). These challenges sparked calls for censorship by outraged parents

Figure 6.4 Early hip-hop pioneers N.W.A., including members Dr. Dre, Eazy-E, Ice Cube, D.J. Yella, and M.C. Ren. Photo by Douglas R. Burrows, 1989.

and some lawmakers, which in turn were met with the legal defense of "free speech" protection under the First Amendment.

Finally, in the decades since those early years, hip-hop evolved and mutated into various subforms, some of which returned to a more cerebral, politically engaged form of social commentary and some of which moved toward an embrace of money and luxury goods, inspired partly by the rising commodity value of the art form itself. Some artists, including those who had come of age in the conditions captured by "The Message" now became multimillionaires, bought mansions, and vacationed on the French Riviera. Their music bragged of economic success, disproving the "haters" and seeking empowerment in becoming rich and famous. These were, in other words, values that were no longer specific to the inner city, or to the ethnic and racial communities that occupied them. They were rather more akin to wider American values that grew more popular with the rise of the Internet, e-commerce, tech company start-ups, and social media. Hip-hop, brought by immigrants and migrants to urban centers where it was used to reclaim public space, became a huge business.

The story of hip-hop culture's rise in American and global culture serves as but one example of the battle over place. It mirrors broader changes in law and society throughout these years. It illustrates the important social construction of "place" through cultural practices and provides an example of how seemingly disempowered communities—ones evidently marginalized with respect to law and politics like the "outsiders" of Sander County or the undocumented targeted by IRCA and NAFTA—can reclaim their spaces, contribute to the culture, and in some cases take control of their destiny in an environment that may view them as alien.

CONCLUSION

"Place" is a social concept that combines physical locations large or small with a sense of meaning shared by those who inhabit it. Indeed, sharing in these meanings is part of what helps to define people as members of a community. That means, in turn, that the concept of "outsiders" is almost always already built into the idea of "place." Often, law and legal institutions play an active role in formulating insider and outsider status, and they therefore are fundamental in defining place.

This chapter illustrated this by looking at migration, trade, and culture. Migration has been a key part of the history of mankind, but its modern variant—in which people move across national borders, values, and languages—seems to frame migration as a deeply political act that challenges "insiders." The arrival of new residents in a community forces people to confront their own values and assumptions, which are otherwise easily taken for granted. David Engel's Sander County study illustrated how local assumptions about legal culture—in which people should invoke formal legal process only as a last resort—become challenged when new residents sought redress. Since they lacked the insider social networks to find remedies outside the law, the courthouse became for them the most democratic means by which to seek righting of wrongs. Yet by pursuing claims through state institutions rather than through social networks, new arrivals also perpetuated their status as "outsiders."

In Sander County outsiders came at a particular historical moment when industry began replacing agriculture as the dominant economic force in the region. A new factory invited outsiders from beyond the county, the state, and even the country to come work the assembly line for a steady paycheck and benefits. This industrialization of the rural landscape was part of a larger historic shift in America when postwar society demanded more foreign-born workers to support the growing population and economic growth.

With the new economics came undocumented immigration from Mexico and Central American nations. Economic development south of the border stagnated, while even further south this led to extreme inequality and political instability, pushing millions to seek better conditions by crossing the border illegally. Seeking to control this flow, the 1986 IRCA and 1994 NAFTA agreements represent high-level national and international policies with macroeconomic goals but also with local effects that went beyond what policy researchers might have predicted. Two such local effects were the rise of MS-13 and the wave of Central American refugee children that together provoked substantial nativism in the United States.

The rise of MS-13 to transnational syndicate status beyond the scope of single national law enforcement agencies was also a manifestation of a more global drift away from nation-state sovereign authority. Countries like Germany and France had long realized that they had to form regional alliances in trade and development if they were going to rebuild and survive in the new world order. The continuing formation of such alliances in the late twentieth and early twenty-first centuries similarly represents a potential decline in the power of the nation-state.

Locally, however, law's control over "place" was also called into question by new urban cultural forms pioneered by the children of migration. While this was true all over the developed world, from Berlin, Germany, to Sydney, Australia, it was especially true in places like Los Angeles and New York, where intercultural mingling and free expression were perhaps most extreme.

Drawing upon artistic and technological forms familiar in the Caribbean, the first signs of hip-hop music appeared in New York in the late 1970s and quickly spread around the United States over the next few years. By the mid-1980s, N.W.A. and other "Hardcore" rap groups spoke directly about local drug culture, law enforcement repression, and unfairness in a justice system that sentenced blacks eight times more than whites for certain drug crimes.[12] Blaring this commentary loudly across urban spaces, hip-hop became the object of obscenity and incitement challenges and therefore was eventually much more than just a social commentary. It was also a sociolegal battleground.

By the 2000s, it was also a big business. Early hip-hop pioneers became wealthy moguls investing in new economy businesses and "giving back" to their communities by discovering and producing new artists who pushed the form even further. A bit like the regional cooperation of Europe, or the labor power of Mexican workers at different times, hip-hop artists realized that their stability lay in economic if not political citizenship and participation. Their "place" was still restricted, but it was clear.

Throughout this discussion, the importance of economy has been undeniable. It played a key role in pushing and pulling migrants from home countries to new lands. It established the demand for national and international trade relations that would ensure peace even after intense conflicts. And it came to allow "dangerous" cultural forms like music and dance as commodities that were therefore safe for mainstream society.

In this process, the size of "community" has also evolved. Whereas we once used to think of community as all those surrounding us whom we might "know" or speak to, cultural and technology changes have made it a name for any size group with shared interests and values. Today, we speak of the "online community," the "intelligence community," and the "legal community," not to mention the "black community" or the "Indian community." Community, and its shared sense of "place," real or virtual, have thus also exploded in scale from the local, to the regional, to the national, to the global. The next chapter pushes these scales even further to consider transcendent, shared visions of the worlds beyond this one, as well as, of course, law's role in those visions.

CHAPTER 6 REVIEW

Key Terms

- Place
- Rural
- Urban
- Fordism
- Chattels
- Pull factors
- Push factors
- Asylum
- Bracero Program
- Fieldwork
- Supranational
- Regional integration
- Economic union
- Customs union
- Free trade agreement
- Foreign direct investment
- Private military company
- Plenary power
- Washington Consensus
- Public square

Further Discussion

1. What does the concept of "place" mean to you? Does this resonate with the definition given at the top of this chapter?
2. What are push and pull factors? Are they ever connected to each other?
3. What is regional integration, and how does it affect "place" on either the geopolitical or the personal level? Give examples.
4. Why do migration, trade, and culture all form parts of a discussion on law and constructions of "place"?

Further Reading

Gutierrez, David. *Walls and Mirrors: Mexican Americans, Mexican Immigrants, and the Politics of Ethnicity*. Berkeley: University of California Press, 1995.

Kelley, Robin D. G. *Race Rebels: Culture, Politics, and the Black Working Class*. New York: Free Press, 1996.

Zinn, Howard. *A People's History of the United States*. New York: Harper Collins, 2005.

Religion

Place is the combination of location and meaning that members claim to hold in common. But nonmembers are usually free to embrace their own meanings and, as seen in urban cultural forms, to reinscribe physical spaces with their own meanings. Often, meanings about space are challenged because of deeply rooted beliefs that members come to embrace or that nonmembers like new immigrants introduce into a community. For much of human history, these deep beliefs have come from conceptions of a Creator, an afterlife, and a conviction that nonbelievers will be punished when they die. These features characterize most of the world's largest religions, and they all indicate an assumption that our world and our bodies within it are temporary moments of a larger story.

The preceding chapters covered key social institutions under the influence of legal norms. They described history, family, and place, all key facets of social being without which individuals can survive and live, but without which society as we know it does not exist. This chapter examines constructions of law and society at the site of religious belief, belonging, and organization. Our tendency is to think of religion as less tangible than those other spheres of social life; whereas those are close to our daily experience, religions deal inherently with spirit, other worlds, and destiny. More precisely, religions deal with abstractions; how then can we talk about them as *social* institutions?

Modern science, technology, and medicine have answered many of the great mysteries to which humans once turned to religion for answers. What were once considered religious miracles have often been reexplained by scientists as obeying a set of "rules." Perhaps for these reasons religious belonging has observably declined in the United States since approximately 1960.[1] Meanwhile, the percentage of people reporting their religious affiliation as "none" or "undesignated" has risen from 2 percent in 1950 to 16 percent in 2010.[2] Tangibly, this decline translates into fewer people attending "church," less money being given to religious charities, and fewer inhibitions about social behaviors such as business on Sunday. For many who believe religion provides an important irreplaceable backbone for society about questions of "right and wrong," these developments are most alarming. But, for others, significant gains have resulted from the decline of religious enthusiasm in the West. One is a growth in so-called **liberal toleration.** Liberalism is the philosophical tradition dating from the European Enlightenment which held that political and economic leaders should govern their communities separate and apart from the social differences that may exist within them. The purpose of modern government, according to this tradition, is to ensure basic freedoms, and doing this requires ignoring social differences as much as possible. This "blind eye" toward social differences—including ethnic, racial, and religious differences—was considered a form of extreme tolerance. But some would argue political leaders should do more than ignore differences, they should protect them. The debate between these positions rages on into the present day; but the general consensus in the West has been that natural and elected human differences generally have little role to play in the peaceful and efficient governance of society. The decline of religious fervor over the past one hundred years is, for strict adherents to liberal toleration, a good thing because it removes political biases toward the most dominant religions. In Europe and North America these are most clearly Protestant and Catholic Christianity.

The decline in Western religiosity may have even more significant gains than the promotion of liberal toleration. It also has allowed Westerners the opportunity to encounter and embrace aspects of Eastern religions. In particularly cosmopolitan cities such as Los Angeles or New York, for example, it is not unusual to find advertisements for meditation, yoga, tai chi, Sufi drumming, or Kabbalah. These five practices alone derive from major world religions founded outside Europe and North America: Buddhism, Hinduism, Confucianism, Islam, and Judaism. In many cases Westerners adopt these practices with little or no interest in the broader histories or cultures from which they derive. But the basic lesson—that there is valuable wisdom in religions of other communities— is hard to deny. So while religion as we know it is measurably on the decline, for many of us it is reemerging in a new form, one that is more open to the coexist-ence of differences and the embrace of those unlike ourselves. Under these con-ditions, members of non-Western communities have come to the United States and Europe, in search of better lives, with the knowledge that they will be safe and secure in practicing the beliefs that help them make sense of a complex world. In that sense, either by causation or by correlation, diversity has increased as religiosity has partly faded.

Nevertheless, this arrival of new differences has brought something of a backlash. Whereas countries like Canada, the United Kingdom, and the United States have long avoided claiming an official national religion, the arrival of more and more outsiders has encouraged a renaissance of Christianity among a minority of the native-born populations.[3] The return to religion has been has-tened in particular by the perceived threat of certain Eastern faiths, notably Islam. Though not the first attacks of their kind on US soil, the 9/11 hijackings were the most visually shocking and frightening to Westerners. The United States had historically intervened in the Middle East, and those interventions likely caused offense and instability for many living in the region. But when the attacks took place, the images of the attackers were released, and the stated ide-ology behind their motives was publicized, many perceived 9/11 not as a politi-cal response to historic provocations but as a sudden outburst of anti-Western hatred cultivated by the Muslim religion itself. Experts drew upon a few con-servative scholars of the Middle East to conclude that this was a "clash of civili-zations" and that the enemy was an entire religion. The problem was, many million members of that religion called Western countries, notably France, the United Kingdom, Canada, and the United States, their home, and many more were scheduled to travel to these nations as regular students, workers, and tourists. The result was a massive increase in security and surveillance research and spending, and these came with an accompanying reduction in the legal protections citizens could claim against restrictions on their freedom. In other words, in the decades since 9/11, the West's rediscovery of religion has in large measure been through the negative experience of securitization of Islam, one of the fastest- growing religious faiths today.[4]

September 11 was also a key feature of a new **millenarianism,** a belief that the world would soon end. Insofar as it was the opening salvo in a new "clash" of religions, the likely result of that clash could be destruction of much of the world's population. Christianity in Western countries also saw an increase because many needed to make sense of their place in the supposed "end times." A decade after 9/11, when the world had not yet been destroyed by East or West, many embraced a theory about planetary alignments and ancient pre-dictions leading to the belief that 2012 would bring about the end of the world. Numerous books about the topic were released, and one Hollywood film even used modern computer special effects to show how it would all end. Needless to say, the 2012 theories did not prove correct, but they were an extension of a return to spirituality brought about by the cataclysmic imagery of 9/11. Since 9/11 and 2012, climate change has become the source of new justifiable fears about the "end of the world." The phenomenon itself, in which centuries of human pollution and overdepletion of natural resources have palpably changed earth's temperatures, damaging the ecological balance beyond repair, is real. But the effect it has had on the collective psyche, restoring the value of religion to make sense of helplessness and fear, is still unfolding.

This chapter is about this restoration of religion in the spaces between law and society. The next section considers in deeper detail whether religion can be considered a "social" institution. The section after that examines the key sources for religious freedom laws in the United States. And the final section compares those sources and their protections with religious freedom abroad. Ultimately, this section returns to the United States to explore one of the most significant religious freedom cases of the past ten years. The case, *Burwell v. Hobby Lobby,* also affords a discussion of new conceptions of the person, ones that may have been unthinkable during the days of early liberal toleration.[5]

A SOCIAL INSTITUTION?

When people go to churches, mosques, temples, or other sites of religious meaning, what are they aiming to do? Many would say the answer is simple: pray. Prayer can rely upon sacred texts or verses, or it can mean any direct, free-form communication with God, saints, or spirits. Religious sites are often important because the site itself has been determined to be a place where that communication is clearest. Most churches, mosques, and temples, however, are not on particularly sacred ground; in the Western world, they are built in communities with many followers, and where there is resulting need for a common place of worship and communion. But if people could also easily pray at home, why is there this need? If religion is about spirit, why is it almost always practiced with *others?*

The French sociologist Emile Durkheim had a *lot* to say about this. He dedicated much of his life's work to understanding the role religion played in the modern world. To accomplish this, Durkheim examined what religion meant to societies far away from his own in both time and space. Many of those societies still adhered to **totemism,** a form of "primitive" religious belief that members of a community, often tied together through kinship relations, were common descendants from a single animal, plant, or geological formation. Durkheim saw commonalities between so-called primitive religions and their more "modern" offspring. In common, he said, both held that certain features of their environments were **sacred**—held in highest esteem—while others were **profane**—or shunned as dangerous, evil, or impure. Further, Durkheim found that *all* religions held in common the function of bringing people together into organized collectives. To do this, they had to not only bring people into common spaces like villages or temples but also bring them into common mind-sets, or **collective conscience.** By focusing members of communities on a single God or network of gods, and by governing them with a singular web of rules, sanctions, and punishments, religions provided the common mind-set people needed to truly *be* together. Indeed, Durkheim's whole definition of religion came down to this community-building function: "A religion is a unified system of beliefs and practices relative to sacred things, that is to say, things set apart and forbidden—beliefs and practices which unite into one single moral community called a Church, all those who adhere to them."[6]

So even though religion is a spiritual and moral system of beliefs and practices, influential writers have long considered it a preeminently *social* system. People do not just want to worship, they want to do it together. For many, this togetherness may mean God is more likely to hear their prayers because in chorus their voices are louder. For others, it may simply mean that they get to see people once a week and on big holiday feasts. In our modern, urbanized lives where people move to new cities in nuclear families detached from extended kin, churches can serve some of the functions of the once-large communal family. In the decades before urbanization, church meant that rural farmers and farmworkers who toiled during the week on large tracts of land far from neighbors could periodically see and be with "their community."

This sociality of religion helps to explain why people get so much out of its formal spaces. But it should also be said that the sociality of religion helps keep its traditions, practices, and beliefs alive over years and years. And while it is certainly true that religion can change and respond to change, the fact that churches may boast dozens, hundreds, and even thousands of members means that the way churches practice their faith cannot simply change over night. For these two reasons, religion is far more than just spiritual belief: it is both social *and* an institution. It is a social institution.

Insofar as this is true, religion, like the family, can be said to serve several key roles in society. When discussing the family, I said that scholars have fought over whether the family serves structural or functional purposes in society. On balance, we surmised, the family clearly serves both functions by allowing people to situate themselves structurally in relation to their wider kin group, and to help assure one another's functioning and thus survival in a hostile world. In recognizing religion to be a social institution as much as a system of belief or practices, I want to add a third social role to this broader discussion of law and society.

In addition to structural and functional roles, some aspects of social life may serve a **symbolic** role. *Symbol* in this context means an object or idea that exists unto itself but that also always refers to something outside itself. A flag is a piece of cloth attached to a pole or ceiling or a wall, but it is also the larger idea of state, nation, or people to which it refers. In the United States, the "stars and stripes" flag refers always to itself as well as to the country that displays it and to the unique history that produced that country. Within a large country like the United States, other flags such as the flag of California or the flag of the Confederacy are also potent symbols for better and for worse. Language, words on a page, is also an important system of symbols. *This* sentence is a group of letters organized into words, but it is also a collection of about twenty symbols to convey their combined meaning. When people organize themselves into collectives big or small, they rely upon symbols to communicate what they are thinking, how they are feeling, and what they would like one another to do. They use symbols to "make sense of" the complex world around themselves.

Religion, then, is not just a social institution, it is one that serves a key symbolic function in human life and may do so increasingly as environmental conditions prove hostile, unpredictable, and unnerving to people.

RELIGION AND POLITICAL LEGITIMACY

In the United States, religion is so fundamental a part of social life that it appears prominently in the First Amendment to the 1789 Constitution. That provision, which also notably includes freedom of speech and the press, protects religion in two key fashions. The First Amendment reads: "Congress shall make no law *respecting an establishment of religion,* or prohibiting the *free exercise thereof;* or abridging the freedom of speech, or of the press; or the right of the people peaceably to assemble, and to petition the government for a redress of grievances."[7]

The first important thing to note here, as in other constitutional amendments, is that it is articulated in the negative. By restricting "Congress," the **framers** of the Constitution said implicitly that citizens cannot be limited in their religious belonging. The limitation on Congress has two features. The first says that it shall not make law with respect to the "establishment" of religion. This is often called the "establishment clause." The principle it refers to is usually called the "separation of church and state," or **separation doctrine.** It may seem obvious today, but it was not in the founding moments of the United States. At that time, many early nation-states had official, state-sponsored religions. That meant religious buildings such as churches and cathedrals were paid for out of public tax funds. Since the sixteenth century, for instance, England has had the Church of England as its official religious institution. Most countries in the Middle East and Asia, meanwhile, are officially Islamic. In those countries, not only do tax revenues help pay for religious sites, but religious clerics are given a powerful voice within government to ensure that political decisions are in line with theological beliefs. It can be no surprise that religious pluralism—the quality in which several different religions might be practiced by members of a single community—remains low in those countries. The framers of the US Constitution, descendants of political and religious exiles from England, chose not to reproduce the state-religion links they had left behind. Instead, informed by the new liberal philosophy emanating from French and English intellectuals, they wanted a state that would support pursuit of the "good life" while remaining largely neutral with respect to what that term should mean to people or what moral authority informed it. Today, the supreme legal test for conflicts over religious establishment is called the Lemon Test—after the 1971 case *Lemon v. Kurtzman.* The court said that state actions affecting establishment (1) must be secular in their purpose, (2) must be secular in their primary effect, and (3) must avoid excessive entanglement in religion.[8]

The second key phrase from the First Amendment immediately follows the establishment clause: "or of the free exercise thereof." This "free exercise clause" concerns people's right to practice religion freely, without the encouragement or discouragement of state officials. Whereas the establishment clause is about discriminatory state support for religions, free exercise is about the state interference with regular people in their practices. Together, these two clauses form the bedrock on which American religious freedom is built. Note that by prohibiting Congress from acting in these ways, they enable the citizenry to act in other ways. This illustrates the difference between what the philosopher Isaiah Berlin famously called "negative" and "positive" liberty.[9]

The prohibition on Congress here creates a negative liberty among American citizens and residents to religious practice and congregation. It says that people shall be free from government interferences with religious establishments (e.g., favoring one over another) and shall have free exercise of religion.

A prominent "establishment" doctrine is not by any means unique to the United States. Whereas countries like Poland formally espouse Catholicism and countries like Pakistan formally espouse Islam, countries like France have formally separated their government from religious groups and beliefs. If in the United States this doctrine came in 1789 under the founding constitution, in France it came relatively recently in 1905 with the passage of a public law by the French national legislative body called the Conseil d'Etat. Whereas the United States from its foundation had been home to numerous Christian sects, France had predominantly been occupied by Catholics and thus had strong ties to the Catholic Church. Previous French republics had seen considerable involvement of Catholic clergymen in state affairs, and the famous 1901 Dreyfus Affair—in which a Jewish army officer was wrongfully convicted of espionage, setting off a peaceful but divisive national conflict—was blamed on Catholic dominance in the military and the state.[10] The 1905 *laïcité* law was very much the product of the Dreyfus Affair and was immediately meant to secularize public authority and participation in full realization of France's liberal commitments to equality and freedom.

In the early 2000s, the French *laïcité* law encountered its first large existential challenge. Over the preceding four decades, immigration into France from

> **BOX 7.1**   Positive and Negative Liberties
>
> A negative liberty is a right you or I have to be free *from* something. The general rights to pursue happiness or maintain private property are negative liberty in the sense that no one can guarantee we *will be* happy or well-endowed with property; they can only hold back other people's interference with our pursuit of these things. Positive liberty might be considered a strong form of "entitlement"; it is things we have the right to have or to do, such as voting in most Western democracies. Much debate rages on, today more than ever, on whether health care, family leave, and social security constitute "rights" of this kind. No explicit provision for them as positive liberties was made in the US Constitution, but this does not mean they are not implicit there.

the French colonies in North and West Africa had soared. For some, such as the Algerians, French colonial rule had been so direct and so strong that citizenship in the metropole was relatively easy to establish. The French had viewed Algeria as an extension of its own soil, and many Algerian-born French whites were given automatic citizenship in the home country. Algerian Arabs arrived in France in large numbers, in part to support the labor needed for rebuilding Europe as promised in the Treaty of Paris. Although faced with more legal obstacles to immigration, people from neighboring countries like Morocco and Tunisia, as well as Senegal and Ivory Coast, also came in large numbers. By the late 1990s, after the first Gulf War had increased inequality in the Arab world, many Arabs turned to religion to make sense of an unfair and fast-changing world. In this period, Islam grew in population as well as in public visibility. After the 2001 terrorist attacks in New York City, many in both the United States and Europe suddenly perceived this growing religious community as a security threat. In the ensuing years, French schools began noticing an increased presence of Islam in the form of young females dressing in traditional Muslim attire—particularly the Islamic headscarf known as the *hijab.* By 2004, the French public was so alarmed by this trend that it supported passage of a new law under the tradition of the 1905 rule on *laïcité* banning religious signs from state-run public schools.

The new law prompted the immediate withdrawal of hundreds of French-Muslim school girls, whose only choice was to attend correspondence, parochial, and boarding schools. It later gave way to another law banning the full female head coverings known as the **niqab** and the **burka.** Both laws had the support of the public, and both were justified on security as well as on cultural grounds that France is and always has been a secular nation. As a legal anthropologist I conducted several years of fieldwork in France at the time these laws were developed and passed.[11] Living in Paris between 2002 and 2005, I noted

Figure 7.1 Women wearing the hijab (headscarf) at the Women's March on Washington, January 21, 2017. Photo by Jerry Keisewetter (Unsplash License).

that even the organizations that described themselves as "antiracist" were in support of these laws banning public signs of religion. Many felt that women covering themselves in these ways was un-French, un-modern, or un-Enlightened. They viewed the headscarves as a sign that Arab-Muslim male subordination of women was spreading and would overtake their own culture if not stopped right away.

This form of aggressive church and state separation appears at first glance somewhat similar to the United States' separation doctrine. If the state and therefore the taxpayers pay for public schools, both countries say, why should public schools "favor" one religion over another? But whereas in the US courts would take issue only if the school was *supporting* one religion—for instance, by offering Bible study—in France lawmakers took issue, so they said, with any religion showing its presence in the state-funded learning environment. Thus the infamous law of 2004 was drafted generally so that it could apply to Islamic veils, Jewish *kippah*s, and Christian cross pendants. The theory behind this prohibition was that *any* religion in the public spaces could prove invasive to people of any other faith, or to those of an increasingly large atheist population in France.

American commentators were generally surprised that a nation would ban religious signs from public view. Why? Weren't they too worried about Islam in the post-9/11 aftermath? Why didn't America's lawmakers pass a similar law? The anthropologist Carol Greenhouse explains this seeming paradox in a very subtle way. She says that the separation doctrine, as it has come to be understood in the United States, does not intend to rid all state-sponsored activities of religion at all. Greenhouse says that in the United States, unlike France, religion gives a moral foundation to political authority. "The separation of church and state in the United States does not by itself create a secular state—and even less so, a secular public sphere. On the contrary, the constitutional requirement of separation can be (and is widely) read as a necessary connection between political legitimacy and religious pluralism—a proposition that carries significant if changeable cultural content in the United States today."[12]

To maintain the support of its people, a state must have legitimacy. This political legitimacy comes only from the sense that the state is acting on the side of Right in its actions—even ones that might harm or kill some (e.g., criminals, terrorists) in the name of the majority. This sense of righteousness must come from somewhere outside the state itself, somewhere among the people represented by it. Religion has always been an obvious source for ideas about right and wrong. Therefore, Greenhouse says, the United States cannot maintain secularism in the sense of French *laïcité* because religious beliefs provide the necessary moral foundations of political legitimacy.

If all of this makes it seem as if religion behaves differently in the United States than abroad, that is because it does. As Carol Greenhouse also points out, the German sociologist Max Weber captured this in an essay entitled "The Protestant Sects and the Spirit of Capitalism."[13] Weber said Protestant church membership brought a variety of social benefits that would permit the United States and its economy to develop in a fashion that proved very useful to American capitalism. Where, for example, Christians in Europe attended church for the religious services, or for spiritual renewal, American Southern Baptists, Weber documented, used church as a forum for business contacts, financial lending and borrowing, and employment opportunities.

More importantly, membership acted as a form of credit; it enabled people to relocate to new communities if they felt there were greater economic incentives there. Arriving in a new town or village, a household could, through its church, make contacts with the residents and find out were jobs might be available. In the cases Weber studied, he particularly noted the ways that church attendance affected creditworthiness in business transactions. Business works on webs of contracts, and contracts always come with certain risk. People would be much more willing to take risks with others they knew attended church—preferably their own—than those they knew did not. Church membership was thus a tool for mobility, a source for trust, a guarantor of good credit, and even a kind of proof of the Self. "As is well known," he wrote, "not a few (one may well say the majority of the older generation) of the American 'promoters,' 'captains of industry,' of the multi-millionaires and trust magnates belonged formally to sects, especially to the Baptists."[14] These "captains of industry" made church membership a significant part of their social life, and it allowed them to conduct business—sometimes in cutthroat fashion—under the rubric of community service and moral righteousness.

Theorists like Max Weber teach us that religion has been a fundamental feature of modern societies. Some would argue that it is a form of superstition, a holdover from primitive beliefs in magic and sorcery. These skeptics, seeing the many ways in which religious belonging and religious belief have divided human beings, suggest that it is a sign of humanity's moral and intellectual weaknesses; we *need* religion because we are scared of the natural and social worlds we inhabit.

But the Weberian view says otherwise. Religion is a powerful political and organizational feature of *modern* society. While it may present ideas about the afterlife, morality, and humans' place in the natural world, it does this with the express purpose of organizing people into groups and binding them together. Accordingly, a new family moving into the state of Georgia in the early twentieth century might know not a single person there. But on arrival, upon finding a suitable church, they would have a new community that brought business, employment, legal and medical advice, and countless other valuable services to make social existence possible. Moreover, as Weber says, by maintaining religious piety through church attendance, the most successful in these communities—the "titans of industry"—represented two glaring realities: that religious faith appeared to be requisite to business success, and that business success appeared to be strong proof of religious faith.

Hobby Lobby

This connection was seen once again in the 2014 US Supreme Court "term." That year, the Court agreed to hear a challenge to the new health care law developed under President Barack Obama, passed by both houses of Congress and then signed into law by the president. This law, the Affordable Care Act (ACA), was meant to decrease the number of uninsured people living in the United States. Until then, the country, influenced in part by a powerful insurance industry lobby in Washington, D.C., had never seriously considered a "national health system" of the kind England and most European countries have. People either purchased health insurance through their employers or received medical coverage directly from the federal government or their state if they lived near poverty levels. The remainder, a shocking 18 percent of the US population, lived without any health insurance.[15] Most of these people lived without any meaningful health care at all, or they used hospital emergency rooms for every basic need—a most inefficient use of precious resources.

The ACA managed to reduce the uninsured rate to just 10 percent. How? First, it legally required insurance companies to remove their exclusions from coverage for adult dependents, making it possible for parents to insure their kids until age twenty-six. Second, it required that insurance companies remove exclusions on people with "preexisting conditions," that is any kind of health problem from before coverage began. Next, the ACA set up an elaborate system of statewide insurance marketplaces where people could review competing plans and select the most effective and cost-effective one for them. Finally, the act established a tax penalty for every person not obtaining insurance coverage by a certain deadline. The ACA did many, many more things to "nudge" people to buy and maintain insurance, but these were the most salient innovations, thanks to which the fraction of the general population with medical insurance rose to an all-time high of 90 percent.

Despite this gain, many were left unhappy. In the case of private health insurance companies, the ACA immediately harmed their profit margins. But also, because the act mandated employers above a certain size to offer insurance, it compelled many businesses to help cover premiums that would go toward a wide array of medical treatments and products. One of the most complicated issues came from women's reproductive and family-planning coverage. The ACA had authorized the US Department of Health and Human Services (HHS) to issue a list of contraceptive drugs and treatments that large employers (with fifty or more employees) would be required to help cover. HHS at the same time provided an exception for religious clerical organizations (e.g., churches but not hospitals) that fell under the definition as "employers" and for whom the contraception mandate would violate "deeply held" religious beliefs central to their mission.

In 2010, the large chain retailer Hobby Lobby, along with a few other companies, filed a lawsuit against HHS for violation of its right to religious freedom. Hobby Lobby at the time sold $4 billion a year of arts and crafts supplies through six hundred stores across the United States. The case was very unusual and important as one of the few times when a corporation was asserting its membership and faith in a religion. If it had been simply a person, or indeed if it had been the kind of business that was owned by one person (and therefore synonymous with the beliefs of that individual), then the case would have been clearer. But Hobby Lobby was neither of those; it was a "closely held" corporation, meaning that it belonged not to one individual and not to a large body of shareholders but rather to a small group—all members of the Green family of Oklahoma City. The Greens were devout Christians who maintained the $6.4 billion company according to the tenets of their faith, including a policy of business closure on Sundays. In an open letter issued by CEO David Green, "Honoring God is more important than turning a profit."[16]

The Green family argued that the HHS rule violated its right to religious free exercise and that this was prohibited under a 1993 law known as the Religious

Freedom and Restoration Act (RFRA). In particular, they said that the requirement that their company pay the full cost of certain contraceptives called abortifacients—those that stop pregnancy after life has been "conceived" rather than before—violated their moral opposition to abortion. Prior to the RFRA, any laws that placed obstacles to the exercise of religion could be challenged only if they did so *deliberately.* Many felt that there were a host of circumstances in which free exercise would be burdened indirectly, through more general law. The RFRA, then, sought to broaden the protection. It said that "government shall not substantially burden a person's exercise of religion even if the burden results from a rule of general applicability."[17] Any rules violating this standard would henceforth be subject to the Supreme Court's most stringent test for validity known as **strict scrutiny.** The Greens argued the contraceptive mandate from HHS under the Affordable Care Act should receive this scrutiny because it violated their free exercise of religion. There was just one problem. The Greens did not operate a church, nor did they argue that the rule interfered with their ability to attend a church or other place of worship. They felt that their operation of Hobby Lobby was itself a form of religious exercise. Could, then, a corporation be capable of religious expression deserving of protection under the RFRA? If so, couldn't other large corporations, fast food or casinos for example, claim religious beliefs that would exempt them from certain laws?

The US Supreme Court, in a five-to-four majority opinion written by Justice Samuel Alito, sided with the Greens. First, it adopted the strict scrutiny standard requiring that the HHS-mandated coverage for contraceptives be the "least restrictive means" of serving a "compelling state interest." Whereas the Court abstained on the question of whether women's reproductive health was compelling, it said that, even if it were, the HHS rule was not the least restrictive means to achieve it. It noted that the relevant treatments could be obtained by employees without their employer "cost sharing."

And perhaps most importantly, it addressed an important issue regarding the **corporate personhood** of Hobby Lobby and its companion companies in the suit. HHS had already acknowledged in the law that individuals and non-profit corporate entities possessed religious freedom rights under the RFRA. It had remained silent on for-profit corporations. Lower courts had sided with HHS because, they said, for-profit companies are in business only to make money and not to exercise religious beliefs. Alito and the majority disagreed. They said that for-profit companies often articulate noncommercial corporate missions and that there was little reason to distinguish nonprofit and for-profit entities with respect to religious free exercise.

In a scathing dissent from Justice Ruth Bader Ginsburg, and signed by Justice Sotomayor, a minority of the justices argued that the extension of religious freedom protection to corporations would create a slippery slope in which any commercial entity, including publicly traded ones with thousands of stockholders, could lay claim to the First Amendment to evade all kinds of legal requirements. Companies like Google or Facebook, for example, could argue moral opposition rooted in religion to any and all violence and therefore claim exemption from their corporate tax obligations that help pay for missiles and fighter jets.

But, in siding with Hobby Lobby and the Greens, the Court said any assertion of religious exemption under the RFRA had to show "sincerely held" religious beliefs—not just any interest in religion. It also made a fundamental distinction between companies like Hobby Lobby and most others. Alito wrote that the decision would apply only to **closely held corporations**, that is to say companies whose shareholders consist of only a handful of individuals, usually family members. According to the US Internal Revenue Service, a company is "closely held" if "more than 50 percent of the value of its outstanding stock [is] owned (directly or indirectly) by five or fewer individuals at any time during the last half of the tax year."[18] Recalling that the HHS rule applied only to employers of fifty or more employees, this meant that the Court's decision exempted employers of only a fraction of US workers—although how big remains to be seen.

Near-total reliance on private employers to provide health care coverage for their employees was somewhat unique to the United States among developed countries. Health care is one of the welfare features supported by strong social democratic states like Sweden, described in chapter 5. But in the absence of a public health service like that of England and Canada, the United States has relied on a private insurance industry system delivered primarily through employer cost sharing. In other words, the ability of adult men and women to access key health care needs has long depended upon the will—inherent or required—of small and large private companies. For these companies, the corporate form has long been a key legal technology allowing groups of people to work together, combine resources, make bets on their decision making, and generally operate free from the burdens of individual liability. It has also allowed corporations a certain degree of "personhood," that is, a measure of autonomy and civil liberty to conduct business to maximize economic opportunity. The corporate form has created, in this regard, only partial persons: they gain many of the benefits of legal personhood while shielding themselves from many of the burdens. Whereas most of us are personally responsible for risks we take, such as overspending our income or betting on the wrong decision, corporations may be institutionally responsible, but they shield their individual decision makers from liability.

The past few decades have seen a change in this arrangement. Over the years, large corporations have enjoyed more and more the *benefits* of legal personhood and have felt few of the *burdens*. The Hobby Lobby case represents, in effect, the extension of religious free exercise protections to a commercial enterprise. Even though its favorable ruling was limited to just "closely held" companies, Hobby Lobby itself employs thirty-two thousand employees in forty-seven US states.[19] Does it make sense that such a large entity can "exercise" religion?

Why not? Just five years before Hobby Lobby was decided, the Supreme Court decided another important case recognizing that companies have "free speech" rights under the First Amendment. In *Citizens United v. Federal Election Commission,* the Court ruled that political campaign contributions from all companies, including nonprofit corporations, for-profit corporations, and labor unions, could not be limited by dollar amount without violating those entities' First Amendment rights.[20] Despite this decision, individual contributions from private citizens remain limited under the Federal Election Commission. Dissenting justices and critical academics and journalists responded that this asymmetry between the speech rights of companies and those of individuals would favor the voices of wealthy corporations and potentially undermine American democracy. These two examples, *Hobby Lobby* and *Citizens United,* have become potent symbols of the spread of corporate personhood against the wider decline of individual power in law and society.

As such they remind us that the First Amendment's establishment and religious free exercise provisions lie at the root of religious life in the United States, but also that religion itself in this environment is a highly contested *social* institution. The dispute in *Hobby Lobby* was, after all, not a dispute over whether the Greens believed in Christian doctrines against abortion, or whether they feared repercussions for acting against those beliefs in the afterlife. The question was how far they should be permitted to enact those beliefs in their social life. As the Supreme Court said in its opinion, those who would support HHS want to limit the free exercise of religion to that which takes place in church on Sunday mornings. Alito and the majority accepted the company's argument that this was wrong and that the exercise of their religion permeated all of the Greens' social entanglements—particularly those relating to a company that professed to have a faith-based mission.

In the same period that this was all taking place, American lawyers were making the most of the new social citizenship of corporate organizations. *Hobby Lobby* came near the end of the Great Recession, a global economic crisis spurred by widespread irresponsible bank lending that had offered home loans to people who would likely have problems repaying this debt and who would end up losing their homes if interest rates changed even slightly. Banks could bundle and sell these loans to other financial institutions, but the transactions they conducted created risk for both the people living in the homes and the companies who were buying up debt. Nevertheless, they argued at the time, these risks were okay because they were promoting access to home ownership at rates not seen since the postwar period. Many of the new home buyers they catered to were, it turned out, low-income and ethnoracial minority borrowers who had little choice but to accept the risky deals. Banks for a time prided themselves on the housing "access" they were creating through risky debt

> **BOX 7.2**   Corporate Law Meets Business Ethics
>
> Around the same time as the *Hobby Lobby* case, corporate lawyers devised a new form called the benefit corporation or B Corp. First adopted in Maryland in 2010, benefit corporation laws spread to more than thirty US states over the next five years. B Corps are for-profit companies that espouse a particular social mission intended to benefit workers, their community, or even the environment. They differ from traditional C Corp corporations in that C Corps maintain primary duties toward their financial stakeholders, usually just their public or private shareholders. B Corps, meanwhile, include as well duties toward "nonfinancial stakeholders," in other words the community or the environment. The benefit corporation applied new ideas from the field of business ethics. It allowed socially conscious founders to raise money among venture capitalists and equity firms— thus giving them a stake in the company—without losing control of the special mission they devised when they started.

creation. Like Hobby Lobby, some came to view and defend this as part of their corporate mission.

The blending of social citizenship and for-profit corporate organizational form was an important feature of American life in the years before and after *Hobby Lobby*. It is therefore not altogether surprising that the Supreme Court decided the way it did. Even at a time when religious membership among Americans was sharply in decline, certain companies, even very large ones, had gained religious freedom. Where this left the many thousands of female employees and *their* religious views was another question.

CONCLUSION

Emile Durkheim's view of religion as a social institution came at an ideal time. Modern societies such as his own were treating indigenous and colonial peoples, in American Indian country, in Southeast Asia, and in Latin America, to name just a few places, as "savages" because their spiritual belief systems differed so much from Christianity. Religious belief was a continuum that connected all humankind, and it sprang in large part from a need among all people to commune with one another. Durkheim's key work on religion came just a few years after France's famous Dreyfus Affair, a political and legal scandal that brought *laïcité*: the end of state Catholicism and the infamous law on establishment.

Establishment doctrine in the United States is softer than that found today in France. Whereas in France it is now unlawful for young Muslim girls to wear

a religious headscarf on public school property, in the United States accommodations for religious belief—especially in education—are common. *Establishment* in the United States refers to the doctrine of state nonpartisanship when
it comes to the endorsement of religion. That means that while most religious
symbols are formally welcome in venues like public education, neither state nor
federal governments are allowed to offer funding or resources to favor one religion over another. That means that if a school is available for church Bible
study on Wednesday after school, it must be available for Qur'an classes and
Buddhist meditation as well. Thanks in part to the Lemon Test, there have been
relatively few efforts to ban the presence of religion entirely, in the way we have
seen in the French context. Recent scholars have said this is because religion
can never be too far away from US political authority; it gives politicians' decision making a sheen of moral authority and earns the support of many. The
image of political candidates and officeholders praying with followers is often
an example of this.

The "free exercise" doctrine, meanwhile, prevents state actions that unduly
interfere with the right to practice one's religion. In a few high-profile
instances, this has led to disputes over the use of drugs and other banned substances in ceremonies of religious worship.[21] Concerns about weakened religious freedoms in the post–civil rights era gave rise to the Religious Freedom
Restoration Act of the 1990s, a rule that returned in 2015's *Hobby Lobby v. Burwell* to support a private corporation's search for an exception to the new
national health care law requiring coverage for sensitive contraception medicines. The company's argument that *Hobby Lobby* should be exempt from covering those medicines because of deep religious beliefs depended on a finding
that corporate business and decision making could itself be an expression of
religious belief. The Green family argued their stores reflected their own family's Christian values. The dissenting judges on the Supreme Court said companies could not "exercise" religion. But the deciding majority said they could, in
certain instances, if they were "closely held" by a small number of owners with
bona fide religious views of their own.

The surprising finding meant that wealthy business owners were practicing
religion even during the week, and even in their workplaces. This mixing of
business and belief, however, was not new. As Weber had already long since
identified, American Protestantism long served a vital business function at a
time in the US economy when people left behind community ties and needed
often to find new ones. Churches were like credit agencies; they could vouch for
a person's good faith and fair dealing, and they could supply lists of successful
businesspeople with whom to collaborate, or make deals.

The foregoing reinforces the main point of this chapter: that religions are
social institutions. Without the interpersonal sociality that religion brings,
basic historical developments such as capitalism in America would not have
succeeded to the extent they did. But we might conclude with another, more

extensive observation. Religion in the work of Durkheim and Weber brought an important kind of social citizenship in which individuals and families joined up with others to form larger value communities. But in the late twentieth and early twenty-first centuries, religion appears to be on the decline among individuals. Some would tie this to social citizenship to conclude that feelings of social belonging are everywhere on the decline. Abandonment of mental health patients, school shootings, health care policies, and even education financing all point to the lack of empathy for the collective by the individual.

But meanwhile, as individuals find themselves to be less social creatures, corporations find themselves increasingly social. *Hobby Lobby* shows that they can express religious values of the kind Carol Greenhouse said are endemic to US political authority. In other cases like *Citizens United*, they hold political opinions and earn the right to protection for them. Social values, in other words, remain strong. But they are exercised less by people and more by institutions, and increasingly by commercial ones at that.

This may be a dark thought. But it confirms what we have been saying to ourselves. Religion is a social building block affected very directly by legal decisions and the legal culture that informs those. The locus of religion may have shifted slightly over time—from the church to the corporate human resources office—but the importance of it in social construction remains undeniable in our age.

CHAPTER 7 REVIEW

Key Terms

- Liberal toleration
- Millenarianism
- Totemism
- Sacred
- Profane
- Collective conscience
- Symbolic
- Framers
- Separation doctrine
- Niqab
- Burka
- Strict scrutiny
- Corporate personhood
- Closely held corporations

Further Discussion

1. If religion is about spiritual belief and the afterlife, how can it be a social institution?

2. Why do similar countries like the United States and France practice liberal toleration differently?

3. Describe the role of the "separation doctrine" in American politics according to Carol Greenhouse.

4. Does *Hobby Lobby* challenge or confirm Weber's description of religion as important to American "titans of industry"?

Further Reading

Durkheim, Emile. *The Elementary Forms of Religious Life*. Translated by Karen Fields. New York: Free Press, 1994.

Greenhouse, Carol J. *Praying for Justice: Faith, Order, and Community in an American Town*. Ithaca, NY: Cornell University Press, 1986.

Weber, Max. *The Protestant Ethic and the Spirit of Capitalism*. Edited by Peter Baehr and Gordon Wells. New York: Penguin Books, 2002.

Class, Race, and Gender

Religious faith, or its absence, is just one of many features that make up an individual's sense of "self." Ask someone, "Who are you?" and he or she will describe any one of a dozen facets of the modern human condition. The answer could be "Buddhist," "a person of color," "middle class," "female," or "Scotch-Irish." Or it could be all of these things. They belong to the many intersecting categories of identity. Identity is who we think and say we are. But these are two different things. Who I *think* I am might be aspirational; it can be anything I want. Who I *say* I am might be subject to social constraints, feelings of pride, or feelings of shame. The law can intervene in both of these facets of identity formation. Before explaining how, we should consider why this is significant for society at large.

We tend to think about identity as an individual matter, and it is. But it is also much more. How we describe ourselves is intimately tied up in the social categories that are readily available to us. The most salient today, according to sociologists, are class, race, gender, and sexuality. So, to begin with, my notions of how to describe a *sense* of self are already delimited by my social surroundings. *Society helps me be myself.* But also, by declaring myself and participating in one or another of these things—for example middle class—I am contributing to that group as a

> **BOX 8.1**　　Critical Race Theory
>
> Critical race theory is an intellectual movement greatly overlapping with the priorities of law and society. It emerged during the 1980s after traditional law scholars like Derrick Bell drew attention to the inherent power asymmetry of modern legal institutions. Younger scholars like Kimberle Crenshaw and Mari Matsuda then argued that the law was inherently implicated in the maintenance of racial hierarchy and repression. Crenshaw's further writings developed the concept of "intersectionality," the condition whereby class, race, and gender can combine in the identity formation of individuals and groups in ways that distinguish their experience and legal treatment from those of the rest of society. Critical race theory views the law as complicit in widespread social inequality, but it also proposes several solutions to systemic problems, including, among other things, the emphasis on narrative—personal testimony and voicing—to restore power to victims of exclusion.

member. *I help society be itself.* In this way, the relationship between self and society is circular; it is engaged in a feedback loop where the one always partly shapes the other. So where does law fit in?

Many of the categories we invoke to describe ourselves are shaped by law and legal institutions. Laws inscribe the **rights** that members of any group can enjoy. They define the remedies people can seek when they are deprived of those rights. Legal institutions like courts or police set up the affirmative protections people can expect in exercising their rights. And in many specific cases, law explicitly states the language in which our identities can be expressed. So, for instance, as law and society scholars like Ariela Gross and Ian Haney López have shown, racial categories like "white" or "Indian" have been litigated in American courtrooms, with parties arguing vigorously that they "belong" to that group and then being told by judges that, on the basis of factual evidence, they do or do not.[1] So not only is identity intimately connected to the makeup of society at large, it is also shaped directly by how the law says people can and cannot identify. Law and society scholars who study this phenomenon are known as **critical race theorists** (see box 8.1).

As suggested in the early portions of this book, both law and society are capable of immense and steady changes over time. The US Census, a federal government survey administered every ten years for the purpose of population mapping and election planning, has used different terms to describe the same groups, including *free person of color, Negro, black,* and *African American.* Although the survey asks people to "self-identify," it clearly delimits the terms along which a person can do this. Moreover, other constraints including unequal protection under law for people identifying in this category, or public scorn for claiming minority status when one does not "look" the part, may heavily influence people's choices. Law, in other words, may supply the terms by which we can identify ourselves, but it also goes further to establish the risks and benefits that come with these choices.

This chapter is an exploration of law and society at the sites of class, race, and gender identity. At bottom, it asks whether we are free to choose who we are or whether these choices are ultimately given to us by forces well beyond our control. To answer this, it first examines key theories of identity coming from some of the most influential social theorists of all time. This section ranges from considering traditional differences like class and race to considering more modern ones like cyborgs and virtual reality identity formations. The next section then delves deeper into law's role in defining socioeconomic class. It examines in particular law's relationship to labor, social welfare, neoliberalism, and the Occupy Wall Street uprisings. The section after that explores race and ethnicity. More than any other category of collective or individual identity, race and ethnicity have depended closely on battles and reforms in courtrooms and legislatures. After that, the discussion turns to law and society's treatment of gender and sexuality and movements to bring about equality for these under law.

IDENTITY AND CHANGE

When expressing "who I am," how free am I to answer? For instance, I can proclaim confidently that I am a card-carrying *Freedonian*.[2] This identification might mean a great deal to me; perhaps it represents my resistance to natural-born citizenship, or perhaps it describes a utopian belief system where all members are equal. And you might respect that. But would any of this matter if you did not know what any of this meant? If my identification in this way does not help others to place me in boxes of their own understanding, what good is it? Identity may be a matter of our own choice, but its social importance comes from its meaning to those around us. It helps others quickly "know" things about our background, our loyalties, and our likes and dislikes. In this regard, identity is only as "free" as it is socially significant.

Social philosophers have been saying this for some time. Some have found identity to be an "iron cage," a limiting cap on the human spirit.[3] Others have said lack of identity causes dehumanization.[4] None knew this better than the German social philosopher Karl Marx. Marx, later associated with a whole political economic system and ideology, initially concerned himself with the freedom of humanity under its new industrial world order. The onset of the new economic system called **capital** deeply concerned Marx. He studied it in several different locations, including Germany, England, and the United States, and found that everywhere it went capital divided its participants up into owners and workers. Because owners wanted to sell their products at the cheapest prices to attract the most consumers, they paid workers the lowest wages the "market" would allow. Workers were thus valued only by the goods they produced. Any surpluses generated from these sales were then reinvested into equipment to expand operations or were taken out by the employers. The economic benefits of this system, Marx said, flowed almost entirely from the laborers to the owners. This was, for him, a form of voluntary enslavement. Why did people agree to it? One reason was that under the law they had little choice. English common law and European civil law had evolved to protect private property interests, and therefore to maintain wealth in the hands of those who already possessed it.

But workers also participated in this system because of their identity. They came to see the value of their work and time—their lives really—through the eyes of their employers, the ownership class. This, Marx said, was **alienation**; laborers had stopped viewing themselves and their value through their own eyes and were thus alienated from themselves. Because of this, the working class had tacitly agreed to accept very poor conditions. Factory conditions were dangerous and unhealthy, working hours were long and harsh, and family and community life were suffering because men, women, and children were all toiling—at work, in the home, and in the streets—to support this system. The ravenous economic priorities of capital were, in short, harmful toward society itself.

Given the general costs and benefits of this larger economic system, was worker alienation helpful for society, and, if not, was there anything to do about it? Marx argued that there was, and that it was simple. To escape from this dehumanizing system, workers needed only to shift their perspective to view their work through their own eyes and to value it from the perspective of what it cost *them.* The products they were making, in other words, could be sold at prices that better reflected the human relations that went in to making them. Workers, the demographic majority of Anglo-European society, needed only to identify themselves as the *center* rather than the *margins* of this system.

Marx's university education had been in law. Although not essential to his analysis, he knew law to be an important fixture in maintaining the economic system that restricted most of the population. Followers of Marx have since argued considerably over whether law is an essential feature of the economic system, the "base," or a cultural construct added on as "superstructure" to justify it. Today, the difference is hard to see. Since we no longer rely primarily on factories manufacturing widgets to generate economic "value," law's control as a form of economic activity and its control as a type of cultural constraint are almost one and the same. What we need to realize, then, is that either way the conditions of life under contemporary capitalist economy are the product of both economic activity *and* the legal norms and institutions required to hold that in place. Indeed, the more alienated the economy becomes—as in the outsourcing of jobs from the American Midwest to Asia or Latin America—the more important law becomes to prevent anger and frustration from boiling into social unrest. Through its influence on individual and group identity, Marx teaches us, law helps to stabilize an otherwise inherently unstable system.

For the sociologist Erving Goffman, however, the power of identity went well beyond its role in the modern-day class system. While that surely was an important consequence, Goffman recognized that identity was shaping and reconciling many more worldly contradictions than just those surrounding class. He found that individual identity formation was also key to perceptions about reality itself. This is because people's sense of themselves does not exist free and apart from others'. The circular nature of identity formation means that once I develop a sense of myself as "professor," for instance, I am likely to view the world around me from the perspective of a university educator. More importantly, I will then share with other professors a similar or overlapping view of the world. As mentioned in chapter 4, this aspect of identity in relation to worldview became known as "framing." Framing is extremely important for understanding law and identity. Normally law and facts about the world are considered two distinct but significant elements of legal reasoning. As the next chapter will explain, "thinking like a lawyer" almost literally means being able to separate law and fact when making arguments about the world. Frame analysis, in which the perspective of worldly actors is studied sociologically, finds that "facts" are viewed commonly by groups of people sharing the same frame. So, for example, the wave of police killings documented in the early 2010s is a real-world fact that cannot be disputed. But people disagree about its interpretation on the basis of their framing. From the perspective of minority communities in American inner cities, not to mention critics of state power more broadly, the killings are a clear example of police overreach and aggression toward racial minorities. From the perspective of law enforcement officers, administrators, and their families and communities, the killings are simply an indication of the considerable fear and stress police work under when the public distrusts them.

Framing has an important implication when it comes to the study of law and legal change. In the United States basic civil rights and civil liberties are "guaranteed" under the Bill of Rights; but that text has not changed in the more than two hundred years since its creation. What has significantly changed is **jurisprudence**—judicial reasoning surrounding that document and its complex meanings. As late as 1857, the Supreme Court held that African Americans, whether freed or slaves, could not be considered "citizens" of the United States.[5] From 1896 to 1954 the Court maintained that it was perfectly legal to separate nonwhite U.S. citizens from white ones so long as conditions were roughly "equal."[6] In 1954 the Court finally decided that this was unacceptable and outlawed formal racial segregation by law.[7] What had changed between these years? In the text of the Bill of Rights, nothing. The end of the Civil War had brought about the **Reconstruction Amendments**—three constitutional amendments freeing the slaves and protecting the rights to equal protection under law and universal (e.g., nonwhite) male voting. But the Equal Protection Clause of the Fourteenth Amendment really only restated and strengthened what had already been said in the Fifth Amendment's equal protection clause.

By the time *Brown v. Board* was decided in 1954, ending legal segregation, what had most clearly changed was the framing of the African American civil rights struggle in America. After the Civil War, US blacks recently freed from slavery were expected to be grateful for their freedom. Their participation in civic life was new and therefore did not, in the minds of white society and its public officials, require "full" benefits. But in the ensuing decades writers like Frederick Douglass, W. E. B. Du Bois, and Zora Neale Hurston—all three eloquent masters of language and rhetoric—called for fuller participation in ways that began to appeal to more and more white, especially northern and urban citizens. During World War I and World War II, African Americans served a vital support function in the US military both as combat soldiers, sailors, and pilots and as logistical support crew. With their return home, advocacy groups like the NAACP called for greater equality to reward the veterans who had sacrificed much to protect a country that had kept them marginalized. By the time the Supreme Court heard *Brown,* the position of African Americans had changed from that of "freed persons of color" to hardworking partners in a modern democratic society. Their position, in other words, had been reframed, and the court hearing *Brown* would have likely viewed racial segregation from the new perspective. Framing, in other words, has been a critical feature in attaining legal recognition and protection of what later become "natural" equal rights.

Framing has another important implication. Besides evolving over time through deliberate political and social activism, peoples' perspective on themselves and the world also shifts when they move around. The great writer James Baldwin knew this well. He was born in Harlem, New York, the grandson of African slaves. He was raised to become a Baptist minister and worked in his youth to help support eight younger siblings. He then moved out of his house to become a writer under the mentorship of the famous Richard Wright. After struggling, he moved to France, and it was there, Baldwin said, that he truly became aware of himself, and his condition, as an African American. His novel *Giovanni's Room,* for instance, is the story of an American expatriate soldier viewed through the eyes of his French associates, who are themselves viewed through the eyes of Baldwin. The transatlantic move—with only forty dollars in his pocket and contact information only for Wright, who had himself moved abroad two years earlier—gave Baldwin a unique frame through which to view American race relations and spiritual redemption. Both Wright and Baldwin joined a group of African American writers, poets, and musicians, whose dislocation in Europe was a source of insight into and criticism of the naturalized race relations of their home country.

If dislocation has been a powerful force in framing and identity formation, so too has been **disembodiment.** Literally describing the separation of "self" from the human body, disembodiment has become an object of intense debate among writers of science and technology studies. The anthropologists Emily Martin and Donna Haraway each wrote seminal books in the 1990s documenting the ways in which human beings—through biomedical advances and communication technologies—were being freed from the limits of their physical bodies. This was followed by researchers in cyberspace documenting the experience of identity formation in new **virtual** spaces like chat rooms and bulletin boards. Information technology advanced quickly in the ensuing years so that people young and old began establishing their online presence through sites like Friendster, My Space, Facebook, Instagram, Snapchat, and so forth. In these formats, people could pick and choose images, text, and even music that would depict who they were to the world. In many cases, this was a reinvention of the self: not a representation of one's real-world life and interests but rather an all-new identity detached from appearances and life chances in the physical human world. The term *catfishing* came to describe a kind of identity fraud in which people online using others' images and information lured others into relationships and transactions that could never be verified or secured in the real world.

The advent of this new virtual identity was both a blessing and a curse for many. On one hand, it meant we could be free from the political and social constraints mentioned previously. Suddenly, "who I am" could be constructed from data readily available online and from all over the world. This "freed" people from the limitations of class, gender, and race. It also, by hybridizing identity in general with a combination of real and virtual presences, led to a new flexibility in real-world identity and social interaction. A metropolitan, middle-aged, African American woman could join Web-based video games like Warcraft alongside suburban white youths. On the other hand, identity theft became a big business in terms of profits from both stealing and selling data and the market for identity protection software and services. In short, as identity became more flexible with technology, it also became more of a commodity to be purchased and sold.

And as identity has evolved because of social change, so too has the law. High-technology law has, as a result, also grown in popularity and demand. This includes legal practice in intellectual property, cybercrime, online contracting, and big data management. But recent history suggests that the classic social categories that make up identity continue to be important. Online, people can construct themselves however they choose; but in the real world socioeconomic class, gender, and race seem to have grown *more* rather than less important.

CLASS

Socioeconomic class refers to the position a person or group occupies in relation to economic resources in the broader society. This position can be a function of income, the amount one earns in a month or a year, and wealth, the amount one has already accumulated. Income even in one single employment niche can depend on regional costs of living variations or on contract negotiations. Wealth, meanwhile, is built up over time or inherited from others who have accumulated it over many years. For this reason, the wealthiest institutions and families are ones in the United States who have been around for many generations. Yale University, for example, was founded in 1701 and has accumulated approximately $25 billion in its endowment fund. Similarly, the Winthrop family, descendants of Massachusetts Bay Colony founder John Winthrop, is one of the wealthiest clans in America still today.

The historian Nancy Isenberg writes that socioeconomic class inequality has been with the United States since the colonial period. With the prospect of starvation, sickness, and death facing new colonists, many recruited to journey from England to the New World were from the English lower class and prisons. Most of these came over as "indentured servants" indebted to wealthy families for the price of the ocean voyage, which was to be paid back over a number of years, usually four to ten. These indentured workers were later supplemented by chattel slaves bought from traders in West Africa and shipped over in the thousands. Of those who arrived with wealth, little could be done to convince them to partake of the hard work building a new colony would require; servants and slaves, therefore, formed the backbone of colonial labor in the early days of the country and were responsible for most of the development and urbanization efforts.

With the end of indentured servitude and slavery, adults were free to work in any vocation, and class became less a matter of bondage and more a relationship to production. As already mentioned, Marx studied this relationship closely to find that those who owned capital—the means of production—had different social interests than those who operated those means. Workers in nineteenth-century America were largely agricultural and industrial manufacturing labor. Their conditions were harsh, their days and weeks were long, and the extraction of value from their toil was extreme. Under "high" capitalism, however, this was considered to be the most efficient arrangement for strong economic production.

As in other Western countries at the time, modernization in the United States brought millions of individuals and families out of the country and into big cities to join an urban labor force geared toward manufacturing. To be sure, the production of **raw materials** such as coal, steel, crude oil, cotton, and so forth was an important foundation of the new economy. But a rise in factory work and a decline in agriculture concentrated more people in smaller spaces within the big cities (see figure 8.1). Specific industries varied by region, but each of the big cities produced something important, and a set of secondary industries emerged around shipping goods to markets all over the country, and later the world.

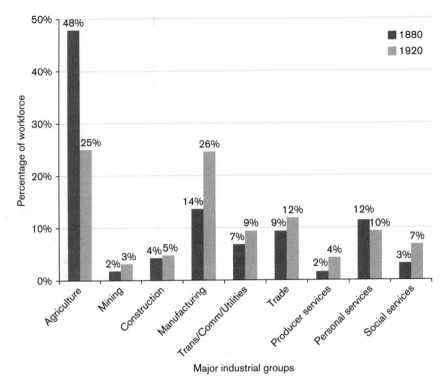

Figure 8.1 Percentages of workforce in US industrial groups, 1880 and 1920. Source: Charles Hirschman and Elizabeth Mogford, "Immigration and the American Industrial Revolution from 1880 to 1920," *Social Science Research* 38, no. 4 (2009): 897–920.

This growth in the urban workforce meant that workers were suddenly more aware of one another, communicated quickly among themselves, and educated each other and the wider public about their conditions. All of this proved useful when, following the stock market crash of 1929, America and the industrialized world slipped into a deep economic depression that saw real gross domestic product (GDP) fall by 30 percent. At the peak of the crisis in 1933, one in four American adults was unemployed. With this large pool of unemployed workers, the value of labor among those who retained manufacturing employment declined further.

At the time, there had been few federal laws in place to protect the American worker. Factory work was still a relatively new foundation to the economy, and many saw labor laws as an artificial constraint on the "freedom of contract" so important to capitalist economic efficiency. On the basis of pure supply and demand, many said, labor should be paid only what it was "worth," and worth should only come down to what the "market" said it was. During the

Depression, this led to especially harsh and dangerous conditions for the American worker. But because employment was so scarce, few were willing to risk livelihoods to protest bad employment conditions.

Labor unions had been strong in the decades before the crisis. The Industrial Workers of the World, for instance, was founded in 1905 and saw its peak membership in 1917 at 150,000 members. The American Federation of Labor, founded in 1886, was an even larger organization, with membership hitting roughly 500,000 in 1900. By the time of the Great Depression, however, membership in all unions had declined substantially. Workers who could find employment made it through the period on their own, and few substantial gains were made in trade union or labor reform activity. Indeed, employers had been able to use the high unemployment rate of the Depression to undermine union solidarity and bargaining power in a manner that, without broader federal legal support, would spell the decline of organized labor.

But by the mid-1930s, the economy began to recover thanks to a series of reforms passed by President Franklin Roosevelt, a Democrat and staunch union supporter. Roosevelt and his advisers believed that American long-term economic stability depended not solely on sound banking and monetary policies—the absence of which had caused the Great Depression—but also on basic stability in the lives of American workers. Capitalism, under Roosevelt in other words, could not simply be about making the most money at the lowest cost to ownership. It had to support worker families and communities—the *social* bedrock on which the industrial manufacturing economy was based.

In 1935, Roosevelt signed into law the National Labor Relations Act (or Wagner Act), aiming to protect on a national scale the rights of employees to organize, unionize, and bargain for better conditions. Its passage was premised upon a realization that workers in the new industrial economy—in which large companies had disproportionate power over the lives of their workers—enjoyed unequal constitutional rights to associate and to contract freely. The act therefore rectified "inequality of bargaining power between employees who do not possess full freedom of association or actual liberty of contract and employers who are organized in the corporate or other forms of ownership association."[8]

The Wagner Act also set up a standing Labor Relations Board to oversee that protections guaranteed in the statute were being respected nationwide. This moment has been considered one of the high points of the American labor movement. Although union membership at the time was not at its peak numbers, the movement had sufficiently influenced the federal government to enact policies that would place economic ambitions and social protectionism on a level playing field.

The moment also demonstrated the power of social movements in law. The Wagner Act was the result of a collaboration between the activism and organizing power of US trade unions and electoral politics and elected officials. Whereas these centers of political power are often viewed as separate in modern history, this represented one of several moments in which they converged to bring about lasting legal reform with direct impacts on society. Mobilization of labor and support from elected officials like President Roosevelt also depended heavily upon the identity formation work of labor organizers at the time. What capitalist owners tried to frame as unfair collusion between workers the workers themselves framed as "solidarity" based on a common social condition and on pride in their daily work.

The New Deal period brought other substantial legal reforms that would establish the American welfare state. One of these was the 1935 Social Security Act. The act set up a fund into which all American employees would pay through a universal payroll tax. As part of the new social security program, Americans would be able to receive benefits on retirement to ensure that elderly persons beyond the working age would not have to live in poverty. Another benefit to this program was to encourage retirement at a reasonable age, thereby freeing up employment positions for new generations of American workers. This would have been particularly important during the "Baby Boom" years, when the adult population swelled as an echo effect of the high birthrate following World War II. A second key benefit, added in the 1960s, was the Medicaid program, which acted as a kind of health insurance to low-income individuals and families. Finally, the low-income program Aid to Families with Dependent Children and its successor Temporary Assistance to Needy Families served as public assistance to families below the poverty line. In these programs, public benefits were never intended to serve as a "government handout" in the way critics later argued. They were, rather, meant to ensure the health and well-being of American citizens and residents subject to the ebbs and flows of prosperity of the global marketplace.

But by the end of the 1970s the Baby Boom generation, now in its thirties, had achieved historic levels of economic prosperity under the protections of gains made by the labor movement and New Deal social welfare programs. Many were educated under the new higher education subsidies. Many bought homes under the Federal Housing Authority low-interest loan programs. Large numbers settled in the American suburbs as the metropolitan inner cities saw waves of factory closures resulting from the shift to a global information economy. This **deindustrialization** completely transformed the American city. Neighborhoods deep inside the large manufacturing towns like Detroit, Milwaukee, and Chicago saw rising unemployment. Longtime white residents left these areas for suburban life; but for new immigrants from Latin America and Asia, as well as urbanizing African Americans, these were some of the only affordable places to live. Residents forced to live there struggled to find gainful employment, and many were roped into crime as a means to subsist. Many more were forced to apply for and remain permanently in the AFDC and Medicaid programs once intended only as a "safety net." Caught in a cycle of low income, low rents, low property taxes, poor schools, high crime rates, and survival on government benefits, deindustrialized American inner cities became ground zero for a new battle over the role of the state in ensuring the "general welfare."

The rise of a new conservatism in the 1980s came with a wave of changing attitudes about the role of law and policy in the lives of everyday citizens. Popular leaders like Ronald Reagan argued that social welfare benefits cause people to become dependent on the government, force state agencies to enlarge beyond necessity, and require working people to pay higher tax rates than they otherwise should. The funds demanded in taxes, Reagan and his advisers said, would be better left in the hands of citizens to spend as they wish. More importantly, the wealthy could receive tax "breaks" to encourage them to spend more on consumer and luxury goods, thereby stimulating economic demand, production, and growth. This became known among the public as **trickle-down economics**," or Reaganomics.

Among scholars of law and society this has been seen as part of the larger movement called **neoliberalism**. Neoliberalism draws its name from "classical liberalism," devised during the late seventeenth and early eighteenth centuries in Scotland, England, and France. Classical liberalism held that human freedom and equality were paramount goals of political society, that these were the only true ends of organized government, and that democratic representation and market economy were the best means of achieving these ends. Governments could provide for their people only to the extent that the free market would not, but it would stay out of market activity unless doing so would permit socially destructive behaviors. One example was in the criminal law. People could certainly justify criminal activity such as selling stolen property or agreeing to commit a murder for hire on the basis of "freedom of contract," but the social effects of stealing and murder were so harmful that these would be areas in which the state could justifiably limit human freedom. Outside of these areas, however, people would be "free." Freedom in those days, of course, was limited largely to men of European descent and often only those with real property to their name. Nevertheless, within a highly bounded notion of "free men," all were considered free.

Neoliberalism as it arose in the late 1970s embraced these concepts but took them further. It agreed with the fundamentals like freedom and equality, but it believed that almost any government intervention either for or against behavior was an artificial limit on freedom. Therefore, taking money from the public in taxes to redistribute in social welfare was considered to be a move against freedom itself. In this light, the many gains that the labor movement of the pre– and post–New Deal eras achieved were reframed as anticompetitive, antimarket, and thus harmful to society. Under Reagan, therefore, trade unions saw their protections weakened, and recipients of welfare benefits like AFDC saw their living conditions reimagined. Suddenly, struggling mothers in urban housing projects were called "welfare queens," and the conservative press portrayed these households as "living it up" on government assistance checks that only grew the more children they produced. This reframing of the archetypal social welfare recipient destroyed public confidence in the social protections that had helped so many over the years and led in great measure to their dismantling over the ensuing decades. Here the relationship of law and social identities was unmistakable. Legal provisions for social welfare were acceptable after the Great Depression, when the average recipient was a white working-class laborer. But these policies were deemed "handouts" once, thanks to the shifting economy and urban space, persons of color were among those most in need of help. The 1990s and 2000s saw legal reforms to try to shift these people off government assistance into programs labeled "workfare," where they would have to enroll in job search programs or work in menial roles to receive the same benefits. This placed added stress on single mothers whose demand for welfare was, in the first place, heightened by children to care for and no spouse to support the household.

The rollback of public assistance was not limited to welfare recipients. On a much wider scale, public subsidies for education across the United States were shrunk under the new neoliberal movement called the **new public management (NPM).** NPM advocates believed vital public programs like higher education could and should be run much like private businesses. Their new key functions would be to deliver a profitable service to the public but also to draw in revenues from those services to offset much of their own costs—in other words, to make institutions commercially independent and self-sustaining. Lawmakers sold this shift to the general public as a means to lower taxes and keep more private wealth in the hands of private citizens. Needless to say, the move most benefited those with wealth already in hand. It also forced individuals and families to absorb more of the costs associated with **public goods** like education. Whereas having an educated society was an important social priority to postwar legislators, the new style of lawmaking viewed it as a **private good**—a way for individuals to increase their own capital, personal brand, and thus value in the market economy. Universities, forced to accept meager state subsidies, had no choice but to raise (and raise) tuition prices. For families of the middle and upper classes, wealth was already available to offset these costs. For the working class and the poor, student loans were the only solution.

Realizing this, many low-ranked colleges, universities, and trade schools began catering to low-income students. While most of these were **nonprofit** entities—designed to meet their operating costs and retain any modest surplus—many new **for-profit** institutions sprang up in this period marketing themselves to poor and working-class students through television, radio, and Internet advertising that capitalized on people's desire to better themselves through education. They also capitalized on the almost unconditional availability of federal student loans, which the school would receive directly and which the students would be forced to repay with interest for the rest of their

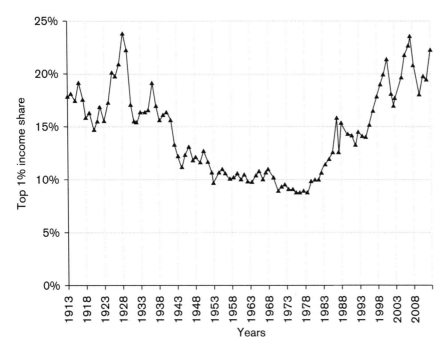

Figure 8.2 Top 1 percent income share in United States, 1913–2010. Courtesy Emmanuel Saez.

lives. The period from about 2003 to 2017 saw total federal student debt levels explode from $250 billion to $1.4 trillion. A disproportionate share of this debt was generated by for-profit colleges. And a disproportionate number of students attending those institutions were from the lowest income brackets.

Aware of this gross transfer of wealth from public to private sectors, the Occupy Wall Street movement arose in the wake of the financial crisis of 2009 to demand new laws that could bring rampant inequality back under control. Figure 8.2 above shows the share of total US income enjoyed by the top 1 percent of earners over time. As is plainly visible, since the turn of the twenty-first century income inequality has reached levels not seen since the 1920s—right before the Great Depression and New Deal legal reforms.

In 2011, Occupy protesters proposed legal remedies for this dire inequality. Among other things, the proposal called for new, stronger banking regulations, prosecution of financial misfeasance leading to the crisis, reversal of the *Citizens United* case (discussed in chapter 7), and more rigorous tax laws to collect a "fair share" from the rich and from corporations.[9] Other proposals included universal free education. Three years after these proposals were floated, the Occupy movement turned to runaway student debt and began advocating for loan forgiveness for some of the most precarious students. In September 2014, for instance, the group acquired $4 million of student debt generated by Everest College, a subsidiary of the embattled for-profit conglomerate Corinthian Colleges.

Occupy Wall Street never fully realized its goal of greater civic equality between working-class individuals and corporations and their wealth investors. Some argued that the movement was too diffuse in its focus or too radical in its tactics. But like many social movements, Occupy was successful as a symbol in and of itself. It showed that many thousands of people were once again forming their identities around economic precarity and class politics. It showed that people on the losing side of the global economy could still frame their reality in a positive, hopeful manner. It showed that collective action in the name of socioeconomic class—much like that of the labor movement of the twentieth century—was alive and well. Finally, it showed that people faced with gross injustice still looked to law and legal reforms for solutions to reshape their world.

RACE

Around two years after the Occupy movement began, a second mass protest movement emerged in the United States known as Black Lives Matter or BLM. Like Occupy, BLM got its start initially online with the **hashtag** #blacklivesmatter.[10] People began using this tag to annotate their outraged responses on social media to three key incidents involving the use of force against black men in the United States. In one case, a civilian named George Zimmerman shot and killed the teenage African American Trayvon Martin, who was walking home alone in a hooded sweatshirt through his father's fiancée's suburban neighborhood in Sanford, Florida. The homes in the neighborhood of Twin Lakes had declined to 50 percent of their initial value by the time of this incident, thanks to the global financial meltdown. Perhaps because of the new sense of precarity, the community had organized a "neighborhood watch" group that included George Zimmerman, a twenty-eight-year-old Hispanic man. Zimmerman was walking the neighborhood at the time carrying a loaded firearm when he spotted Martin and confronted him on the sidewalk about his right to be in the community. There was a verbal and then a physical altercation, and as the two men wrestled on the ground, Zimmerman drew his gun and by his own account shot Martin in self-defense. Trayvon was killed on the spot, effectively just for walking home.

This incident sparked widespread outrage. An audio recording made its rounds on television news and social media, while people debated online in the new virtual public square about the potential for justice in the case given racial divides in the United States. After the election of President Barack Obama in 2008, many said the "Dream" had been realized and anything was now possible.

America would henceforth be a **postracial** society. Now, with the senseless death of a young boy in the name of neighborhood "self-defense," this sounded even more far-fetched. The not-guilty verdict for Zimmerman in his subsequent murder trial shocked many. In Florida, it turned out, a person under threat in an altercation like this one had the right to "stand your ground" under state law. This meant that the killing was legally interpreted as justifiable **self-defense.** But publicly, it was symptomatic of systemic injustice.

This was further confirmed over the next several years when law enforcement officers in Ferguson, Missouri, killed Michael Brown, a black eighteen-year-old who only days earlier had graduated high school. Details about the altercation remain in dispute, but the agreed-upon facts say that the police killed Brown only ninety seconds after encountering him and a friend in the street, and that Brown was entirely unarmed. The incident sparked mass protest in the Ferguson suburb of St. Louis, to which activists and public intellectuals traveled from all around the United States at the time. The officer who killed Michael Brown was cleared of any wrongdoing in court.

A third such incident occurred in 2014 in the New York City borough of Staten Island. There, forty-three-year-old Eric Garner was detained outside a convenience store on suspicion of selling loose cigarettes. Police forced Garner to the ground and held him in a chokehold for nearly twenty seconds. Video of the event captured Garner begging the officers to release the pressure and stating clearly, "I can't breathe!" By the time they let go Garner was dead. Once again, national outrage erupted quickly thanks to the widely circulated video and the very sad but memorable phrase Garner squeezed out with his final breaths.

All three incidents contributed to the growing sense among many Americans, whites included, that justice was still beyond the reach of racial minorities. It was, in a sense, a confirmation that the country was in no way "postracial" and that rather the divisions and fears that prevailed in the wake of chattel slavery lingered. The election of Obama in 2008, if anything, had provoked new resentments that would ultimately spill over in the 2016 election year.

The expectation that the election of one black president would erase centuries of legal racism and resentment was always unrealistic. As the critical race theory scholars point out, courts have often tried to decide questions of racial identity. The historians Michael Omi and Howard Winant, for example, explain that specific legal cases in the US South decided who had to be "white" or "black" using a formula that dated back to the dawn of racial science. The so-called "one-drop rule" said that individuals with even a single trace of African blood in their system would be classified as "black" under law and entitled to only the rights and privileges reserved for that category.[11] In a similar example of racial identity jurisprudence, a case about jury composition in Texas led to the conclusion that Mexican Americans would no longer be considered "other whites"; they were their own ethnic group deserving of equal protection under the Constitution.[12] This was a departure because up until the late 1940s, Mexican Americans had been legally considered "white" for purposes of civil rights and civil liberties.[13]

Before this, Asian Americans had been deemed nonwhite in 1923. That year, the Supreme Court heard the fascinating case of *U.S. v. Thind*, in which an Asian Indian Sikh man living in California sought to **naturalize** as a US citizen.[14] Immigration law at the time limited naturalizations to "free white persons." To acquire land in California under that state's Alien Land Law of 1913, Thind would have to be a citizen. Relying on a similar decision regarding a Japanese American one year earlier, the Court under Chief Justice William H. Taft said that Thind was not a "Caucasian" as that term was popularly understood. Thind had argued that northern Indians were technically "Caucasian" as they derived from the same region and linguistic roots as Europeans. But the court rejected this scholastic interpretation of the term, which would have made the racial grouping of "white" more expansive and more enfranchising.

With the identities of black, Latino, and Asian Americans determined as "nonwhite" in the highest legal institutions in the United States, the other question was what rights they would enjoy or be barred from. In the period from the Civil War to the civil rights era, American blacks were formally "equal" under the law, but they enjoyed limited rights compared to white Americans. Everything from their ability to ride in train cars to their ability to stay in hotels, eat in restaurants, or study in school was shaped by policies of discrimination that allowed owners and operators to exclude those they considered to be African American. The separation of the races was not simply a practical holdover from the days of slavery. It reflected an ongoing belief that interracial mixing was against the tenets of Christianity, or against the "law of nature." These beliefs continued well after schools and public accommodations were formally desegregated. As late as 1967 it was illegal for white and nonwhite couples to intermarry in many of the southern states. Only the dramatic case of *Loving v. Virginia* changed this to guarantee the right to marry to all couples of mixed racial and ethnic origins. This case would be reinvoked time and again in the battle over same-sex marriage—itself not nationally protected until 2015's *Obergefell v. Hodges*.

Law's ability to shape and reshape racial identity and attitudes remains very current today. Hard-fought battles in the highest court forced the equality of nonwhite groups into mainstream reality, but these gains have been piecemeal and have come only after substantial social movement activity and agitation. Equal rights, in other words, were not "given"; they had to be *claimed* by racial minorities, who suffered substantial casualties in the struggle. Popular historical accounts that celebrate the multicultural experience in the United States as one of increasing equal protection under the rule of law fail to appreciate the deep-seated traumas felt by people of color in achieving those gains. That means the struggle today remains incomplete.

This can be seen in at least four large areas of law and society. The first is immigration law. The national-origin preferences of the 1924 Immigration Act may have been lifted in 1965, but similar policies—such as contemporary preferences for immigrants with substantial wealth or with advanced education—continue to perpetuate a racialized screening process for becoming American. The battles over refugee and asylum policies seen in the Central American refugee crisis described in chapter 6, and seen more recently in the very low numbers of Syrian refugees accepted into the United States, are further instructive. The origin countries in both cases—El Salvador, Honduras, and Mexico on one hand and Syria and Iraq on the other—are clearly ones whose people hail from non-European genetic stock, cultural formations, and religious faiths. The public outcry that resulted when refugees began arriving from these places—ones ravaged by violence in which the United States had a hand—says much about the willingness to embrace nonwhite immigrants as "new" Americans, even when they need help the most. More recent history, including the 2016 push to build a southern "border wall," as well as the child-separation policy of 2018, suggests that the United States may be in a moment of heightened intolerance sanctioned by law.

Police violence in the cases described above is another example. In the cases of Trayvon Martin, Michael Brown, and Eric Garner, all three victims were African American, male, and physically large individuals. The acquittal of the wrongdoer in each case—plus many more that have followed since—instructed the entire world that it was both rational and legally justifiable to kill another human being when that person's physical body (and little more) put you in fear for your own life. It was, in other words, "reasonable" to consider any black man on the street a threat to personal safety almost irrespective of what he was doing. Some cases even suggested this was true for black women.[15]

All of this points further to the massively disproportionate rates of incarceration among US minorities. African Americans, who make up just 13 percent of the US population, make up roughly 40 percent of those in jail or prisons.[16] Alongside this figure, it must be noted, the population identified as "white" makes up 64 percent of the total population but only 39 percent of those behind bars. There are many things to say about these comparative statistics. Whether one believes they are the result of a "structural" tendency toward criminal behavior or a highly lopsided justice system, the broader conclusion must be that the "system" on one level or another "sees" race and racial identity in determining the fates of average people. Racial identity has not only been decided by law, it has been rewarded and penalized by it.

Finally, racial inequality is sewn into the fabric of legal advocacy itself. If more African American males are in prison than in college, what are the chances that many will go on to earn degrees and pursue graduate school? Without college degrees, how many will be able to go to law school and become attorneys? And with few attorneys in their communities, how well will African

Americans be represented in the justice system? This documented absence of minority lawyers in the United States has been part of a "justice gap" for some years. It has meant that, faced with civil legal problems like bankruptcy or a car accident, many will simply be unable to afford legal help and will represent themselves or default in their case, so that they will be held liable at a disproportional rate. The lack of well-trained African American and other minority attorneys in the legal profession is still further evidence of the lingering disadvantages racial identity can bring to those said to receive "equal protection under law."[17]

Law has been both friend and foe for minority groups. Whereas it has played a role in their search for and near achievement of equal protection, it has also been the legitimating basis on which that protection had long been denied. Even when the law changed because the Supreme Court "saw the light," law enforcement and legal practice were able to thwart full implementation of equal rights for all racial identities. To the extent that law did play a role in achieving some measure of justice, professional lawyers were at the center of these struggles. Some of them became very famous as a result. In the case of Thurgood Marshall, lead counsel in *Brown v. Board* and graduate of Howard Law School, a seat as the first African American judge on the Supreme Court was a symbol of national gratitude for what he had accomplished. But the lingering underrepresentation of minority lawyers to this day suggests that the profession remains out of reach for more nonwhite students. This may not be the case because anyone wants it this way. It is more likely the result of the structural exclusion so many experience on their way through youth, higher education, and early adulthood. Even where they are welcomed to join the legal profession, recent evidence suggests they are recruited into low-ranked, low-performing law schools with a higher risk of underemployment and heavy debt on graduation.[18] The result is that professional law does a great job speaking for minorities, but it has yet to find a way to help them speak for themselves.

GENDER AND SEXUALITY

Integration of the legal profession by gender has been similar. White women have been allowed to appear in court for quite some time. The first recorded case in the United States was Margaret Brent in 1648. Far ahead of her time, Brent became adept in colonial property law and came to manage the estate of her own family as well as estates of others. In 1869, Arabella Mansfield became the first woman to be admitted into a state bar in America. A resident of Iowa, she was sworn in during the year that this state became the first to admit women attorneys to practice law in its courts. Both Brent and Mansfield are considered early feminists. Mansfield was an avid supporter and participant in the women's suffrage movement—the first modern forerunner of the women's movement of the late twentieth century.

It is appropriate that some of the leading early feminists were lawyers. Law would come to play an important role in the shaping of gender and sexual identities in modern US history. The women's suffrage movement is an apt example of this. Under the leadership of Susan B. Anthony, the suffragists had already become active before the Civil War as they mobilized to end slavery. By the age of seventeen, Anthony had collected signatures to abolish slavery, and in her midthirties she became head of the New York State chapter of the American Anti-Slavery Society. Once the Civil War ended and President Lincoln freed the remaining southern slaves, the women of the abolitionist movement turned to their own civil rights and liberties. Their first order of business was to change the laws preventing women from voting in the United States.

Through the nineteenth century, women were not given a voice in electoral politics. They stood as supporters and symbols of virtue and domesticity next to their husbands, who, if they were running for office, needed the appearance of moral virtue to convince the male voting public that their civic intentions were true. But this exclusion was only the tip of a very large iceberg. Women were also not allowed to own private property, for example. Once they married, any land or valuables they acquired or inherited became the property of their husbands under the rule known as coverture (see chapter 4). Women stuck in bad marriages had to receive permission from their husband to divorce, and the law in many states protected the rights of men to "discipline" or beat their wives as a form of household order.[19] The women's suffrage movement, which focused overtly on winning the female right to vote, was therefore really about something much bigger. Hoping for the right to voice their grievances through the election of public officials, the suffragists really aimed for a wider transformation of woman's role in the society through law. Known today as the "first wave" of US feminism, the suffragists' ultimate victory in the passage of the Nineteenth Amendment of 1920 was a glimpse of things to come.

This wider transformation was placed on hold through the early twentieth century. In that time, the West fought through World War I, a Great Depression, and then World War II. Legal change to achieve social equality—outside of the labor movement class victories described above—would have to wait. However, these historic global events in their own way hastened the changes in society necessary to support broader legal advances for gender equality. The Nineteenth Amendment had followed on the heels of the First World War. Then, during the Great Depression, a period when one out of four adult men were out of work, many women had to innovate ways to provide for their families. Men's role as sole breadwinner came into question, as did the power that came along with controlling family finances. In the Depression years, there was little to control.

Figure 8.3 Female laborer at work on Consolidated bomber, Consolidated Aircraft Corp., Fort Worth, Texas, during World War II era. Source: Library of Congress.

Finally, during World War II, as men were deployed overseas in the largest numbers ever seen, many women not only had to provide for their families but also had to enter the workforce to support the war effort itself. US military propaganda films famously showed women, dressed in jumpsuits with their hair tied up high, working as mechanics, drivers, and assembly line workers (see figure 8.3).

The result was a further transformation of traditional gender roles, at least for a time. At the end of the war, soldiers returned home and more families had children than ever before in the United States. Women were again expected to support the household and take a backseat to the career objectives of their husbands. Whereas those who had worked in factories and warehouses had spent the war gaining experience in the company of other women, they were now asked to forget their new skills and live a more isolated, domestic reality.

But it was too late. Expectations had been changed. By the 1960s, following a period of dramatic economic expansion in the United States, women were needed in the workforce and many became working mothers. Here, they confronted what would remain a problem to this day: an income gap in which women would be paid a fraction of what their male counterparts might earn. This was justified on the basis of the "family wage," the idea that men should earn enough to support whole families, while women worked for "pocket money." The income gap was just one of numerous workplace discrimination conditions that would become the subject of feminist criticism and activism in the 1960s and 1970s. Women's groups such as the National Organization of Women emerged in this period as part of what is now called the "second-wave" feminist movement.

Besides employment and income discrimination, a key target for this movement was reproductive and privacy rights. For centuries, safe family planning had been beyond the reach of women in the West. In 1873, the United States passed the Comstock Act prohibiting the very mention of birth control. The first well-known women's birth control clinic in the United States was opened in 1916 by Margaret Sanger, but it was repeatedly shut down and prosecuted for "public nuisance" and other violations. The Comstock ban was lifted in 1938, and in 1960 the first birth control pill was approved by the US Food and Drug Administration. As one might imagine, this biomedical innovation would have a dramatic influence on adult female social behavior in the period. Suddenly, "the Pill" enabled women to have sexual encounters with less risk of having their lives altered by reproductive consequences—as men had been able to do for all of history. Availability of the Pill was uneven across the states, with many taking the position that it was immoral to interfere with reproduction and that it encouraged promiscuous behavior among women. Finally, in 1965, the Warren Supreme Court heard *Griswold v. Connecticut* and held that married women could not be denied the right to contraceptive medicines on the principle that reproductive choice was a matter of family privacy.[20] "Privacy," the Court said, may not have been an overt statement in the Bill of Rights, but it emanated from the first ten amendments the way light emanates from the sun even when blocked by an eclipse—you may not see it, but the right is there. Over the next decade, the right would be expanded to all adult citizens irrespective of marital status, and many new contraceptive medicines and devices would be developed by the growing pharmaceutical industry. While it may not seem like a specific gender rights issue, the advent of female contraception and the legal right to use it were important steps in the march toward gender equality by second-wave feminists. From the right to vote and the right to employment equality, women had, by neutralizing the argument that their sole purpose was reproduction, advanced their standing as social beings.

Still, even as more and more women entered the workforce and were able to plan family life after *Griswold,* several problems lingered into the 1980s and 1990s. Many of the professions, law included, remained largely off limits to women. The US military, for instance, did not allow women in "assigned" combat roles until 2013. Many believe fear of allowing women to fight and die in combat helped to defeat long-standing efforts at an Equal Rights Amendment

(ERA), which had been pursued by both first- and second-wave feminists and was nearly passed in 1979. Some of the ERA's most outspoken critics were certain conservative women, who felt that the special role women played in families and society would be diminished if they were placed on equal footing with men in political and economic life. Without the ERA, however, a "third wave" of feminist activism grew in this period, focusing on integration of the working professions, furthering changes in social expectations (such as who pays on dates, or who studies to earn a doctorate degree), and especially extending the struggle over gender equality into the realm of sexual minority rights. From this, the lesbian, gay, bisexual and transgender movement took root in cities and towns across the country, focused on the principle that people's bodies and private lives are not the business of legal or social rulemaking. Although this movement had in fact been around since the 1960s, it was not viewed as a national mainstream movement until roughly 1998, when the student Matthew Shephard was savagely beaten and abandoned to die near the University of Wyoming. Shephard's murder drew unprecedented attention to the fear and hatred experienced by LGBT youth in the United States, but it also led to the Shepherd/Byrd Act of 2009—a comprehensive anti–hate crime law signed into effect by President Obama.

The LGBT and women's movements are not nearly one and the same. However, they have drawn attention to many of the same issues of identity, discrimination, and law in a society that thinks of itself as "modern" and "civilized." As of this writing, treatment of transgender Americans—the 'T' in LGBT—remains the next frontier for legal protections from abuse and fear. The right to use public restrooms and the right to serve and die in the US military are both topics of recent debate as the country struggles to decide how law should reflect morality as it pertains to people's freedom to identify.

CONCLUSION

In a world where we celebrate the freedom to pursue private property and individual happiness, we tend to think of ourselves as free to identify as we choose. Some sociologists have argued that it is even this freedom that distinguishes "modern" life from all that came before it.[21] But the sections of this chapter have challenged that belief. Identity, it turns out, is highly delimited by the principles and institutions of our law and therefore is subject to historical and political contingencies.

There is much at stake in identity formation. Marx's theory of class liberation depended upon a reidentification of the modern laborer as the center of the capitalism economy. Goffman's theory of framing said identity could influence how we view and interpret reality. And science and technology studies researchers found that modern technology has made the human body less determinative of identity than ever before. Yet, as if to confirm that importance of law in identity formation, a discussion of class, race, and gender suggests that freedom to identify is subject to always-present legal constraints. Even when people appear to gain their freedom, they remain indebted to the institutions of law for "granting" them that right.

CHAPTER 8 REVIEW

Key Terms

- Rights
- Critical race theory
- Capital
- Alienation
- Jurisprudence
- Reconstruction Amendments
- Disembodiment
- Virtual
- Raw materials
- Deindustrialization
- Trickle-down economics
- Neoliberalism
- New public management
- Public goods
- Private goods
- Nonprofit
- For-profit
- Hashtag
- Postracial
- Self-defense
- Naturalize

Further Discussion

1. How might the online world of cyberspace affect racial identification, and how might law augment or limit these changes?
2. What would critical race theorists say about the killings of Trayvon Martin, Michael Brown, and Eric Garner?
3. Why were labor unions stronger before the Great Depression than they were just after?
4. What concept helps to explain the multilayered identity of real people who may be part of class, race, and gender minority groups? How so?

Further Reading

Delgado, Richard. 2017. *Critical Race Theory: An Introduction.* 3rd ed. New York: NYU Press.

Ehrenreich, Barbara. 1983. *The Hearts of Men: American Dreams and the Flight from Commitment.* New York: Knopf/Doubleday.

Gross, Ariela. 2008. *What Blood Won't Tell: A History of Race on Trial in America.* Cambridge, MA: Harvard University Press.

Roediger, David. 2017. *Class, Race, and Marxism.* London: Verso Press.

SOCIAL CONSTRUCTIONS OF LAW

3

In the last unit you read how law helps "construct" the very notion of society by reinforcing some of the basic building blocks of human communities. The major strands tying community together—history, family, place, religion, and identity—are now often the subject of legal debate, agreement, and formalization. But this is only the beginning. On close inspection we see that law itself is also a deeply social practice. Unit 3 of this book examines some of the ways in which our understandings about law are themselves socially constructed. That is to say, law does not precede society any more than society precedes law. In chapter 9, we see that lawyers—the professionals charged with legal expertise and ethical duties to promote justice—are created through an intensive socialization process running from legal education to professional practice. Chapter 10 then turns toward the criminal and civil justice systems for a look at how procedure and reasoning—learned behaviors central to legal practice—are designed and passed on through the generations. Finally, chapter 11 pans out to review how popular portrayals of legal actors and proceedings educate the public on what lawyers do—even if exaggeratedly—and sets expectations for what people can accomplish by appealing to legal expertise.

The Socialization of Lawyers

Much of our social interaction has been dramatically altered by new technology. Text and video chatting have made distance communication faster, cheaper, and more efficient. Digital banking and e-commerce have made buying and selling things quicker and more frequent. And online learning has made "going to school" a lot easier for those who traditionally could not do so because of family, work, or geographic limitations. Will new technology similarly revolutionize law?

Already legal information once limited to law libraries, from court cases and statutes to practice tips and forms, has become available online. This information is more readily found, but so is a legal expert through the use of Internet searches that can narrow attorneys by location and practice areas. One of the newest innovations has been the advent of "artificial intelligence" (AI) lawyering. Whereas clients once had to visit an office to consult with a licensed attorney on any new case, AI is making it possible for people to enter information online and interact with a "chatbot" or other program that can walk them through the steps of client **intake.** A world in which most of this preliminary legal work is done by AI may be fast approaching. But it is not here just yet.

For now, clients must still consult directly with a licensed attorney or their assistants by phone or in person before a relationship can be established. Once one is, the attorney and their office are bound by specific **rules of professional conduct** that govern everything from lawyer solicitation and advertising to billing of fees and retention of client money. In establishing the **attorney-client relationship,** experts are expected to comport themselves as members of a profession. But what does this even mean, and how is it learned?

The reproduction of professional behavior is a complicated process rooted in more general social learning. It is a process, therefore, of **socialization.** But it is not only a matter of learning how to behave; it is also the product of substantial knowledge acquisition—of literally studying rules and understanding how they play out in actual disputes or transactions. All this sounds like the business of law schools.

Law schools have, for over one hundred years in the United States, been the main avenue for gaining legal knowledge and attaining lawyer socialization. Before them, as in the early days of the American republic, aspiring lawyers generally "read" law as an apprentice of a practicing lawyer and then gained experience on the job in their office. Over the years, certain firms became better adept at preparing apprentices, so they took on more and more for the sole purpose of teaching them for a small profit.[1] One by one, these early firm schools were bought out by local universities and became departments within the structure of those institutions. Surprisingly, Yale Law School, often considered the premier law program in the United States and perhaps the world, was acquired in this fashion long ago.[2] Whether and how such law schools have been successful in preparing new generations for the bar exam is another matter entirely—one about which much has been written in recent years. Just the fact that the production of legal expertise is the product of this storied history and contemporary debates is a strong indication about its role in law and society.

Legal education and the legal profession, I suggest in this chapter, are social phenomena. Although they deal in the transmission of knowledge and its practical application, mastery of the law depends upon social relations between creditors and debtors, teachers and students, and administrations and faculty, as well as among institutions. This chapter describes key features resulting from these relationships. The first section below describes how law schools conceive of and cultivate "thinking like a lawyer." This boils down to two major ways of dividing the world up for expert legal processing: facts versus law, and issue spotting. The next section looks at the socialization process in three phases of becoming a lawyer. From joining a law school to learning within its walls to exporting its knowledge out into practice, this section explains that there is a clear and direct process of initiation into the professional community. Throughout, the social contingency of legal professional knowledge should become clear as but one more way in which law and society are intimately self-supporting.

"THINKING LIKE A LAWYER"

US law schools underwent considerable challenges in the years after the Great Recession of 2009. Many blamed the financial crisis on a weakening of state financial regulations by lawmakers who espoused the neoliberal mantra that "the market knows best." Overzealous banking speculation led to a global economic downturn, which in turn caused credit to dry up, corporate finances to dwindle, and the number of international business transactions to shrink. Companies that would normally have hired the world's largest law firms could no longer easily afford to and had less reason to. When they did, they demanded that legal services be performed by well-trained and experienced **partners** and **senior associates** rather than by brand-new junior and summer associates, as had been done in the past (see figure 9.1). Whereas firms could once pass work to neophytes and bill their services at standard firm rates, they now had limited work to justify young hires and expected midlevel and senior lawyers to put in more hours to stay afloat.

The lack of profitable work meant that large firms could no longer hire large cohorts of junior attorneys. This shrinkage in big firm hiring meant that law graduates had to accept less lucrative employment in smaller firms or that they remained unemployed for a longer time. As many as 40 percent would find no stable legal employment at all.[3] One solution could have been more solo and small firm law practices opening up around the country. But there was a problem.

The shift to small firm hiring and solo practice was severely limited by the kinds of education law schools had been producing for the past one hundred years or so. Whereas early law schools had taught students how to apply practical skills, the absorption of most legal education into large academic universities shifted the focus of US law schools from skills to knowledge. In the early twentieth century, Dean Christopher Columbus Langdell introduced the "case method" of law teaching to the classrooms of Harvard Law School. From there, Langdell's method spread across the East Coast, then the Midwest, and finally reached the West Coast. This expansion took place in part because, as the demand for lawyers grew out west, and as more and more law programs opened around the country, schools wanting to hire the "best" professors gravitated to Harvard Law graduates. This made their way of teaching—itself contingent upon their way of learning the law—the industry standard.

Through this process, the case method spread quickly as the dominant mode of law school pedagogy. In it, students in a classroom are not expected to recite or overtly discuss legal **doctrine** or rules. Rather, under the case method, law students read and dissect legal cases through the opinions written by the judges deciding their outcomes. Sometimes, ancillary documents such as briefs, jury instructions, and relevant statute laws are introduced to supplement the opinions. But the goal in reviewing these materials is to discern several key features of every legal case in the common-law system. That is,

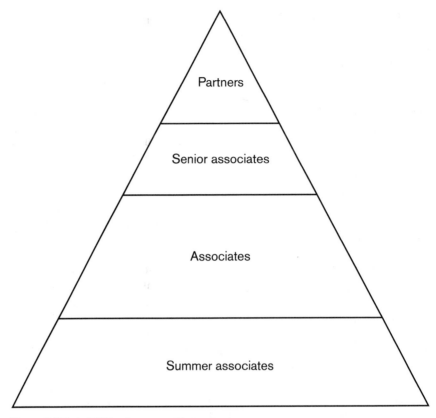

Figure 9.1 Typical US law firm pyramid structure.

students are expected to identify clearly the **facts,** the **issue,** the relevant **rule,** the **reasoning,** and the court's final **holding.** In class, the professor engages a student over these elements in a particular case and then raises difficult questions about them. In many instances, the teacher poses similar cases with differing outcomes to provoke the students to recognize subtle differences. Ultimately, students are expected to take away from all of this not simply the rules as they exist in real time in the **jurisdiction** but also the reasoning that courts are likely to apply using those rules. So where do students learn the rules if not here? For that, students in the United States have historically had to look outside the classroom. They have devised a battery of extracurricular methods for learning the law, including study aid books, study groups, and sometimes even separate prior crash courses in legal doctrine. If professors were not teaching "the law," what were they teaching? Until very recently, most professors would have simply said, "Thinking like a lawyer." They meant that the rules could be found, and could be memorized, but that what students were expected to learn from them was how to *read* cases and how to *discuss* and *apply* them meaningfully—that is, in proper professional spoken language.

FACT VERSUS LAW

"Thinking like a lawyer" means two main things for professors. The first is a separation of the world into fact and law. Most lay persons tend to believe that "the law" is pretty formulaic. This is captured in some common clichés we hear in everyday life, but ones that easily represent that layperson's legal education. "You do the crime, you do the time." "You break it, you buy it." "A man's home is his castle." The first captures the obligatory connection between act and punishment in criminal law, the second the nexus between injury and liability in civil justice, and the last the idea that one has autonomy in use and enjoyment of one's own real estate. But if law were this simple, there would be far less demand for lawyers. Take, for instance, a car accident between you and a teenager named "Little Timmy" in a midwestern state like Illinois. An auto accident between two civilian drivers is probably a negligence case, and it therefore falls under the state law of torts. Most people would want to know the specific law that relates and would then simply apply it to the story. Let's assume that the law simply says, "All car collisions must be compensated." You now have two pieces of information, a fact and a law. Putting them together, you have:

Fact: In his car Little Timmy collided with you.

Law: Victims of all car collisions must be compensated.

From this, it is not too difficult to arrive at a result in this case:

Result: You must be compensated.

But you may already have several objections. How do we *know* Timmy collided with you? How *bad* was the collision? *Who* is supposed to do the compensating? We know Timmy is responsible simply because it says so. The fact might have been different (e.g., that you collided with Timmy), but because it is given in this way it must be accepted as given. Any questions about the authenticity or accuracy of this statement fall under the law of evidence and must be handled preliminarily by the judge (not the jury). In the English and American common-law systems, authentication of evidence, much like questions about the relevant law in general, is handled by a judge. Questions of fact are handled by the judge or jury. By the time a decision is required, all available facts are known and clear. So, in an example such as this, particularly in the US law school classroom, anything given as "fact" cannot be disputed. That is how we know Timmy collided with you. Similarly, the severity of the collision is not relevant here. That is because the law as stated includes nothing about "how bad" it must have been. Ostensibly, the *amount* of compensation will depend on the *amount* of damage done, but again this is covered in a host of rules called the law of remedies. To assess blame or liability in this instance, under the available material "how bad" does not matter. Finally, *who* should compensate the victim remains open ended. There is no reason for suggesting that it *has* to be Timmy, but neither does it have to be anyone else. Even where liability may attach to Timmy for this accident, someone else may pay for the damage. Who? Timmy, like many of you reading this, probably has a contract with an insurance company to cover damages in cases such as this—what is often literally called "liability insurance." So the ambiguity in the law as stated leaves open the likelihood that Timmy's insurance will—much as in the real world—pay for this.

But clearly it can't be this simple. What does it mean to "do crime," "break something," or have a "home"? Law, even in the English, American, and European systems, is not as formulaic as it seems. The great anthropologist Clifford Geertz spoke critically about this learned separation between fact and law. To an audience at Yale Law School in 1981, Geertz explained that while English and American courts have come to base their entire universe of legal reasoning on the separation of fact and law, many if not most non-Western societies do otherwise. Drawing on his own fieldwork experience across Morocco and Indonesia, he was able to compare fact versus law in Islamic, Hindu, and Malay cultures—three of the most widespread cultural systems in the world. In all three, Geertz said, he could identify important cultural concepts that bridged the worlds of fact and law in important, reality-shaping ways. "'Law,'" Geertz said, "here, there, or anywhere, is part of a distinctive manner of imagining the real."[4]

What this means, in other words, is that for many societies separations between fact and law are not so clear and may indeed be harmful to the very idea of justice or its local equivalents. This also means that the separation is something specific to Western, if not primarily common-law, legal thinking. And even though Western lawyers study rigorously in the separation of fact and law, it is the difficulty executing this that gives lawyers their "expertise" and makes them valuable in our society. What law students in fact learn in school is not some new truth about the natural and social worlds around them but rather a new way of using language to translate back and forth between facts and law.[5]

You might be asking yourself how law can be *both* a separation of fact from law *and* a translation between these. This all stems from law's foundation in language. Although we invoke the law when we have real-world, practical problems like a drunk-driving citation or a neighbor building a fence on our property, these problems only set the law in motion. Once it gets going, it requires that we translate the real-world problem, the facts, into language that a court or administrative office will easily understand. It also requires that we ask for a specific legal remedy for our problem—also to be couched in clear, technical language. Sometimes this language uses terms, like *profit a prendre* or *mens rea*, that come directly from older non-English languages in which our law has its roots.[6]

ISSUE SPOTTING

Returning to the story of Little Timmy, we saw above the basic facts and the law to be applied, as well as the result that this gave us, based on a simple "plug and play" approach to legal reasoning. This easy result was in part the product of the specific language used: I said that Timmy "collided" with you, the **plaintiff,** and that the law happened to require damages for all "collisions." In this case there can be little room for interpretation. But, in the real world, Timmy, as the **defendant,** in other words the person accused of causing the harm, would likely have a good lawyer trained to argue that he did not in fact "collide" with anyone. Sure, he might have "tapped," "bumped," "scraped," or even "swiped" your car, but this was hardly a "collision," the lawyer would likely say. This may seem like a cheap trick to the average layperson, but note that the defense attorney has a professional obligation to assert the best arguments to defend their client in a case. The attorney in this case is disputing the basic fact that there was a "collision" and rightly so; in the absence of this fact the law may not apply. If a judge believes this disagreement is reasonable and cannot confidently resolve it alone, they will likely send this question to a jury, and the whole case may depend upon whether a jury of nine "reasonable" people would call the incident a "collision" or something else. The whole thing, you see, can come down to this basic translation of events that transpired in the real world into the term required by law to obtain a remedy.

The ability of an attorney to hear the client's story and pick out this kind of ambiguity is called "issue spotting." Issue spotting is the second key feature of "thinking like a lawyer" and it is one of the key skills a student learns in law school; indeed, most first-year law school exams are structured around two or three basic issue-spotting questions to be answered by the students in essay format as thoroughly as possible in a short two- to three-hour time frame. Some highlight the fact that issue-spotting exams are nothing like the real world; the professor often crams dozens of disputes and harms into a single story running just a few pages in length. In the real world, some say, attorneys usually have to deal with only a few problems at a time and often get accustomed to seeing the same sets of problems from a narrow community of clients—technology software companies or local police, for example. This may be true, but the issue-spotting final exam format forces students to train themselves beyond the competence needed in the real world. It also may not be so far off; nonexpert clientele probably do not understand the idea of a legal

Figure 9.2 Rodin's famous sculpture
Le penseur or *The Thinker*. Source: Library
of Congress.

"issue" and therefore recount dozens of extraneous facts and anecdotes before
the attorney or her assistants can properly discern where the legal arguments
and their weaknesses will lie.

Issue spotting and separating fact from law are two major facets of "thinking like a lawyer." They are both, as you probably found out, highly conceptual
skills closer to philosophy than to taking apart a carburetor. On one hand, we
think of lawyers as highly intelligent, abstract thinkers able to draw big connections and pierce through logical inconsistencies. But on the other hand, we
want them to be able to *do* the tasks of lawyers—tasks such as legal research
and document drafting.

Although these two things are by no means mutually exclusive, American
law schools have seen heavy criticism over the years for emphasizing the
former, philosophical reasoning, over and above practical lawyering skills. This
tendency reflects the broader social ambivalence on whether to see lawyers as
philosophers or as mechanics.

Professors at the "top" law schools, from Stanford and Columbia to Washington University and Vanderbilt, have long emphasized the philosopher role.
This does not mean they saw their graduates as Rodin's "Thinker," perched on a
stone with chin on fist (figure 9.2).

It meant that they saw their students as going on to **appellate law** practice,
public policy making, and the judiciary.[7] They expected, in short, that their students would become social and political leaders more than small firm practi-

tioner foot soldiers. Meanwhile, law schools outside the "top" forty or fifty schools assumed their students would fulfill the roles of daily legal practice. The result was a bifurcation between the public policy and practitioner-based law programs.

From about the mid-2000s, experts of legal education and the legal profession began debating the merits of this bifurcated approach to training lawyers. In one camp, some said that the division was not clear enough. Some two hundred law schools were accredited by the American Bar Association (ABA) through its Council of the Section of Legal Education and Admission to the Bar. All of those schools were, as a condition of accreditation, required to abide by a 143-page handbook called the Standards and Rules of Procedure for Approval of Law Schools. Compliance with these many rules—about such things as admissions rigor and faculty governance—was sometimes challenging and expensive. But the cost of noncompliance was loss of accreditation and, in turn, loss of federal student loan eligibility. So every single law school in the United States, from the very highest- to the lowest-ranked program, was forced to spend its resources to maintain accreditation. Critics said these expenses forced law schools to be overly costly, to charge exorbitant tuition amounts, and to obligate students to incur substantial debt. Repayment of this debt would in turn force many to take only the highest-paying law jobs (e.g., defending corporate interests or designing mergers and acquisitions) and to ignore the needs of middle- and lower-income individuals in both the inner cities and rural communities.[8] The split between "high" and "low" law schools, many felt, was not wide enough.

But some on the other side of this active debate were saying the division was already too wide and should be narrowed. They pointed to several items. First, they said, the American system is supposed to have only one *kind* of lawyer capable in theory of handling any type of case. For this reason, formal legal specialties are rare in the United States. Indeed, other countries like Great Britain and Australia have a "dualist" legal profession with two kinds of lawyers—one to handle high-level cases and the other to take on more daily transactional and small litigation work. In its revolutionary tradition of democratizing law and justice, the United States chose not to adopt this dualism. But law school rankings, developed around the mid-1980s, created a split between "top" schools and all the rest.

Second and perhaps worse, there were palpable social inequalities between these high- and low-ranked law schools. As one might expect, the "top" law schools at East Coast Ivy League institutions tended to be the province of students from wealthier families. Moreover, until recently they were often populated with primarily white Protestant students. Yale Law School, for instance, admitted its first Jewish students in the 1930s, though it seemed to limit their numbers until the 1960s.[9] Black students were admitted in low numbers much earlier, but they too remained a disproportionately small population until recently. In the intervening years, dozens of new law schools cropped up around the United States to admit specifically more Jewish, Catholic, and later black, Latino/Latina, and Asian American students.[10] In the years after the global financial crisis of 2009, many turned to these groups as a new recruitment market, making sure their seats would be filled amid declining application numbers. This all led at least one observer to call the new admissions attitude "diversity as survival strategy."[11] In my own research, I have written extensively on the application of this attitude among ABA-accredited for-profit law school programs.[12] Beginning in the early 2000s at a time of rapidly increasing demand for legal education, for-profit law schools were founded with money from private-equity investors looking to make fast and large returns on investment. The plan, apparently, was to sell the new schools in a period of five or ten years, but this was thwarted by the law school enrollment bubble bursting around 2012. The result was a turn to diversity as a survival strategy, and a move to offer disproportionately minority students a thinner, lighter legal education than their peers were receiving at more established law schools. This arrangement, critics like myself have been saying, creates a new dualism where "low–ranked" means racially diverse, and racial diversity means low quality.[13]

The great problem with for-profit and low-ranked law schools was that their approach to minority access would brand those students as lower quality by skimping on the key programs that focus on lawyer socialization—programs like clinics and lecture series. Those schools could perhaps teach "thinking like a lawyer" in the classroom, but that was only a small part of what it meant to actually be a lawyer. They could even focus on "practice-ready" skills sets like motion and contract drafting, but that too was only a part of being a professional.

SOCIALIZATION

Professional training is a **socialization** process. For those studying them, modern professions are unique subsets of society with several key features. One of these is a "monopoly" over key socioeconomic activities. In law it is the practice of law or application of legal expertise. In medicine, it is the practice of medicine or application of medical expertise. Both law and medicine demand that practitioners be licensed, and they erect steep barriers to attaining that license; this is commonly justified as a marker of high quality, but it is also a form of monopoly on the economic activity itself.

To become a lawyer or medical doctor, one must achieve a certain level of excellence in higher education, gain entry to a graduate institution, and pass a certification exam upon completion of study. In the case of medicine, more emphasis is placed on clinical education—learning by doing—and the stage just after licensure is itself a brief period of on-the-job practical learning called "residency." One of the main purposes of residency in medicine is to learn a "bedside manner," the proper professional social demeanor that allows doctors to approach patients with caring formality and makes patients so universally trust in their physician. In law, clinical learning is a growing part of the curriculum, but it is by no means yet required across the board. Similarly, no hands-on experience after admission to the bar is required before opening one's own legal practice.

Nevertheless, lawyers do go through their own socialization. For the most part this is brought about in three stages. First, lawyers' professional socialization occurs through the basic encounter with the law school experience itself. Before even beginning the course of study, law school applicants begin learning how to *be* as lawyers simply through the structural features of legal education: the ways the program of study is divided and organized, priced and financed, and processed and delivered to students.

All new students quickly learn that law is taught unlike any subjects they have previously learned. On arrival, first-year students or "1Ls" are expected to abide by a fixed class schedule preestablished by the school administration. This arranges the students into "sections" in which they remain for the entire 1L year. Some find these sections a bonding experience, while others find them to be socially constraining. Either way, the grouping of 1Ls into sections of fifteen to twenty students has the effect of simulating a legal work environment. Because grades are "curved" with only so many A's and B's available in each term by section, this brings intense pressure. Pressure to compete leads on one hand to social tensions, but it can lead on the other to bonding and collaboration—it all depends on the individuals and personalities involved. Regardless, as many would say, this high-pressure 1L experience is meant to parallel the social conditions of being a lawyer, where competition and collaboration are both part of the game.

Given this, 1L students are also quickly advised on "professionalism." They are reminded that their reputation in the legal community is already being built and that how they treat one another in class will follow them for the remainder of their professional lives. Integrity, formally so important to lawyering, is a large part of this reputation, so matters such as cheating and plagiarism are handled with great severity. Similarly, social demeanor affects professional reputation, so the students are instructed to exercise caution in social gatherings and in online forums such as social media or class Web pages.

Students are also given a set list of books to buy. These are primarily "casebooks" designed as compilations of appellate court opinions organized by subject matter under large legal areas corresponding to divisions in the curriculum. About these books there are two key facts to keep in mind. One is that they are extremely expensive. Although they could be made as paperback books on cheap printing paper, they are instead leather-bound hardback books made to look like the case reporter books of libraries and law firms. And because they are so thick—often eight hundred to one thousand pages—these books are also extremely heavy. For a student who has three classes in a single day, plus a laptop computer to carry, the standard school backpack might give way to a rolling suitcase just to save one from back pain and injury.

Casebooks are the direct result of the case method approach to teaching described earlier in this chapter. It has long been believed—by most anyway—that since attorneys practice from authoritative cases, law students should learn the law from them. But this means that although a rule or principle could be summarized in a sentence or two, it is usually taught using dozens of pages of small case excerpts and high-intensity discussions between the professor and students in front of a large group classroom. Increasingly, these large classrooms are "high-tech," with projectors, computers, microphones, and public address speakers.

CURRICULUM

Every classroom is organized by divisions in the 1L curriculum. That curriculum, after a century of evolution in the Anglo-American tradition, typically breaks out into eight subjects, depicted in table 9.1.

Torts is a subject that groups together the law of accidents and the law of intentional wrongs. Accidents are fairly recognizable; basic ones include car crashes and slip and fall cases, but more complex ones might involve industrial or environmental disasters where the harm produced is more widespread or more scientifically complicated. Intentional wrongs are things like fist fights, nuisance cases, and even defamation, as discussed in chapter 4. Torts casebooks are special because they often include old common-law cases from England and Australia, harkening back to a time with the British Commonwealth applied one "common law" for civil wrongs, and reminding us that our system is a direct descendant of English law. In that way, the 1L case method is often an exercise in legal history—another overlap between legal education and the themes discussed in chapter 4. But insofar as students continue to read famous cases like Australia's *The Wagon Mound* or England's *Rylands v. Fletcher*, this is also a reminder that American classroom education in law school is decidedly not always aimed at preparing for legal practice.

Contracts is, as it sounds, the law of mutually agreed-upon binding agreements. Cases read in this course range from ordinary small business transactions to disputes involving a rich elderly man who promises to pay his grandchild if the youngster will stop smoking cigarettes. In most cases read during this class, the agreement has somehow gone awry. Either the basic elements needed to form a contract are missing, or the contract was fully formed but later broken by one of the parties. Other interesting issues arise when the contract is supposed to benefit a third person, or when the buyer or seller is a commercial entity expert in trading goods or services of this kind. In the latter case,

Table 9.1 Typical Law School First-Year Curriculum

First Semester	Second Semester
Torts	Criminal Law
Civil Procedure	Professional Responsibility
Contracts	Constitutional Law
Legal Research and Writing	Legal Research and Writing

the rules of contract law are often codified in what is called the Uniform Commercial Code (U.C.C.), developed by a group of contracts scholars and adopted ultimately by most of the fifty United States.

Property class is less self-evident. It deals almost exclusively with *real* property or land. You might assume that this is the same as real estate law, but it is not. Whereas some of this course involves full sales of land in its entirety, the bulk of it—indeed, what makes it so complicated—consists of the many cases in which only certain rights to the land are traded. For example, an **easement** is a kind of right to use someone's land for a particular purpose. The utility companies in your area probably have easements to access electrical or telephone boxes on private property. A neighbor whose house is tucked away from an access road may have an easement to use her neighbor's driveway. The list goes on. As already suggested, many of these land transfer and use rules go all the way back to Roman and English common law, and they therefore contain terms that sound like another language. Because most law students have not, by their 1L year, purchased or sold real property, the property class is sometimes the most abstract.

But thanks to the Civil Procedure class it usually is not. Civil Procedure or "Civ Pro" is the study of how cases get filed, advanced, and resolved in the American civil justice system. Note that this is different from the criminal justice system, for which there is a different class entitled Criminal Procedure. In Civ Pro, students learn solely about prosecuting and defending cases in the civil system—meaning only cases involving the above three subject areas. This class teaches students *who* initiates a case, *how* the initiator sets it in motion, *where* a case should best be heard, *how* a defendant part responds, *how* evidence can be obtained on either side, *how* requests for early dismissal or early judgment can be made, and *what* a losing party can do if it disputes the outcome. As you can see, this is a fairly abstract and technical class primarily because most students have never seen its principles in action. Increasingly, law schools are moving toward teaching civil procedure in clinical settings, or in combination with some of the other 1L courses.

Constitutional law, on the other hand, is a topic many new students have familiarity with. Political science, the most common undergraduate major for law students, usually presents its students with one or more courses on the Supreme Court, or key areas like free speech or freedom of religion jurisprudence. But what most do not initially appreciate is the delicate analysis required to resolve new cases that arise under constitutional law. Whereas the threshold question may be "What right has been violated?" the next question becomes what constitutional "test" should be applied in evaluating the law or other state action that caused the harm in the first place. It is the memorization of these various tests and mastery of their application that students in "Con Law" are most tested on.

Although Americans do not make this distinction, European systems consider constitutional law a subtopic of "public law"—the kind of legal subject matter involving the state or the public. For them the second public law area is criminal law. For 1L students, Criminal Law is the sixth major course required in the standard curriculum, and it too is one students are sometimes familiar with. Most legal drama programs on television or in movies entail a simplified criminal law scenario, and terms in this subject are some of the most commonly used in vernacular English. *Guilt*, for example is the term for what the civil justice system calls *liability*. Laypersons speak of guilt all the time, yet they are largely ignorant of the meaning of *liability*. Criminal law is also interesting because the factual problems are some of the most fascinating to the human imagination. From murder and arson to burglary and assault, there are often deep emotional and psychological motivations to why people commit these crimes, and their study serves as a kind of research into human nature itself. If you do not believe this, consider the "heat of passion" defense; this rule permits a defendant otherwise guilty of murder to argue that he did the crime in an emotional rage—over something like lover's jealousy—and therefore was not thinking straight. A successful argument of this kind will often get a reduced conviction (e.g., manslaughter) and therefore a lesser sentence.

Legal research and writing and professional responsibility are two specialty areas that are both highly important and yet subject to different institutional variations. In some law schools research and writing are taught "in house" by full-time professors. In others they are taught by adjunct instructors from the practicing legal community. Professional Responsibility courses, otherwise named as Legal Profession, Professional Ethics, or Legal Ethics, study the rules and guidelines governing lawyer behavior. These too vary in how they are taught, but they generally employ a full-time faculty member specialized in this area. Professional responsibility is the only subject with its own separate "bar exam," and the only one offered to students *during* their law school tenure. Interestingly, with law schools themselves coming under intense scrutiny for possible fraud, discrimination, and breach-of-contract cases, and with practicing attorneys sometimes at the center of gross financial and accounting misfeasance cases, some have asked whether professional ethics need to be more centralized in the law school experience.

CLASSROOM

The curriculum itself is the first general step toward a unique socialization for aspiring attorneys. Through it, they learn to conceptualize all the legal problems in their world (really only the common-law world) as fitting into one or another of these boxes. Diving in a little deeper, they then experience the law school classroom itself. There, social learning about what it means to become a legal professional only accelerates. The law school classroom is a very unique learning environment; although it appears to resemble the typical college lecture hall, the similarities do not run deep. That is because everything depends upon the *social* encounter it creates. Let us compare the differences for a moment. Table 9.2 sets up, side by side, a comparison of key features in undergraduate and in law lecture-based courses. Your experience—especially if you are in a small liberal arts college—may differ. But consider this a rough approximation of how the two experiences stack up against one another per lecture.

While all of these comparative differences are extremely important, particularly if you are considering going to law school yourself, perhaps none is more significant than the "Socratic" style of teaching referenced near the middle of the table.

The so-called Socratic method for teaching is named for the Greek philosopher Socrates. He famously never wrote books or articles (at least none preserved for history), but his lectures were captured in the writings of his even more famous student Plato. Those writings spoke of a thinker who taught the brightest young minds of ancient Greece from his academy in Athens. There, legend says, Socrates would teach his students about ethics, science, mysticism, and dozens of other subjects by asking a question, eliciting a response from a single student, and then engaging in a back-and-forth conversation with follow-up queries. This discussion-based or dialogic method was thought to encourage deeper reflection, understanding, and curiosity than mere lecturing would. It remains a preferred pedagogical technique in some of the liberal arts, but it has become nearly synonymous with law schools in the United States. In combination with Langdell's case method, the Socratic teaching style lends itself to simulating the attorney-judge interaction that professors say lies at the heart of common-law advocacy. This back-and-forth interaction is often tense and adversarial, and you can imagine how—in front of ninety competitive law students vying for top grades in a class—it becomes stressful and discouraging, particularly for those whom psychologists might call "introverted." On the other side, it encourages students who enjoy public attention and performance, and especially those who might have insight into the professor's mental processes and line of reasoning. How could that be?

The sociologist Pierre Bourdieu believed that the things we possess in common with other people, from common experiences to shared interests, are rarely coincidence and are more often the result of shared determining factors.

Table 9.2   Comparison between Typical Undergraduate and Law School Lecture Experience

Points of Comparison	Undergraduate Lecture	Law School Lecture
Homework	20–60 pages / 1–2 hours	40–100 pages / 2–6 hours
Preparedness expected	Basic familiarity	Verbal command
Participation	Optional (if any)	Mandatory (for some)
Classroom technology	Variable	High-level
Teaching style	Monologue w/ Q&A	Dialogue or "Socratic"
Teacher-student relation	Polite or indifferent	Adversarial
Student-student relation	Polite or friendly	Competitive or polite
Subject matter taught vs. tested	Direct relation	Little relation (rules not stated but tested)

He called these determining factors "sociological predispositions." For example, two students attending Harvard College on full need-based scholarships as undergraduates might never meet one another until they sit in adjoining lecture hall seats. But once they get to talking, they find out that they like the same music, the same style of dance, or similar clothing. Some might say, "What an amazing coincidence!" Bourdieu would say they were predisposed to finding kinship in their tastes. Need-based scholarships imply a certain socioeconomic status. Socioeconomic status implies a set of geographic (e.g., city, neighborhood, community) backgrounds. Students from the same or similar geographic backgrounds are likely to share similar youth culture references. And these shared reference points, especially if they differ greatly from those of other Harvard College freshman, will likely "unite" the two students in friendship. All of these things make up what Bourdieu labeled the **habitus.** They are the features that make our identity less about ourselves and more about our contexts.

In law school, the professors likely share a narrow habitus as well. They are almost all lawyers, mostly trained at top-twenty law schools, generally academically gifted, and quite frequently themselves from upper-middle-class backgrounds. Until recently, unfortunately, they were also overwhelmingly white and male. In presenting the facts, issue, rule, analysis, and holding of a case to a group of ninety students, which of those students might be most likely to follow the professor's train of thought—especially when "legal reasoning" can be so far removed from common sense? Perhaps you are skeptical of this question; legal analysis, you say, is universal and analytical. Like philosophy, it takes nothing for granted. This commonly held belief is false.

What law faculty call legal analysis is not universal or bias-neutral at all. On the contrary, it assumes all kinds of things about human behavior that in fact depend on the habitus concept just described. It also tries to exclude questions about "right" or "wrong" by substituting a value-free notion of legal judgment. But the very idea that a person's childhood should not matter, or that a drug deal is worse when it involves a high-crime neighborhood, is itself a value judgment that becomes submerged in the technicalities of evidence, procedure, and analysis. If you do not believe this, consider research by the anthropologist Elizabeth Mertz. In the mid-2000s, Mertz and a team of research assistants observed law school classroom teaching in 1L courses at eight schools across the United States. They recorded student-teacher conversations in the famous Socratic method, and they hired a student note taker to keep detailed notes about the body language and tone of the speakers recorded. Mertz believed that if she could capture the language in which law classroom exchanges took place she could unlock the secret to lawyer socialization starting in the 1L year. But what she found was even more important. Not only did professors commonly steer students away from using commonsense terms like *right* and *wrong* and toward using technical jargon like *liability* or *no liability*, it was a process that catered more to some students than others in the room. The team found that students of color and female students had a more difficult time adjusting to the morally neutral language expected of them. They found, in short, that socialization through language seemed to favor white male students.[14] Minority and female students, on the other hand, tended to answer the professor's queries and follow-up questions with language rooted more in notions of right and wrong, or everyday social experience. The study proved that "thinking like a lawyer" is in part a function of language use and that this in turn depends upon ethno-racial and gender identities and experience.

This type of research is paradigmatic for **empirical,** or real-world, studies in law and society. It identifies a problem area, poses direct and answerable questions, gathers appropriate data, and then uses a formal process for analyzing that. In Mertz's case, her team used a kind of linguistic analysis. Other researchers have a dozen related methods at their disposal. But commonly, for studies involving legal education and legal practice, language is central.

PRACTICE

Another group of researchers, for instance, looked at the third and final phase of lawyer socialization worth noting here. That is, if learning to participate in the social world of lawyering begins with the law school curriculum and accelerates inside the law classroom, it certainly continues in the attorney's early years of practice. *Practice* refers to the period after an attorney has both graduated law school and passed one or more state bar exams. Although practical experience may be accrued before this, rules of professional responsibility dictate that law practice, consulting with clients and pursuing or defending their case, cannot ethically take place until an individual is duly licensed in the state of practice. A whole set of rules specifies what counts as practice, how to define the state in which the practice was conducted (e.g., nowadays much is done remotely) and when exceptions can be made.

These ethical norms, spelled out clearly in the Model Rules of Professional Conduct, also define the attorney-client relationship itself. This relationship can begin from the moment a client walks through a lawyer's office door, and it is judged on the basis of an objective standard for what the average reasonable client would believe the relationship to be from that moment. For this reason, lawyers are expected to be very clear in advising any new individuals on whether they intend to take their case and what should be said in the initial consultation. These draconian rules may sound overly complicated, but they are there to protect the public, and their mastery—verified by passage of the MPRE or ethics bar exam—is a key requirement to lawyer socializations.

Once the attorney-client relationship has been established, the mode of communication between lawyers and clients parallels the formality identified in the Mertz study just described. Researchers Austin Sarat and William Felstiner studied attorney-client consultations in dozens of divorce cases back in the 1980s. They recorded 115 such conferences and transcribed their tapes into written form that they could then analyze for the language used. What they found was striking.

In divorce cases, which are often highly charged with emotion and personal trauma, attorneys tended to use language that would steer clients *away* from assignment of blame to their spouse's past behavior. Clients, who tended to want to make sense of the past, since it had led their relationship to go wrong, often made character judgments about their spouse in assessing past and present behaviors. The attorneys, aware that past motives were largely irrelevant to the fact of the conduct itself, tended to use only language that described the past and present "situationally," in ways rooted in the social or economic situations in which they took place. But in discussing the future, including courses of action for the divorce proceedings at hand, their attorneys seemed to be willing to ascribe values to character and personality traits of the opposing spouse. In other words, they were willing to judge that person's motives toward the future whereas for actions present and past they were not. Borrowing from classic sociological theory, Sarat and Felstiner label this "motive mongering" and find it to be an integral part of the practice of law in the context of family law and particularly divorce. Zooming out for comparison to the law classroom, this also suggests that legal practice continues the trend of lawyer socialization at the level of language. To this we might add one additional observation related to law and society: by speaking to their clients in a linguistically lopsided fashion—where the past elicits certain words but the future different ones—lawyers act as teachers. They effectively instruct their clients, primarily laypersons not trained in legal discourse or reasoning, that justice requires they embrace this terminology and apply it accordingly. While this is only one large, empirical example of this, how many more can you think of in which practicing attorneys, using the skills of their professional socialization, serve as instructors on justice by simply practicing law among the general public?

CONCLUSION

Becoming a lawyer clearly entails much more than simply earning the necessary degrees and license to take on client cases. It means learning to see the world in the way lawyers are expected to. It also means learning to represent—that is, to talk about—the world in new and sometimes counterintuitive ways.

For aspiring attorneys entering law school, these new ways of seeing and speaking can be learned and mastered in several ways. The first is through encounters with a new mode of thought called "thinking like a lawyer." This is put before students in the classroom in the two important ways of separating "fact versus law," and taking apart client problems through "issue spotting."

The second is through the broader socialization process that begins from the moment of enrollment and continues through the practice of law itself. Encounters with the unique curriculum of law school subject matter teach students how to divide the world accordingly into legal practice areas. Student-faculty exchanges in the classroom suggest that new language is necessary to avoid judgments about right and wrong. And "motive mongering" by practicing attorneys is meant to steer clients away from emotional reactions toward the past while focusing more on legal strategies toward the future.

All things considered, these observations suggest that becoming a lawyer entails much more than memorizing the rules of the law. Unfortunately, however, this means that it remains subject to the limitations of discrimination and framing brought about by differences in social identity as conveyed in the last chapter of this book. Given that, it can be of little surprise the legal profession, so much a social institution in its own right, is the site of ongoing inequalities and tensions that parallel the society surrounding it.

CHAPTER 9 REVIEW

Key Terms

- Intake
- Rules of professional conduct
- Attorney-client relationship
- Socialization
- Partners
- Senior associates
- Doctrine
- Facts
- Issue
- Rule
- Reasoning
- Holding
- Jurisdiction
- Plaintiff

- Defendant
- Appellate law
- Socialization
- Easement
- Habitus
- Empirical

Further Discussion

1. How is "thinking like a lawyer" different from the way people usually think about the world?
2. In what ways is the law school experience different from college? Should it be different?
3. If Mertz was correct in finding that law professors seem to favor certain groups in the classroom, should this be changed?

4. Should the legal profession try to eliminate its own inequalities described in this chapter, or are those inequalities justifiable because they mirror broader social world?

Further Reading

Mertz, Elizabeth. *The Language of Law School: Learning to "Think Like a Lawyer."* Oxford: Oxford University Press, 2007.

Rhode, Deborah. *Access to Justice*. Oxford: Oxford University Press, 2005.

Tamanaha, Brian. *Failing Law Schools*. Chicago: University of Chicago Press, 2012.

Tejani, Riaz. *Law Mart: Justice, Access, and For-Profit Law Schools*. Stanford, CA: Stanford University Press, 2017).

Criminal and Civil Justice 10

I n the last chapter we saw some of the ways in which
people wanting to be lawyers are initiated into the values and behaviors that characterize attorneys as a
group. Indeed, those values and behaviors have everything
to do with why we call their particular kind of group a
"profession" rather than a trade, guild, or community. We
learned that aspiring lawyers pick up these values and
behaviors by participating in the education process—law
school—which the profession has endorsed as the nearly
sole pathway to official legal expertise in the United States.
The process began with entry into the distinct first-year
curriculum, continued with the classroom experience,
and finished with time spent in the practice of law through
lawyer-client interactions. But how do the social practices
learned through these experiences *express* themselves in
our legal system itself?

In a general sense, the legal system can be divided
smoothly into criminal and civil justice systems. The
criminal justice system, consisting in many states of its
own courts at the trial level, is concerned foremost with
the liability of individuals suspected of violating a criminal statute. This is significant because it means criminal
law is usually a matter of state legislation, and it can usually be found in well-organized penal codes—different, for
example, from the judge-made case law that constitutes

much of civil justice. Violations of the criminal code are considered harms against the state, or against the people of a given jurisdiction; for this reason, you may have heard the names of criminal cases written as "People v. John Doe" or "State v. Doe." Criminal law is similarly classified as public rather than private law, though the victim is sometimes a private citizen. The penalties for violating criminal law usually include community service, monetary fines, or **incarceration.**

All of this contrasts with civil justice. In areas like tort law, the rules are said to derive from judge-made case law, often handed down from England through the centuries. Tort law generally applies only to "private wrongs," so case names tend to refer only to the two parties—the plaintiff or victim on one side and the defendant or wrongdoer on the other. Finally, the types of remedies available in the civil justice system do not include incarceration. They usually entail payment of a monetary damage award, or performance or abstention from an act or service.

With this in mind, chapter 10 separates itself into three main sections. The first begins by looking at the criminal justice system with particular emphasis on a major Supreme Court case that changed, partially, how this system should work. The second section then turns from criminal to civil justice—the area in which defendants aren't locked up in jail but rather are subject to civil *liability*, or money damages, for injuring one another. The last section examines several key features of procedure—the formal steps by which claims are decided in the criminal and civil justice systems.

Procedure refers to the formal steps required to bring new cases into the system or move forward ones already in it. In the United States we live with two sets of procedure: criminal and civil. Each is found in thick rulebooks often called the Code of Criminal Procedure and Code of Civil Procedure in each state and often modeled on the Federal Rules in each system. Above all else, this well-developed body of procedural rules is a testament to what Western countries have come to call the "rule of law" (see chapter 3)—an idea that law rather than any person dictates what is permissible in society. Legal procedure also ensures that every participant using the legal system is following the same set of norms, and therefore behaviors. This ensures minimal efficiency; for example, courts can process documents faster if everyone submits them on the same size, shape, and even thickness of paper—or increasingly in the same electronic file format! So procedure is important—almost as much as the substantive law itself—for promoting the rule of law and judicial efficiency.

Jurisprudence, meanwhile, may be akin to the rules of legal decision making. When judges decide cases, how do we know that their decisions are not just based on mood or social prejudice? Ideally, we know this through the reasoning given by the case opinion. A series of decisions taken together forms the jurisprudence on a particular topic. So the US Supreme Court jurisprudence on "freedom of the press" currently holds that journalists enjoy a special privilege when criticizing government officials. This comes not from one case alone but from a series of cases in which the famous *New York Times v. Sullivan* is considered a centerpiece.

Many lawyers and law scholars would say that jurisprudence is not just the reasoning behind a decision but also a *distinct* form of reasoning that is unique to "our" legal system. By *our,* these experts mean the English common-law tradition inherited when law was first established in the US colonies. So free speech jurisprudence may be one thing in American law, and it may be another in French civil law. Both are forms of reasoning that explain why the law is what it is and how contemporary decisions come out the way they do. As described in earlier chapters, one of the single greatest distinctions in US jurisprudence happens to lie between formalism and realism (see Introduction)—the ideas that outcomes are based on formal application of rules to facts and that outcomes are decided first while rules are used later to justify those.

Whereas legal reasoning is the substance of applying rules to facts and thus is assumed by their separation, procedure is the process by which we separate these two things and then document the application of the one to the other. In this chapter, I claim simply that legal reasoning and procedure both depend upon social relations and symbols to maintain a stable legal system.

CRIMINAL JUSTICE

The criminal justice system is motivated by three different but related goals. The first is **retributive justice**—the idea that making someone pay for a harmful act even when that payment does not restore the victims is still important. Retribution sits alongside other key approaches to criminal justice, including **restorative justice**—the idea that victims can be made whole by certain acts of repentance by a convict—and **rehabilitation**—the notion that individual criminals can and should be rehabilitated or brought up to good standing for productive membership in their society.

There is therefore often substantial disagreement over the "best" course of action in many types of cases. Should a murderer, for instance, be executed under a legal death penalty? Many would say "yes," "an eye for an eye." Many others would say "no," "two wrongs don't make a right," and would point out that the execution will do nothing to bring back the lost victim. Legal anthropologists, meanwhile, have studied the ways in which public executions—present in many societies around the world—play an important, ritual healing function in a community that has been already traumatized by a homicide. These are just some of the many complex arguments in play when we are talking about the role criminal justice should play in a society.

Another key topic has been the very basic rights accused criminals should possess when they are drawn into this high-stakes system. Today, it is widely understood that the loss of one's freedom (and certain other basic social rights) due to a criminal conviction is extremely serious. We recognize the importance of a strong legal defense for criminal suspects facing imprisonment. But this was not always the case.

In summer 1961, a fifty-one-year-old man by the name of Clarence Earl Gideon was on trial in Florida. He was accused of stealing fifty dollars in cash and a few bottles of beer and soda from a pool hall. At his trial, due to prior minor run-ins with the law, Gideon faced a maximum sentence of five years' imprisonment. A suspect with an ace defense attorney could probably have avoided this stiff penalty, but Gideon did not have that. Instead, he had only himself; he was too poor to afford to pay an attorney to defend him. To his credit, he filed his own documents and made his own arguments. One of these was a petition asking for the appointment of a state-sponsored defense attorney. The trial judge in the case denied this request, as there was no law in Florida at the time requiring him to do otherwise. As you might imagine, Gideon was convicted at the end of his trial and sentenced to the maximum five years' incarceration.

Before moving on to learn of his fate, we might pause to ask how we feel about this. Was Gideon right in asking for the state to give him a "free" legal defense? Who would ultimately be paying for this? Was the trial judge right in denying Gideon this freebie? In this case it was just one poor man's fate at stake. But there could be thousands more convicts who would claim the same expensive benefit. Was it not their responsibility to avoid criminal activity in the first place, the way most in society do? Finally, if we agree with the judge's denial here, what are we saying about justice in American society? Should it be the privilege of only those with money?

Once imprisoned for the five-year term in Florida, Gideon had time to read or, more properly, study the law. He felt with the wisdom of an untrained citizen that something was not right about the way he could lose his freedom without any expert advice or support and the way wealthier members of society could retain theirs for worse offenses just because they could afford a lawyer. The difference spoke to the larger problem of "**access to justice**" in the American system. Here, *justice* refers not to the "right" outcome in a case but rather to the benefits of the justice system in its entirety. These benefits accrue most to people who can seek out and retain the expert advice of licensed legal counsel. Normally, as in the case of luxury goods like cars, jewelry, and new technology, we accept that only the rich can access certain things. But *justice* has always been an important feature of our democratic society; we like to think of it as offering equal access to everybody. For Gideon, his treatment by the Florida trial judge after requesting an attorney was in violation of this principle.

So he wrote to the Florida Supreme Court using a petition for **habeas corpus.** This form of legal petition has existed under English common law for centuries, and it allows an imprisoned person to ask the sovereign—a king or a

> **BOX 10.1**   The Legal Services Corporation
>
> The relationship between neoliberalism and access to justice may not be obvious, but it is strong. In the United States, in the decades since the 1980s, government expenditures on public welfare have steadily shrunk, on the belief that people are better off when they receive less public assistance. One of the key assistance programs affected has been the legal services corporation (LSC). Created under the Ford administration in 1974, the LSC is a congressionally funded nonprofit law firm that provides legal assistance to poor clients around the country. Supported by the Carter administration in the late 1970s, the LSC had its budget cut by 25 percent under Reagan—far less than the zero funding the president had then sought. This was restored over the next decade until the 1994 midterm elections, when Republicans gained control of Congress and again cut the LSC's budget by roughly 40 percent. At present, the funding for the nation's largest legal aid resource is a topic of debate. When fiscally conservative leaders seek to reduce public spending, it becomes a popular target.

government—to "deliver the body" from its detained state. When the original US colonies broke from monarchic England, they incorporated habeas corpus into their federal constitution in the form of the "suspension clause" found in article 1, section 9, which says that "the privilege of the writ of habeas corpus shall not be suspended, unless when in cases of rebellion or invasion the public safety may require it." Famously, this privilege was twice suspended: first during the Civil War and then during World War II for reasons of national security. When President Bush sought the same suspension for Guantanamo Bay's high-security prison after the 9/11 terrorist attacks, the effort was rebuffed.[1] All criminal sentences come with the right of appeal through the state and federal courts, but this can expire or be exhausted permanently. The habeas corpus petition can be filed many years after a suspect's conviction in the criminal system. For this reason, and with advances in DNA science (see chapter 13) and other new evidence, we have seen since the mid-twentieth century a growing "innocence movement" consisting of law and society scholars and activists around the world seeking to overturn **wrongful convictions**—some decades old—through petitions for habeas corpus.[2]

Gideon's petition to the Florida Supreme Court was denied. Under the rules of federal jurisdiction, the last remaining recourse was to appeal to the US Supreme Court, the highest court in the nation. The Supreme Court's jurisdiction to hear the case was not based on substance—Gideon had violated no federal criminal statute. It was rather based on **appellate jurisdiction** established by the Constitution itself, saying that decisions from state supreme courts can usually be appealed *directly* to the highest court in the land. But because

Gideon was so poor—and now a state prisoner—his only resources to make this plea were a pencil, some paper, and his own limited readings of the law.

The author Anthony Lewis wrote of Gideon's story in the prizewinning book *Gideon's Trumpet.* There Lewis vividly describes the manner in which the unassuming prisoner filed his documents with the court.

> In the morning mail of January 8, 1962, the Supreme Court of the United States received a large envelope from Clarence Earl Gideon, prisoner No. 003826. . . . Like all correspondence addressed to the Court generally rather than to any particular justice or Court employee, it went to a room at the top of the great marble steps so familiar to Washington tourists. There a secretary opened the envelope. As the return address had indicated, it was another petition by a prisoner without funds asking the Supreme Court to get him out of jail. . . . A federal statute permits persons to proceed in any federal court *in forma pauperis,* in the manner of a pauper, without following the usual forms or paying the regular costs. . . . It also says that *in forma pauperis* applications should be typewritten "whenever possible," but in fact handwritten papers are accepted. . . . Gideon's were written in pencil. They were done in carefully formed printing, like a schoolboy's, on lined sheets evidently provided by the Florida prison.[3]

Here the ingenuity of Lewis's writing shines bright. What seem like literary details—the size of the envelope or the lines on the paper—are actually key elements for the student of procedure. Courts across the United States, both state and federal, specify very carefully the requirements of all filings, including font sizes, ink colors, and margin widths. In conveying Gideon's document details, Lewis tells the reader a lot very quickly: that there are specific rules to follow; that Gideon did his best to comply with them; that he still failed to match the professionalism of other filings; and that the Court might still tolerate all this under a rule that seemed to help poor people gain access to the Court. But if the Supreme Court was going to hear Gideon, he would have to do more than simply be a poor prisoner. He would have to assert a compelling argument under established law, and do so in a way relevant to the entire nation. Without these, the Court would feel hard pressed to expend its precious time on one single individual's case. Remarkably, the nonexpert Gideon managed to comply with most of the basic rules for appealing to the Supreme Court.[4] He filed within the ninety-day time limit. He enclosed the lower court documents, including his petition for habeas corpus and the order denying it. He included the all-important motion to be permitted to file as an indigent.[5] And he included the main request, the petition for **writ of certiorari**—the request for hearing that must begin every Supreme Court case.

Gideon had tried to make a compelling legal argument. He said that his conviction violated the due process clause of the Fourteenth Amendment. This fundamental legal precept says that all individuals before the court must receive fair treatment according to the same procedures as everyone else. In this case, Gideon argued that "to try a poor man for a felony without giving him a lawyer . . . was to deprive him of due process of law."[6] He even mentioned that the US Supreme Court had itself said this was the law. Unfortunately, he got the law wrong. The Supreme Court's own case law about this said otherwise. In *Betts v. Brady,* decided twenty years before *Gideon,* the Court held that any fundamental right to counsel did *not* apply to state criminal trials.[7] Under that case, the only reason an indigent defendant deserved state assistance of counsel was if failure to do so was a "denial of fundamental fairness." In later cases, this rule was further defined to require illiteracy or mental illness. Clarence Gideon, perhaps unaware of *Betts,* had a different notion: that he should be provided counsel *irrespective* of circumstances. He even told his trial judge that the Supreme Court "says I am entitled to be represented by counsel." But this was flat wrong. As Anthony Lewis points out, however, this did not mean it always had to be. Perhaps Gideon could get the nine justices on the Court to change their position. If so, this would be one of the most momentous uphill victories ever won in US legal history.

And it was. Gideon ultimately won his case in a unanimous decision that changed national law and attitudes about the right to counsel in the United States.[8] Thanks to Gideon, today no suspect can lose his or her freedom in federal *or* state court without the help of licensed legal assistance. In theory, this boosts the validity of the criminal justice system, since anyone convicted must have a stronger case stacked against them. But unfortunately, in practice the reality is different. State-appointed defense attorneys are often overworked, underpaid, and sometimes not the most zealous advocates for their clients. Many do their best to **plea-bargain** their client's case, forcing him or her to accept some blame and punishment in exchange for a lesser penalty. But some have been found to be entirely incompetent. Unfortunately, whereas incompetence in civil court may mean the loss of property or money damages, in criminal court it often means loss of freedom. In addition to the reopening of old cases through new evidence, the postconviction justice movement has therefore directed much of its resources to examine the competence of state-appointed defense attorneys in cases all around the United States. While it is a shame that "expert" attorney conduct must be reexamined in this way, this has benefited prisoners after the fact on numerous occasions and has helped to marginally raise the bar in criminal defense lawyering.

Gideon's case tells us many things. To begin, it offers a window onto the intricacies of US criminal procedure and shows us how individuals can change it. Much like the case *Miranda v. Arizona* (1966), *Gideon* tells us that if defendant rights are not respected early in a criminal investigation or prosecution, then subsequent dispositions of their case can be overturned or invalidated.[9] When you watch a television crime drama and see police detectives "reading" a suspect his or her rights, you can know that this step is an element of criminal apprehension required across the United States under *Miranda.* In that case, a defendant had disclosed information to police under the false impression that he *had* to. Police had not informed him that this was not required. So evidence obtained from the defendant was ruled invalid because it was obtained without such a proper disclaimer as "You have the right to remain silent." Like *Gideon, Miranda,* a case about one single criminal defendant, changed the entire landscape for US criminal procedure.

Another thing *Gideon* teaches us is that the US justice system can be highly unequal in the way it treats people. For those who study race relations and history, this is a pretty commonplace observation. But *Gideon* was a poor white man, and his case shows that race is not the only disadvantage in the system. The ability to afford strong legal counsel can make all the difference in retaining one's freedom in the face of imprisonment, and one is far more likely to be incarcerated if one is poor than if one is not. This was of course true before *Gideon v. Wainwright.* But unfortunately it is still true today. Even though suspects now "enjoy" the right to state-appointed counsel in criminal trials where imprisonment is a penalty, the variable quality of attorneys who take such cases means they may in some cases be worse than no attorney at all. Partly as a result, US prisons today harbor a population of inmates that has grown 350 percent over the past thirty years.[10] That population is disproportionately poor to begin with; it comes from average income levels roughly half the national average.[11]

CIVIL JUSTICE

Another limitation of the outcome in *Gideon* is that applies only to criminal cases. Criminal justice makes up only half of our system. The other half, civil justice, consists of all legal claims and cases involving the other kinds of disputes: accidents, property claims, contract battles, civil rights violations, and so forth. Even fraud cases, which require a mental state to deceive someone, are usually civil offenses. In purely civil disputes, imprisonment is never a viable penalty. The primary result of civil liability is monetary damages—a defendant must pay the plaintiff for the harm that has been created in the past, the present, and sometimes even the future as a result of his or her wrongful actions. This means that the most a person can usually lose in civil court is money.

Yet a good defense is no less important. For low-income defendants—for instance, an uninsured minimum wage worker who accidentally hits a pedestrian while driving—the consequence of losing in civil court can be almost as bad as imprisonment. As the sociologist Matthew Desmond illustrates, many Americans live in conditions of precarity where the loss of even one paycheck can set off a chain reaction that results in loss of their home, their property, their job, and even custody of their children.[12] The chances of someone in this situation affording a civil attorney are far lower than those of wealthy Americans. Like *Gideon,* they might be able to represent themselves, but doing so would almost certainly mean quitting their job, and very likely losing to an experienced plaintiff's attorney. One likely scenario, then, is to simply not show up, receive a "default judgment," and then wait until the court enforces this judgment by seizing property and other assets. For these reasons, many today believe that *Gideon* should apply to civil justice and that the state must be willing to provide attorneys to indigent clients faced with only civil penalties. To understand how such attorneys might help, a closer look at civil justice is instructive. For the average person of modest means, an encounter with civil justice is most likely to arise from tort law.

If *tort* sounds like an "ugly" word in English, it is because it is meant to. The word comes to us from the Latin *torquere*, meaning "to twist," via Old French and Middle English. It is still used in modern French to mean "wrong." The word is only used when something is amiss, out of place, or offensive.

In contemporary English the word *tort* is only ever used in discussions about law. In fact it describes an entire body of "civil wrongs not arising out of contract or property."[13] What does this mean? First, it is organizational; it means we will not find tort law described in books about the law of interpersonal or business contracts. Those books describe rules and cases about disputes between people relating to their formal agreements. Most contract cases are about written agreements, but some can be verbal as well. Property disputes, meanwhile, are always about people's relationship to parcels of land. Often property disputes are about the land itself—what shape it should be or who really "owns" it. But just as often they are about the *use* of that land, since uses can be divided up and sold, leased, or loaned out to nonowners. If the power company representative walks onto your property to read the meter for billing purposes you may wonder why he or she has the "right" to do so. It is likely because your utility agreement—or some other agreement attached to your property when you bought it—grants their company an **easement** to enter the premises for this purpose. The key is that there is one designated purpose; if the company decides to erect a utility pole on your land, that would probably exceed the scope of its easement and give you a strong claim under property law. So much for contract and property; tort law as we defined it above is basically everything else. Car accidents, libelous news stories, factories emitting noxious pollution, and even medical doctors making mistakes are all governed by tort law.

Tort is a form of civil wrong distinct from, but not unrelated to, criminal law. Sometimes tort law overlaps with criminal law. Intentional physical harms like assault and battery are ones that often appear in both fields and are subject to liability under both systems depending on the precise actions. Take, for example, a "bar fight"—the kind of physical altercation that erupts in a public place where people have consumed alcohol and are, perhaps, emboldened and uninhibited. Assume that this fight injures one combatant more than another and that the defeated fighter is upset about that. The latter may choose to file a police report that would then open an investigation under the criminal code, which probably has a section prohibiting assault and battery. If investigators consider this serious enough, they will bring the other fighter into custody where they must be charged with a specific crime and **arraigned** or brought to criminal court. If so, then the case will always be titled something like *State v. John Doe* or *People v. John Doe.* But since both parties were fighting, the loser may not wish to involve the police; they could rather contact a personal injury attorney and file a civil suit for battery. Notice that the civil suit requires no formal "code" violation. Instead the civil suit for the tort of battery will be treated as a potential violation of tort law itself and will be filed under the title *John Roe v. John Doe* or something similar.

What is the significance of all this?

Tort law is a form of "common law" rather than statutory law, meaning it is only the sum of all cases that have been decided in the relevant jurisdiction. Furthermore, tort law is *state* law, so it is slightly different in each of the fifty US states. While most of these states inherited the English principles that came over at the start of US history, each has modified them in different ways specific to its terrain, industries, climate, and culture. And the states have had roughly two hundred years to do so. For this reason, Supreme Court Justice Louis Brandeis famously called the states "laboratories of experimentation" for civil law. This echoes a sentiment in the Western legal tradition that law should be custom fitted to the peoples of each geographic location and cultural value system, though the problem comes in delineating how and where the separations between them should lie.[14] Comparing tort to criminal law, then, we find that although some of the same actions could land you in either type of liability, tort violations stem from judge-made, "decisional" law, whereas criminal violations stem from legislative statutes devised by government representatives and "enacted" by lawmakers.

Accidental versus Intentional Harms

The world of judge-made tort law can be divided neatly in the following way. The first general division is between "intentional harms" and "accidental harms." As you might imagine, this general division comes down to what the actor who caused harm was thinking at the time of the action. If their mind was not on doing the act that caused injury, it can be considered "accidental." If their mind was focused on committing the act, then we consider this "intentional." But notice two things very important here: the accidental action need not be the underlying conduct that might be considered "normal" under most circumstances; and the question of intent is not about the harm but about the action that produced it. So a person need not be *driving* by accident (e.g., unknowingly), but they may have swerved into a person accidently. Perhaps a tree fell in their way, or a turn-off sign had fallen down. Likewise, a person who chooses to crash their car into a pedestrian may not intend to paralyze the victim and may only intend to break their leg (a terrible thing either way!). But the

> **BOX 10.2**   General Outline of U.S. Tort Law
>
> - Intentional Harms
>   - Claims
>   - § Assault
>   - § Battery
>   - § False Imprisonment
>   - § Trespass to Land
>   - § Trespass to Chattels/Conversion
>   - Defenses
>   - § Defense of Person or Property
>   - § Private Necessity
>   - § Public Necessity
>   - § Discipline
> - Accidental Harms
>   - Negligence
>   - Defenses
>   - § Contributory Negligence
>   - § Assumption of Risk
>   - Strict Liability
>   - § Abnormally Dangerous Activities
>   - § Respondeat Superior/Vicarious Liability
>   - § Products Liability
> - Privacy and Reputational Harms
>   - Defamation
>   - Public Disclosure of Private Facts
>   - Intrusion on Seclusion
>   - Misappropriation
>   - False Light
> - Nuisance

latter driver will not be able to call this collision an "accident" just because the injury produced was accidentally greater than the driver intended. The action, in other words colliding with a pedestrian, was intended, and therefore so, according to tort law, were any resulting injuries.

Zooming in for a moment on accident law, there are really two types of this. The first we call *negligence*. Negligence liability is, by far, the most common type of tort claim in the English common-law system. That is because people moving about through urban spaces typically do not intend to hurt one another, but they often take extreme risks. Running to catch a train, speeding in traffic, playing contact sports, even leaving children in the care of strangers—all of these somewhat routine activities actually come with measurable risks from a few different angles. When they go wrong and someone is indeed hurt, it is usually because one or another party made a temporary lapse in judgment. The activities themselves, running, driving, playing, and trusting, are not in themselves negligent or unlawful. But combined with a lapse in judgment, for instance texting while driving, they are. What are normally just risky behaviors become negligent ones. Negligence is the form of tort law that must analyze these occurrences and determine whether the behavior merits legal liability.

To do so, courts require a showing of several key elements. First, the defendant must have owed a *duty* of care to the plaintiff in the first place. We all should be nice to one another, but we do not owe a legal duty to be careful toward strangers unless we know they exist, they come close enough to be relevant, and they are not themselves there to help or protect us. Second, courts want to see that the defendant *breached* that duty to the plaintiff. Showing a breach of duty requires showing what the actor in fact "did"—for instance, look down at their phone while driving—and comparing this to what they in theory "should have done" given other, probably safer versions of the same activity.

The plaintiff must then show that the defendant's breach *caused* the harm in question. Causation is surprisingly complicated to show; this is because the world around us is complex and often multiple actors in the environment contribute to a single incident. For this reason, tort law has evolved the subelements of factual cause and proximate cause. Factual cause describes the one decisive act without which the harm would not have occurred. So for instance, if a rancher sues because their house burned down in a forest fire, the defendant smoker may try to argue that the fire was caused by heavy winds, or by failure to fireproof one's house. But they will not be able to argue that the fire would have started without their tossing a cigarette into the bushes a mile away. That single act—smoking in a dry forest area—would be the factual cause. But the defendant smoker does have a point: What if they were smoking five hundred miles away? Would they then still be responsible? This question is one about "proximate causation." How close, it asks, must the defendant's action be to the plaintiff's injury to be considered *the* cause? This is one of the most tricky decisions courts have to make under tort law, and it often comes down to public policy about how we want to allocate responsibility and which behaviors we want to reward. Smoking in dry wooded areas seems pretty egregious, so it is conceivable a court might still consider this a proximate cause even five hundred miles away from injury; the question about "proximity" is therefore a relative one.

The last element of a classic negligence claims is the *harm* itself. The plaintiff must argue in their complaint that everything the defendant did wrong actually resulted in measurable injury: a burned house or a broken leg. If it did not, or all it resulted in was hurt feelings, a court will likely dismiss the claim even if all the other elements have been proven with certainty. Except in rare circumstances, pure emotional harms like fear, embarrassment, or sadness are not recognized or compensable harms. Why not? There are two main reasons. The first is that they are difficult to *verify:* How does anyone know for sure whether a plaintiff was made fearful or sad, and how does this compare with their state before the injury? Second, the *measurement* of the harm is impossible in absolute terms. What units of measurement can be applied to fear, embarrassment, or sadness? Perhaps hours spent hiding under the covers, or ounces of teardrops shed?

All of this raises an important point about tort law generally and the harm element in particular. Compensation of injured victims is not the primary purpose of this area of law—righting the moral imbalance or injustice is. To accomplish this, plaintiffs must translate their injury into money—dollars and cents—so that the court can decide whether to hold the other side liable in this amount. Emotional harms are difficult if not impossible to translate into money, and, even if this were not true, their reimbursement in money, as Pound told us in chapter 2, might not by fitting. Having said all of this, courts usually do *add* emotional harm onto personal injury and property loss to assess damage awards in those types of cases. The reason is simple: where life and limb or personal property have been harmed, some form of verifiable injury has already taken place and any emotional collateral damage is likely to have genuinely occurred.

So much for the law of negligence. Everything said so far in this section applies to activities that are, in themselves, reasonable. Driving—although dangerous—is not inherently unreasonable under most conditions. Setting off fireworks—although involving minor amounts of gunpowder—is also not in itself unreasonable (though it may be illegal in your state). Most of our daily lives consist of dozens of mildly risky activities that can go wrong but are not in themselves considered outrageous. Doing them reasonably—even if they result in accidental injury—will probably not get you into legal liability.

But notice that some activities *are* inherently dangerous. These are things that, even when executed with the highest levels of care, are still likely to go wrong and produce injury. The first example might be the transportation of explosive chemicals. Unfortunately, we live in a world where dangerous chemicals are all around us—usually in small amounts. Liquid bleach, fertilizers, air conditioner coolant, and pesticides are just some of the inventions of modern chemistry designed to make our lives easier—and they do—but they carry with them unusually high risks. A small bottle of any of these items is not particularly special. But imagine where that bottle has come from and you will probably picture a chemical factory with large metal vats of noxious substances and workers dressed like astronauts to protect themselves. Now imagine that those substances travel to and from this factory in large containers carried on the backs of trucks or trains. Then think about how trucks and trains get from one side of the country to the other; although trucks on the nation's roads have

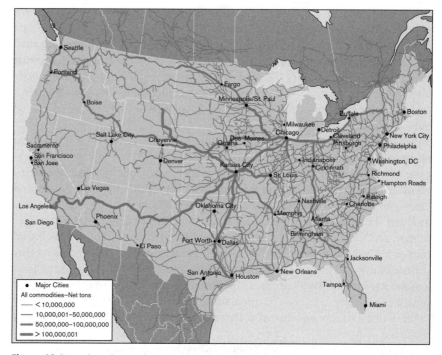

Figure 10.1 Freight rail map of the United States, 2010, showing Chicago and Kansas City as two major hubs. Source: Federal Railroad Administration.

much greater flexibility, one quickly realizes that both networks of railroad tracks and interstate highways often pass through large, densely populated urban areas like Detroit, Chicago, or St. Louis (see figure 10.1).

Once you have imagined all of these things, you are closer to understanding the second major area of accident law known as **strict liability.** Strict liability is the kind of tort law applied in cases when the activity in question could not be made much safer through the conduct of the person doing it. A conductor of a train carrying thousands of pounds of ammonium nitrate—the active ingredient of most fertilizers with potential to be used in bomb making—might be the most careful driver in his company and still experience an unusual incident like a spark from the tracks or a broken railroad switch. These things are beyond the company's control. Yet if they occur, the results, particularly in a populated area, will be devastating. Such incidents have occurred on several occasions, causing the spillage of noxious, combustible chemicals and the evacuation of entire communities, often at great economic expense to their residents.

To deal with this type of problem, strict liability simplifies the calculations otherwise required by negligence law. Instead of telling chemical companies they have a qualified duty to act reasonably and then spending considerable effort litigating whether they did so after an accident, tort law eliminates the negligence standard altogether. It says such companies have an "absolute duty" to avoid such accidents and that this comes with an absolute obligation to compensate victims when one occurs. There are several important justifications for this. First, inherently dangerous activities usually bring greater wealth to their actors—otherwise why would they feel motivated to take such risks in the first place? As you may already know, therefore, the petrochemical industry worldwide is one of the most lucrative—yet most dangerous. So tort law says these actors can better afford to compensate people for harms they create. Second, this added duty forces such companies to make very careful choices to minimize risks to the public. If ammonium nitrate is highly combustible, perhaps it need not be transported through downtown Chicago. Moving shipments *around* rather than through cities might be more costly to companies, but at least this is cheaper for them than paying certain damages to victims for harms likely to occur. Finally, tort law chooses activities like this for strict liability because they are so explosive and devastating that often they destroy the very evidence courts would need to determine reasonable conduct before the accident. Without it, in other words, companies might be rewarded for doing so much damage that they could not be proven responsible.

Accidental and intentional harms make up the majority of tort law claims. There are, indeed, a few separate claims distinct from both of these, but they tend to overlap with other areas of law like contract and property. This section has highlighted the largest body of tort law to give you a close-up picture of at least one field of civil justice aimed at remedying wrongs between citizens and requiring clear, distinct elements for a claim to go to trial in our system. Comparing negligence and strict liability further offered a glimpse beneath surface rules at the underlying public policy issues these laws have emerged to address.

Key Features: Juries, Insurance, Contingency Fees

The US civil court process was inherited largely from England, but it has evolved several distinct features that bear mention. First, the use of the **jury** is somewhat unique. Under the Seventh Amendment to the Constitution, individuals bringing or responding to suits in civil court are actually guaranteed a right to trial by jury.[15] While this provision formally applies only to the federal courts, in practice it is generally respected by the state courts as well. Furthermore, findings of fact made by juries are virtually sacrosanct; they cannot be questioned by judges at trial or on appeal. This gives juries extraordinary power in our system. For this reason, when judges are weighing evidence to determine if parties may continue in their suit, they do so "as if" the jury were already present, trying, for example, to determine whether "a reasonable jury" would consider that the evidence to prove an element was "more likely than not" met. Additionally somewhat unique is the fact that our juries are intentionally picked for their ignorance of the law; they are "lay" jurors, not experts. This differs from countries in Europe that have specialized professional jurors trained to hear and respond to evidence. Our use of lay jurors is not without controversy: some think it forces people to decide from instinct or implicit bias, while others feel it preserves the community wisdom considered latent in the common law.

A second fundamental feature coloring civil justice is the widespread presence of insurance. Insurance is a massive $80 billion business in the United States alone.[16] It specializes in risk. Experts known as **actuaries** tell insurance underwriters the amount of risks that people and situations represent statistically. So, for instance, they might study adult mothers who have smoked since age fifteen to determine that these individuals tend to die before age sixty at a particular rate. They might also find that athletic adults who participated in college sports and consume less than one alcoholic drink per week tend to die before sixty at a far lower rate. Which do you think will be charged more for life insurance (e.g., the kind of insurance that pays your children for your unintentional death)?

In the US justice system, life insurance is just one of several forms of insurance that become relevant in the typical dispute. While life insurance may matter most in the case of someone who dies without a written will—thereby leaving surviving family to argue over who gets what—**liability insurance** is probably more commonly relevant in cases of tort law. There, the insurance was purchased in the first place to offset the very risk of injury being caused to self, other persons, or property. Most states now have mandatory automobile insurance laws requiring everyone to carry liability coverage for driving. As you probably know, it costs more to buy auto insurance for a teenager than it does for a middle-aged parent. The experts have assessed the risks taken by each group and priced the product accordingly. Although their costs to buy insurance may vary, a pedestrian accidentally hit by either of these drivers will likely take the presence of insurance into account when they sue the driver in court. Significantly, however, courts themselves—judges and juries—are not allowed to consider the presence of insurance relevant in determining damage awards.

A third feature related to the insurance question is the **contingency fee** arrangement. The United States is one of the only countries in the world that permits attorneys to work for clients under this arrangement. *Contingency* essentially means "depending upon" some other event. In this case, that event is winning at trial. So the contingency fee is a payment system where an attorney might work unpaid for a period of months or years pending the case outcome but then would be entitled to a percentage as high as 45 percent in some cases if they do win (figure 10.2). If you have seen advertisements for personal injury lawyers saying, "You pay nothing unless we win your case!" it means they are proposing to work for a contingency fee. Often, however, such proposals come with fine print that does charge clients for fixed costs like photocopies, phone calls, and travel. Can you think of the pros and cons of a system that

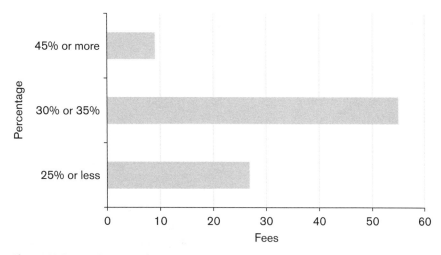

Figure 10.2 Typical contingency fee rates.

allows for such agreements? Does the fact that these are lawyers—sometimes considered "officers of the court"—play into your opinion?

Table 10.1 lays out some of the common pros and cons about contingency fees. On one hand, they are a bad idea. They encourage attorneys to act like salesmen in the way just mentioned. They encourage lawyers to go looking for or soliciting new cases among victims of injury. They can result in attorneys taking large—perhaps too large—chunks of the final damage award. They can be misleading if clients think they will have no expenses. They can encourage attorneys to claim exorbitant damages—perhaps millions in personal injury harm for spilled coffee or millions in pain and suffering for lost dry cleaning.[17] And maybe most common of all, they can encourage attorneys to pressure clients to settle their claim with big companies more interested in making the trouble disappear than in correcting any injustice, or harmful corporate policy. Some firms specializing in filing cases against big businesses to extract quick damages in this way have been called "settlement mills"; in them clients describe being treated as a case number more than a person and may say they rarely if ever got to speak to an actual attorney.

On the other hand, contingency fees allow for some important dynamics in our system. If, for example, you are a college student who has been hit by a driver while biking to class, you probably would never have several thousand dollars lying around to hire an attorney—even if you knew you were not at fault. Now imagine the millions of people who are not students but nonetheless travel to and from minimum wage work each day just trying to feed their families that month. Indeed, there may be some reason to think low-income people are more likely to suffer personal injury harm than middle- and upper-salaried workers. If

Table 10.1   Pros and Cons of Contingency Fee Agreements

Cons	Pros
Encourage solicitation	Promote access to justice
Permit taking chunk of damages	Encourage zealous advocacy
Can be misleading (fine print)	
Encourage exorbitant claims	
Encourage settlement	

they are not injured traveling *to* work, they are probably more likely to suffer harm *at* work. The contingency fee arrangement allows them to engage an attorney without money up front and in this way may promote access to justice.

Additionally, the arrangement gives attorneys a direct stake in their clients' outcomes. If they were paid only up front, they way, say, a public relations expert is, they might be the most diligent workers and advocates but they would see no added financial benefit from actually winning. True, their reputation might suffer in the long run and they would lose that way, but in the short run they would be immune. The contingency fee encourages *zealous* advocacy on the part of lawyers because their own livelihood is made to also depend on the strength of their work.

It is very noteworthy that our cousins in England and Australia—systems sharing our ancestry in English common law—do not permit contingency fees in the way we do. In those places, the dangers of soiling the professional reputation of attorneys—particularly through commercialization—outweighs any potential benefits. But there is also something else that makes their strict view possible. If table 10.1 above seems imbalanced to you in a manner that may favor abolishing the contingent fee in our system, consider the following. Access to justice by itself may be the *most* important feature in that whole table. Without it, the democratic nature of our legal system is entirely undermined. Countries like England and Australia worry less about this because they always have two kinds of lawyers available—one expensive and more highly trained, the other more affordable with less expensive education. The two work in separate courts, so there is rarely a problem of inequality in expertise. On the contrary, in England and Australia average citizens may be more likely to retain an expert, since the affordable kind are more readily available to all. In the United States, we do not yet have such a bifurcated system, and therefore the first expert available to even the poor is likely an expensive one.

One final distinction separates our civil justice from that found elsewhere. It too pertains to finances—namely the payment of court "costs." In the United

States we observe a rule that says each side—plaintiff or defendant—pays its *own* costs: attorney fees, court filing fees, expert witness fees, and so on. Unless previously agreed otherwise, say in the form of a contract, American litigants pay their own way. If they lose in court, they still pay only their own costs. This has been called the **American Rule.** In England, meanwhile, it is the opposite. The loser in a court battle is required—unless agreed otherwise previously—to pay the winner's costs. As you can imagine, this makes losing particularly costly there. But it also does something else. It makes being confident in your case much, much more important in the decision to file suit or in the decision not to settle one. Who benefits most from this added incentive? Given the resources potentially saved, probably the courts themselves do, as in turn do their creditors: the taxpayers.

PROCEDURE

A typical lawsuit is organized into roughly five procedural phases: pleadings, pretrial motions, discovery, trial, and appeals. The pleadings are all of the written documents that get the process into the court system. Courts require first that the person injured, the plaintiff, file a **summons** and a **complaint.** The summons is the formal request that the injuror, the defendant, appear before the court. The complaint is the first formal assertion of what the defendant did wrong. This must include a statement of the legal principle violated, the basic facts of what happened, and the nature of the injury that resulted. Already at this stage, the judge can begin to determine whether a valid claim exists or whether the plaintiff may be simply airing a grievance. Often plaintiffs want courts to do something about some offense they have suffered, but there may be no legal rule addressing this, or remedy available. The plaintiff must also **serve process** on the defendant through one of several available means; this means that the defendant must receive adequate written notice that they are named in a suit and potentially subject to liability. Once served, the defendant has the opportunity to respond to the complaint with their **answer.**

The next phase is that of **pretrial motions.** As the name implies, this is a period before trial begins when parties "move" in writing to have the judge make a procedural decision. If the defendant feels that the complaint is without legal merit, they can file the pretrial "motion to dismiss." This is a special motion that asserts that, *even if* all asserted facts were true, no legal remedy allows the defendant to be held liable. A clear example would a terrible insult. The defendant may have said in front of an onlooking crowd that the plaintiff "sucks at chess," but there is no law against such a statement. The motion to dismiss essentially says, "Sure, I did insult the plaintiff in this way, and sure, she may have lost people's respect as a result, but none of this is unlawful." Sometimes the plaintiff is permitted to amend their complaint because relevant law does exist, and they may have failed to say this. An "insult" may border on defamation, for instance, and as we have seen, there is substantial law about that.

If the judge decides the amended complaint is satisfactory, he or she will permit the case to proceed to discovery. In the discovery stage, the parties have a set amount of time to request key information from one another. Discovery requests come in a few common varieties such as interrogatories, depositions, and document requests. The United States is different from countries in Europe in this respect: here discovery is driven by the parties themselves, while there it is conducted by the court directly. One of the results from our approach is that parties often can and do overwhelm the other side with requests for information or with release of information. In large, complex litigation, for instance, one multinational company may "respond" to its competitor's request for documents with millions of individual files and folders. Fortunately, this document production and review can take place largely electronically today. Legal consulting firms do good business specializing in what is known as "e-discovery." Some of these firms have developed advanced software for searching and coding documents on the basis of the relevant needs and content. Unfortunately, sorting through all these files, even in electronic format, still requires a real person with eyes and critical thinking skills, so large firms engaged in e-discovery must often use their own attorneys or hire contract attorneys to pore over the mass of documents. As you would guess, this can get very costly. Yet from a strategic position that is the point: flood the other side with information and run up your opponent's legal bills in the hopes that they will withdraw or surrender. In European courts, such tactics would only burden the institutions themselves and would therefore prove counterproductive to all sides.

After all this information has been gathered and processed, either party may raise the second major pretrial motion: the **summary judgment.** A motion for summary judgment asserts that there is "no genuine issue of material fact": in other words, the parties agree on all facts and the judge can decide the case without even needing to consult a jury. Remember, if all facts are agreed upon, there is nothing for a jury to do in a trial. Most suits in the US courts that make it this far will end at this stage.

Only approximately 5 percent of all civil cases make it past summary judgment. Of the remaining number, even fewer end with a jury verdict. That is because the trial phase is full of hurdles to surmount. The first is the **burden of proof,** or the responsibility allocated to one side or the other to produce sufficient evidence. The plaintiff carries the burden of proof for the basic elements—duty, breach, causation, and harm—in a tort suit. The defendant carries the burden for any defenses. Meanwhile, either side can offer evidence and argue to undermine the opponent's evidence. In civil court, the standard for this burden is the preponderance standard: all evidence must be shown to make a fact "more likely than not" true. In criminal court, the standard is higher; evidence must be proven "beyond a reasonable doubt." If a defendant can weaken a plaintiff's action by creating substantial doubt about, say, causation, he or she can undermine the whole case. During trial, as each of these arguments unfolds, either party can also make motions for things like excluding evidence, or stopping the trial and deciding the case outright (**directed verdict**). If the claim survives all of these hurdles, a jury that has heard the entire story will be given specific instructions and asked to produce a verdict. The US system requires only **general verdicts.** This means the jury is asked only for an "up or down" decision on a general question, such as "Do you find the defendant liable for damages?" Rarely are juries asked to provide a **special verdict,** that is to say a decision with specialized reasoning such as "Do you find the plaintiff has met his burden of showing duty, breach, causation, and harm?" Before dwelling on juries further, it should be said that the trial jury verdict is far from the final word, yet very powerful in itself. It is not the final word because the loser possesses the right to appeal to the next level of court—usually the federal or state "appellate court"—assuming they follow proper timeliness and formatting procedures, as we saw in *Gideon* earlier in this chapter. But the jury is powerful in the sense that no judge, even among the higher courts, can question the verdict in its substance—even where that substance lacks explanation. Although higher courts can question the instructions given, and can undermine a verdict in that way, judges lack the power to overturn juries directly.

REASONING

Anthropologist Larry Rosen has said the power of common-law juries stems from their "oracular quality."[18] What does this mean? In the study of myths and legends undertaken by experts in folklore and cultural anthropology, a common figure or character has often been the oracle. An oracle is someone or something that possesses secret wisdom and dispenses it out to special individuals— usually the main character in the story. With that information, the character is then empowered to complete a journey or task to achieve his or her purpose in the whole narrative. Juries, Rosen says, operate in a similar fashion.

They do this because of their combination of importance and secrecy. Juries are important for reasons already hinted at: they bring an air of common sense and morality to key questions in a dispute. Although they can decide only factual matters, often these are highly subjective matters. For example, is the witness of sound character so that their testimony may be believed? The opposing lawyers will argue they are not by pointing to various past incidents of lying, cheating, or stealing. This is called **impeachment.** The other side will then argue before the jury that these acts came under pressure in the circumstances and are not part of the witness's character. In the end, it is up to the jury to decide the believability of whatever that witness says on the witness stand. The jury may be charged only with fact finding, but its nonexpertise is meant to represent the average judgment of the community with regard to uncertain information. That this judgment would be represented in a formal courthouse is said to bolster the legitimacy of the court process in our system. Without it, people would feel judged by the officials themselves and might never be truly certain that their legal fates were not arbitrary or political in some fashion.

Juries also reflect something else about legal reasoning. As we saw in the last chapter, it separates the world into questions of fact and questions of law. But if the facts in each case are slightly different—as they are bound to be—how can they ever be decided on the same principles? The answer lies in a device literature scholars call **metaphor.** Anthropologists like Rosen say metaphor applies far beyond literature and may in fact be endemic to all of human creativity.[19] More to the point, metaphor is what allows common-law legal reasoning—a progression from one case to the next without changing drastically the rules of decision.

How so? Suppose in 1905 a case involved a horse and buggy driving negligently on a narrow country lane. A jury in that case found that the driver had been intoxicated with alcohol, and the court imposed liability for injuries sustained by a pedestrian and her dog. Now suppose a case arises in 2019 involving a self-driving car and a teenager on the sidewalk riding a "hoverboard"—the kind of electronic two-wheeled scooter kept balanced by gyroscopic motors and sold as a kid's toy. Clearly the cases are quite different, separated as much by time as by technological advances that would take days to fully understand. But perhaps your mind is already past that. Maybe you are already thinking the cases are actually similar—at least in some ways. If so, then you are exhibiting the kind of metaphoric thinking Rosen referred to. This thinking is endemic to the **analogical reasoning** required by our common-law system. Here the facts change quickly, but the law evolves slowly over time. Both the horse and buggy and the self-driving vehicle are modes of individual transportation. Both are probably owned by a single operator. And both are designed for short (versus transcontinental) journeys. Similarly, the injured victim in both cases appears to be "innocent," having done nothing blameworthy. And both possess personal property that may have suffered injury as well. By *analogy*, the cases are similar, and the reasoning that decided one could very well be applied to the other. More likely, however, a series of thousands of other cases fall in between these to help evolve the deciding principle and prepare it for the current high-tech era. In this way, metaphor, so important to ancient mythology and human creativity, may lie at the heart of our legal institutions and be yet another reminder of the delicate dance between law and society.

CONCLUSION

This chapter has been about procedure and reasoning at the sites of criminal and civil justice. It looked at some of the social implications underlying criminal law and criminal procedure, and it examined up close some of the values that structure civil justice and civil procedure, ending, just now, with an explanation of the importance of the jury system and its place within the legal reasoning of our institutions.

Together, these topics further support a conclusion that the formal practice of law is a deeply social practice. I have called this unit "Social Constructions of Law" to denote the depth of this connection. *Construction* is in many ways the perfect term; it is not simply that our education, profession, procedures, and reasoning support or engage with social values and tendencies. It is that those elements of our law are actually *made out of* these things.

The opening chapters of this book introduced the concept of social constructivism, but this chapter is the culmination of it so far as law and society today is concerned. Constructivism, I said, does not mean that our world is an illusion, or that the rules and processes we have seen so far are somehow less than "real." Quite the opposite: the constructed nature of law predetermines that it will act more severely against some members of society than others. Unfortunately, since the advent of Western democratic liberalism itself, law generally has favored those with wealth, and those at the center rather than at the margins of society. Fortunately, however, in piecemeal fashion, this system has surprised us by giving opportunity to those who would be forgotten, where otherwise they might have none at all.

CHAPTER 10 REVIEW

Key Terms

- Incarceration
- Retributive justice
- Restorative justice
- Rehabilitation
- Habeas corpus
- Wrongful convictions
- Appellate jurisdiction
- Writ of certiorari
- Plea bargain
- Easement
- Arraigned
- Strict liability
- Jury
- Actuaries
- Liability insurance
- Contingency fees
- Access to justice
- American Rule
- Summons
- Complaint
- Serve process
- Answer
- Pretrial motions
- Summary judgment
- Burden of proof
- Preponderance standard
- Directed verdict
- General verdict
- Special verdict
- Impeachment
- Metaphor
- Analogical reasoning

Further Discussion

1. Was it fair for Gideon to expect the state to pay for his defense attorney? Why or why not?

2. What are the pros and cons of a contingency fee system for accident law?
3. If juries serve as oracles—answering questions with wisdom from outside the law—where does this wisdom come from? Do we need this in our legal system?

Further Reading

Abraham, Kenneth. *The Forms and Functions of Tort Law*. New York: Foundation Press, 2012.

Lewis, Anthony. *Gideon's Trumpet*. New York: Random House, 1964.

Rosen, Lawrence. *Law as Culture: An Invitation*. Princeton, NJ: Princeton University Press, 2006.

Justice and Popular Culture

One of the main drivers of this book is the notion that ideas shape reality, either because they color the lenses through which we view the world, or because they translate into things we do, say, or build. Moreover, because none of us exists in a vacuum, our ideas are always influenced by and influencing those around us. Therefore, the opening chapters of this book introduced the concept of social construction in order to ask the fundamental question of how law participates in this phenomenon. Unit 3 then inverted this question to ask how law itself is the result of a socially constructive project—whether by design or by accident. It has so far asked how becoming and being a lawyer is a social practice. If the last two chapters focused on the social underpinnings of formal law—legal education, profession, rules, institutions, and processes—this chapter pans back out to the level of society once again. It asks a broader question: How does **popular culture** influence the way the general public views law, and how might it shape the expectations people have for what "the system" can do for them?

This question invites us to examine products of pop culture in some detail, so this chapter may be a fun one; it allows us to think and talk about film, television, and the Internet. While of course by no means the only genres of

BOX 11.1   Film and Video Technology

When delving into the substance conveyed by film, TV, and the Internet, it is useful to consider the media themselves—particularly as they may begin to seem more old-fashioned with the rise of even newer media formats. Not that long ago, both film and television were extremely cutting-edge technology. Both arose to capture light from a source—for instance, the beautiful Monument Valley in Utah and Arizona (figure 11.1)—and to imprint the image created by that light onto a physical medium. In the case of film, that medium was originally celluloid film—quite literally a photosensitive chemical liquid trapped between two sheets of rudimentary plastic known as celluloid. This substance dates back to the 1860s in origin, it was used widely in the production of moving picture film, and then it was phased out in the 1950s. Whereas the replacement substance *acetate* would be more stable, celluloid was very flammable, which—combined with the high heat generated by film projectors—led to accidental fires in editing rooms and theaters.

If the large-budget movie industry today relies on acetate film, lower-budget or independent filmmaking relies now on digital camera recording. Engineers since the 1980s have developed better and better ways of capturing images as digital information—the same ones and zeros that recorded this book manuscript as an original word-processing file before its production. This information must then be stored on a movable object like a disc or tape, or else it can go directly onto a hard drive like the one in your computer, tablet, or smartphone. For makers of digital film recording gear, it was this second part that was most challenging historically—moving picture files take up considerable memory, and building storage devices large enough for moviemaking took a while. As with all technological evolution, however, storage devices eventually caught up with the demand, and today most filmmaking entails digital recording, or digital transfer of original film footage. Once fed into computer editing software, digital film files have become easy to edit, process, and distribute. As a bonus, the quality of imagery has improved—at least in its detail and fidelity to the original.

For television, the evolution was very similar except that videotape became an important intermediary step between film and digital recording. In the 1960s, engineers created ways to store moving images on magnetic tape reels that could be housed as cassettes. One of the earliest popular but rudimentary video reels is that of Lee Harvey Oswald, the named assassin of President John F. Kennedy, being shot in front of live TV cameras while being transferred between jails in Dallas days after the assassination. Video also played some role in the documenting of violence both in Vietnam during the latter years of the American war there, and in the Chicago 1968 Democratic Convention riots. TV news of both events shocked average Americans and really captured the era as one of change, repression, and resistance. Video and television, therefore, were pivotal in ushering the cultural shifts of the 1960s.

Figure 11.1 Monument Valley, scene of many Hollywood western films during the first half of the twentieth century. Source: Carol M. Highsmith Archive, Library of Congress, Prints and Photographs Division.

pop culture to speak of, those three media have been the most influential throughout recent Western history.

VISUAL CULTURE

When we speak of film and television as evidence about society, we are really speaking about them as **visual culture.** This is a term sociologists and anthropologists use to describe a particular kind of cultural form created and transmitted through visual media like those just described—but print forms like newspapers and magazines would count as well. Visual culture predates modern life. Evidence suggests early humans exhibited visual culture specifically; the famous cave paintings at Lascaux, France, are a prime example (figure 11.2).

Discovered in 1940 by an eighteen-year-old boy, the cave at Lascaux is said to contain roughly six thousand figures painted from naturally available pigments and preserved from the elements by their depth underground. Some convey quite complex scenes of animals fighting or groups of humans engaged in hunting. These are said to be approximately seventeen thousand years old. Contemporary visual culture is actually not that different from what was found at Lascaux. If those ancient images appear simple on the surface, consider our

Figure 11.2 Cave paintings at Lascaux dating to approximately seventeen thousand years ago. Source: Wellcome Library, London. Wellcome Images (Creative Commons).

now common practice of conveying messages—sometimes at the highest levels of national government—via Twitter, Facebook, Instagram, or Snapchat. Both types of communication must be deliberately brief, to the point, and yet referential toward often very big issues. How can this be? How can the most simple of communications—a cave painting on one hand and a "tweet" on the other— convey so much meaning with so few words?

The answer may lie in **semiotics**—the observable relationship between words or images and their meanings. Semiotics is a key tool in the study of visual culture. It was developed by early linguists and anthropologists, but it was later extended in application to myths, literature, and of course popular culture. It is therefore crucial to the discussion below about cultural constructions of expectations about law.

According to semioticians, the experts specializing in this field, every visual object can be considered a **sign.** A stop sign is a "sign." The word *stop* is a "sign." And a picture of a car coming to a stop is a "sign." All three of these convey roughly the same meaning. A sign therefore breaks further down into a **signifier** (the thing representing something) and a **signified** (the thing being represented) (see figure 11.3).

Interestingly, some experts even consider the "signified" itself a "sign." So, the word *bird* consists of the word itself and the bird someone imagines when they

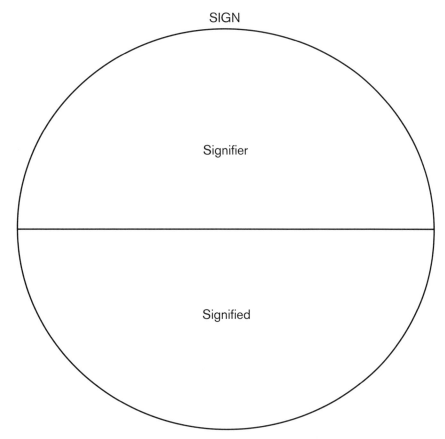

Figure 11.3 Sign/signifier/signified.

read the word. But if we see that bird in the real world sitting on a branch in a tree by the window, it too can be considered a "representation" of a bird. At this point, hard scientists and regular people would probably object by saying reality is not a "representation of reality." This is the kind of topic college students might debate late into the night at a campfire or party, and it is not one we need to resolve here. For our purposes, the implication of semiotics is more straightforward.

The implication is that all images you see on a screen—whether on film or on television—convey a message, and sometimes do so without us knowing. A scene with police detectives interrogating a suspect has become quite common in film and TV crime shows. Sometimes the scene includes an ashtray with a burning cigarette and the ashes from much smoking before it. A semiotician would say the ashtray conveys a sense of "time." It is a sign representing the passage of many minutes or hours, and suggests that the interrogation has taken long, that the suspect may be uncooperative, or that the detectives are relentless. Note that it can also convey a message of poor health conditions; the detectives are so committed to their work they will do anything to stay on the job longer—including risking lung cancer. Finally, the ashtray may represent the conditions in the interrogation room: stuffy, congested, claustrophobic, and hazy.

All of this "analysis" comes from one detail in the scene. Critics of semiotic theory—and cultural studies more generally—would say we are reading our own interpretations into the imagery. They would also say we are imputing our perceptions to other viewers. They have a point. So more rigorous interpretive social scientists would then observe and document how actual people or groups of people interpret the images. They would then generalize from that data. They too have a point. While the imagery of the sign alone is one kind of data, it may be incomplete without the other kind of data—the observed reactions of real people. Without this, isn't the semiotician merely generalizing his or her own interpretive posture onto others?

That question is important—if a little geeky—but it is not by itself our purpose here. I have covered the basics of film and TV recording and semiotic theory only to make a more general point before delving into some real examples. The point is that film and TV producers, directors, editors, and writers have to make choices, and their choices are usually deliberate. Because one cannot show an entire world on screen in thirty minutes, or one hour, or even three hours, the images we see in our film and TV programming have been selected purposely by the creators in order to convey a specific feeling, idea, or message. Not only that, but as an audience we are meant to receive that feeling, idea, or message, but sometimes we do not. The French theorist Louis Althusser—now considered a giant in cultural studies—called this part of the process **interpellation.**[1] The term means to "hail" or "call upon" an audience, but Althusser meant this in a deep sense: the images assembled by popular culture are meant to convey a common sentiment, but also our ability to join the community as it reacts uniformly becomes an important marker of our membership, or belonging in that community. If, for example, I laugh out loud at an onscreen murder in a crowded theater, the people around me might think I am different, poorly socialized, or psychopathic. My interest in being one of them requires me to react the way they do. Others in the audience will feel similarly. Together, we may not naturally be all the same, but we will act that way. The movie we are watching, therefore, does not just appear to its audience, it also helps to *create* it. The audience is interpellated.

"POPULAR" CULTURE

From visual culture, popular culture is a small jump. If all societies have exhibited some form of visual culture since prehistory, popular or "pop" culture is a much more recent phenomenon—though not as recent as you might think. Much related to the notion of *imagined community* described in chapter 4, popular culture seems to have arisen with the advent of mass media; in its earliest days this took the form of print formats like newspapers and novels. The first newspaper was said to have appeared in Germany in the early seventeenth century. This makes sense in part because the printing press first appeared in Germany just 150 years earlier. The earliest newspapers contained news about the business world, though a new version of single-sheet papers called "broadsides" later emerged to declare the guilt or innocence of criminal suspects before public executions.

Newspapers developed to disseminate news of the day, but they took on entertainment roles as well. In doing so, they began a split between "high" and "low" culture that lingers well into the present. "High" culture was often understood to be the cultural forms embraced by the elites and the wealthy. Classical music, critically acclaimed literature, and certain performing arts like ballet and theater all fitted this description. "Low" culture, meanwhile, was the opposite; it was embraced by the "masses" for what was said to be the purpose of distraction or amusement only. Whereas high culture was said to offer some redeeming edification value, low culture was said to "just pass the time away."

This distinction may be illusory, and it may be political. The original plays of William Shakespeare, for instance, were not intended to be "high" culture. On the contrary; they presumed a raucous audience that might throw objects on stage or yell at characters they found distasteful, or heroic. Yet the plays of Shakespeare—less accessible to a general public today because so much of their English is obsolete—are now considered "high" culture.

High culture is defined by its appeal to the elites of a society. Much of that appeal comes from a kind of exclusivity. So for instance, many of the brand names for clothing or fashion accessories are worn by the very wealthy only. The high prices of these items nearly ensure that the general public will not have access to them. This makes their possession by elites even more symbolic: it shows to the world at large that the wearer can access items very few people can. Exclusivity becomes an essential feature of "high" status.

Another more obvious feature is wealth. Because luxury fashion items come with very large price tags, they signal to the world that the wearer is in possession of great wealth, and with it likely also status. Note that the quality of the item may not correspond to the elevated price tag at all. This is made abundantly clear in cases of "high fashion T-shirts" where the same cotton T-shirt one would buy for ten dollars can sell for one hundred dollars if imprinted with the logo of an important designer. This is, of course, an extreme case, and some such items really do come with higher quality, or greater lifelong warranties by the brand that sells them. Overall, however, there is a demonstrable class distinction between "high" and "low" culture that transcends cultural forms from art, literature, music, and fashion.

But this class distinction is only the beginning of a very long conversation. From it spring the many interesting ways in which popular culture becomes a site for resistance, and the ways in which this resistance is then itself bought and sold by elites as a commodity. In our discussions about "place" in chapter 6, we considered some of the ways in which hip-hop music and culture express political resistance to spatial exclusion from the dominant culture. In chapter 12 in the next unit, this role is discussed even further. Racial and ethnic minority youth sometimes relegated to conditions of low socioeconomic status have channeled creative energies into art forms ranging from rap music and graffiti art to break dancing and car customization. As cultural historians like George Lipsitz and Robin Kelley have long said, these artistic creations signal efforts by minority youth, often dispossessed from the larger economy under neoliberalism, to reclaim urban space and find value in a world that would otherwise render them valueless.[2] Many of these new forms have gone on to become successful, multi-billion-dollar industries. Rap music, for example, evolved from a renegade street music in the late 1970s into a prolific wealth generator characterized by luxury fashion, expensive cars, and highly entrepreneurial kingpins. The onetime gangster rap artist Dr. Dre—former member of N.W.A., whose album *Straight outta Compton* told of poverty, crime, and police brutality in South Central L.A.—has today become one of the wealthiest hip-hop artists of all time from the sale of his company Beats Electronics to Apple in 2014 for $3 billion. Once upon a time this outcome might have been a problem for a bona fide rap artist—it is literally what artists once decried as "selling out." Yet today even the renegade "low" forms of pop culture glorify wealth and celebrate elitism and exclusivity in ways that make Dre's story a compelling one that only boosted his credibility.

One reason for this is a general trend in popular culture called **co-optation.** Co-optation is what happens when the new creative acts of resistance, such as the *Straight outta Compton* album, become taken up and taken over by those far beyond its target audience. In the case of gangster rap, this process had already begun in the 1980s, when millions of suburban, white teenagers discovered the new music and embraced it as a general form of teenage rebellion. This helped boost sales of the records beyond what was ever expected, but it also meant that the message about daily life in the inner cities was lost in translation. It also meant that music and television industry elites could profit off of this new minority art form in a way that perhaps did not benefit the communities from which it sprang. Quickly, the path to success as a hip-hop artist became getting "discovered" by a music industry scout and getting "signed" by traditional music executives to large, vertically integrated entertainment companies. Such companies did not want to "rock the boat" too much, and some encouraged the artists to soften their political messages or shift the topic of discussion. It was in that context that the focus of hip-hop music shifted from documenting inner-city life as it existed toward obsessing about wealth and luxury goods as a sign of success. Finally, perhaps the most interesting twist in all of this has been the emergence of hip-hop as a legitimate object of cultural study in anthropology, sociology, and literature departments at Harvard, Yale, and Princeton, among other places. All of this is to illustrate the fact that the distinctions between "high" and "low" culture have been—in the past few decades, thanks in part to urban culture and suburban youth's demand for authentic expressions of angst and resistance—to a great extent turned upside down.

The most relevant feature of forms of popular culture is their ability to express elements of legal culture. **Legal culture** describes the symbols, practices, and values pertinent to a society's conception of rules, institutions, and dispute resolution. Early hip-hop music was often an expression of frustration with inner-city law enforcement, as well as with the court system and prison industry. It conveyed an attitude of hurt and mistrust built up over decades—if not centuries—between the African American community in particular and the legal systems of urbanizing America. It reflected a legal culture full of ambivalence, injustice, and speaking "truth to power."

But it was not the first to do so. Urban music developed in the 1980s was actually joining a long tradition of popular culture portrayals of law and justice. America's fascination with law had long drawn the attention of film and television writers and directors; the courtroom did, in a sense, long serve as a kind of "stage" on which dramatic events and interpretations could be replayed to fixated audiences. Portraying law on film and on television was therefore an efficient and sure way to ensure maximum drama.

LAW IN FILM

The medium of motion picture film was invented in the late nineteenth century as an outgrowth of still photography. Film editing, in which two more sections of film are spliced together, did not emerge until the turn of the century. Synchronous sound—that is the recording and replaying of sound as it occurred in the scene on film—did not arise until the 1920s. This chronology is important because, almost from the very beginning, as early as 1907, motion pictures took law or legal institutions as their subject matter. The first and most remembered high-quality feature film about litigation is *Young Mr. Lincoln*, about the early trial practice experiences of Abraham Lincoln in Springfield, Illinois. Starring Henry Fonda and directed by John Ford, it appeared in 1937, capturing the courtroom like a "stage" that would translate well onto film and thus the "silver screen." In treating the courtroom as stage, or the litigation process as **plot,** filmmakers engage in the very constructive process of visual storytelling. As described above, they make deliberate choices about what to show and what not to show the theatrical audience. Before the advent of videocassettes, movies were watched exclusively in theaters around the country, and therefore in public groups. Portrayals of law thus had to speak to actual people witnessing the projection in real semipublic spaces.

A list of all the films covering litigation of some form is too long to reproduce in any substance here. This section highlights only the key types of portrayals that have emerged over time. The first involves depictions of lawyers specifically. One type of portrayal might be called *lawyers as virtuosos.* Virtuosos show mastery over the world around them; they appear to possess knowledge, skill, or power beyond the average person, and this gives them an almost supernatural quality over and above their fellow men and women. Obviously, in the real world, some lawyers are "better" than others. This is usually measured in terms of case outcomes—who wins most often. But on film, all we usually see is *one* case. For that reason the virtuosity of the really great lawyer must be communicated in more obvious ways. So, on-screen, we see the skilled attorney making an ingenious tactical move on cross-examination, locating an essential missing piece of evidence, provoking heartfelt reactions from the jury, or giving a rousing closing argument. Sometimes we even see all of these in one film. In *To Kill a Mockingbird,* the 1962 film adaptation of the Harper Lee novel, the main character's father Atticus Finch (played by Gregory Peck) must legally defend a poor black man in the rural South during Jim Crow. Near the movie's end, Finch gives a rousing closing statement about prejudice and humanism that is directed not only at the on-screen jury but also at the theatrical audience in mid–civil rights era America. Finch is portrayed not only as a virtuoso (and a virtuous attorney) but also as a virtuosic father; confronted by his two children's fears and flights of fancy, Atticus is always calm, soft-spoken, firm, and wise in his response. In some ways, by combining the ideal father figure with the ideal advocate, author Harper Lee created in Finch the archetype lawyer-as-guardian of justice. As Steven Lubet has said, "No real-life lawyer has done more for the self-image or public perception of the legal profession."[3]

Just a few years earlier, United Artists released *Inherit the Wind*, featuring Spencer Tracey as Henry Drummond, a well-known defense attorney asked to represent a southern schoolteacher prosecuted for teaching evolution in his class. If this sounds familiar it is with good reason. *Inherit the Wind* is adapted from a play that was a fictionalized account of the "Scopes Monkey Trial" of 1925. The Scopes Trial was a high-profile case in which a substitute teacher had dared teach evolution in a Tennessee high school, contrary to a state law prohibiting this. In the real-life story, Drummond was actually the famous attorney Clarence Darrow. Much like the celebrity defense attorneys of a later era, Darrow had become notorious and respected for winning other high-profile cases like that of Chicago teenage murder suspects Leopold and Loeb. A staunch opponent of the death penalty, Darrow used the strategy of getting the defendants to plead guilty and then claiming they had a mental defect during the sentencing trial. In a famous twelve-hour closing argument, he argued that social context and psychological disturbance caused the boys to murder a neighbor just for the "thrill." There he succeeded in allowing the pair to escape a death sentence.

In a similar theatrical fashion, Darrow made the unusual move during the real-life Scopes trial of calling opposing counsel William Jennings Bryan, a former US secretary of state, to the witness stand as an "expert" on biblical interpretation. During his questioning, Darrow asked whether Bryan took the Bible—in which it was said God created Man and Woman—literally. Bryan was forced to say "no," and his statements were reproduced in the print media in a way that turned public opinion against dogmatic prohibitions on teaching evolution. In the movie *Inherit the Wind,* Drummond also examines the opposing lawyer Matthew Brady. The camera takes frequent close-up shots of the pair, with Drummond looking exhausted at times, leaning into the witness stand, and with Brady sweating profusely but defiant in his responses.

"Is it possible, that something is holy to the celebrated agnostic?" Brady asks Drummond.

"Yes!" Drummond replies pointedly—as if stating the punch line for the entire film. "The individual human mind."

Both *To Kill a Mockingbird* and *Inherit the Wind* depict a certain kind of virtuosity among on-screen lawyers: they are well-regarded, respected professionals "serving" on a seemingly doomed case with grace and courage. Public opinion is against the lawyer in each case. But through the sheer power of their professional acumen, they are able to turn that opinion around—even if they ultimately each lose. And maybe that is the point. On-screen, virtuosic lawyering may not be about "winning" in court; it may define winning as success in a broader social, moral context.

A second major theme in the on-screen portrayal of law is the lawyer as a kind of buffoon—someone who appears to be foolish and ill prepared in some ways but then displays unexpected talent in legal reasoning. One high-profile example is the title character from *My Cousin Vinny* (1992), portrayed by Joe Pesci. In the film, Pesci's character has little litigation experience and no successes to his name, but he is asked to travel from New York to rural Alabama to defend his teenage cousin from a murder charge. Both Vinny and his girlfriend, played by Marisa Tomei, are portrayed as stereotypical New York area Italian Americans— a fact meant to play humorously against the southern community residents seen in the film. At several points, the judge, played by classic actor Fred Gwynne, cannot understand Vinny's basic English pronunciations. Made to look nervous, out of place, and incompetent throughout most of the trial, Vinny has a sudden epiphany while questioning a key witness and raises evidence that her eyesight may have prevented her witnessing the crime. Unlike the virtuosic portrayals above—in which the hero-lawyer does *not* win the case—Vinny actually succeeds in exculpating his cousin and friend. In that way the lawyer-as-buffoon narrative may be inverse to the lawyer-as-virtuoso: its power comes from winning when one's own apparent skills suggest that one will lose.

Legally Blonde (2001), featuring Reese Witherspoon, supports this theory. In it, a fashion-minded sorority girl from Los Angeles is dumped by her law school–bound boyfriend for being too airheaded just prior to the latter's departure for Harvard Law. In an attempt to win the boyfriend back, Witherspoon's character Elle Woods makes an unusual and comedic application to the same school complete with a kind of "audition tape" video. Not only is Elle admitted, she is placed in a class with the boyfriend and his now-new girlfriend—a more brainy, somber student, played by Selma Blair, who is from a Brahmin family. Needless to say, despite being a student, and despite being considered airheaded, Elle is asked to represent a wealthy widow on trial for murder after her own professor is dismissed by the client. She of course wins, but it is *how* she wins that is most memorable: Elle shows that the victim's own daughter—who claimed to be washing her hair at the time of the crime just hours after getting a "perm"—actually committed the crime. Anyone who gets that many perms, she said, would know not to wash so soon after the hair treatment. The film pitches the victory as a win for blondes everywhere who would be prejudged on their looks. Yet the whole film needs that prejudgment to succeed as a comedy. Just like *My Cousin Vinny*, it shows an attorney (or law student) succeeding against all indications of skill and knowledge of law. But also it gives would-be law students a certain hope that their failure to stand out intellectually in the past is not a predictor of future success as a lawyer, so these films that feature a buffoonish lawyer may provide some of the more democratizing images of the profession.

In all of these films, though to varying degrees, the court is a setting, the place where the core drama unfolds and where the greatest dramatic tension is created. In another sense it is also a player in the story. This is because the judge him- or herself is often a key focal point. As law professor David Papke points out, judges are often portrayed as strict, authoritarian, and humorless characters in the courtroom.[4] In that sense, they are the perfect "straight man"; in a comedy their unflappable seriousness makes the main character—like Vinny or Elle Woods—look even more outlandish and funny. But the judge is only one figure in many trial settings. The other, the jury, is equally dramatic.

Several courtroom drama films have succeeded in making the jury the focus of the narrative. This may not seem surprising if you consider that juries of nine or twelve laypeople are bound to have disagreements and alliances. But if the purpose of any narrative is to zoom in on the experience, inner monologue, and feelings of one or two main characters, it is surprising that jury films are able to keep focus and attention enough to develop these characters. Two noteworthy films do this especially well.

The classic jury film is *Twelve Angry Men* from 1957. The story is based on a play from 1954 in which a jury deliberates on the guilt of an accused murderer. The jury itself is nearly unanimously convinced of the suspect's guilt, except for one holdout juror—an architect—who raises doubts throughout the deliberations sufficient to change the mind of several of his co-jurors. The film makes a point of depicting the twelve jurors as distinct individuals with names, professions, and personalities. It thus differs considerably from other trial films in which the jury is treated as one single mass. *Twelve Angry Men*'s jury includes a high school football coach, a bank teller, a businessman, a stockbroker, a young sports fan, a painter, a salesman, an architect, an elderly man, a mechanic, a naturalized German watchmaker, and an advertising executive. On one hand, it is easy to criticize this lineup from the 1957 adaptation as uniformly white and mostly middle class. In later versions like the 1997 adaptation, African American and Latino actors are used to play several of the key jurors. But one has to remember that in 1957 America civil justice, not to mention on-screen popular culture, was heavily skewed toward white, middle-class demographics. This does not excuse the homogeneity shown in the earlier film, but it does contextualize it as part of a larger pattern that bears remembering.

Runaway Jury (2003), based on a John Grisham novel of the same name, does not make that mistake. Its jury is much more of a cross section of the American public, including ethno-racial minorities, a military veteran, and of course a number of female jurors (conspicuously missing from the early *Twelve Angry Men* versions). The film is an ambitious story covering a list of key topics about the civil justice system. First, it is foremost a jury film in that the jury, one juror in particular, not the lawyers or the judge, is the main focal point. Second, it attempts to show the role moneyed interests play in the US civil justice system. The romantic view considers juries the "oracular" element infused into the legal system; by representing community it legitimizes the courts and eliminates fears of corruption or tampering. *Runaway Jury* suggests juries can be easily tampered with or manipulated. And indeed, doing so at high cost are jury consultants hired by major corporate defendants willing to pay millions so as not to lose at trial. Finally, although lawyers are not the primary focus, they are an important feature. Viewers see the defense counsel, who is seemingly working as a puppet of the consultants and the defendant corporation, juxtaposed against the plaintiff's counsel—played by Dustin Hoffman to great effect—a heroic, morally searching, and emotionally invested southern lawyer. Equally on display, therefore, is an opposition between slick northern, urban legal experts, ostensibly from New York or Chicago, and a southern small-firm attorney.

Jury films are a subset of the trial film genre made popular since the early days of American cinema. They are particularly intriguing since, although some people have served on juries, most people do not really know how juries operate behind closed doors. Film dramas about juries therefore open a window onto this idiosyncratic institution of our system. But they also reflect back to us what a cross section of our population looks and sounds like when locked in a room deciding the fate of an accused human being, or a multinational corporation. Nevertheless, everything shown on screen in these films, as with all trial films in general, is carefully chosen and survives the editing process. If film editing begins with hundreds or thousands of hours of raw film footage, one has to imagine that the 90 to 120 minutes of film left in the "final cut" was the most important imagery the director had assembled. Films are costly to make, so these decisions usually, but not always, are also meant to be the most efficient way to communicate a message to the audience. Less costly than film, though no less deliberate, is television.

LAW ON TELEVISION

Television technology is slightly younger than film, but its origins may also be older than you would think. The first moving pictures transmitted wirelessly were sent in the 1910s. The first US patent for TV-like transmissions was granted in 1925, and the technology remained crude up through the Second World War. In the 1940s, wireless communication and amplification advances made consumer-level television more possible, and within ten years TV became the predominant means of affecting public opinion in the United States. Between 1942 and 1949, roughly 3.5 million TV sets were sold in the United States. Between 1950 and 1959 that number was roughly 63 million. The 1954 TV broadcast of *Twelve Angry Men* could have reached as many as 35 million viewers,[5] but perhaps more important is the fact that TV program producers turned so quickly to courtroom drama to fill the new airwaves with compelling content. The same period saw the advent of TV "cop shows" like *Dragnet* (1951–59), which was actually a radio program adapted for the visual medium. *Dragnet* claimed to be the reenactment of investigations from actual case files taken from the Los Angeles Police Department. Other police and detective shows from this classic era include *Charlie Wild, Private Detective* (1950), *Highway Patrol* (1955), *Perry Mason* (1957), and *Peter Gunn* (1958).

There have been several explanations for why law enforcement dramas became so popular in the 1950s. One is that they are, in a sense, easy. If *Dragnet* is any example, these stories needed little creativity if they could be simply pulled from the headlines or police files and adapted directly to the small screen. Those that had been radio shows were especially ripe for transfer to the visual medium. But on a deeper level, some believe American society "craved" these kinds of programs. The 1950s were a period in which many adult men— roughly sixteen million—had just returned from serving in World War II in Europe and the South Pacific. The onset of the Cold War brought fears of foreign ideas and surreptitious "infiltration." And the late 1950s brought the desegregation and early counterculture movements. It was, in short, a time of fragile peace on the American home front; soldiers returned from war to start families but retreated to suburbs where racial integration and crime were believed to be remote "threats" to domestic living. The law enforcement shows of this period, in short, reminded TV set owners that the world was divided easily into "good guys" and "bad guys" and that professional "good guys" out there were keeping "bad guys" in check. We might also note that this was a heyday for cowboy western shows, where good and bad were depicted often in the opposition of light and dark skin seen between "cowboys and Indians." This all brought a sense of comfort and moral certainty to a public trying to avoid thinking about the moral ambiguities of a world war.

The television cop dramas saw a decline during the 1960s. Many believe this was in part due to the rise of student protests and the Vietnam antiwar movement—two contemporary trends that made state authority and law enforcement less popular themes among the youth. Nevertheless, as the late 1960s and early 1970s saw the decline of those movements, many began to view the "hippie generation" as one riddled with new problems emergent out of the "free love" and drug cultures. The 1970s, therefore, brought a return of law enforcement in TV dramas with shows like *Baretta, Kojak, Police Woman, CHiPs,* and *Police Story.* Cop shows of the 1970s brought darker themes than the earlier period, and they made use of new technological advances in production such as full-color recording cameras, new synthesizer music, and more lightweight equipment allowing the rise of the now infamous TV car chase scene.

Today, cop shows focus often on crime investigative technologies themselves. *Crime Scene Investigators* (*CSI*) became one of the most popular and long-running crime shows, airing from 2000 to 2015. *CSI* featured a forensic crime lab team trying to solve mysteries each week through the gathering and analysis of physical evidence. The main characters, meanwhile, were the investigators themselves. whose personal issues and character flaws become the source for dramatic irony, tension, and humor. *CSI* was so popular it spawned a wave of spinoff programs such as *CSI: Miami,* and *CSI: New York.* These programs are just some of the many examples where law enforcement television has turned increasingly to crime laboratories for content and has therefore shown the public that criminal justice is increasingly merged with hard science.

But just as crime TV turned to science, courtroom shows focused on the dramas of being a lawyer. Beginning with *L.A. Law* in the late 1980s, interest in life inside the US law firm seems to have grown over the years. *L.A. Law* premiered in 1986 and set the tone for many of the courtroom programs of the next decade. With high-quality writing and a large group of up-and-coming actors who would go on to become very successful, *L.A. Law* won fifteen Emmy awards during its run. It also sparked a major uptick in the number of law school applications in the late '80s. Subsequent shows like *Ally McBeal* kept the public interest in the topic alive. *Ally McBeal* was significant, as it featured for the first time a young woman in the lead role of white-collar professional navigating the distinct stresses of being female and junior in the hierarchical, male law firm environment. *Boston Legal* and *Franklin and Bash,* in more recent years, took this focus on lawyer personal idiosyncrasies to another level by showing the moral trade-offs made by both male and female attorneys as they engaged in open conflict and romantic relations with one another, with their clients, and even with adversaries.

Finally, no overview of law on TV could miss the rise of the reality courtroom program. Beginning in the 1980s with *The People's Court,* these programs show disputants appearing in front of a "judge"—often a retired judge or arbitrator—for a real-life hearing. In reality, these are not formal "courts" at all but rather forms of alternative dispute resolution to which parties must agree before appearing on camera. Whereas this genre began with only one or two programs, it has since exploded into dozens of programs on most major networks broadcasted usually in the midday period. Judge Judy has become the most flamboyant, quotable example as she admonishes the parties for spinning the truth by saying, "Don't pee on my leg and tell me it's raining!" Courtroom reality shows may be part of a larger trend toward "reality TV" in the last several decades. The programs are fast and easy to produce, and audiences become hooked on what they perceive to be the real-life problems of people just like themselves. They dispense with the boring, technical details of legal procedure—details that most of the judicial system is geared toward respecting—and instead focus right in on the interpersonal, emotional conflict behind most legal disputes. Some of these programs are less reality than others too; they have been known to hire amateur actors to play out cases "as if" they were really unfolding in front of the judge. In this way too, by blending "real" and "fiction," they truly are of a piece with contemporary television culture and its influence on politics and law in the so-called real world around us.

LAW ONLINE

After film and television, online communications beginning in the 1990s became the next major medium for the transmission of popular imagery about law, lawyers, courts, and disputants. Online communications consist of a wide variety of idioms from ordinary text that we read on screen, to video clips watched by millions on YouTube, to social media sites like Facebook and Twitter where people rapidly share all of the above. This rapid sharing may be what makes the online environment so special. Whereas the texts and clips themselves can be conventional—akin to newspaper stories or TV commercials—their "sharing" has revolutionized information flows about law and society today.

Facebook and Twitter are but two examples of social media—the kind of online communication where people connect to one another on the basis of shared interests or experiences and then pass information to and from one another through those connections. On a platform like Facebook, users have their own profile in which personal information like age and education are filled in, and they can post new stories and events to that page as often as they like, but they also see a "newsfeed" of their contacts and their stories and events. The result is a virtual public square in which the individual feels part of a community. Twitter is much like Facebook but without the wide latitude in what can be posted; there messages are limited to 280 characters, and abbreviations and code-speak are more common. Twitter can still share news stories linked to the *New York Times* or newer outlets like BuzzFeed, as well as more recently video and photos.

The technicalities of these media are less important than the content people share through them. Without this content they are just databases. Indeed, the sites themselves are constantly gathering data on user behavior, preferences, and dislikes, and they have gained attention for sometimes selling that data to corporations for marketing and behavioral research.

Because they are content driven, and because stories and events can be shared so easily, these media have also shaped what counts as news. Just in the past several years, large geopolitical events have been triggered because an average person shot video or still images with a cell phone and transmitted that to their own friends, who in turn transmitted them further, and so on. In the United States, this has been seen time and again with cases of excessive police force. Video footage of such cases goes at least as far back as the March 7, 1991, video of Rodney King being kicked and clubbed by a half-dozen Los Angeles police officers. At that time, the video was shown in clips across TV news stations. By the time the officers were acquitted of wrongdoing a year later, the general public had a pretty good sense about the anger and frustration and were less surprised by the L.A. riots that resulted. But the video itself was not the focal point.

Today, when such cases arise, the video—sometimes captured by police body cameras but more often by bystander cell phone camera—gets shared via social media and spreads like wildfire. In the case of Eric Garner, a 350-pound, asthmatic African American man apprehended by police in New York for allegedly selling untaxed cigarettes, the video was outrageous. It showed three police officers wrestling Garner to the ground outside a liquor store and pinning him with a chokehold, as Garner gasped for air while screaming, "I can't breathe!" roughly eleven times. Once Garner lost consciousness the officers released their hold but made no effort to perform CPR. Within minutes, Garner was dead. A bystander captured video of this horrible scene and shared it quickly on social media. It left no ambiguities about Garner's suffocation and his ultimate death. The video was shared millions of times across Facebook, Twitter, and the like. It did much to galvanize the movement already taking shape known as Black Lives Matter.

The sharing of videos on social media does much to influence people's views of the law and law enforcement. In the above cases, it leads many to conclude—upon seeing the way law enforcement treats people of color—that there are two different justice standards in the world today. But these videos also take on new meaning when the officers responsible for these incidents are exculpated of wrongdoing by review boards, judges, and juries.

Another, very different implication of the online environment for messages about law pertains to the legal profession and practice of law. Lawyers have long been limited in the kinds of advertising they are permitted to conduct in attempting to recruit new clients. Prior to the 1977 Supreme Court case of *Bates v. Arizona,* lawyer advertising itself could be banned in any given state by the relevant state bar authority.[6] *Bates* held that lawyer advertising was protected commercial speech and therefore subject to constitutional protections that prohibited an all-out ban. Since then, the doors have opened to newer, more creative forms of attorney advertising. The most common include TV ads seen on daytime television and bus stop ads, both aimed heavily at potential personal injury (PI) clients. The modern rules on lawyer professional conduct specify certain requirements for advertising now, but within those limits is considerable latitude for "creative" claims about "reasonable" fees and satisfied clients.

The online space has opened up new avenues for advertising of this kind. Today lawyers are able to purchase ad space on websites directly targeted to the clients they wish to find. This is no different from other kinds of online advertising, but note that it could run afoul of existing ethics rules. For example, lawyers are not permitted to hang around emergency rooms to recruit personal injury clients in the real world. But they probably are permitted to advertise PI legal services on websites for pharmacies, urgent care, and medical devices.

Not only that, but there has been a marked rise in the number of attorney blogs and podcasts. Blogs, or "weblogs," allow users to post stories and update their website easily as often as they like. Blogs have become a major source of local news for people, and many have gained huge followings or been purchased and absorbed by traditional outlets like the *New York Times.* Attorney blogs are frequently about contemporary legal questions like "Are Uber or other ridesharing service companies 'common carriers' for liability purposes?" or "How can I copyright my own online independent music?" Law firms today often hire clerks who specialize in writing up these kinds of stories. Some have gone farther to record and post "podcasts"—essentially audio discussions of the same kinds of issues, sometimes with guests and experts. These kinds of blogs raise a number of issues. Is their publication tantamount to legal advice? If so, does its transmission across state lines constitute unauthorized practice of law without a license? And do all readers and listeners of this information become prospective clients of the authoring firm? Many of these questions will need to be resolved in the coming years. Until they are, it suffices to say that the explosion in online communications has changed the way lawyers engage with the society around them.

The last important thing new communications have affected is access to legal authorities and legal expertise. Whereas one used to have to visit a law library or speak to an expert in person, today most of the initial research for these things takes place online. First of all, one can easily search Google for preliminary information about a kind of claim, procedure, or institutional forum. Sites like the Cornell University Legal Information Institute have published a legal dictionary and federal and state authority information online since the 1990s. Other for-profit online resources include LegalZoom and Legal Shield. The latter offer printable forms and task-based services and advice. Many are talking about all new artificial intelligence or chatbot lawyers that will be able to give online advice directly without human contact at all. But for those still in need of traditional lawyering, finding a licensed expert has become easier through searchable databases like Martindale-Hubbell, AVVO, and the state bar website of most jurisdictions.

CONCLUSION

Greater ease in finding the law or finding an attorney is just the latest outcome of an increasing presence of law and lawyers in popular media. That presence has deep roots in the early film and television portrayals that are nearly as old as film and television themselves. Content producers early on realized that few things are more dramatic and theatrical than the drama and theater of real life, and law has been a key site for stimulating those. The choices made by film and TV directors to show some images and not others are deliberate. Whatever imagery and sound we see in the final "cut" of a movie or show is the result of considerable editing in which hours and hours of footage have been spliced together to maximize audience impact. Usually far more footage has been cast away in the process.

Audience impact from these images is the result of the semiotic process described at the top of this chapter. Each picture we see evokes an idea in our mind, and knowing this, directors can depict scenes without showing too much at all. One thinks, for instance, of the image in early black-and-white films of the curtains blowing in an open window to stand in for a love scene, or the silhouette of a man with an inverted knife raised high in the air to stand in for the direct portrayal of a murder. The minimalist imagery often evokes a lot more than a highly realistic portrayal of romance or violence does. Not only that, but individual audience members want to see these images in the same way as their peers. This interpellation process has been a key feature of visual culture for as long as humans have kept records. In part for this reason, some cultural artifacts appeal as "high" culture while others appeal as "low"—both have their place in our society, but each is marked by the class dimensions of its interpretation.

Film, TV, and Internet forms of culture seem to transcend these divides today. While early black-and-white films and programs might be considered to be "classic" and therefore to suggest establishment, tradition, and historic values, they are equally accessible to most members of the society through DVDs, online streaming, and remaining theater and cable TV showings. Similarly, the Internet is generally—especially since the advent of wireless data streaming—accessible to all. Meanwhile, the rise of popular culture as a legitimate field of study in colleges and universities has further upended the distinction between high and low. The Broadway musical *Hamilton*, made popular in 2015, is perhaps one recent example of this; its popularity spread thanks in part to social media. Depicting classic scenes from American history through the medium of hip-hop music and the acting talents of people of color, it rose to become the most popular Broadway show of all time.

Portrayals of lawyers, juries, and judges on film, TV, and online can educate the general public about the legal system and the pursuit of justice. They serve, in a sense, as a public relations extension of legal education and the legal profession. Popular culture depictions of law, therefore, further drive home the point that law is itself a form of social practice.

CHAPTER 11 REVIEW

Keywords

- Popular culture
- Visual culture
- Semiotics
- Sign
- Signifier
- Signified
- Interpellation
- Co-optation
- Legal culture
- Plot

Further Discussion

1. Are popular portrayals of law and lawyers good or bad for justice in society? Why?
2. Do portrayals of law and lawyers make for good evidence about the way society views these important players? Or are they merely entertainment?

3. What new formats or technologies for cultural content do you foresee emerging in the next decade, and how might these too become sites for expressing legal culture?
4. Is there a meaningful difference between "high" and "low" culture? What role might law play in this?

Further Reading

Althusser, Louis. "Ideology and Ideological State Apparatuses (Notes towards an Investigation)." In *Lenin and Philosophy and Other Essays*, 85–126. New York: Monthly Review Press, 2001.

Lubet, Steven. "Reconstructing Atticus Finch." *Michigan Law Review* 97, no. 6 (May 1999): 1339–62. doi:10.2307/1290205.

Papke, David Ray. "The Impact of Popular Culture on American Perceptions of the Courts." *Indiana Law Journal* 82 (2007): 1225–34.

SPECIAL TOPICS OF ADVANCED SOCIOLEGAL CHANGE

4

Unit 3 made clear that law and legal expertise are preeminently social constructs. Professional lawyers enter the legal education process as regular men and women but come out "thinking like" or "speaking like" a lawyer. This transformation could not take place without the direct, one-to-one interaction between students and professors, and later between junior and experienced attorneys. Once inducted, new lawyers must follow specific forms of reasoning and procedure unique to the legal environment. These are the components that make up the larger notion of legal practice. Finally, we saw how popular cultural forms—such as television and film—contribute to social expectations for what the law is supposed to do. All of these observations help explain why law is both flexible and slow to change. As a product of social construction, it can neither lag too far behind social norms nor move too quickly to change them.

Unit 4 looks closer at changes taking place in fast-moving areas of sociolegal life. Chapter 12 examines "Art Forms"; eschewing the stand-alone term *art* for a more self-conscious title, it describes law's role in helping to decide what even counts as art in our society. Chapter 13 looks at technology, with specific emphasis on genetics research and information technology. DNA, we will see, has revolutionized aspects of criminal law, while social media have given rise to new harms under libel law. Chapter 14 looks at nature, or more specifically the environment, as a final important site for intense sociolegal change. Interested in complex developments like climate change and the arrival of the Anthropocene—both of which could signal a turning point for human planetary survival—this chapter is in some senses a rallying cry for attention to the more urgent changes in law and society today.

Art Forms

On the surface, "art" and "law" appear to have little in common. Art seems to deal with the world of images, colors, creativity, and fashion. Law is said to be logical, black and white, formal, and slow changing. Humanists, those who study the experience of being human, might say that each represents a different facet of the human condition: one seeks free-flowing expression and the other seeks order and security. But on closer inspection these two spheres of experience overlap at some very specific and illuminating sites throughout the social environment. Moreover, by focusing in on those sites, students of law and society can learn something altogether new about the relatedness of these two realms. Art is therefore an intriguing site for advanced study and application of sociolegal knowledge. This chapter takes up this subject by focusing on several key examples where art and law have met each other with fascinating results.

For instance, in 1980, the New Jersey Supreme Court heard a case in which an artist got word that a collector outside New York City had three paintings identical to ones she had lost decades earlier.[1] The paintings, she said, had been stolen from her companion's own gallery in Manhattan all the way back in 1946. The defendant collector said that he had rightfully purchased the pieces from a gallery in Princeton, New Jersey, the previous year. He argued that even if the paintings had once been stolen, so much time had since passed that the original artist could no longer claim them as her own. Why all the hassles over a few small paintings?

The artist was Georgia O'Keeffe—one of the most important American painters from the twentieth century. Whereas the value of the paintings was reported around $150 at the time of the original theft, O'Keeffe had become very popular in the intervening years, to the extent that she was known as the "mother of American Modernism."[2] By 1975 those paintings had a value of approximately $35,000—or close to $200,000 in today's money. By 1980 that value would have only increased further given O'Keeffe's stature. So, given the amount of time passed and assuming the paintings were indeed stolen, how should the court handle this?

O'Keeffe had brought the claim as an action for **replevin.** Replevin is a cause of action derived from the courts of equity once common in New England following the legal traditions of Great Britain. Under **equity,** claimants could argue essentially that a ruling in their favor was a matter of basic fairness and justice rather than formal common-law norms. *Replevin* comes from an Old French word meaning "to recover"; the claimant uses it to recover goods from an adverse party immediately, on the theory that to allow delay would be to permit injustice or waste. In O'Keeffe's case, her opponent argued that too much time had passed to grant her request for replevin. All legal claims are typically barred by a **statute of limitations** preventing people from coming back years after an incident when evidence was lost or murky. In New Jersey at the time, the statute of limitations for replevin was six years, and this term is common across the United States. But, argued O'Keeffe's lawyers, there was one problem. How can a plaintiff assert a claim within six years after a theft when the theft may be undetected for a matter of decades? It was this question that persuaded the New Jersey Supreme Court to change state law. Rather than uphold the rigid statute of limitations, the court decided to apply the **discovery rule,** a principle stating that the clock measuring statutes of limitations only begins to run once the underlying injury has been discovered. This rule, they said, was particularly important to apply in the world of collectible art. Can you guess why?

In the first place, valuable art thefts are *frequently* undiscovered until years after their occurrence. Paintings, sculptures, photographs, and the like are often stored in deep, climate-controlled cellars, vaults, and storage rooms around the world. These are places where their absence may remain unnoticed for some time.

In the second place, collectible works of art accrue in value over time. This was true for O'Keeffe, just as it remains true for most of the artists described later in this chapter. That being the case, the would-be art thief would gain a major incentive to commit crimes because they could count on receiving the full future value of the stolen goods so long as they could keep the theft undetected for six or more years. By departing from the standard statute of limitations rules, the New Jersey Supreme Court recognized that art bandits should not benefit from the passage of time after their underlying offense. They should not, in other words, be rewarded for being especially *good* criminals.

These considerations of time and value as they pertain to artwork are actually far more illuminating than initially appears. O'Keeffe's was a case in which the economics of the art world likely played a role in the court's retooling of procedural rules, as well as the artist's own case outcome. But as I have suggested throughout this book, law's embrace of neoliberalism has been in the making since the latter half of the twentieth century. This chapter, therefore, continues that suggestion by applying it to visual arts—a field fraught with difficulties in valuation, physical preservation, and public/private property distinctions. In this chapter, the central question may simply be whether and how any one work of art will be deemed legal or illegal. I maintain that since the latter twentieth century it is economics that most frequently determines the answers to this question. In other words, whether a work of art becomes classified as an improvement or an affront to society through law is often a question of the wider economic implications of the work itself. In that regard, although we might often view paintings, murals, photos, and the like within a bounded frame separate from their worlds around them, they are in fact symbols of wider social contexts that can determine their legality.

To support this point, this chapter traverses several key topics. The first section deals with the meanings of "art" itself. Clearly, these meanings are always contested and shifting; nevertheless, the battles over meaning tell us as much about the social world as do the works of art themselves. In particular, we will be interested ultimately in the role law plays in those battles. The second section looks closer at specific forms of public art and urban culture. What kinds of artwork embellish public spaces, and why are some treasured and others vilified? This section also requires that we consider the role of "urban culture" more generally—a concept that has appeared in previous chapters but one whose aesthetic dimensions have so far been only lightly treated. The last section zooms in further on the work of one public artist in particular, the international art provocateur who calls himself "Banksy."

MEANINGS OF ART, CULTURE, AND LAW

Visual arts are nearly as old as human beings themselves. The previous chapter mentioned the cave paintings at Lascaux as one of the earliest examples of humans attempting to visually depict the world around them in a medium—in that case paint and stone. The works are estimated to be approximately twenty thousand years old.

From 2600 to 1100 BC, the Minoan civilization of the European Bronze Age mastered several art forms, including pottery, fresco painting, and jewelry, in

Figure 12.1 Minoan ceramic jar dating to at least the twelfth century BCE. Photo by Zde (Creative Commons).

ways that ushered in the Greek classical age and have influenced Western art ever since. While these early artistic works appear at the beginning of most art history textbooks, they are significant in that they were primarily functional objects or architectural features. They were, in that sense, decorative of otherwise valued objects. They also represented the world in ways that were natural, albeit stylized (see figure 12.1).

What this means is that the images depicted on works like this Minoan vase were intended to evoke the real animal—a serpent, for example—rather than draw attention to human perceptions of it. This approach was replicated throughout classical art; it can be seen in the extremely faithful marble sculpture work of the Romans in the first century AD, or the Christian biblical scenes depicted in Byzantine frescos from the sixth to tenth centuries.

Following a period of political fragmentation and infighting known as the "Dark Ages," the European Renaissance brought a renewed wealth and prosperity such that patron families like the famous Medici banking clan of Florence became the supporters of numerous influential artists of the age. Leonardo da Vinci, Rafael, and Michelangelo all received financial backing from members of this wealthy family and produced several of the most revered works of the Renaissance as a result. In all cases, however, the style of this

Figure 12.2 Claude Monet, *Haystacks*, 1891. Musée d'Orsay.

period was conservative. Indeed, with advances in the physical tools of art production, Renaissance painting became even more "realist" than classical art had ever been. Wealthy benefactors like the Medicis wanted their artists to paint portraits of themselves and their friends, or else religious scenes that would elevate the family in the graces of a Christian God. Even the Renaissance's new interest in landscape paintings pursued the most realistic reproduction of scenes of nature. There was a direct correlation between the political-economic security enjoyed by an artist and that artist's approach to visualizing the world around him. In this way, the very definition of art was dependent upon the tastes of the wealthy.

Jumping ahead in time several centuries, artistic taste saw its next major upheavals during the period now referred to as "modernism." Modernist art began to play with the idea of representing the world. Whereas most of its predecessors believed that the most faithful depiction of a person, a place, or a thing was the best way to reproduce the experience of it, modernists began to realize and then practice an idea of art as simply evocative of that experience. Therefore, painters or photographers no longer needed to capture the world most accurately; on the contrary, to the extent that their works showed dramatic departures from "real" images—departures like exaggerated shadows, blurred lines, and even distorted shapes—they could *better* illustrate what it was like to be in the moments they depicted. Perhaps the greatest example of this would be *Haystacks*, a series of paintings composed by Claude Monet around 1890 (see figure 12.2).

The series is significant for a few main reasons. First, it depicts a mundane landscape scene from late nineteenth-century rural French life. In that period, landscape painting tended to show more dramatic subjects like forests or mountains. From his rural retreat in Giverny outside Paris, Monet simply painted scenes of ordinary nature or peasant life in the community around him. In that sense, *Haystacks* is a soft chronicle of farm life at the time. Second, the artist chose to depict the subject some twenty-five times in different color palettes and from different angles. None appears to show a perfect reproduction of what the human eye would have seen. All play with color and light in dreamlike fashion, giving one the feeling that one is looking upon a farm in the predawn hours before one's eyes have fully even opened. For that reason, the paintings have both a natural and otherworldly feeling about them. Above all else, Monet, like his impressionist contemporaries in Europe at the time, made no effort to conceal his own brushstrokes. The paintings seem almost like a mosaic of discrete artistic movements memorialized on the canvas. In each of these ways, *Haystacks*, like most of this artist's other work, is a paradigmatic example of early modernism. This movement would develop further through the 1970s both in Europe and across the rest of the world. It is significant, however, that it found one of its most formidable opponents in the World War II era.

In Nazi Germany, art was viewed as a powerful tool for political mobilization and consensus building. Adolf Hitler, himself a failed painter, came to resent the wealthy financiers of Berlin, who tended to sponsor rising artists other than himself and who happened to be ethnically Jewish. Through his rise to power and notoriety, Hitler famously drew sketches of Nazi uniforms, monuments, and buildings, making robust use of his aesthetic training and practice. He also went so far as to sponsor exhibitions of "degenerate art"—a term broadly applied to any forms of what is now understood as "modern" art, but one that tended to target Jewish and communist artists. In Munich in 1937, the *Entartete Kunst* exhibition attracted over two million visitors and was designed to generate public reaction against modernism. It displayed the works of artists like Paul Klee, Marc Chagall, Hans Richter, and Piet Mondrian—people whose work today is considered highly valuable. Beyond these kinds of grotesque exhibitions, the Nazis also burned thousands of valuable pieces in the name of aesthetic purity.

It is significant that the archetypical regime of European fascism chose to fight one of its most remembered cultural battles at the site of visual arts. Hitler's repression of modernism stemmed in part from his own vendetta against the art world. But it was also based on his understanding that social control depended in part on the control of aesthetic taste. Whereas, independently, individuals can often disagree over what constitutes "good" aesthetics—whether in music, art, architecture, or poetry—a tightly controlled civil society will exhibit uncannily uniform attitudes toward styles and fashions. In effect, this is a hallmark of fascism itself. But this point has larger implications for a chapter on law and society. Law, we saw early in this book, is in large part a tool for social control, and Western liberalism tries to place that tool in the service of human "liberty"—often construed as freedom to act in open markets. Socialism, by comparison, tries to place that tool in the service of the "greater good," or at least one party's conception of that. And Islamic legal cultures use it in the service of religious piety. The fascists of Nazi Germany were keenly aware of the control capacities of law as applied to visual arts, and their blanket attack on "degenerate art" offers a stark illustration of the relationship between power, law, and the meaning of "art."

Two later movements round out a very loose chronology of Western art history relevant for this chapter. Those are "pop art" and "postmodernism." Pop art was a movement active from the 1960s through 1990s that construed everyday objects and images of popular culture—items like soup cans or laundry detergent boxes—as objects of art. Pop art was conceived and promoted by several highly trained American artists with names like Roy Lichtenstein and Andy Warhol. But one of its hallmark contributions was a democratization of the fine art world. If paintings of soup cans could now be considered priceless and hung in the most elite galleries, then the meaning of "art" could now include items barely touched by an artist's hand at all. If so, then anyone could create it, and it could be found almost anywhere. Pop art, therefore, set the stage for what would arise in the subsequent decades on the streets of American inner cities when cans of paint would wind up in the hands of untrained urban youth.

The second movement with similar significance was postmodernism. This style—considered to have emerged in the 1970s—was in effect an amalgamation of virtually all art styles that came before it. This mishmash style was labeled *pastiche* by art critics. Along with these multilayered references to other styles, postmodernism refers to historical eras of the past and reveals the artistic process to the viewer in ways modernism only touched upon. In effect, postmodernism further democratized art by making even the works of "high" artists appear to be improvisation—a kind of do-it-yourself. This, of course, further opened up the world of art to more peoples and styles.

Visual arts in the United States, perhaps even up until the present, are often dominated by white, middle-class artists. To dedicate one's life to producing painting, sculpture, and the like has often required certain privilege that was inaccessible to working-class Americans or people of color. For that reason, culture in those communities tended to historically evolve as "folk" art—productions that were made largely in the home outside of "normal" working hours. But, beginning around the 1970s, new genres of urban culture began to emerge that would become truly distinct, valued art forms authentically emergent from poor and working-class neighborhoods in American inner cities.

URBAN CULTURE

Art forms can be dangerous. They are capable of encouraging viewers and listeners to reimagine the world around them in ways that display more justice, caring, and basic fairness. As expected, authorities often find this capacity threatening to the established order in society. The Nazi hatred for modernism was a prime example of that. But another perhaps closer to home has been the period of political and legal crackdowns on urban youth culture. This phrase refers to the forms of popular culture found commonly—and usually pioneered—by ethnic, racial, and class minority youth in large cities. There people live in denser neighborhoods, often speak in non-English languages and dialects, and usually incorporate elements of style and design imported from another land of emigration. At numerous points in time, authorities in the United States have moved in to repress or to sanction the repression of urban youth exhibiting forms of popular culture that—in their critical nature—seem to challenge accepted social norms.

A few examples of this are especially instructive. The first is the infamous Zoot Suit Riots of 1940s Los Angeles. At that time, L.A.'s Mexican American population was already strong in its identity. Thousands of Mexicans had remained in Southern California since the days of the Spanish colony, and thousands more had been arriving in the early twentieth century to work in the city's growing industries. Meanwhile, L.A.'s population expanded rapidly, with many southern blacks leaving the Jim Crow South in search of better opportunities out west, and many white migrants from Oklahoma and Arkansas arriving during the Dust Bowl era, fleeing desiccated farmlands.

In the early 1940s, when the United States entered World War II, basic materials like sugar and flour, as well as metals and fabric, were in especially high demand and short supply. Americans were expected to "serve" the war effort by cutting back their consumption of these raw materials. Meanwhile, Mexican American youth in Los Angeles began to embrace the "zoot suit," a kind of flowing men's fitted suit with inflated shoulders and pant legs, often in bright colors, and topped off sometimes with a wide brimmed felt hat, as seen in figure 12.3.

Public wearing of a zoot suit in early 1940s Los Angeles meant one of two things. It meant the wearer was particularly "hip," aware of and ahead of the latest trends in fashion and style, or it meant he was a traitor, purposely using up extra fabrics to stymie the war effort and help the Axis Powers—America's enemy at the time. Police began responding to individual altercations between patriotic white youth and Mexican American zoot suiters in the city before finally, in late May 1943, a group of white sailors confronted a group of zoot suiters in downtown L.A. and a fight broke out. In the aftermath of that incident, police and off-duty military servicemen—many hailing from the Deep South, where lynchings were common—poured into downtown. It all

Figure 12.3 Three men wearing versions of the zoot suit. Photo by Ollie Atkins, 1946. National Archives, Richard Nixon Library and Museum.

culminated in one incident on June 4 in which two hundred white men in twenty taxis rode to East L.A.—a primarily Mexican enclave—and attacked a group of young boys, stripping them of their zoot suits and burning the garments in a pile. From there, similar incidents spread across the city.

Most significantly, then-governor of California (and future Supreme Court chief justice) Earl Warren ordered an investigation of the riots. The McGucken Report held that racist targeting of "pachucos" or Mexican American zoot suiters was the cause of the violence. Notably, it found that this violence was actually abetted by L.A. law enforcement in the early days of the violence, meaning that—in short—it was a state-sanctioned attack on the ethnic community. Whereas the explanation given was animosity caused by the zoot suit phenomenon, the underlying cause was more likely interethnic tensions that had been simmering in a city of increasing ethno-racial diversity. Notably, the sternest reactions came only after the Mexican government lodged a complaint with

Figure 12.4 1963 Chevy Impala lowrider custom demonstrating hydraulic lift modifications. Photo by Jarek Tuszyńsk, 2011 (Creative Commons).

the US State Department threatening to suspend trade. Since Mexico was its largest trading partner, California responded with the McGucken investigation. Once more, economic considerations influenced the search for justice.

The Zoot Suit Riots were a reaction by white Americans against not simply the presence of Mexican American youth in wartime Los Angeles, but also their reassertion of identity and claims on urban space. At a time when all were expected to fall into step with the economics of the war effort, pachucos wanted to stand out as style pioneers, in an aesthetic departure from the crew cuts, slacks, and cotton shirts of middle America.

A similar reassertion would follow that era in the form of lowrider car culture. Lowriders are a form of customized automobiles where the owner lowers the car body by modifying key components of the car including the block, the shock absorbers, and the spindles (figure 12.4). In addition, lowrider owners frequently painted their cars bright custom colors like turquoise, magenta, and the like so that they stood out on city streets against the dominant black-colored cars available in the late 1940s. By the late 1950s, these colors were becoming standard on American cars, but this shift was arguably influenced by the customizing counterculture of the lowriders.

Significantly, the movement also started in postwar Los Angeles among Mexican American men of the **barrios,** or Latino/a neighborhoods. According to the cultural historian George Lipsitz, lowrider customization among these communities was seen as an ironic commentary on the highly standardized American auto-manufacturing norms of the era.[3] Not unlike the zoot suiters of the previous age, the lowriders were seeking a form of distinct communal

identity when faced with pressures for extreme conformity and deindividuali-
zation in postwar American society.

Also not unlike their pachuco predecessors, the lowriders were promptly
met with legal reaction meant to discourage their stylistic choices under color
of law. In 1958 the California state legislature adopted Vehicle Code section
24008, making it illegal to have any part of a motor vehicle below the car's
wheel rims—effectively banning lowriders from city streets. While initially a
setback to the burgeoning subculture in places like East L.A. and the San Fernando Valley, inventive auto mechanics developed a hydraulic switch system
allowing the driver to lower and raise the car on a moment's notice. This system remains one of the key characteristics of L.A. area lowrider vehicles to this
day, and it is captured famously in the late 1990s hip-hop music videos of artists like Snoop Dogg and Dr. Dre.

From its early days, lowriding led to "cruising," a social ritual in which youths
in small groups piled into vehicles—though not always customized ones—to
drive slowly down select "strips" around Los Angeles to see and be seen among
one another. If the Champs-Élysées and the Boulevard St. Germain were once
public catwalks for fashionable people in Paris, France, key thoroughfares like
Van Nuys Boulevard and Whittier Boulevard were the car-culture equivalents
on the US West Coast. Cruising predates lowriders, but it certainly received
more energy and more color once car customization became part of the mix.
Unfortunately, residents of surrounding communities also came to view the
influx of youth, particularly Mexican American ones from the 1960s into the
1970s, as a threat to public safety. This perception was exacerbated by the rise of
L.A. gang activity in the late 1970s. By the end of that decade, the law further
intervened at the municipal level to prohibit "cruising" on key strips like Whittier Boulevard, effectively crushing this ethnic subculture and sending it underground. While lowriding persisted through the 1990s and into the present era,
it did so as a cult movement rather than a widely accessible public form of social
expression. Like the repression of the zoot suit before it, then, the legal response
to lowriding in California succeeded not by eliminating the practice outright
but by removing it from public view, thereby reclaiming the urban space as one
belonging to the dominant middle-class society.

A third historic movement in US urban culture worth noting is b-boying,
breaking, or break dancing. Deeply tied to the rise of hip-hop music in New York
in the 1970s, *breaking* refers to a style of dance emerging among African American and Latino/a youth that set the heavy drum and bass rhythms of early rap to
bodily movement. If the late '70s saw the rise of hip-hop through warehouse and
block parties fueled by Jamaican-style sound systems (see chapter 6), break dancing was a similarly public art form in which the dancer often blasted loud music
from a "boom box" or "ghetto blaster" portable transistor stereo (itself a recent
invention from the period), laid down a slab of cardboard to protect him- or herself from the concrete below, and then "popped and locked" in styles that seemed

to mimic the machine-like movements of robots and manufacturing equipment from industrial production. In addition to the area of public space claimed by the dancer's cardboard floor, a large area of three-dimensional space was occupied by the dance itself through headspins, backflips, moonwalking, and the like. Break dancers also partook of the boastful, self-inflating talk of wider hip-hop culture as they "battled" one another for domination of a street corner, a park, or a neighborhood as the loud music permeated the urban landscape. Although break dancing itself was never made explicitly illegal, break dance battles were often broken up for creating a public nuisance or because they might have led to other criminal activity. Zoot suits, lowriding, and breaking all represents phases of urban artistic culture pioneered by American ethnic communities as part of the way they made public spaces their own and reasserted identity in times of exclusion or forced conformity. These movements offer a backdrop to the real subject of this chapter on art, law, and society. Moving back to a more literal meaning of art as a visual expression of individual or collective sentiments about the world, one direct descendant from all three of the above movements has been **graffiti** culture.

GRAFFITI

Graffiti is an art form. Let's start with that. Although it may consist only of letters or rudimentary pictures, it gets its primary significance not from the technical prowess of the artist but from the often jarring locations in which it is found. It becomes more significant the more inappropriate it appears within its context. Examples of this illicit form of expression have been found inside ancient Egyptian temples, in Renaissance era cathedrals, and even on the coronation chair inside Westminster Abbey—where British monarchs have sat for centuries to be crowned king or queen. If the illicit nature of graffiti gives it its power, then the more sacred its location the more powerful it feels. In the case of these historic examples, however, so much time has passed that the graffiti itself also becomes sacred and worth protecting.

In modern times, the contexts in which graffiti is found have everything to do with how long it lasts, how quickly it is "cleaned up," or how valuable it becomes as an art form. Modern-day graffiti is closely associated with the emergence of hip-hop and b-boy cultures in the inner cities. For that reason, one of its main breeding grounds was New York City.

The sociologist Richard Lachmann was one of the first to systematically study graffiti artist culture and social organization in New York in the 1980s. Lachmann found that contrary to popular visions of graffiti artists as mere guerrilla vandals or opportunistic fame seekers, they actually followed mappable "career" paths not unlike other vocations.[4] Moreover, he wrote, graffiti artists partook of the worlds of both social "deviance" and high art. In that

Figure 12.5 Graffiti murals at 5Pointz in Queens, New York, 2013. Photo by Dare 2 Create (Creative Commons).

respect, their lives were shaped by both the social networks where they emerged—who their mentors and adversaries were—and the way their audiences reacted to their work.

Graffiti in New York in that era could be divided into two forms that remain significant for this chapter. The first was "**tagging**"; this referred to a most basic form in which the artists painted or "wrote" his or her name—usually a nickname such as "Nightcrawler" or "Jeeves 101"—in unlikely but conspicuous locations such as on the side of active subway trains, or on billboards high above the street. Because of these precarious contexts, the works themselves were not elaborate; to a layperson they looked like thin letters scribbled together hastily. Sometimes they were barely legible as words. But within the tagging community, the artists began to recognize one another's monikers, and they began to confer respect on those they saw more often, or in more dangerous locations. In Los Angeles, by comparison, the famous green directional signs above freeways were often a popular target for tagging, since they were seen by hundreds of thousands of people a day, and the danger in approaching them was high indeed.

The second major form of graffiti was **muralism.** With mural painting, the artist often had more space and more time. Figure 12.5 shows a graffiti mural taken from New York City. The work still revealed a name or a word. It still was usually signed by the artist, often under a moniker. But notice in the figure how much more elaborate the work is in terms of both design and execution.

Lachmann wrote that some taggers graduated up to mural painting. They might do so by serving as a kind of apprentice to a known muralist. There they learned the techniques and styles of the experts, and they learned to develop their own approaches over time. Successful graffiti muralists could reach great heights as legitimate artists. In the mid-1980s, New York City art collectors began buying graffiti-style paintings to display in expensive penthouses or in upscale office buildings. This new demand changed the sociology of the graffiti subculture in the city. Prestige artists once congregated at important walls around the community, and around them gathered the younger generation that learned by watching. The advent of gallery-collectible graffiti sent the best artists of the era into workshops to work their magic not on concrete but on canvases, albeit big ones. This shift effectively broke the social bond between graffiti muralists and younger taggers, in turn sparking some tensions between the groups.

Meanwhile, out on the streets, the criminalization of graffiti as part of New York's effort to clean up its image further altered the subculture. On one hand, it appeared to be an effort to protect the property rights of real estate owners in the city. New York Public Law 145.60(2) lays out the basic elements of the criminal complaint for graffiti. It requires in addition to the simple act of painting or carving onto another's property two key requirements that are sometimes difficult to prove. The first is "intent to damage." The artists must conduct his or her act without the belief that doing so will somehow "improve" the owner's property. While improvement might be relative in aesthetic terms—some might argue that graffiti looks better than a plain wall—the fact is that improvement in this context has an economic meaning that implies an increase in market value. On that account, almost no artists can justifiably claim that their graffiti increases a building's market value.

The second key prong of New York's antigraffiti law requires that the artist execute the work "without permission." In most cases of prosecution, this is true and easy to show. However, there are some cases when an owner invites neighborhood artists to decorate a wall with a mural. The belief is that an empty wall will be a target for unauthorized painting or tagging and that an authorized mural is preferable and indeed may show support for the customer community. But the very definition of graffiti as "illicit" may make such consented paintings less attractive or less prestigious to certain types of artists. Yet with increased enforcement of the criminal laws against graffiti, and with urban renewal projects around the country in formerly blighted inner cities, the spaces for the most elaborate graffiti art have dwindled, making permitted spaces not only more attractive but highly valued in their communities.

No case illustrates this better than the 5Pointz community of New York's Long Island City in Queens. In the wake of the 1980s crackdown on widespread urban graffiti in New York, artists sought out safe spaces to continue their craft. A deactivated water meter factory in Queens had just the right qualifications to become the center for graffiti artists. A two-hundred-thousand-square-foot building with vast cinder block walls, the space was acquired by a New York developer in the 1970s with intent to develop the property. Instead,

Figure 12.6 5Pointz artist collective in 2009, well before its destruction. Photo by Nigel Morris (Creative Commons).

the owner, Jerry Wolkoff, began leasing the space to various businesses and then ultimately to artists as studios in the 1990s. Permission was granted to artists to paint on the building itself. In 1992, a disabled plumber by the name of Pat DeLilo started a group called Graffiti Terminators to combat New York's graffiti problem by offering artists alternative spaces to practice their craft. With permission from Wolkoff, DeLilo set up the Phun Phactory as a kind of open-air gallery and practice space.[5] From then, the building grew in reputation, with newspaper and magazine write-ups from Japan to Germany. International graffiti artists began making the pilgrimage out to Queens, and by the early 2000s the space came to be known as "Aerosol Arts Center." From the 2000s through 2013, hundreds of artists left their mark on the property. The new curator, a veteran tagger named Jonathan Cohen, took over supervision of the property, vetting any artist who wished to propose and execute a new mural. For this reason, substantial planning, consent, and timing went into the creation of most of the elaborate works adorning the walls of 5Pointz. Figure 12.5 above showed an example of one such mural, and figure 12.6 gives a view of the building as a whole.

In the twenty-some years that 5Pointz operated as a site for sanctioned graffiti art, New York real estate prices skyrocketed, with the notable exception of the years following the terrorist attacks of September 11, 2001. In other words, Wolkoff had increased incentive to eject the artists and develop the property into the most common type of development project—multitenant condominium buildings. Indeed, the gentrification of New York neighborhoods like Williamsburg and Park Slope in neighboring Brooklyn pushed consumption of luxury housing further and further out into Long Island, making 5Pointz a likely target for development. Beginning in 2011, Wolkoff began the formal steps to tear down 5Pointz. In winter 2013 the resident artists of the building were all evicted. The artists filed suit in federal court to protect their works but lost their bid for an injunction. Months later, without any notice, Wolkoff had the walls of 5Pointz shoddily whitewashed. Later in 2014, he ordered the entire building at 5Pointz razed to the ground, and so it was.

With the help of artist-friendly attorneys in the city, twenty-one of the muralists at 5Pointz sued Wolkoff in a Brooklyn federal district court, arguing that their rights to their work had been violated by the sudden whitewashing and demolition of the building. The artists used the Visual Artists Rights Act (VARA), a 1990 federal statute protecting the **moral rights** of artists and adopted by Congress after the United States finally acceded to the Berne Convention for the Protection of Literary and Artistic Works in 1988. *Moral rights* refers to the types of artistic authorship rights that are more commonly protected in civil law countries. These include rights of attribution, rights to anonymous publication, and rights to the physical integrity of the work. As adopted in the United States, moral rights under VARA are more limited in scope than in other countries. Rarely tested in US courts, VARA requires that the artistic work be of "recognized stature" in order for the artist's moral rights to be legally protected. Whereas one might hope this phrase had been defined through previous common-law jurisprudence the way other legal standards often are, in fact it was still too new to be of initial practical help. Certainly, many in the graffiti world, hip-hop music culture, or New York art and architecture would easily testify that 5Pointz was a treasured landmark, but chances were high that national art "experts" would have never heard of it. Sadly, this conflict of opinion led to a major loss for the artists in 2013 when they filed for an **injunction** to stop the destruction of the property, also under VARA. At that time, the presiding judge concluded that 5Pointz was not properly a "work of art," and that destruction of it would not be considered "irreparable harm" since so many photographs existed. The building was subsequently demolished under apparent sanction of law.

In 2017, years after the murals were themselves reduced to dust, the artists got their day in court at the actual trial for damages suffered by infringement of their moral rights. Again arguing under VARA, the artists this time asserted that while the developer certainly had the right to dispose of his own real property, they should have received ninety days' notice to protect and possibly remove their works—many of them world famous by this time—before destruction. Stunningly, the presiding judge this time allowed the claim to go to trial, and, at the end, a six-person jury held for the artists. They won. In

February 2018 the judge awarded the group of 5Pointz muralists a total of $6.7 million for the destruction of their work and violation of rights under VARA.[6] The outcome promised to encourage other artists to seek similar remedies and gave art attorneys similar incentives to take such cases.

The delicate balancing of rights at play in the 5Pointz case is worth emphasis in this chapter and in the context of the larger themes of this book. American law, most would say, is generally an institution aimed at balancing rights of various kinds: individual versus collective, public versus private, and positive versus negative. In this case, as with most property use cases, the balance is between the rights of owners to "use" their property with the maximum freedom afforded by law (e.g., not to engage in criminal activity) and the above moral rights of the artists who had invested so much of themselves into adorning the 5Pointz blighted factory with colorful works of art that attracted thousands of visitors annually. Whereas cases involving property use normally require a balancing of competing economic interests—for instance, whether a factory's pollution may be worth the number of jobs it results in—economics was only one side of this case. Indeed, the final outcome in 5Pointz reflects an unusual reassertion of the moral against the economic. But this reassertion can be considered exceptional. For the most part, artists' works in public spaces will not be protected unless they serve to economically "improve" the property. This is well illustrated by rounding out this chapter with a look at the mysterious international artist known as "Banksy."

TRANSNATIONAL PUBLIC ART: BANKSY

In the late 1990s a new artist began gaining fame for simple, creative stencil paintings offering biting social commentary on issues from police violence to environmentalism. Stencil art uses the same basic tools as ordinary graffiti, paint on concrete or brick, but it employs the stencil—any flat hard screen cut out in the negative of an image, or image with words. Whereas graffiti artists arrive at a wall surface and apply paint from a can or brush in "freehand" style—the way painters always have—stencil artists place the flat screen on the surface and then simply cover the relevant area with paint. In that sense, stencil-based graffiti appears less technically savvy and more accessible to the layperson. But meticulous work often goes into carving the stencil screen in the first place, and just as much effort may go into transporting screens to and from a site undetected.

The new artist called himself "Banksy." His first major work was a freehand mural in the English town of Bristol in 1997, but by 2000 he had moved entirely to stencil works (figure 12.7). Most importantly, the appearance of Banksy's name on new, highly creative stencil paintings spread around other cities in England, and then across the channel to Europe, and then across the Atlantic

Figure 12.7 Banksy, *Flower Thrower*, as seen in Jerusalem, ca. 2005. Photo by David Silverman/ Getty Images.

to North America. By approximately 2005, Banksy was "world famous." When his paintings appeared, they began to attract tourists, photographers, and even art collectors looking to acquire portions of wall, or billboards that had been adorned by his hand. The works themselves were often jarring. One example includes "Untouchables," a black-and-white painting stenciled on the side of a run-down brick building in Chicago's West Loop. The image shows an old-fashioned baby carriage tilted in a downward direction high up on the side of the building. The baby is visible inside only because its legs are outstretched and it has released its rattle into the air. The baby feet and floating rattle give a sense that the stroller is in rapid motion, downward. And most importantly, the artist placed the stencil just above a brick pattern left from what was once a staircase attached to that side of the building. The staircase pattern is still discernible from the wear and tear on the exposed brick. It looks, in other words, as if a baby stroller is falling down a staircase toward disaster. The image creates a sense of anxiety and urgency in the onlooker. In that way, it is immediately memorable and jarring.

What are the implications of this painting being placed on the outer side of a run-down city building? In 2013, Banksy arrived in New York City to conduct a thirty-one-day residency in the city. The idea was to complete one new work of art per night, and these were placed at various locations across the five boroughs of New York. Examples of work produced in this period included "The Street Is in Play"—an image of a child reaching out for a can of spray paint on an antigraffiti sign.

As pointed out by several commentators, Banksy's arrival in New York that year—an internationally significant event in an art world whose headquarters is arguably New York City itself—really put the city's antigraffiti law (and law enforcement) to the test. Recall that in New York the definition of graffiti requires that the work be made with intent to damage and without the owner's permission. Once the work meets this definition, it is punishable by fine or by imprisonment, depending upon the severity and sequence of other prior criminal acts. Once the work is defined as graffiti, it has been criminalized and can be scheduled for removal. When entry-level taggers mark up a storefront wall and sign it with their moniker, these requirements are usually met. Ordinary graffiti by a new artists brings no benefit to the property and is considered to be essentially vandalism. So what about the elusive Banksy?

The appearance of a Banksy stencil work on a storefront is said to *increase* the property's value. The new work tends to attract new visitors to an area (ideal for commercial spaces), and it puts the neighborhood "on the map"; some owners have been known to take affirmative steps to preserve the work, and in a few cases sections of concrete have been sold at auction at high value because they have been marked by the world-famous artist.[7] In other words, the addition of a stencil piece to a building by Banksy may no longer come with "intent to damage" or without the owner's permission. On these accounts, law enforcement would likely have a hard time making the case about illegal graffiti so far as a Banksy work was concerned. So much for the different legal implications of graffiti art completed by socioeconomic and ethno-racial minority youth and by a world-famous English artist.

The social implications of these differences are very telling about the relationship between law and society. In effect, Banksy illustrates a distinction between "high" and "low" graffiti art. On one hand, part of the definition of graffiti is its illicit quality. While the style of New York taggers and muralists can be copied or transferred onto large canvases and sold in galleries, the work produced for that purpose is not graffiti in the common sense of the term, or in the legal sense for which there are criminal penalties. But the art produced in that style is still evocative of the illicit origins of graffiti art. Even the rich collector who purchases a canvas from a gallery does so in part because the piece adds an urban, edgy, or deviant quality to his or her collection. It shows that the collector is in touch with, sympathetic toward, or perhaps ironically allied with the aspirations of the inner-city youth who produced modern graffiti in the first place.

On the other hand, not all graffiti art generates such a response at all. On the contrary, most does not. Most of the general public tends to view urban graffiti as an eyesore, a sign of urban decay and of impoverished conditions. The criminal justice concept known as "broken windows theory" is evidence of this perception. Under this theory, any small sign of decay—typically a broken window but also graffiti—can serve as license in the community for more criminal or deviant behavior. So what distinguishes the works that become collectible art masterpieces from those that are better off whitewashed?

In the case of 5Pointz, the ornate murals in the classic New York City style were in the wrong place at the wrong time. Many had the same look as that found in certain Manhattan galleries—and they even shared the same author in some cases. But because they sat on private property, the absolute right to **dispose** of which has historically been granted to the owner, they were permitted to be destroyed. Only some years later—when it was effectively too late—were the artists' moral rights recognized and their damages compensated. Again, their remedy could only be money; the vindication of moral rights, however, may have repercussion for artist rights that will be priceless.

But Banksy's works have been treated very differently. During his residency in New York City, for example, law enforcement was trained and instructed not to destroy, and in some cases to protect, any new stencil works that appeared across the boroughs. The presence of the internationally acclaimed artist seemed to elevate the prestige of the city in the art world—to which it has historically been a cultural center. For the property owners whose walls have had the unique honor to be adorned with an original Banksy, the artwork can bring immeasurable attention, value, and prestige. To the city of New York, or others in which the artist has been active, his once-illicit guerrilla paintings are now a marker of relevance and distinction in the global economy.

CONCLUSION

The stories of Georgia O'Keeffe, Nazi "degenerate" art, lowriders, zoot suits, break dancing, graffiti muralism, and Banksy all have something in common. All illustrate unique attempts by different societies in different times to apply the formal rules and reasoning of law to the shifting and aesthetically subjective world of arts and culture. Certainly, there can be clear consensus at times about what constitutes "good versus bad" or "beautiful versus brutish" products of the art world. There can even be legitimate agreement over the very boundaries of that world. But the application of legal institutions and processes to fix those distinctions seems always temporary or inadequate. At the same time, these cases reveal, once again, the role that politics and economy play in the uses and extensions of law to society. The remaining chapters look for similar evidence in two more fast-changing areas of the world around us.

CHAPTER 12 REVIEW

Key Terms

- Replevin
- Equity
- Statute of limitations
- Discovery rule
- Barrio
- Graffiti
- Tagging
- Muralism
- Moral rights
- Injunction
- Dispose

Further Discussion

1. Do you agree or disagree with the way the common law handled the stolen art case of Georgia O'Keeffe?

2. What are some of the main differences between graffiti tagging and graffiti muralism? How did the sociology of these two art forms evolve in late twentieth-century New York?

3. Should artists possess "moral rights" in their works? If so, should these rights be extended to cover graffiti?

4. Why might the title of this chapter be "Art Forms" rather than simply "Art"?

Further Reading

Hickey, Dave. *Air Guitar: Essays on Art and Democracy.* Los Angeles: Foundation for Advanced Critical Studies, 1997.

Lachmann, Richard. "Graffiti as Career and Ideology." *American Journal of Sociology* 94, no. 2 (1988): 229–50.

Lipsitz, George. *The Subcultures Reader: Cruising around the Historical Bloc.* New York: Routledge, 1997.

Science and Technology

Human beings have always had an ambivalent relationship toward their own tools. On one hand, tools—by which we mean any instrument of natural or manmade origin used to assist with human survival or success—have been at the center of great leaps forward in human progress throughout the ages. The opening sequence of the classic science fiction film *2001: A Space Odyssey* makes this clear. There, an individual ape, a member of a small group, discovers that it can dominate its surrounding peers by using a leftover animal bone as a club to bludgeon any competitors. The audience sees the ape toss the club into the air, sending it spinning, and the director Stanley Kubrick then cuts to a shot of an advanced space station spinning similarly in deep space, implying that there is a direct link between the first-ever primate hand tool and the most complex technological wonders humanity has created for space exploration.

On the other hand, demonstrated just within the scope of this opening scene, the human interest in tools is not without negative consequences. For the apes, the discovery of the club leads to increased internecine violence. For the humans in space, the very ship that was designed to serve as a home in the hostile vacuum of the universe turns against its creators. Immediately, two themes emerge: the connection between technology and harm, and the potential for technology to outrun the intended purposes and intelligence of its creators. In short, technological development has been at the center of human progress, but it has also been a key object of law's effort to regulate society.

Like the world of art in the preceding chapter, the world of technology offers a fascinating vantage from which to examine law and social change. Technology is sometimes—as in the examples later in this chapter—the catalyst for rapid and robust change. It sparks developments in everyday behavior, often before human beings are collectively aware of it. The mobile telephone, to name just one obvious example, made private conversations about business or love suddenly public as speakers engaged in dialogue on city streets and public transportation. From that, the unspoken rules about public utterances and eavesdropping on affection have shifted.

If technology has been a driver of social change, law has sometimes struggled to keep up. But technology has also permitted vast changes in the practice, accessibility, and enforcement of law. The use of DNA analysis—most notably in post-conviction justice for severe crimes—may be the most extreme example of advances in molecular biology being translated into novel forms of evidence collection and testing, and resulting ultimately in the exposure of grave inaccuracies in the criminal justice system (ones often colored by race and class discrimination). So while technology has pushed society to change in unforeseen ways, it has also permitted law and its agents to refine the administration of justice.

This chapter is about all of these things. The first section below offers a broad overview of three areas in which technology has affected law and legal studies. The topic can be and often is the subject of its own book, so this overview will by necessity only scratch the surface. The second section will inventory some of the major technological advances that have come in the last several decades, focusing primarily on those that resulted in changes in social behavior or social structures with legal implications. Zooming in on one of those—social media—the third section will examine the now widespread problem of online speech and reputational harms, what experts have occasionally referred to as "Twibel." Is such a new label necessary? What makes it different from traditional defamation? These questions will guide that section in a manner that allows us to more accurately assess the relationship of law, technology, and social change. But even increased understanding of this relationship will fail to entirely overcome a problem first pointed out by Roscoe Pound himself: the inadequacy of law in remedying certain specific harms. It is on this last point that the final section will dwell.

LAW AND TECHNOLOGY

The story of law and technology forms a significant plotline in the bigger story of law and social change. Since the Age of Enlightenment (roughly 1685–1815)—

if not earlier—human beings have vigorously pursued advancement in applied science, leading to periodic great leaps forward amid a larger background of slow and steady progress. The discovery of microorganisms in the late seventeenth century could be considered one such turning point, after which medical doctors finally knew the root cause of many diseases. The discovery of penicillin—the first true antibiotic drug—two centuries later could be considered another one. Suddenly, with the advent of a drug to eradicate bacteria that infect the body, mothers in labor, soldiers on the battlefield, and children bedridden with fevers could be treated and cured. These types of leaps forward in science have been called "scientific revolutions" by the famed historian Thomas Kuhn.[1] Kuhn has said that they consist of major paradigm shifts in human understanding about the natural or biological worlds.

But science clearly goes beyond medicine to improve human quality of life in ways not directly related to health. The discovery of the molecule gave way to the observation of electrons, which in turn gave rise to an electronics revolution, which in turn made possible the development of modern computers. In that case, computer science engineering owes its birth to discoveries in the "pure" scientific fields of chemistry and physics. The latter is an example of technological development. The end result (though not quite the *end*, since it is still very much under development) is a labor-saving tool for human application to all kinds of different areas of life, not the least of which may be clinical medicine. So, if we are being perfectly clear about terminology, we might say that *science* is the search for causal explanations about the natural world, whereas *technology* is the application of those explanations to the creation of new tools. Importantly, such tools can be used in turn to produce new tools, so that technology often begets new technology.

Law has been affected by these histories in a number of important ways. Recall for a moment chapter 3, where we saw some of the ways in which both common- and civil law legal families are descendants of ancient Roman law. For centuries, both systems evolved at a steady pace to cope with changes in the social environment. With an acceleration in technological progress over the past fifty years, however, law in both major families has had to adapt even more quickly to the new factual scenarios that present themselves to law enforcement, courts, and legislatures. Two key examples of this can be seen in the fields of criminal justice and intellectual property.

Criminal justice is the field of law and legal studies dedicated solely to the discovery, investigation, prosecution, and punishment of harms to society. Whereas in most crimes individuals are indeed harmed—a backpack is stolen from a student, or a banking scheme defrauds an account holder—the cases these result in are usually entitled "The People v. Defendant A" or "The State v. Defendant B." This contrasts with the civil system, in which cases are almost always "Plaintiff A v. Defendant C"—an individual against an individual. The reason is that criminal conduct is almost always a violation of a criminal or penal "code"—a form of comprehensive legislation aimed at behavior considered *socially* deviant and institutionally recognized as such. The antigraffiti law of New York City in chapter 12 was a prime example of this. Individual acts of graffiti against property owners may violate aspects of the civil law—of trespass, for instance—but they are prosecuted criminally under the penal code based on sections of code written by lawmakers to prohibit a behavior considered to be socially destructive. The last chapter showed, if nothing else, the cultural relativism behind the idea of "socially destructive."

The use of science to solve crimes dates back to at least the late eighteenth century—again to the Enlightenment period, when human reason was said to displace religion and superstition as the pathway to understanding the world.[2] But whereas science generally seeks to find explanations for naturally occurring events like storms, diseases, or astronomical changes, the new **forensic science** sought to solve crimes using the same principles of cause and effect. Early examples of forensics included the matching of bodily bullet wounds with a suspect's firearm, or the use of chemical testing to find trace amounts of poison in a dead body. Much like the scientific methods of the early period, these forensic methods depended greatly on visual observation, physical testing, and logical deduction.

The twentieth century brought a new "scientific revolution" in the form of the electron microscope. Traditional microscopes allowed the forensic researcher to see particles as small as a cloth fiber or a fleck of skin, and these forms of evidence gained increased acceptance in criminal cases over time. But they also tended to break down quickly both in the natural environment and in investigative custody. Meanwhile, the methods for storing and preserving valuable police evidence were—and arguably continue to be—very imperfect. With the leap forward in molecular biology, however, forensic scientists gained access to a critical type of evidence that has since come to revolutionize the justice system: DNA.

DNA, or deoxyribonucleic acid, is a substance found within the cells of every living organism. It consists of four base molecules: cytosine, guanine, adenine, and thymine—otherwise abbreviated as C, G, A, and T. This "macromolecule" was famously first modeled by the Cambridge researchers James Watson and Frances Crick in 1951, but scientists had been aware of its likely existence since at least 1869. Watson and Crick's innovation was to model the macromolecule as a "double helix" (see figure 13.1)—a kind of dual-stranded spiral where each side connects to the other through pairings of the C, G, A, and T submolecules.

Importantly, this model allowed Watson and Crick to theorize about the significance and replication of DNA. Scientists had already suspected that these combinations of base pairs contained the fundamental information all living cells need to operate—kind of like an instruction manual for all the myriad microfunctions of the living world. Should a cell grow hair, should it release

Figure 13.1 DNA molecule featuring characteristic double helix structure (Creative Commons).

digestive acids, should it replicate itself, or should it attack another cell? Each cell's own DNA would answer these questions and therefore tell it what to do. Scientists have since likened this cellular instruction manual to a "code"; much like the kind of code that tells computers how to operate, DNA consists of a very simple language assembled in infinite combinations of clusters that give operationally essential directions that shape the overall system. And there's one last important point: despite substantial overlap across the living world, the complete DNA profile of every organism turned out to be unique from every other. In that way, the macromolecule became more than just the "software" of life, it became a virtually flawless fingerprint.

The implications of DNA for crime investigation were soon acknowledged. If every person had his or her own unique DNA and if this substance was contained in every human cell, and if human beings were shedding cells through skin and bodily fluids constantly, then the prior whereabouts of anyone could be ascertained with a careful microscopic search of the areas of their prior movement. Needless to say, this had a major impact on forensic science. Whereas specialists had previously relied upon literal fingerprints obtained by imperfect law enforcement officers from crime scenes, DNA allowed the scientists to study other physical evidence at the microscopic level to extract DNA strands from articles of clothing, bedding, carpeting, and so forth and then compare those with the DNA found in a suspect's blood sample.

The latter has been called DNA profiling or fingerprinting, and the technique for accomplishing it was developed by Alec Jeffreys in the United Kingdom in 1984. Jeffreys's discovery and development of the new forensic technology set off a revolution in crime scene evidence and crime solving. Early reports boasted of the 100 percent accuracy rate of DNA fingerprinting. And countless suspects were put behind bars on the basis of faith in the new method.

But there were critics from the beginning. At the time, the prevailing rule in the United States for admitting scientific evidence in court was called the Frye Test.[3] Under *Frye,* scientific findings could be admitted into evidence if the method of their discovery had been accepted by a majority of experts in the field. According to early critics of DNA fingerprinting, the method had not yet been generally accepted, as it was still new. Over the next decade, even as the method grew in popularity, others raised objections related to the collection and management of physical evidence by law enforcement. Most famously, the defense team in the O.J. Simpson criminal murder trial cast serious doubts upon the prosecution's case even though the latter had shown DNA from Simpson at the scene of the crime. The defense, a team of flamboyant, high-profile L.A. attorneys, suggested convincingly that the Los Angeles Police Department had contaminated the crime scene and samples from it with Simpson's blood.

DNA fingerprinting technology created a revolution in forensic science and, in turn, a revolution in criminal justice itself. For every new case that can be decided on the basis of this new form of evidence, there remain many more older cases decided before its discovery. Would the application of this new technology to older case files tend to confirm or challenge past convictions? It is with precisely this question that the worldwide **innocence movement** has been concerned. That movement, composed of numerous Innocence Project groups around the United States, Australia, and the United Kingdom, among other places, accepts petitions from convicted prisoners—usually ones serving life sentences—who believe new analysis of their cases in light of modern technology like DNA sequencing could lead to their exoneration. In each instance the Innocence Project must assess the strength of these claims and new evidence, they must file a petition for habeas corpus (literally an order to deliver the body from imprisonment), and then they must often argue the case in federal court in hopes that the judge will order the federal or state prison involved to release the prisoner. In a few cases the court will remand the case back to a state court for review. Studies have shown the success rate of habeas petitions in capital—that is to say death penalty—cases to be as high as 47 percent.[4] Many states have now made available postconviction DNA testing for inmates able to meet minimum application requirements.[5] The innocence movement is one major outcome of the revolution brought to law by DNA technology—itself a by-product of the scientific discovery of DNA itself. A second major development has been the rise of the subfield called intellectual property law.

Intellectual property, or IP, is an umbrella category that covers intangible rights to creative works of science, technology, literature, art, and so forth. Practically speaking, it includes legal theories and claims related primarily to copyright, patent, and trademark.[6] **Copyright** is a form of protection guaranteed by the US Constitution, which states, "Congress shall have the authority . . . to promote the progress of science and useful arts, by securing for limited times to authors and inventors the exclusive right to their respective writings and discoveries."[7] Under this authority, Congress enacted the first Copyright Act of 1790, intended to promote "learning" by securing the rights of inventors. That law has since been amended several times, but it remains in principle unchanged. Thus authors must first file for copyright protection with the US Copyright Office, and once they are granted a copyright to a creative work they hold that right for a number of years. The duration of the copyright has changed over time and remains dependent upon the conditions of creation. Since 2002, the term for individual authors is seventy years following the author's death, and for corporate authors it is 120 years after creation.[8]

Patent, meanwhile, is a separate form of protection administered by the US Patent and Trademark Office. It is intended for inventors who wish to protect the idea, design, or schematics of a new device, process, substance, or more recently code. Increasingly the patenting of biological life-forms such as hybrid plants and animals has become a frontier issue. In the United States, the first patent was issued in 1790 for a new process of producing potash, a substance used in fertilizer production. Whereas patents were typically once issued for entire devices, today's complex technology means everyday devices like computers and smartphones run with hardware and software from numerous authorial sources and may require the use of dozens or hundreds of other patented technologies.

Trademark, meanwhile, is a form of protection for commercial names and images. Whereas patents protect their inventor from having his creation stolen and resold, trademark protects the name or image of that creation from being applied to related or similar objects. Therefore, one of the key standards for trademark violation claims is whether the violating use creates the likelihood of confusion in the marketplace. The assumption behind this protection is that trade names and images that succeed in the market obtain a market value in and of themselves, and that unauthorized uses of these can tend to dilute the value the trademark holder has accrued. One example of unauthorized trademark use is the infamous case *Rogers v. Grimaldi.* There an Italian production company made a feature film (directed by the acclaimed Federico Fellini and starring award-winning actor Marcello Mastroianni) about impersonators of the American performers Fred Astaire and Ginger Rogers.[9] The film itself was titled *Fred & Ginger,* so Rogers sued under a US trademark law prohibiting the "false designation of origin" of a product—a claim intended to prevent the labeling of one commercial product with the valuable name of another. The defendants argued that because their film was an "expressive work"—in other words, not a purely commercial product but a form of artistic expression—they should be freer to use names that might have trade value to someone else. In this case, the Second Circuit Court of Appeals agreed because the names of the famed dancers were being used to reference characters in the original story depicted in the film.

If these are the basic areas of IP protection and remedies in the United States today, the origin of these rights is considerably older. Intellectual property has its roots at least as deep as the eighteenth century. In that era, philosophers theorized about the nature of human economic advancement and political order. John Locke in particular became known for a theory of "political society" rooted in the collective pooling of sovereignty to permit, among other important things, state protection of private property. Writing against other theories that may have believed the government *itself* should own property in the name of "the people," Locke said that government's main role was to enforce the individual's exclusive claims on and rights to dispose of his or her own property. A tyrannical government—one worthy of armed overthrow—would therefore be one that abrogated this duty or tried to take private property for itself.

Another important feature of Locke's theory of the right to property was the origins of the right itself. In his view, one of the key sources of rights in private property was the owner's history of "improving," that is to say laboring and making profit from the property; it was in effect a value theory of ownership.[10] This idea was especially meaningful in England at the time of Locke's writing; there, on a small island nation with very limited borders, most land was owned by the British crown or by noble families. Upon death of the household father, the rule of **primogeniture** required that all land holding pass to the eldest male heir in the family with the main purpose of keeping estates intact rather than divided. Recall from chapter 4, meanwhile, that this rule was one of the main points of contention for property law in the early American colonies. The colonists, now settled in a region of seemingly infinite land availability, rejected primogeniture for an even-distribution rule that would partition real property among all male children of the same generation. Not only that, but the influence of Locke's groundbreaking value theory of ownership was especially appealing to the colonists. It gave an important incentive to early American settlers first to make the dangerous journey to the New World, and then to invest their time and energy farming, mining, or otherwise developing plots of land. We know from the historical record that the Founding Fathers were especially influenced by Locke and that early land holdings were recognized among early commoners—those without prior wealth or status—on the basis of their willingness to work hard. Indeed, the historian Nancy Isenberg has written extensively about the ways in which sloth or laziness was viewed as perhaps the worst possible vice in the early American colonies and that it was used in part as an argument against slave ownership and in part to marginalize the working poor as what she calls an early form of "white trash."[11]

The Lockean theory of property ownership was closely related to a second influential idea, that of utilitarianism, which held that rightful ownership of property should go to the party with the greatest potential to use it for the largest benefit to the largest number of people. Suppose that in a dispute over a natural wildlife habitat, for example, an environmental organization wants to preserve the land for the wider community to enjoy for generations, while an opposing developer has discovered limestone deposits underground that could be mined and used for building materials to benefit the nearest city. The utilitarian view of ownership would want to weigh the costs and benefits of each use and compare those against one another. For this reason, utilitarianism has been abbreviated as "cost-benefit" analysis. However, it is important to note that in its original eighteenth-century form—as developed by Jeremy Bentham and John Stuart Mill most famously—utilitarianism did not treat "benefit" as mere monetary gain, but rather as "happiness" generally. On that basis, the benefit of environmental protection (see chapter 14) could come in the form of total individual enjoyment over centuries from a natural wilderness preserve—by definition a result that is not easily quantified in money. Modern-day utilitarians—of which many are law and economics proponents—would likely prefer assigning a monetary value to this enjoyment, measured by, for example, park entrance and parking fees collected over time.

Both the Lockean and utilitarian approaches to property ownership are examples of the Western moral theories underlying contemporary intellectual property law in its relationship with society. Each in its own way justifies a particular allocation of property rights as "good" on the basis of different reasoning. However, why either of these should be embraced at all is a separate question—one that is concerned fundamentally with the *purpose* of property ownership in the first place. When it comes to intellectual property, the kind of property that cannot be touched or held, the purpose of ownership seems most of all to be innovation. Innovation is the progression toward ever-new variations and uses of an idea or combination of ideas. Taking computer software as a brief example, the kind that drives modern-day computers and smart devices is of course the descendent of software developed five years ago, which in turn derived from software developed five years before that. With each successive wave of engineering, developers build on existing code to create new software codes that lead to new applications—some with benefits for real-world problems. So the extent to which existing software today is protected by intellectual property law will have immediate consequences for innovation of new software to advance computer operations in the next generation. For this reason, copyright, trademark, and patent lawmakers are constantly balancing two competing kinds of rights: those of the original developer to profit from his or her own innovation and those of end users to understand the workings of this product in the hopes of one day building something new.[12]

This problem of rights balancing in IP is especially acute today in at least four major areas of modern industry. The first has already been listed: computer software design. Companies like Apple make the operating code for the iPhone freely available to encourage developers to come up with new "apps" that they can then register and sell through the App Store online. This is because, with each new app created, the iPhone becomes potentially that much more useful as a tool for modern living. Enhanced **virtual reality** games are a good example of how this usefulness changes over time. After the release of Pokemon Go, a smartphone-based reality-enhancing 3D game, in which users moved through real space looking for virtual objects that existed only in the game, the smartphone suddenly became a "tool" for parents to get their game-loving children outdoors and exercising![13]

The second fast-changing industry where IP law has been important is in the development of new personal devices. Famously, Apple guards information about its new hardware very closely prior to any new unveiling. Occasionally, employees have been said to accidently leave early prototypes behind at Silicon Valley bars or restaurants, leading to a public relations frenzy about what the new device contains. Offshoot devices like the smartwatch, the Fitbit, Bluetooth headphones, and home theater TV Web connectors have all emerged out of the smart device revolution. The similarities between these devices may be clear, but each enjoys the substantial protection of IP laws in the United States, Europe, Asia, and elsewhere. And of course, with companies now offering original programs through those devices, their TV and movie content also will keep IP attorneys busy for the foreseeable future.

In the biomedical field, IP laws protect the creation of new biotechnology and pharmaceutical innovations. There, new devices such as arterial stents (used for unblocking arteries for heart attack patients), cancer spit tests, and smart contact lenses are all technological innovations meant to improve the health of at-risk patients, and their creators benefit from the exclusive right to profit from their inventions provided by intellectual property law.

But perhaps the most controversial of modern industries using these protections has been the agricultural industry. Already countless new strains of farm crops like corn, soy, wheat, and barley have been **genetically modified** to resist disease and drought better than their natural predecessors did a generation ago. Should the companies—ones like Monsanto, based in St. Louis, Missouri—be permitted to patent the genome of new seed strains they create? So far, they have been. This means that farmers who purchase modified seeds from the company may be able to cultivate that crop for only one cycle. Either the seed itself will not produce plants that are able to generate new seeds, or the farmer will be required to pay a license fee for using offspring seed in the next generation. In short, companies like Monsanto, under the strict protection of intellectual property laws once aimed to protect "ideas," now enjoy the exclusive right to profit from new strains of "life" itself. But sometimes these strains are not new at all. In the 1990s, for example, Monsanto sought patent protection for its use of the neem plant—a common staple found in over one thousand foods and health remedies in South Asia. The move was blocked by activists and the

Indian government, but not before the label "**biopiracy**" was applied to the practice and this egregious instance of it.

The problem of biopiracy raises a final important issue about intellectual property law, and in fact about property law in general. A primary theme of this book has been to explore the way economics has come to shape the relations between law and society under an ideology of neoliberalism. This example illustrates one of the ways in which law not only shapes economics but creates economic value almost out of thin air. When the law designates something—a piece of land, an inventive idea, or a work of artistic beauty—as property, it gives the owner the exclusive right to use and profit from the object. This exclusivity, it turns out, is the main basis on which that object's economic value now rests. For anyone else to rightfully use or profit from the object, he or she must obtain some right from the original owner. Once the law guarantees the enforcement of that right, no one apart from the owner can usurp it without penalty unless he or she has the owner's permission. The owner, then, is incentivized to profit from giving permission. Most, but not all, do this. So, the law, by recognizing the private right of property, quite literally creates economic value in the possessive differential between the person who owns and the person who does not but wishes to. This, again, is one of the greatest lessons from this brief look at intellectual property law and society.

LAW AND SOCIAL CHANGE

But it is when new technologies are used to solve age-old human problems that they truly usher in social change. One of the key questions in this book has been whether law *responds* to changes in social structure and behavior or whether it drives it. From the twelve prior chapters an implicit answer emerges: both. Depending on the context, law is capable of doing either, and we embrace it in both cases. But when we look closely at science and technology, it appears that the law is often more in its responsive role. That is because neither litigation, legislation, nor dispute resolution is capable of pushing new innovation in science and technology. They can, as the above paragraphs illustrate, help to encourage it, but that is something altogether different from "driving" change.

Three features of law and society make this responsive role all the more striking. The first is the important distinction described earlier in the book between fact and law. In Western legal systems, whether common law or civil law, legal reasoning distinguishes between facts it finds "in the world" as things that happened, or things that exist, and the rules as they apply to those things. American legal education, for instance, requires students to discern the "legal issue" in classroom case discussion because the students read judicial opinions—not party briefs—in which the relevant facts are assumed. The entire civil and criminal procedural systems are similarly designed to carefully distinguish between accepted and disputed facts. Juries are then charged with settling the most significant factual disputes. As the above section suggested, science and technology complicate these steps. They introduce new ways of "making" facts through new instrumentalities of evidence gathering and testing.[14] DNA, and the challenges it posed to the Frye standard for admitting scientific data into evidence, constitute a prime example of this.

Science and technology further relate to a tradition in law and society known as "gap studies." Although no longer fashionable among academics, gap studies was once a paradigmatic definition of what sociolegal studies did: understanding the difference between what law says it does and what law can actually do when it operates in society. Thanks to critical legal studies, law and society, and even the law and economics movement, this "gap" is no longer controversial. But less specifically appreciated is the extent to which it is based in large measure upon rapid advances in science and technology. Whereas in some cases, like DNA fingerprinting, the science helps to make the law more accurate, in others, like new social media interaction, it has done quite the opposite.

SOCIAL MEDIA AND REPUTATIONAL HARMS

In late 2008 there were approximately 100 million users of the social media platform Facebook around the world. By late 2017, that number had swollen to 2.1 billion—a twenty-fold increase.[15] That would place usage of Facebook in the hands of roughly one in four humans on earth. The microblogging site Twitter in 2017, meanwhile, hosted 330 million users, an increase of more than ten times in the same period.[16] Both Facebook and Twitter represent the (not so) "new" normal in social interaction in the early twenty-first century. Increasingly humans connect with and communicate with "friends" through these platforms rather than in real life, or by telephone. Some studies have suggested that the greater networking this brings actually leads to increased feelings of loneliness.[17] One reason can be that real-world connections are being replaced by virtual ones. Another can be that the nature of virtual interaction is far more superficial. Sites have made this easier by including reaction buttons such as "Like" or "Love" in their interface. But even if social media interaction may be a poor substitute for real human interaction, it is capable of creating as much, if not more, personal harm to people. Schools have reported increases in bullying through social media—or cyberbullying, as it is now termed. Identity theft has grown as more and more people "share" information about themselves online. And reputational harms such as defamation are capable of rapid and widespread injury as false information can travel faster and farther than ever before. The US elections in 2016 saw the massive sharing of "fake news" reports on social media, many of which, as it later came out, were propagated by Russian "bots" or fake account holders.[18] But long before that, false information had been doing heightened injury to people since the early days of the Internet. Would individuals seeking a legal remedy for social media reputational harm have greater or lesser protection in this brave new world?

DEFAMATION REVISITED

When social media took hold of Western culture in the 2000s, they seemed to offer the promise of "pure" social interaction. Many speculated about a discrimination-free Internet because qualities like skin color, economic class, and even language itself could be hidden from view behind the codes, algorithms, and interfaces of popular networking sites. Ten years earlier, similar speculation had been made by sociologists of the new medium who were studying chat rooms and online role-playing sites. What in fact occurred was far more complicated and vexing. The promise of a free-identity Internet gave way to the reality that social differences were not only still present online but in some cases exaggerated. To take one example, gender identity, which in the real world has been largely based upon physical appearance (Do you have muscles or curves? Short hair or long hair?) became almost reduced to these qualities. For young kids on Facebook and Twitter, therefore, posting revealing self-images exaggerating muscles or body shape became a heightened problem at younger and younger ages. Meanwhile, it became easier for predators to pose as young male or female account holders online thanks to these superficial markers of identity.

A related phenomenon was the rise of online defamation. Defamation, you may recall from chapter 2, is derived from old English common-law doctrine that protects the right of an individual to his or her own reputation. Not unlike contemporary intellectual property law, common-law defamation recognized a property-like interest in the use value of one's intangible reputation. So the common-law claim required that an injured party show that the defendant "published" "defamatory matter" that was "of and concerning" him or her. Each of these elements worked as a term of art, so *publication* meant release to at least one other person, *defamatory matter* meant false information whose harmfulness was judged according to an objective standard in a bounded community of "right thinking people," and *of and concerning* could mean something as specific as a named individual or as general as an entire sports team.

New York Times v. Sullivan confronted the additional problem of a "public official" being defamed. It asked whether individuals and news organizations should have extra leeway in reporting on public officials given the importance of this information, and given the likelihood that some reports would have false information. Zero liability would provide no incentive to "get it right," but major liability would mean little incentive for journalists to report on potentially true but harder-to-verify information. The Warren Court held that henceforth all such claims by public officials would require an additional showing of "actual malice"—knowledge or reckless disregard for the falsity communicated. This holding was later expanded to "public figures," including the everyday media celebrities who today influence public life.

The birth of the Internet posed new problems for defamation law and social norms in the United States. If the common-law test required a showing of "publication," the question sometimes arose *who* could be considered the publisher of the false and injurious information. In older cases, this question sometimes arose when, for example, a separate newspaper vendor was sued for selling papers commercially published by another company containing stories researched by staff journalists who, in turn, quoted independent sources for evidence. Was the newsstand vendor a publisher just like the newspaper company? The answer often came down to a reasonableness standard: whether the average newsstand would have reason to know the contents of its papers and magazines.[19]

The Internet age introduced a similar but more complex problem. Most text, video, sound, and image content online is posted by individual users—that is where the Web got its democratic promise in the first place. However, individuals rarely "host" their own Web content. Even individuals and small businesses with private websites keep these housed on Web-hosting servers owned by others. But at least in the early days of the Internet such individuals and businesses were the only ones curating their own content as Web pages, blogs, and the like. Still, some of the earliest cases for injury resulting from online behavior involved individuals posting to public websites hosted by Internet service providers (ISPs) themselves. Most readers today will not recognize these providers, but they included names like America Online (AOL), Compuserve, Prodigy, and Earthlink. In the mid-1990s, these companies distributed their software on CD-ROM discs sent through the mail, offered phone numbers for customers to connect using then-cutting-edge dial-up modem technology, and usually charged a monthly fee after a brief trial period. They also offered a variety of base content for users such as an e-mail address and interface, a Web browser, and early social networking platforms, bulletin boards, chat rooms, and newsgroups. It was in relation to these early social platforms that some of the landmark case law emerged.

First, in 1991's *Cubby, Inc. v. CompuServe Inc.*, a court in the Southern District of New York heard one of the first claims by a plaintiff trying to hold an ISP liable for publishing defamatory content about it.[20] Cubby was a business entity that published *Skuttlebut*—an online newsletter. CompuServe published a competing newsletter called *Rumorville*. Cubby asserted that *Rumorville* published false information disparaging its newsletter. This form of defamation is known as trade libel. The court admitted the claim, becoming one of the first to apply defamation jurisprudence to this scenario, but it said CompuServe could not be treated as a "publisher" for the common-law element of defamation. It was, instead, a "distributor" only.[21]

Then, in *Stratton Oakmont, Inc. v. Prodigy Services Co.*, an anonymous user of Prodigy's Money Talk chat room posted comments alleging that the New York financial firm of Stratton Oakmont was committing financial fraud.[22] Given the anonymity of the original poster and his or her likely inability to pay a substantial liability award, the plaintiff's decision to name Prodigy made good lawyering sense. But, in light of the *Compuserve* holding, it was a long shot. Nevertheless, the *Stratton Oakmont* court held for the plaintiff, finding Prodigy could be treated as a "publisher" for purposes of online defamation liability. The case caused such uproar in the US telecommunications industry that it prompted Congress to take swift action.

In 1996, after some lobbying by the telecom industry, Congress passed section 230 of the Communications Decency Act of 1996 (CDA). The CDA was a comprehensive piece of legislation that tried to limit the availability of pornographic and salacious material online in the early days of the new Internet. Perhaps not surprisingly, the antiobscenity provision of the act was struck down in a 1997 landmark case protecting the free-speech character of the modern Internet. But section 230 remained; it provided in relevant part that "no provider or user of an interactive computer service shall be treated as the publisher or speaker of any information provided by another information content provider."[23]

The major test of section 230 came in 1997 when the US Fourth Circuit Court of Appeals heard *Zeran v. America Online, Inc.* The facts were complex. In April 1995 a domestic terrorist bombed the federal building in Oklahoma City killing 168 people, including among them six preschool children. The day after the bombing, an anonymous user posted an "ad" on AOL's bulletin board offering new bombing-themed products such as T-shirts containing distasteful jokes and slogans about the crime and the dead.[24] Interested customers were told to contact Kenneth Zeran by his real home phone number. Zeran was then flooded with threats. After being notified, AOL removed the original posting, but it popped up again separately on the ISP's site before being again removed. Soon after, an Oklahoma City radio announcer read the original ad over the airwaves, causing another frenzy of threats against Zeran, as well as FBI intervention. In the case, Zeran asserted a claim for defamation against AOL, saying that it had negligently published the hurtful, false information about him. The case was controversial in that Zeran's claim was a matter of state tort law, and the injury had occurred before passage of section 230, but the claim was filed after. The Fourth Circuit held that the CDA applied and immunized the ISP regardless of both of these issues. Zeran remains the strongest application of section 230 in the protection of ISPs and other Web hosts, and, as we shall see, remains the basis on which social media platforms are able to operate relatively worry-free despite some of the dramatic harm created by their users.

SOCIAL MEDIA AUTHOR/PUBLICATION

The defamation cases just described all involved bulletin boards or news-groups—features of the early Internet. Once social media emerged, however, many of those forums became obsolete. Social media, for discussion's sake, are the kind of online platforms that allow users to maintain individual, customizable profile pages, link those pages to one another, and then interact regularly through the exchange of text, images, video, and sound data. The profile page becomes the online avatar for the person, allowing him or her to shape a public persona and appearance with the inclusion of personal information. The usual vital information like birthday and occupation can appear, but social media make a special point of emphasizing personal "interests"—things someone does for fun or distraction from the real world. This is especially important, as these sites evolved into pools for marketing data mining. Once companies like Facebook obtained personal "interests" from each of their two billion users, this data became highly valuable to market researchers, who have paid well for their benefit. In this regard, the rise of social media interaction has played a key role in the development of twenty-first-century global capitalism.

But social media platforms have also grown to serve a key news-sharing function. In an age when many no longer trust traditional media outlets, many report receiving and trusting news more when it comes through the new social networking sites than when it comes through television or radio. One reason for this may be the way social networking has generated "**news bubbles**," or zones of the online environment where people of the same political persuasion or opinion tend to gather and interact to the exclusion of opposing views. Another is the appearance of online news as unmediated "raw" information. People tend to think of news spread from microbloggers about, say, a street protest in Ferguson, Missouri, as having more reality than a well-produced, big-budget report of the same event on the evening TV news. Some traditional media like CNN, for instance, have thus encouraged user-generated news content in what has been termed a "crowdsourcing" approach to news gathering. The problem becomes, of course, how to maintain quality control over such a distributed network of lay journalists.

These developments have given rise to a new phenomenon that practicing lawyers have started to call "**Twibel**," a portmanteau of *Twitter* and *libel*.[25] Twitter, most readers may already know, is the social media platform that allows users to maintain a profile page but interact with one another only through short 280-character statements. Users can tag one another or classify their tweet under a "hashtag," a kind of metalabel that places their statement in a list with all others of the same classification. Thanks to its brevity and directness, Twitter has become a favorite for users during big newsworthy events. The various social justice protests related to police brutality and women's equality in recent years have become hotspots for tweeting and have thus spawned their own viral hashtags such as "#blacklivesmatter" or "#nasty-woman." The news coming out of these events directly from users on Twitter has posed a new problem for traditional news-gathering teams. To begin with, the editorial process—in which the journalists themselves review the veracity and credibility of news—is effectively eliminated. Whereas in some instances this is a good thing because news happens fast and lives may be saved by people knowing quickly, lives can also be jeopardized when people learn the wrong information before anyone has the chance to catch and correct it.

Second, the new environment for news has created a pressure among long-time respected news outlets to become the first to report something. National Public Radio (NPR), a staple of American radio news broadcasting for decades, found this out the hard way in 2011. In January of that year, the Arizona congresswoman Gabrielle Giffords was conducting a constituency meet-and-greet at a grocery story in Tucson when she was suddenly shot at close range along with several other people by a deranged young white gunman. NPR, which had a local reporter on the scene very quickly, became the first to report on the incident. But in reporting events over the subsequent hour, the network also reported prematurely that Giffords had died during treatment for her wounds. This information was flat out wrong; worse, it needlessly upset many people. The rush to be first in the age of social media had caused the network to overlook its own long-standing journalistic standards.[26] This was just one high-profile example of the traditional media being pulled in a new direction thanks to the pressures created by outsourced news distribution through sites like Twitter and Facebook.

But perhaps one of the most curious tests for online defamation law was the 2014 case of former Cincinnati Bengals cheerleader Sarah Jones. After retiring from cheerleading, Jones became a high school teacher in her home state of Kentucky. In 2009, two posts appeared on the online gossip site TheDirty.com asserting that Jones carried two forms of venereal disease. The posts were from an anonymous user, but they were tagged with editorial comments signed by the site's manager, who called himself Nik Richie. Jones sued the website and Richie in federal court almost immediately, asserting defamation and several other claims. She was particularly aided by the fact that libel law contains a common-law provision saying that false assertions of a "loathsome disease" require no special showing of damages, in contrast to most other cases, which do have this requirement. Recall also that naming the site and its owner in the suit may have been a risky move; the CDA section 230 had already long been recognized as providing publishers immunity from suit for third-party-posted content. But as a matter of legal strategy, it made sense: despite being a long shot, suing the publisher can often have the effect of "unmasking" an anonymous poster by forcing the website to disclose who its user is. Then again, sites often are reluctant to do this, as it would encourage all users to abandon their services.

At trial Richie's lawyers did assert publisher immunity under section 230. The court rejected this. Can you guess why? It said that Richie's addition of comments and signature raised his involvement to the level of an editor and beyond that of a mere publisher. Once content managers exercise some oversight of the content, they cannot claim that they blindly recirculated it. This would be like the newsstand signing off on newspaper article text before the paper is printed and then sold at its store. The trial court awarded Jones approximately $330,000 in damages in what was considered a blow to Internet content providers everywhere but a victory for individuals managing their reputations in a difficult and sometimes cruel new online world.

Nevertheless, the Sixth Circuit heard Richie's appeal in 2014 and reversed the decision entirely. It held that the trial court had applied the wrong test in determining whether Richie's own contribution to the harm was significant enough. The language the Sixth Circuit favored came from a 2008 Ninth Circuit ruling that held that a Web content manager must influence the "creation or development" of the content itself rather than simply providing an add-on at the very end.[27] Jones's trial court damage award was reversed, and, besides having her reputation now dragged through the mud for a protracted six-year period, she was ordered to pay the court costs for TheDirty.com. On one hand this seemed to be a victory for online bullying. The website was in fact a kind of "revenge site" where disgruntled exes often posted salacious or embarrassing information about their former partners. On the other hand, it was celebrated by commercial Web providers across the United States. Online companies were famously watching the case because its outcome would affect their own liability. Amicus briefs to the Sixth Circuit were filed by no less than, AOL, Inc., eBay, Inc., Facebook, Inc., Google, Inc., LinkedIn Corp., Microsoft Corp., Tumblr, Inc., Twitter, Inc., and Zynga, Inc. All had argued for the expansive reading of CDA section 230 immunity, which the court ultimately adopted and applied.

What can individuals do, then? Whereas the hope of holding companies liable for hosting injurious content is now pretty remote, experts advocate a number of nonlegal "self-help" precautions and remedies for social media–based injury. The first is to remain guarded about what one shares in these venues. The second is to invest in new online "reputation management" services—businesses that will help track what is said about their customers online and report abuses quickly. And the third is to consider new online mediation services that allow parties in conflict with one another over online content or commercial transactions to settle disputes remotely in the same medium where the injury arose in the first place. While all of these may provide some measure of protection or relief, readers will note that they dramatically shift responsibility for harm onto individual users.

The Jones case, along with others like it, returns us to a topic introduced early in this book. Illustrating the gap between what law wants to do (justice) and what it can do (remedies). Roscoe Pound said: "We try to hide the difficulty by treating the individual honor, dignity, character and reputation for purposes of the law of defamation, as assets. . . . But it is not so obvious what else the law may do."[28] He meant of course that the protection of something as important but intangible as reputation requires the law to strain itself translating the injury into a dollar amount. Immediately, this lays bare the problem of always needing to translate justice into money. Yet even though Jones lost her bid for money damages for reputational injury, this translation very much did take place—it was just at an earlier stage in the development of online defamation law. The reason why so many big tech companies filed briefs is the same reason why telecommunications companies lobbied for section 230 in the first place: their business success depended on risk management—in this case management pertaining to the risks of defamatory content spreading like wildfire in the new information technology age. The risk that some will use the new medium to cause injury to others was always there. Policy makers then had the choice whether to allocate responsibility for this to the commercial providers of the medium or to the individual users themselves. Section 230 and the Jones case illustrate in high relief the ways in which this allocation of risk has been driven in large measure by economic reasoning.

CONCLUSION

Legal issues in science and technology further illustrate the dynamic relationship between law and society. Rules and institutions can and do change, bringing with them altered patterns of behavior in the social environment. But social interactions and structures also can and do change first, necessitating in turn adjustments and readjustments among rules and institutions. Certain key cases of scientific and technological change aptly illustrate the latter. They reveal law's occasional slowness as well as agility in adapting to new fact patterns ushered in by human progress. But they also illustrate some of the types of harm that result from this lag or go unremedied as a result of it. The next and final chapter turns to one of the more extreme consequences when scientific and technological progress is placed in the service of industrial growth before legal expertise is able to keep pace.

CHAPTER 13 REVIEW

Key Terms

- Forensic science
- DNA
- Innocence movement
- Intellectual property
- Copyright
- Patent

- Trademark
- Primogeniture
- Virtual reality
- Genetically modified
- Biopiracy
- News bubble
- Twibel

Further Discussion

1. While the use of DNA evidence to exonerate accused criminals has been a positive development, are there any dangers to using molecular biology to identify people and establish their criminal history?
2. Does the concept of intellectual property—including its various legal protections—promote or limit technological innovation and progress?
3. Should companies be able to patent genetically modified organisms such as pest-resistant fruits and vegetables?
4. Is a new word like *Twibel* necessary when we already had *libel*, meaning written defamation?

Further Reading

Biagioli, Mario, Peter Jaszi, and Martha Woodmansee, eds. *Making and Unmaking Intellectual Property: Creative Production in Legal and Cultural Perspective*. Chicago: University of Chicago Press, 2011.

Kuhn, Thomas. *The Structure of Scientific Revolutions*. Chicago: University of Chicago Press, 1962.

Lynch, Michael, Simon A. Cole, Ruth McNally, and Kathleen Jordan. *Truth Machine: The Contentious History of DNA Fingerprinting*. Chicago: University of Chicago Press, 2010.

Nature | 14

In the 1840s, the United States was still a growing nation with borders still in flux and most of the population in the East. The western United States seemed like a wild frontier to most, lawmakers especially. Under what became known as "manifest destiny," they began to view westward expansion across the continent as part of the driving mission of nineteenth-century America. Therefore, any people, animals, and land encountered in the expansion process were to be considered subordinate to the destiny some writers felt was preordained. Indeed, they pointed to specific passages of the Bible that described the earth as existing for the sole purpose of humankind's comfort and sustenance. In the nineteenth century, the United States was thought to be the real-world manifestation of this "divine providence," and Americans its primary beneficiaries.

But some already saw the downsides of this homocentric worldview. The American naturalist John Muir became the most famous of these. Muir immigrated with his family from Scotland at the age of ten. While still young, Muir had memorized most of the Old and New Testaments. But as he came of age into adulthood, he began to lose faith in Christianity and grew increasingly fascinated by science and nature, which he studied avidly at the University of Wisconsin. On completion of his studies, he walked from Kentucky to Florida, studying the natural environments he passed on the way and reporting on them in the book *A Thousand-Mile Walk to the Gulf.* This became the first of many naturalist books Muir produced before he rose to national prominence and founded the Sierra Club. But perhaps his most important feat was to lead groups of lawmakers on camping trips in the wild. Muir felt that if those in positions of power could appreciate the beauty of nature firsthand, they might not be so quick to destroy it in the name of American expansion and industry. In particular, his leadership led to the creation of Yosemite National Park in California, a valley of sheer granite cliffs, waterfalls, and majestic redwoods that stand as a monument to "pure" nature. The beauty of Yosemite and places like it has been described as **charismatic**— as possessing the kind of alluring physical imagery that gets people's attention and causes them to invest in its protection.

Unfortunately, much of nature is not so "charismatic" or as easy to protect. In the years since Muir wrote, the number of national parks has increased, but the magnitude of environmental degradation has too. First, agricultural practices emphasizing large, industrial farming have led to vast quantities of chemicals being released into the soil and water supply. Relatedly, numerous animal, plant, and insect species have been driven to extinction by the increased levels of toxins in nature. Third, fossil fuel extraction and consumption have destroyed many natural habitats and have polluted air and waterways. Similarly, dependence on petroleum-based plastics has caused the global spread of microplastic pollution—particles of disintegrated plastic that are in virtually every water system on the planet. Finally, the buildup of human energy production and consumption has raised carbon dioxide in the atmosphere to historic levels, exaggerating the "**greenhouse effect**" and causing global temperatures to rise several degrees on average. In winter 2018, for example, scientists measured Arctic temperatures forty-five degrees above normal.[1]

These natural changes have been met with a global environmental movement born out of the 1960s social movements but dedicated to the protection of nonhuman life and natural, public land and resources. The environmental movement holds a key place in discussions about law and nature because it is, for the most part, responsible for bringing about the gradual changes in the law so far seen over the past fifty years. This is unusual: law and society frequently often (but not always) evolve in tandem without the intervention of political interest groups. Parties bring claims, claims are heard by courts, and judges decide outcomes that affect the broader society. Not unlike the social justice movements of the 1960s, however, nongovernmental interest groups have played a significant role in bringing claims on behalf of the public for misuse of natural resources, or they have exerted influence on legislative and judicial behavior through their marketing and outreach efforts.

This final chapter of *Law and Society Today*, therefore, covers these diverse topics in law and nature. It suggests that law's considerable struggle to adequately protect the natural environment is a final clear example of the current predicament of law and society. Unlike the previous two chapters in this unit on law and social change, this reveals an area in which both law and society have been painfully slow to change in reaction to rapid developments in the worldly context in which both reside. It suggests that this slowness is a grave symptom of neoliberalism—a kind of economic capture currently limiting our ideas about "justice" today. Supporting this, the chapter first revisits the concept of private property as it relates to nature in the Western world and compares this to other approaches. It then turns to legal authorities and processes as they apply to nature to ask what, if anything, law is good for in the domain of environmental protection. Finally, it examines a relatively new perspective on the law and society of environmentalism that experts have termed the **Anthropocene** approach—a view that nature is now irreversibly altered because of humankind's own actions.

PRIVATE PROPERTY VERSUS NATURE

The story of property in the West usually begins with early land law from medieval Europe and England, imported in turn to the colonies via exploration and settlement. But that tends to ignore the predominant sociocultural approaches to land that Europeans encountered in the New World. Instead of a tabula rasa—or blank slate—in North America, the colonists encountered elaborate indigenous societies that had well-developed approaches to land and the environment. This is contrary to the dominant perspective that Europeans alone had the concept of "property" while the Native Americans had no such thing.[2] The usual story holds that the former endowed the New World with a unique form of ownership that fostered exploitation and "improved" the natural environment into a usable one. But if both culture groups had developed concepts of property, perhaps the key distinction was that the Europeans based their entire framework on the forms of *legal* ownership.[3] To claim land as yours, you must have the "law on your side" in the form of land title or some other equivalent claim. In this regard, manmade law sat above nature itself. For Native peoples, by contrast, any lawlike constraints on how people access and use land were themselves also subservient to nature.

The roots of this distinction run very deep in Western civilization and expansion. Scholars usually tie it to the Judeo-Christian Bible itself—perhaps the single most influential text in the early modern Western world. There, some say, key verses implore human beings to "conquer" nature for their own nourishment, comfort, and enhancement.[4] Some of these verses even suggest that man's dominion over nature should strike terror in other living creatures.[5] But a face-value reading of these verses and practical interpretation of them are two different matters. For legal anthropologists especially, it has always been important not to simply read the authoritative texts of a society's legal culture but to also read those texts through the eyes of the people to whom they are meaningful. At least a few social science studies have indeed documented the effect of religious belief on environmental concern; they find that concern for environmental degradation does seem to lag among groups with stronger Christian theological beliefs.[6] Whether the same correlations are on display among people confessing to other religious beliefs is another question. Preliminarily, however, it is evident that widespread environmental harm from industrial development has emerged in high-growth, high-population countries like India and China. In China, one high-profile example was the alteration of the Yangtze River at the Three Gorges Dam. Currently the largest hydroelectric power plant in the world, the dam created upstream flooding that displaced 1.2 million local human inhabitants, leading to numerous human rights abuses.[7] On one hand the power generated from hydroelectric plants is far cleaner than the many more that burn dirty coal—in plentiful supply in the vast Asian nation. On the other, the dam has irreversibly scarred the natural landscape. The point of this example is that countries far outside the typical Judeo-Christian European and North American theaters have also been responsible for exerting "dominion" over nature—though perhaps it becomes justified on grounds of more pragmatic, human needs.

Returning to North America, it is important to also recall that these underlying beliefs toward land and the "improvement" of nature lie at the heart of our operating political philosophy. The US founding fathers were particularly interested in the writings of English theorist John Locke. As presented in the last chapter, Locke's idea of political authority connected it tightly to the notion of private property. Each individual family held dominion over its own estate. Each could grow that estate through the input of its own labor or capital. But once some did so, they would have larger property holdings than their neighbors. In a pregovernment era, this imbalance, and the imbalance between property owners and people who did not own any property, would create an incentive for outsiders to usurp others' property and leave individuals and families alone to defend their holdings from invaders. As a solution, humankind developed itself into a "political society" governed by a coercive state capable of promulgating laws to protect individual rights such as property, and by most accounts possessing a monopoly over the tools of coercion such as weaponry, courts, and prisons. One implication of this, meanwhile, is that a state that loses this capability or fails to exercise it renders itself illegitimate and subject to potential overthrow. In the last chapter I concluded that the connection between private property and legitimate government was a crucial element of our founding political theory. Here, in a chapter on law and nature, I want to extend this statement a bit further: if the legitimacy of government is tied to the protection of land (among other) rights, and if those rights are premised upon the "improvement" of raw land, then the power of our government institutions *depends upon* their protecting the right to alter or despoil nature itself.

Environmental activists might well say that this is obvious. Large environmental harm could not occur without the failure of the state, the federal government in particular, to limit individual (including corporate) rights to appropriate natural resources for their own gain and to **externalize** the costs of mistakes like oil spills and chemical leaks. Striking examples of such disasters abound; the Exxon Valdez oil tanker spill in Alaska produced horrific images of suffocating seabirds covered in crude, and the Deepwater Horizon explosion produced streaming live video of thousands of gallons of crude oil shooting from the ocean floor at high speed. These kinds of events represent not only the private extraction of natural resources based on some private right secured by law but also the degradation of the surrounding natural "property" at relatively minor cost to the corporation responsible.[8] Some would see such appropriation as the very basis on which the capitalist system—an economic system avowedly secured by our approach to government—operates.

But the US government is far from inactive in developing laws aimed at controlling environmental harm. Since at least the early 1970s it has passed important acts of Congress, overseen pollution permitting through federal agencies, and taken input from respected nongovernmental organizations.

JURISDICTION AND ENFORCEMENT

The year 1970 was an important watershed for environmental law and activism. The early seventies were still very much under the influence of the social movement waves that swept the West between the US civil rights movement and the global antiwar and student free speech movements of the 1960s. In 1970 the very first national Earth Day celebration took place following years of vocal advocacy of peace activist John McConnell and was given formal US government recognition spurred by Senator Gaylord Nelson. In the two years following, the United States saw most of its key environmental legislation produced.

The US federal government gets its authority to act on matters of the environment from article 1, section 8 of the Constitution, which says Congress has the power "to regulate Commerce with foreign Nations, and among the several States, and with the Indian Tribes." Known as the **commerce clause,** this section has become something of a catch-all for congressional acts. The regulation of guns—ostensibly a matter of police power or public health—has in fact been treated at times under the commerce power of Congress. The two most significant federal environmental statutes under this power remain the Clean Air Act of 1970 and Clean Water Act of 1972. Both promulgated under the Nixon administration and amended numerous times since, they marked a turning point in the public consciousness about environmental destruction and in legal efforts to prevent it. This turning point was perhaps triggered by a series of key events in the years before.

One was the famous Cuyahoga River fire of 1969, during which the river in question—a major thoroughfare for industrial production and distribution in Ohio—caught on fire thanks to the high volume of flammable chemicals floating on its surface. Another was the publication of *Silent Spring* by the naturalist writer Rachel Carson in 1962; her book documented the decline of bird species occurring throughout North America as the result of industrial chemicals—notably DDT. Both events were visually striking and emotion-provoking incidents that helped garner support for the building environmental movement, so Nixon's signing of the new legislation came at a time when public support for it was at an all-time high. Nixon's signing of these laws was itself done in heightened ceremonious fashion meant to capture, perhaps, some of the momentousness of the harm being done to nature and his apparent heroic leadership in response.

The Clean Air Act of 1970 came at a time when American cities were choking from car exhaust fumes, industrial smoke, and dirty energy production. Although a Clean Air Act had been in place since 1963, it was largely unenforced. The 1970 law created the Environmental Protection Agency (EPA) to develop acceptable standards and enforce them through permitting and fines. Once in place, the EPA promulgated pollution emission controls, required automobile and industrial emitters to register and forced them to comply with lower emission levels. This, in turn, spurred greater research into pollution reduction technologies. One resulting example was the advent of the catalytic converter, a device in every vehicle that limits the release of nitrogen oxide and carbon monoxide from the standard auto engine fumes. Another was the creation and widespread use of unleaded gasoline. Lead, as readers will know, is toxic to human beings. Prior to the EPA, lead was a common ingredient in gasoline. Starting in the 1970s, the EPA mandated the phaseout and elimination of this ingredient because its use was allowing it to enter the atmosphere and permeate the human environment. Figure 14.1 below shows the average human blood lead levels in the decade after the EPA's intervention.

One recent example of an EPA case brought under the Clean Air Act was *Husqvarna Ab and Husqvarna Consumer Outdoor Products N.A., Inc.* There, a Swedish small equipment manufacturer—think lawn mowers, leaf blowers, and chain saws—was sanctioned for failing to obtain EPA advance certification for its products sold in the United States.[9] The concern was that Husqvarna consumer products could exceed EPA emissions limits and that the company had failed to purchase carbon emissions credits to offset this. The emission credit system is a formal exchange administered by EPA to force large companies to begin to "internalize" the costs of the pollution they create. In this case, on December 5, 2017, EPA entered a judgment and settlement with Husqvarna requiring them to pay a fine of $2.85 million.

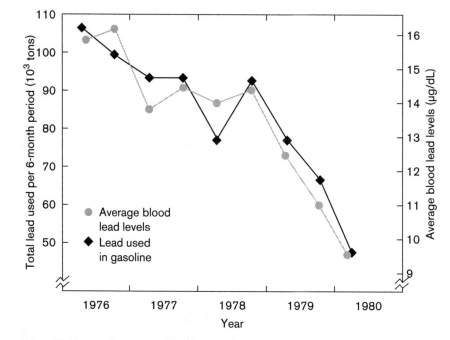

Figure 14.1 Average human blood lead levels under US Environmental Protection Agency (EPA) rules, 1976–80. Source: US Environmental Protection Agency, "History of Reducing Air Pollution from Transportation in the United States (U.S.)," n.d., accessed March 14, 2018, https://www.epa.gov/air-pollution-transportation/accomplishments-and-success-air-pollution-transportation.

Similar cases have emerged over water pollution. When industries pollute protected waterways, the harm tends to be slightly more localized and, therefore, traceable than that of their air pollution equivalents. Such water cases are brought by the EPA under the Clean Water Act, the second of the Nixon administration's large federal policies on the environment. The act began as the Federal Water Pollution Control Act of 1948 but underwent sweeping amendments following the late 1960s' rise in environmental political awareness sparked by the Rachel Carson book and the Cuyahoga fire, among other things. Similar to the Clean Air Act, the Clean Water Act authorized the EPA to set water pollution safety standards and to require a permit from any "point source" pollution into navigable—that is to say circulating—waterways. And it began to address non–point source pollution—things like stormwater runoff from large city streets that brought substances like motor oil and tire residue into the ocean.[10]

By far the most significant Clean Water Act case of the past decade was the Gulf of Mexico oil spill disaster of Deepwater Horizon, a private offshore oil rig contracted by British Petroleum. Following a terrible explosion on the offshore rig on April 20, 2010, that killed eleven workers, crude oil from the ocean floor poured into the Gulf for three months. The total spill amounted to four million barrels of oil over the entire period—and much of that oil made its way into coastal waterways of Louisiana, Mississippi, Alabama, and Florida. The spill ruined the coastal economies of fishing and tourism, affecting so many individuals and businesses that the EPA had to set up an entire separate claims process administered through the federal Eastern District of Louisiana. The total penalties assessed against BP were a record-setting $5.5 billion for violating the Clean Water Act, as well as nearly $9 billion for destroying natural resources—an amount intended to benefit bona fide individual victims of the injury. With such historic damages imposed, one could argue that the Clean Water Act "worked" exactly as intended in this case.[11] On the other hand, the natural habitat of the coastal Gulf States was altered irreversibly in a manner that may far exceed the dollar amounts of even these large settlements.

Both the Husqvarna and Deepwater Horizon cases illustrate some of the key challenges of the approaches to legal protection of nature embodied in the EPA and its enabling laws. Although the organization "requires" permitting for polluters before they engage in harmful conduct, in the most egregious cases it is often limited to reactive (rather than proactive) measures, so that, by the time penalties are assessed, it is too late for the environment to avoid harm. Additionally, the extent to which post hoc penalties can deter future harmful conduct remains questionable. The specific corporation might be forced to change its practices, and in some cases an entire industry might. But disasters caused by private extraction of natural resources or steady production of dirty consumer products continue to occur. One of the key safeguards against these ongoing disasters has been the surprising role played by nongovernmental organizations serving as watchdogs for the public interest.

NONGOVERNMENTAL ORGANIZATIONS

Nongovernmental organizations, or NGOs, have become a fixture of modern civic life around the globe. Whereas classic political theorists talked about "the state" in contrast to "civil society," NGOs seem to bridge this divide by organizing private citizens into politically motivated groups to further unified agendas as if acting with a single will. Although only ever in an advisory role with respect to governments, certain NGOs have become powerful as transnational fund-raisers and resource mobilization bodies. Many have stronger brand recognition than intergovernmental organizations: Amnesty International, for instance, has become synonymous with global human rights protections. The World Wildlife Fund may be the equivalent for animal rights.

The environmental movement has seen the rise of several key NGO players in the United States. Greenpeace may be the biggest brand. Founded in 1971 amid the same social activism that gave us Earth Day, Greenpeace gained considerable notoriety from charismatic actions like their 2015 kayak blockade of an oil rig owned by Shell Oil and bound for offshore drilling in Alaska.[12] The National Resource Defense Council (NRDC) is slightly older and combines activism and protest with scientific, legal, and policy research. NRDC experts have actively proposed new legislation such as the Water Rights Protection Act, designed to protect group water rights for organizations currently forced to surrender those in exchange for using public lands. The NRDC has been active in litigation, with perhaps its most cited victory being the 1984 case *Chevron U.S.A., Inc. v. Natural Resources Defense Council, Inc.*, which held that federal administrative agencies such as the EPA are to receive substantial leeway as they apply federal law.[13] This has come to be called "Chevron deference," and the NRDC's name comes up every time this doctrine is invoked—which is often.

Finally, the Sierra Club is equally known but considerably older. Founded by the naturalist John Muir in 1892, the Sierra Club was initially focused on preservation of natural environments and has enjoyed several major victories. In the 1960s, for example, the US Bureau of Reclamation introduced plans to dam the Colorado River at the top and bottom of the Grand Canyon to generate hydroelectric power for the developing Southwest—experiencing at the time a boom in economic and population growth thanks to the rise of aerospace and information technology industries there. The Sierra Club vehemently opposed the construction of the two dams and took out full-page ads in the *New York Times* and *Washington Post* in 1966 announcing to millions of urban readers that the Grand Canyon was about to be destroyed. The campaign worked, and by 1968 the United States had to abandon the plan. That visitors can, to this day, visit a preserved Grand Canyon owes very much to the work of the Sierra Club among others.

The power and voice of NGOs like Greenpeace, the NRDC, and the Sierra Club are clearly beneficial to the environmental protection cause, but they raise some important issues about the relationship between law and society. First, if the environmental movement was a spontaneous public movement that reflected changing social attitudes about nature, was it a good thing for a handful of key groups to occupy the landscape? What happens to average citizens when advocacy groups become their mouthpiece in politics? And what happens to well-founded social movements when their power and energy are bridled by bureaucratic organizations worried about fund-raising and membership as much as the underlying mission—of environmental protection in this case? These questions are too large to answer in this survey chapter of law and nature, but they reveal the fascinating interplay between law and society on one hand and politics and culture on the other. In some senses, they are more important than ever today, as global society confronts perhaps the greatest ecological threat of all: itself.

THE ANTHROPOCENE

Global society's success is becoming its failure. In a very short (in geologic time) period of a few thousand years human beings went from living in caves and hunting with clubs and spears to exploring space and storing almost all of human knowledge on computers the size of a briefcase. To get here from there, immense amounts of energy had to be harvested and consumed. But the harvesting and consumption of energy have come at a significant price: deforestation on nearly every continent, release of dangerous levels of carbon emissions, and the destruction of animal and plant species at the rate of a minimum two hundred species per year. Figure 14.2 depicts the dodo, the most famous example of animal extinction caused by human beings.[14]

All of these dramatic changes in the natural environment result from human industry, and they have given rise to a new term for the geologic epoch in which we now find ourselves. Physical and social scientists are calling our modern age the *Anthropocene,* a portmanteau word that combines the Greek roots for the word *man* (*anthropos*) and (geological) *era* (*kainos*). Following periods like the Pleistocene and (most recently) the Holocene, the Anthropocene designates a change in the concentration of chemicals and particles found in the soil and rock layers beginning around the time of the Industrial Revolution in the forty years before and after 1800. In that time, the economies of Western countries, notably England and the United States, began shifting from primarily farm-based production to primarily factory-based manufacturing. While both countries still maintained extensive internal and external colonies to extract natural resources from untamed wilderness areas through mining, timber, and the like, the bulk of their economic value production and labor employment began to concentrate in big cities, where factories made use of low-skilled workers in large physical plants and warehouses. These factories utilized new industrial machinery, as well as a division of labor such that specific workers would specialize and concentrate on key elements of the manufacturing process—unlike the previous tradesmen, who had been capable of each building the whole product in various steps. By the early twentieth century this division of labor had been perfected by the likes of Frederick Taylor, an engineer who applied the principles of "scientific management" to the steel production process to minimize the labor steps required to produce a unit of steel product. **Taylorism,** as it came to be called, revolutionized industrial production worldwide by maximizing the value that could be extracted from labor and thereby reducing the cost of making consumer products. But as factory production moved faster, so too did the waste products of factory operations. Most operations involved some form of chemicals to process the raw materials. All involved some form of energy—often coal- or wood-burning generators to power the heavy machinery or conveyor belts moving through increasingly complex factory buildings. All of this heightened production, in short, generated heightened levels of environmental pollution, most notably

Figure 14.2 William Frohawk, painting of the famously extinct "dodo bird," 1905. Source: World Wildlife Fund, "How Many Species Are We Losing?" Panda.org, n.d., accessed March 14, 2018, http://wwf.panda.org/about_our_earth/biodiversity/biodiversity/.

carbon dioxide. From that period onward, elevated levels of carbon and other compounds can be found in the geologic strata, and for that reason many have been quick to accept and adopt the *Anthropocene* as a term for the contemporary period of human-influenced earth chemistry.

But the term has another implication for law and society. The legal scholar Jedediah Purdy has argued that the Anthropocene is not merely a new period of time where humans leave a worldwide trace on the planet. For Purdy, the new epoch also means that there is no longer any untouched, raw "nature."[15] Whereas much of environmental law and policy formerly focused on "preservation" of nature in the tradition of John Muir and his disciples, the Anthropocene requires an acceptance that there is no longer any true wilderness to preserve. Indeed, anthropologists have long pointed out, maybe there never was one. The very concept of "nature" exists in the human imagination only as a counterconcept to "civilization"—the side of the world built by humans to ensure safety and comfort in a way that keeps the wild experience of nature at bay. The average city, with its paved streets, elaborate storm gutters, busy sanitation services, and general rules of traffic and crime, is intended to minimize the natural flow of water, dirt, and animal instincts that characterize nonhuman environments. Nature as a concept appears only once that which it represents has been eliminated from the daily lives of most citizens, and only since then has it become something in need of preservation.

Regardless of this observation, the reality is that the dominant approach to environmental law emphasizing preservation may not be adequate to limit the toll humans are taking on the world around them—whatever we want to call it. At the current rates of population growth and carbon emissions, humans themselves may not have more than a few hundred years to survive on the planet—let alone preserve the trappings of nature on it. Proponents of the concept of the Anthropocene—a vision of the world as "postnature"—suggest therefore that the very survival of humans will depend on drastic new policy.

Opponents have much to criticize about this. Many point out that the world cycles through natural species explosions and extinctions and that the geological record actually shows many shifts of this nature occurring from "acts of God" that range from meteorite collisions to volcanic eruptions. If the dinosaurs, some of the most powerful and widespread species to walk the earth, were susceptible to the march of time, why shouldn't humans also be? Furthermore, even if we made self-preservation rather than environmental conservation our priority, who is to say this could ever work? Humans can't possibly alter the course of earth's life cycle themselves, can they? Nowhere is this debate more salient and consequential today than in the discussions surrounding **climate change.**

Climate refers to general dynamics in earth's patterns. Whereas weather can change drastically from day to day and week to week, climate is historically more stable. Scientists might find natural variations over decades in a region's weather record—for instance, nighttime temperatures can ebb and flow—but they should normally evolve slowly or not change at all. Since approximately the 1970s, scientists have been monitoring global climate indicators such as temperature and carbon concentrations around the world. Their findings—almost without dispute—suggest that the earth is currently experiencing a widespread warming trend. The change in temperatures coincides with elevated levels of carbon dioxide—a compound known to trap solar heat within the atmosphere rather than allowing it to release back into space. The heat trapping has been called the "greenhouse effect," and the condition it has created was first called "global warming" before being modified to "climate change," since in reality unreleased heat was causing greater fluctuations in weather patterns rather than a uniform warming. Indeed, politicians favorable to the industries contributing to the problem have been known to say "global warming" as if to emphasize that it never materialized, when in fact the more accurately named climate change is well documented and clearly behind such dramatic weather events as Hurricane Katrina, Superstorm Sandy, and Supertyphoon Yolanda—record-setting storms all within the past fifteen years.

Climate change might be considered a subtopic in the larger discussion of the Anthropocene. It illustrates an irreversible human effect on the natural environment. Yet it is also something different. Rather than simply indexing a "postnatural" era, or labeling a turning point in the geologic record, climate change poses a significant direct threat to human activity and existence. If temperatures rise, vast beds of Arctic sea ice melt, dumping billions of gallons of fresh water into the world's oceans and causing a rise in sea levels. As this occurs, coastal flooding in many of the most populated urban areas—New York and Los Angeles, for example—is likely. But also, as once-in-a-century storms march in every year, the cost of damage and rebuilding to developed economies is enormous. In the former "Third World" countries, rebuilding sometimes never even happens. The beautiful island nation of Mauritius in the Indian Ocean may soon be entirely underwater as sea levels rise.

All of these examples point to the same conclusion: action is needed. The question for readers of this book becomes this: What, if anything, can law do? The limitations are serious. Traditionally, as the early chapters of this text pointed out, law has been a product of *national* sovereignty. Modern law may have emerged out of the communal or village living of early modern England and Europe, but it got its uniform legitimacy with the rise of the nation-state, so that we came to speak of the "law of England" or "the law of France" or, nowadays "the law of the European Union." When it comes to tackling industrial carbon emissions in the name of the Anthropocene or climate change, the pressing question is whether contemporary law based on the nation-state model is of much use.[16] If France as a country passes a law to limit motor vehicle emissions once a week, this is certainly helpful, but is it consequential given the total emissions produced on the European continent and the circulation of air pollution worldwide? If not, are global solutions the way forward?

Given the planetary scale of climate change, international organizations have long tried to align the industrial powers of the world in emission controls treaties. After the Rio Earth Summit in 1992, 195 countries ratified the United Nations Framework Convention on Climate Change (UNFCCC). The UNFCCC was the first international agreement formally recognizing the need for action on global temperature change. Out of its framework, the signatory countries agreed to the historic Kyoto Protocol, finally setting "legally binding emission reduction targets" for the developed countries of the world on the understanding that these were the nations most responsible for carbon emissions, and the ones whose economic strength could best shoulder any burdens from pollution reduction measures.[17]

Importantly, the United States under then-president Clinton did sign the Kyoto Protocol but failed to ratify it and therefore failed to make it binding law. President George W. Bush then removed the United States' signature altogether, arguing that the limitations would do substantial harm to the US economy in part because it meant shifting toward greater reliance on renewable energy and away from coal production. Moreover, Bush echoed doubts among a minority of the scientific community that climate change was even caused by manmade carbon emissions. This climate-skeptic position has hardened over time, and at times it has been sponsored by fossil fuel energy companies helping to finance scientific research favorable to their business model—one that externalizes the costs of pollution while privatizing the profits attained from natural resource harvesting. The debates over Kyoto have settled in as the structure for most debate about climate change. A majority of scientists hold carbon emissions responsible, they are met with criticism by a few scientists supported by energy corporations, and policy makers rely on this skepticism while speaking to the coal-producing states whose voters rely most on the coal economy, and whose votes in national elections have grown disproportionately important under the United States' unique electoral college system.[18]

A similar result occurred in 2016. In late 2015, members of the UNFCCC gathered for the Paris climate conference, which aimed to, again, refocus global policy on emission reductions. They came to an agreement to reduce the trajectory of global temperature change by two degrees Celsius, requiring, again, the reduction of carbon emissions from at least fifty-five countries accounting for 55 percent of global emissions. Within a year of the conference, the Paris Agreement was ratified by enough nations to bring it into force—much to the celebration of countries in Europe and coastal Asia. But, once again, the United States' signature was conspicuously absent from the treaty. Although the United States under President Obama was a participant in the Paris process, President Trump withdrew the nation in June 2017, stating, "The bottom line is that the Paris accord is very unfair at the highest level to the United States." By this, he meant that it disadvantaged the American economy more than others. This posture was consistent with Trump's longtime promise to "make American great again." But it perhaps failed to recognize that the consequence of nonparticipation decades from now will include additional weather disasters that also cost the US economy dearly. Both observations are rooted in the economic rationality that many in Western law and politics have adopted—and that this book has treated as a dominant theme. But dedicated environmental activists continue to resist this thinking. The health of the planet, they continue to say, cannot be measured by economic metrics. When planetary survival is at stake, no short-term dollar amounts are worth more than long-term emissions reductions. As one expert elegantly said, "Trump just passed on the best deal the planet has ever seen."[19]

LAW AND SOCIAL CHANGE

The struggle over climate change is a political one, but even if it were not, any legal solutions developed would be subject to the key limitations raised by law, limitations that social movements have struggled against for years and that this book has repeatedly discussed. First, how can law—an expert discipline and profession—humble itself to absorb knowledge from other fields like climate science? What research will be the official version of cause and effect, and which studies will influence the potential solutions? Second, how can new legal rules impose negative rights on large industrial polluters, and what enforcement power will back them up? Companies, we have seen, are increasingly transnational in their conduct and organization. At times, as with corporate tax inversion, they have gone transnational specifically to evade the governance of the nation-state. If so, then how do we confront the increasingly autonomous private corporation that lately finds itself beyond the reach of national law and enforcement? Even when new legal solutions are global in scope, they so far depend upon national ratification and enforcement to take effect.

But also, even if law is effective in stopping the runaway trains of industrial carbon emissions and climate change, then what? With Purdy and others we must contend with the idea of a "postnatural" world in which humans really are now stewards of the nonhuman environment, including living animal and plant species, but also "nonliving" rock and mineral formations. First, do we have what it takes to properly *value* these things? To even use the word *value* is to introduce economic reasoning to this conundrum. Yet there is a difference between economic reasoning and "market" reasoning. The word *economy* comes from the Greek word *oikos*, meaning "household," and economic reasoning has been with human beings since their dawn on planet Earth. Managing the household has changed by leaps and bounds, but the underlying endeavor to make life livable and happy so that human beings can reproduce and thrive remains the same. So it is not economism itself that has done human beings a disservice; it is rather the kind of economic reasoning that reduces management of the figurative household—the village, the town, the planet—to a "market" activity, particularly emphasizing exchange for money. Money is that mysterious artifact of modern economics that has both no value and all value at the same time. It is, truly, the driver of modern markets. So the problem with our ability to properly value the postnatural world is not our attachment of value per se—a forest might *mean* everything to us, even or especially when it cannot be converted into cash money—but the incessant need to define that value in market terms.

Second, and perhaps most importantly, can we trust ourselves to rethink homocentrism—the worldview that places human beings ahead of all other planetary creatures and objects? This is a tough proposition if our civilizations were built on the idea of dominion over nature. Yet, a movement in law has emerged to give natural objects themselves their own legal status worthy of protection. In 1972, the legal scholar Christopher Stone wrote a seminal article that was quickly cited in a Supreme Court case dissent that very same year. Stone was concerned that cases involving environmental protection almost only ever weighed the rights of the humans—often a developer or oil and mineral exploration company on one side and an NGO or tribe on the other.[20] In the piece entitled "Should Trees Have Standing?," Stone wrote,

> Unfortunately, so far as the pollution costs are concerned, the allocative ideal begins to break down, because the traditional legal institutions have a more difficult time "catching" and confronting us with the full social costs of our activities. In the lakeside mill example, major riparian interests might bring an action, forcing a court to weigh their aggregate losses against the costs to the mill of installing the anti-pollution device. But many other interests—and I am speaking for the moment of recognized homocentric interests—are too fragmented and perhaps too remote to causally warrant securing representation and pressing for recovery.[21]

Stone was saying that even from a purely human-centered economistic view that all costs are negotiable our legal judgment fails to capture much of what constitutes "cost"—even to just human beings.

But in the decades since Stone raised these important questions about the legal personhood of nature, things have changed. The consequences for inaction have grown only more dire, and now human species survival will depend upon cooperation with the nonhuman environment—permanently altered though it may already be. The anthropologist Anna Tsing writes about this potential for rebirth on the verge of natural extinction in her naturalist ethnography *The Mushroom at the End of the World.* She documents the natural habitat for the matsutake mushroom, a wild fungi that cannot be farmed and primarily grows in forests disturbed by human timber and mining practices. Harvesting matsutake requires the hunter to enter the forest as a forager, the way human ancestors once gathered their daily nourishment by hand. So rare and tasty is the mushroom that it has become the "most valuable mushroom in the world." For Tsing and her colleagues, the matsutake is both a commodity and metaphor for the "possibility of life in capitalist ruins"—a world in which nature fights through the devastation humans have caused themselves by their appetites for more. Much like the concept of the Anthropocene, *The Mushroom at the End of the World* dispenses with caution; it offers a look ahead to rebirth after devastation, perhaps with a belief that that is where the best hope now lies.

CONCLUSION

For students of law and society, these concepts are ideal ones to end upon. The past few decades in this field have seen fascinating conversations develop and unfold in the academic circles of professors and researchers. They have given rise to more graduate and undergraduate programs of study, and options for majors and minors to tackle the questions this book has addressed over the course of fourteen chapters. But those conversations have not yet solved the pressing problems caused by the endless, dynamic interplay between law and society. Like a creature chasing its own tail, law and society continues moving, at times rapidly, but it has yet to achieve its objective of creating legal solutions to better match social problems.

Throughout this series of chapters I have suggested a conspicuous reason for this: those of us studying law and society must better recognize the presence of a third player on the field. Whenever social problems have called for legal solutions, they have always begged the question "What is law?" and, really, "What is its modus operandi?" Many in the nonlegal world would answer succinctly: the purpose of law is justice. Yet this book has illustrated the idealism of that answer. In fact, thanks to a series of historical turns over the past several decades, there is a new logic behind what we often view as legal solutions. This logic, that of market economy influenced most heavily by the moral philosophy of utilitarianism, has been driving legal solutions to large social problems more than any other new approach in the past fifty years. Law and society students must know this if we are to continue the important work of proposing new solutions while fixing old ones.

As with the rebirth of life in the matsutake example, hope lies with the future and not the past. Readers reaching the end of this book for school, for research, or just to learn: that hope lies with you.

CHAPTER 14 REVIEW

Key Terms

- Charismatic
- Greenhouse effect
- Anthropocene
- Externalize
- Commerce clause
- Taylorism
- Climate change

Further Discussion

1. What do we mean when we say aspects of nature are "charismatic" or "not charismatic"?
2. Humans have occupied the earth for many thousands of years. What is new about the Anthropocene?
3. Why are matters of jurisdiction and enforcement so difficult for environmental harm?
4. Do readings and discussions in law and society offer any hope that the problems of environmental degradation could still be solvable through human ingenuity and cooperation?

Further Reading

Carson, Rachel. *Silent Spring*. Boston: Houghton Mifflin, 2002.

Muir, John. *My First Summer in the Sierra*. Boston: Houghton Mifflin, 1911.

Purdy, Jedediah. *After Nature: A Politics for the Anthropocene*. Cambridge, MA: Harvard University Press, 2016.

Stone, Christopher. *Should Trees Have Standing? Law, Morality, and the Environment*. 3rd ed. Oxford: Oxford University Press, 2010.

Tsing, Anna. *The Mushroom at the End of the World: On the Possibility of Life in Capitalist Ruins*. Princeton, NJ: Princeton University Press, 2017.

Notes

PREFACE

1. US Courts, "Federal Judicial Caseload Statistics 2017," 2017, www.uscourts.gov/statistics-reports/federal-judicial-caseload-statistics-2017.

1. INTRODUCTION

1. Jon B. Gould and Scott Barclay, "Mind the Gap: The Place of Gap Studies in Sociolegal Scholarship," *Annual Review of Law and Social Science* 8 (2012): 323–35.
2. William J. Crampon and Alex J. Norman, *Ethnic Disparities in Long Beach, California*, ReThinking Greater Long Beach, 2014, www.rethinklongbeach.org/resources/Ethnic+Disparities+in+Long+Beach.pdf (no longer accessible).
3. Ibid., 3.
4. See generally Kevin R. Johnson, "The Intersection of Race and Class in U.S. Immigration Law and Enforcement," *Law and Contemporary Problems* 72, no. 4 (2009): 1–35.
5. See, for example, Erik Bleich, "The Legacies of History? Colonization and Immigrant Integration in Britain and France," *Theory and Society* 34, no. 2 (2005): 171–95.
6. Pew Research Center, "Technology Device Ownership," October 29, 2015, www.pewinternet.org/2015/10/29/technology-device-ownership-2015/.
7. Asifa Quraishi-Landes, "Five Myths about Sharia," *Washington Post*, June 24, 2016, https://www.washingtonpost.com/opinions/five-myths-about-sharia/2016/06/24/7e3efb7a-31ef-11e6–8758-d58e76e11b12_story.html ?utm_term=.aaac8f05b65a.

2. WHERE LAW MEETS SOCIETY

1. Richard Posner, "A Theory of Negligence," *Journal of Legal Studies* 1, no. 1 (1972): 33.
2. Fred R. Shapiro, "The Most Cited Legal Scholars," *Journal of Legal Studies* 29, no. S1 (2000): 409–26.
3. The so-called Age of Discovery refers only to the period from the fifteenth to the eighteenth century in which European explorers encountered non-European peoples on their home soil. It is therefore "Eurocentric." There is evidence available that non-Europeans had developed technologies sufficient to navigate and travel widely before the Europeans. Easter Island in the South Pacific, for example, a remote island now belonging to Chile, may be just one of several places that the early Polynesians reached by ocean voyages of thousands of miles and settled. See, e.g., Brian Switek, "DNA Shows How the Sweet Potato Crossed the Sea," *Nature*, January 21, 2013, www.nature.com/news/dna-shows-how-the-sweet-potato-crossed-the-sea-1.12257.

4. Pound, "What Is Law?," in *Social Control through Law* (1942; repr., New Brunswick, NJ: Transaction, 1997), 35–62.
5. Ibid., 45.
6. Ibid., 46.
7. Ibid., 47.
8. Ibid., 47–48.
9. Riaz Tejani, "Little Black Boxes: Legal Anthropology and the Politics of Autonomy in Tort Law," *University of New Hampshire Law Review* 11 (2013): 129.
10. Lawrence Rosen, *Law as Culture: An Invitation* (Princeton, NJ: Princeton University Press, 2006), 68–70.
11. Pound, "What Is Law?," 59–60.
12. See, e.g., Mitchell Crusto, "Federalism and Civil Rights: The Meredith Case," *National Black Law Journal* 11 (1989): 233.
13. Gene Marine, "The Free Speech Movement," *Nation,* December 21, 1964, https://www.thenation.com/article/free-speech-movement/.
14. Antonia Molloy, "Tom Cruise Settles $50 Million Defamation Case over Claims He Abandoned Daughter Suri," *Independent*, December 23, 2013, www.independent.co.uk/arts-entertainment/films/news/tom-cruise-settles-50million-defamation-case-over-claims-he-abandoned-daughter-suri-9022484.html.
15. There are exceptions; see, e.g., Carol Burnett v. National Enquirer, Inc., 193 Cal. Rptr. 206, July 18, 1983.
16. Molloy, "Tom Cruise Settles."

3. COMPARATIVE LEGAL COMMUNITIES

1. In the US criminal justice system, "guilt" and punishment are determined in two separate phases of the legal process.
2. Paul Raeburn, "Too Immature for the Death Penalty?," *New York Times*, October 17, 2004, www.nytimes.com/2004/10/17/magazine/too-immature-for-the-death-penalty.html?_r=0.
3. "Excessive bail shall not be required, nor excessive fines imposed, nor cruel and unusual punishments inflicted." U.S. Const. amend VIII.
4. Roper v. Simmons, 543 U.S. 551, 578 (2005).
5. Roper v. Simmons, J. Scalia Dissent, 543 U.S. 551, 624 (2005).
6. The Roman Empire includes the Byzantine Empire, also known as the Eastern Roman Empire, which lasted until 1453 A.D.
7. This is an important fact because common-law countries use organized "rule books" that collect and reproduce the law. They are here called "treatises" or "restatements of the law." These collections, however, are considered merely gatherings of law as created by cases, they are only "persuasive authorities," and they are generally not adopted by state or federal governments.
8. For more on the rich history of this distinction going all the way back to Roman law, see, for example, Ugo Mattei, Teemu Ruskola, and Antonio Gidi, *Schlesinger's Comparative Law:*

Cases, Text, Materials, 7th ed. (New York: Foundation Press, 2009).

9. This removes a major financial obstacle to bringing suit, but that obstacle may be reinserted by holding the loser accountable in most civil law countries for the court costs and attorney fees of both sides rather than having each side pay its own way, as in the United States.

10. Peter De Cruz, *Comparative Law in a Changing World* (London: Routledge Cavendish, 2008), 43.

11. Many of these espoused Marxist doctrine, but some held to other versions of socialism.

12. This has been called the "statist catastrophe." See Richard Gilman-Opalsky, *Precarious Communism: Manifest Mutations, Manifesto Detourned* (New York: Minor Compositions, 2014), 4.

13. Duane P. Schultz, *A History of Modern Psychology*, 9th ed. (Belmont, CA: Thomas Higher Education, 2008), 47–48.

14. Mark F. Griffith, "John Locke's Influence on American Government and Public Administration," *Journal of Management History* 3, no. 3 (1997): 224–37.

15. This influence came at the least via Voltaire. See, e.g., Alex Calinicos, *Social Theory: A Historical Introduction* (New York: NYU Press, 1999), 16–17.

16. There are indeed four main schools of jurisprudence in global Islamic law. See, e.g., Mattei, Ruskola, and Gidi, *Schlesinger's Comparative Law*, 377.

17. Rosen, *Law as Culture*.

18. Mattei, Ruskola, and Gidi, *Schlesinger's Comparative Law*, 282.

19. Ibid.

20. Ibid.

21. Ibid., 31.

22. Alan Watson, *Legal Transplants: An Approach to Comparative Law* (Athens: University of Georgia Press, 1974).

23. De Cruz, *Comparative Law*, 11.

24. Mattei, Ruskola, and Gidi, *Schlesinger's Comparative Law*, 98.

4. HISTORY

1. See, e.g., G. W. F. Hegel, *Lectures on the Philosophy of History*, trans. H. B. Nisbet (New York: Cambridge University Press, 1975).

2. See, e.g., Karl Marx and Friedrich Engels, *The Communist Manifesto* (Sweden: Chiron, 2016).

3. Eric Hobsbawm, "Introduction: Inventing Traditions," in *The Invention of Tradition*, ed. Eric Hobsbawm and Terrence Ranger (Cambridge: Cambridge University Press, 1983), 1.

4. Ibid.

5. Paul Quigley, "The Birth of Thanksgiving," *New York Times*, November 28, 2013.

6. Benedict Anderson, *Imagined Communities: Reflections on the Origin and Spread of Nationalism* (1983; repr., London: Verso, 2016), 49.

7. "Congress shall make no law respecting an establishment of religion, or prohibiting the free exercise thereof; or abridging the freedom of speech, or of the press; or the right of the people peaceably to assemble, and to petition the Government for a redress of grievances." U.S. Const. amend. I.

8. Whitney v. California, 274 U.S. 357 (1927).

9. New York Times v. Sullivan, 376 U.S. 254, 270 (1964).

10. Ibid., 273–74.

11. Ibid., 276.

12. Peter Irons, "Morally Sinful by the Word of God," in *A People's History of the Supreme Court* (New York: Viking Press, 1999), 11–13.

13. Ibid.

14. U.S. Const. art. 1, § 2.

15. Elizabeth Mertz, "The Uses of History: Language, Ideology, and Law in the United States and South Africa," in *The Law and Society Reader*, ed. Richard Abel (New York: NYU Press, 1995), 361–80.

16. Austin Sarat and William L. F. Felstiner, "Law and Social Relations: Vocabularies of Motive in Lawyer/Client Interaction," in Abel, *Law and Society Reader*, 403–28.

17. Ibid.

18. United States v. Associated Press, 52 F. Supp. 362 (S.D.N.Y. 1943), quoted in New York Times v. Sullivan, 376 U.S. 254, 270 (1964).

19. Recall that England had cut down much its natural-growth forests by the eighteenth century.

20. Lawrence Friedman, "American Law in the Colonial Period," in *A History of American Law* (New York: Simon and Shuster, 1973), 36–39.

21. Irons, "Morally Sinful," 3–8.

5. FAMILY

1. See, e.g., Aristotle, "The Politics—Book I: The Household and the City," in *Justice: A Reader*, ed. Michael Sandel (Oxford: Oxford University Press, 2007), 264; G. W. F. Hegel, *Elements of the Philosophy of Right* (1821; repr., Cambridge: Cambridge University Press, 1991), 219; and Alexis de Tocqueville, *Democracy in America*, vol. 2, ed. Francis Bowen, trans. Henry Reeve (Cambridge, MA: Harvard University Press, 1862), 238.

2. Gregory Bateson, *Naven*, 2nd ed. (Stanford, CA: Stanford University Press, 1958), 74–77.

3. Obergefell v. Hodges (U.S., 2015).

4. Loving v. Virginia, 388 U.S. 1 (1967).

5. Gustavo López, *Hispanics of Mexican Origin in the United States, 2013: Statistical Profile* (Washington, DC: Pew Research Center, 2015), www.pewhispanic.org/2015/09/15/hispanics-of-mexican-origin-in-the-united-states-2013/.

6. World Bank, "GDP per Capita, PPP (current international $)," World Development Indicators Database, updated December 16, 2016, http://data.worldbank.org/indicator/NY.GDP.PCAP.PP.CD.

7. Child Welfare Information Gateway, "Intestate Inheritance Rights for Adopted Children," 2016. https://www.childwelfare.gov/pubPDFs/inheritance.pdf#page=2&view=Adoptive%20parents%20and%20adopted%20children.

8. David Meyer, "Parenthood in a Time of Transition: Tensions between Legal, Biological, and Social Conceptions of Parenthood," *American Journal of Comparative Law* 55 (2006): 2106–7.

9. Recall that courts require parties to a case to meet their "burdens" of proof which vary depending on the case. In standard civil cases like auto accidents, the standard is simply "more likely than not," sometimes phrased as a "preponderance of the evidence." For standard criminal cases the standard is "beyond a reasonable doubt," a very high standard that reflects the severity of criminal punishments such as imprisonment or death. And in between these is "clear and convincing" evidence, a standard applied in constitutional law cases as well as, among other things, family law paternity cases.

10. US Department of Health and Human Services, "Indicators of Welfare Dependence: Annual Report to Congress, 2008," December 20, 2008, https://aspe.hhs.gov/report/ indicators-welfare-dependence-annual-report-congress-2008.

11. Devin Leonard, "Michael Jackson Is Worth More Than Ever, and the IRS Wants Its Cut," *Bloomberg Businessweek*, February 1, 2017, https://www.bloomberg.com/news/features/2017–02–01/michael-jackson-is-worth-more-than-ever-and-the-irs-wants-a-piece-of-it.
12. Ibid.

6. PLACE

1. Nicholas Lemann, *The Promised Land: The Great Black Migration and How It Changed America* (New York: Alfred A. Knopf, 1991), 6.
2. Kitty Calavita, *Inside the State: The Bracero Program, Immigration, and the I.N.S.* (New York: Quid Pro, 2010), 1.
3. David Engel, "The Oven Bird's Song: Insiders, Outsiders, and Personal Injuries in an American Community," in *Law and Community in Three American Towns*, ed. Carol J. Greenhouse, Barbara Yngvesson, and David M. Engel (Ithaca, NY: Cornell University Press, 1994).
4. Ibid.
5. Max Weber, "Politics as a Vocation," in *From Max Weber: Essays in Sociology*, ed. H. H. Gerth and C. Wright Mills (New York: Oxford University Press, 1958), 78.
6. Associated Press in El Salvador, "A Day without Murder: No One Is Killed in El Salvador for First Time in Two Years," *Guardian*, January 12, 2017.
7. Adam Isacson, "Migration Patterns in 2016: A Look at the Numbers," WOLA: Advocacy for Human Rights in the Americas, November 15, 2016, https://www.wola.org /analysis /migration-patterns-2016-look-numbers/.
8. Ibid.
9. U.S. Const. art. 1, § 8, clause 4.
10. U.S. Const. art. 2, § 2.
11. John Williamson, "What Washington Means by Policy Reform," in *Latin American Readjustment: How Much Has Happened?*, ed. John Williamson (Washington, DC: Institute for International Economics, 1989), 7–20.
12. Danielle Kurtzleben, "Data Show Racial Disparity in Crack Sentencing," *US News and World Report*, August 3, 2010, https://www.usnews.com/news/articles/2010/08/03/data-show-racial-disparity-in-crack-sentencing.

7. RELIGION

1. Tobin Grant, "The Great Decline: 60 Years of Religion in One Graph," *Religion News Service*, January 27, 2014, http://religionnews.com/2014 /01/27/great-decline-religion-united-states-one-graph/.
2. Heidi Glenn, "Losing Our Religion: The Growth of the 'Nones,'" NPR.org, January 13, 2013, www.npr.org/sections/thetwoway/2013/01/14/169164840/losing-our-religion-the-growth-of-the-nones.
3. While the United Kingdom has no official religion, England, its largest constituent country, has long embraced Anglicanism as the official state religion.
4. John Blake, "Four Ways 9/11 Changed America's Attitude toward Religion," *Belief Blog*, CNN.com, September 3, 2011,http://religion.blogs.cnn.com/2011/09/03/four-ways-911-changed-americas-attitude-toward-religion/.
5. Burwell v. Hobby Lobby, 573 U.S. ___ (2014).
6. Emile Durkheim, *The Elementary Forms of Religious Life*, trans. Karen Fields (New York: Free Press, 1994), 33.
7. U.S. Const. amend. 1, emphasis added.
8. Lemon v. Kurtzman, 403 U.S. 602 (1971).
9. Isaiah Berlin, "Two Concepts of Liberty," in *Four Essays on Liberty* (London: Oxford University Press, 1969), 118–72.
10. Piers Paul Read, *The Dreyfus Affair: The Story of the Most Infamous Miscarriage of Justice in French History* (London: Bloomsbury, 2012).
11. Riaz Tejani, "'A Logic of Camps': French Antiracism as Competitive Nationalism," *Political and Legal Anthropology Review* 38, no. 1 (Spring 2015), https://papers.ssrn.com/sol3/papers .cfm?abstract_id=2602830.
12. Carol Greenhouse, "Separation of Church and State in the United States: Lost in Translation?," *Indiana Journal of Global Legal Studies* 13, no. 2 (2006): 494.
13. Max Weber, "The Protestant Sects and the Spirit of Capitalism," in *From Max Weber: Essays in Sociology*, ed. and trans. H. H. Gerth and C. Wright Mills (1906; repr. New York: Oxford University Press, 1976), 302.
14. Ibid.
15. Tami Luhby, "The Truth about the Uninsured Rate in America," CNNMoney.com, March 14, 2017, http://money.cnn .com/2017/03/13/news/economy/uninsured-rate-obamacare /index.html.
16. David Green, "Column: Christian Companies Can't Bow to Sinful Mandate," *USA Today*, September 12, 2012, https:// usatoday30.usatoday.com/news /opinion/forum/story/2012–09–12/hhs-mandate-birth-control-sue-hobby-lobby/57759226/1.
17. 42 U.S.C. § 2000bb-1.
18. US Internal Revenue Service, "Entities," IRS.gov, n.d., accessed July 31, 2017, https://www.irs.gov/help-resources/tools-faqs /faqs-for-individuals/frequently-asked-tax-questions-answers /small-business-self-employed-other-business/entities/entities-5.
19. Hobby Lobby, "Our Story," accessed July 31, 2017, www .hobbylobby.com/about-us/our-story.
20. Citizens United v. Federal Election Commission, 558 U.S. 310 (2010).
21. Employment Division v. Smith, 494 U.S. 872 (1990).

8. CLASS, RACE, AND GENDER

1. Ariela Gross, *What Blood Won't Tell: A History of Race on Trial in America* (Cambridge, MA: Harvard University Press, 2009); Ian H. López, *White by Law: The Legal Construction of Race* (New York: NYU Press, 2006).
2. This fictitious nation appears in the 1933 Marx Brothers film *Duck Soup*.
3. Weber, *Protestant Ethic*.
4. Karl Marx, "Economic and Philosophical Manuscripts of 1844," in *The Marx-Engels Reader*, 2nd ed., by Karl Marx and Friedrich Engels, ed. Robert Tucker (New York: Norton, 1978), 66–125.
5. Dred Scott v. Sandford, 60 U.S. 393 (1857).
6. Plessy v. Ferguson, 163 U.S. 537 (1896).
7. Brown v. Board of Education of Topeka, 347 U.S. 483 (1954).
8. National Labor Relations Act, 29 U.S.C. § 151 (1935).
9. GandhiKingMindset, "Forum Post: Detailed List of Demands & Overview of Tactics for DC Protest," *Occupy Forum*, September 28, 2011, http://occupywallst.org/forum/detailed-list-of-demands-overview-of-tactics-for-d/.
10. A hashtag is a writing device used on social media to link a piece of text with other pieces of text on a similar topic.
11. Christine B. Hickman, "The Devil and the One Drop Rule: Racial Categories, African Americans, and the U.S. Census," *Michigan Law Review* 95, no. 5 (March 1997): 1161–1265.

12. Hernandez v. Texas, 347 U.S. 475 (1954).

13. Mendez. v. Westminster, 161 F.2d 774 (9th Cir. 1947); Ian Haney López, "Race, Ethnicity, Erasure: The Salience of Race to LatCrit Theory," *California Law Review* 85 (1998): 57–125.

14. United States v. Bhagat Singh Thind, 261 U.S. 204 (1923).

15. Mythili Sampathkumar, "Charleena Lyles: Police Officers Shoot and Kill Pregnant Black Woman after She Reports Burglary," *Independent,* June 19, 2017, www.independent.co.uk /news/world/americas/charleena-lyles-seattle-shooting-pregnant-black-mother-of-four-brettler-family-place-a7797971 .html.

16. Peter Wagner and Bernadette Rabuy, "Mass Incarceration: The Whole Pie 2017," Prison Policy Initiative, March 14, 2017, https://www.prisonpolicy.org/reports /pie2017.html.

17. The fraction of attorneys from every racial minority group is disproportionately low. As of 2010, the US Census Bureau counted the Asian American, "Black," and "Hispanic" populations of the United States at 4.8 percent, 13 percent, and 16 percent, respectively (US Census Bureau, "Overview of Race and Hispanic Origin: 2010," March 2011, https://www.census.gov/content/dam /Census/library/publications/2011/dec/c2010br-02.pdf). According to the American Bar Association ("ABA National Lawyer Population Survey 10-Year Trend in Lawyer Demographics," 2018, https://www.americanbar.org/content/dam/aba /administrative/market_research/National_Lawyer_Population_ Demographics_2008–2018.pdf), the fractions of the legal profession from each of those communities were 3 percent, 5 percent, and 4 percent, respectively. American Indians and Alaskan Natives made up 1.7 percent of the population and roughly 1 percent of attorneys in 2010. All four have therefore been numerically "underrepresented" in the legal profession to varying degrees. In the case of Asian Americans, this situation contrasts sharply with the medical profession; as of 2008, Asian Americans accounted for about 13 percent of all US physicians (Association of American Medical Colleges, "Diversity in the Physician Workforce Facts & Figures 2010," 2010, https://members.aamc.org/ eweb/upload/Diversity%20in%20the%20Physician%20Work-force%20Facts%20and%20Figures%202010.pdf.

18. Riaz Tejani, "Professional Apartheid: The Racialization of U.S. Law Schools after Global Crisis," *American Ethnologist* 44, no. 3 (2017), https://doi.org/10.1111/amet.12521.

19. Ward Farnsworth and Mark Grady, *Torts: Cases and Questions,* 2nd ed. (Austin, TX: Aspen, 2009).

20. Griswold v. Connecticut, 381 U.S. 479 (1965).

21. Anthony Giddens, *Modernity and Self-Identity* (Stanford, CA: Stanford University Press, 1991).

9. THE SOCIALIZATION OF LAWYERS

1. A. Benjamin Spencer, "The Law School Critique in Historical Perspective," *Washington and Lee Law Review* 69 (2012): 1949– 2063.

2. Robert Stevens, "History of the Yale Law School: Provenance and Perspective," *History of the Yale Law School: The Tercentennial Lectures,* ed. Anthony T. Kronman (New Haven, CT: Yale University Press, 2004), 1–16.

3. Jordan Weissmann, "The Jobs Crisis at Our Best Law Schools Is Much, Much Worse Than You Think," *Atlantic,* April 9, 2013, https://www.theatlantic.com/business/archive /2013/04/the-jobs-crisis-at-our-best-law-schools-is-much-much-worse-than-you-think/274795/.

4. Clifford Geertz, "Local Knowledge: Fact and Law in Comparative Perspective," in *Local Knowledge: Further Essays in Interpretive Anthropology,* 3rd ed. (New York: Basic Books, 2000), 184.

5. Elizabeth Mertz, *The Language of Law School* (Oxford: Oxford University Press, 2007).

6. Like an easement, *profit a prendre* refers to the transferred right to a specific use or benefit from a piece of land. For instance, it might include hunting, fishing, mining, or timber rights. *Mens rea* refers to the criminal "state of mind" required (among other things) for a "guilty" finding under criminal law.

7. Appellate law is that form of legal advocacy practiced at the intermediate court of appeals and court of last resort in common-law systems. In most instances it requires no further showings of evidence and focuses rather on arguments over interpretations and applications of law alone. It is usually considered a more elite level of law practice.

8. Deborah Rhode, *Access to Justice* (Oxford: Oxford University Press, 2005); Brian Tamanaha, *Failing Law Schools* (Chicago: University of Chicago Press, 2012).

9. Dirk Johnson, "Yale's Limit on Jewish Enrollment Lasted until Early 1960's, Book Says," *New York Times,* March 4, 1986, www .nytimes.com/1986/03/04 /nyregion/yale-s-limit-on-jewish-enrollment-lasted-until-early-1960-s-book-says.html.

10. Bryant Garth, "Crisis, Crisis Rhetoric, and Competition in Legal Education: A Sociological Perspective on the (Latest) Crisis of the Legal Profession and Legal Education," *Stanford Law and Policy Review* 24 (2013): 503.

11. Aaron Taylor, "Diversity as a Law School Survival Strategy," Saint Louis University Legal Studies Research Paper No. 2015– 1, February 2015, https://ssrn.com/abstract=2569847 or http:// dx.doi.org/10.2139/ssrn.2569847.

12. Riaz Tejani, *Law Mart: Justice, Access, and For-Profit Law Schools* (Stanford, CA: Stanford University Press, 2017).

13. Tejani, "Professional Apartheid."

14. Elizabeth Mertz, *Language of Law School: Learning to "Think Like a Lawyer"* (Oxford: Oxford University Press, 2007).

10. CRIMINAL AND CIVIL JUSTICE

1. Boumediene v. Bush, 553 U.S. 723 (2008).

2. For a good introduction to this movement, see Gwen Jordan et al., "Contemporary Perspectives on Wrongful Conviction: An Introduction to the 2016 Innocence Network Conference, San Antonio, Texas," *Hofstra Law Review* 45, no. 2 (Winter 2016): 365.

3. Anthony Lewis, *Gideon's Trumpet* (New York: Vintage Books, 1966), 3–4.

4. Ibid., 5.

5. This was his second try; his first lacked this motion and was sent back.

6. Lewis, *Gideon's Trumpet,* 8.

7. Betts v. Brady, 316 U.S. 455 (1942).

8. Gideon v. Wainwright, 372 U.S. 335 (1963).

9. Miranda v. Arizona, 384 U.S. 436 (1966).

10. Sentencing Project, "Trends in U.S. Corrections," fact sheet, January 2016, https://sentencingproject.org/wp-content /uploads/2016/01/Trends-in-US-Corrections.pdf.

11. Bernadette Rabuy and Daniel Kopf, "Prisons of Poverty: Uncovering the Pre-incarceration Incomes of the Imprisoned," Prisons Policy Initiative, July 9, 2015, https://www.prisonpolicy .org/reports/income.html.

12. Matthew Desmond, *Evicted* (New York: Crown Books, 2016).

13. Kenneth Abraham, *The Forms and Functions of Tort Law* (New York: Foundation Press, 2012), 1.

14. Charles-Louis Montesquieu, *The Spirit of the Laws*, trans. Ann M. Cohler, Basia C. Miller, and Harold Stone (1748; repr., Cambridge: Cambridge University Press, 1989), 231–33, 310, 311.

15. U.S. Const. amend. VII: "In Suits at common law, where the value in controversy shall exceed twenty dollars, the right of trial by jury shall be preserved, and no fact tried by a jury, shall be otherwise re-examined in any Court of the United States, than according to the rules of the common law."

16. Statista.com, "Value of Gross Premiums Written by General Liability Insurance Companies in the United States from 2009 to 2025 (in billion U.S. dollars)," n.d., accessed March 12, 2018, https://www.statista.com/statistics/422059/general-liability-insurance-sector-usa/.

17. See, e.g., Stella Liebeck v. McDonald's Restaurants, P.T.S., Inc. and McDonald's International, Inc., 1995 WL 360309 (Bernalillo County, N.M. Dist. Ct. 1994).

18. Rosen, *Law as Culture*, 83.

19. Ibid., 9–10.

11. JUSTICE AND POPULAR CULTURE

1. Louis Althusser, "Ideology and Ideological State Apparatuses (Notes towards an Investigation)," in *Lenin and Philosophy and Other Essays* (New York: Monthly Review Press, 2001), 85–126.

2. George Lipsitz, *Dangerous Crossroads: Popular Music, Postmodernism and the Poetics of Place* (London: Verso, 1997); Robin D. G. Kelley, *Race Rebels: Culture, Politics, and the Black Working Class* (New York: Free Press, 1996).

3. Steven Lubet, "Reconstructing Atticus Finch," *Michigan Law Review* 97, no. 6 (May 1999): 1339–62, doi:10.2307/1290205.

4. David Ray Papke, "The Impact of Popular Culture on American Perceptions of the Courts," *Indiana Law Journal* 82 (2007): 1225–34.

5. Assuming all TV owners would have tuned in to CBS at the time.

6. Bates v. State Bar of Arizona, 433 U.S. 350 (1977).

12. ART FORMS

1. O'Keeffe v. Snyder, 83 N.J. 478 (1980), 416 A.2d 862.

2. Erika Kim, "Why Georgia O'Keeffe Is the Mother of American Modernism," *Sleek Mag*, July 14, 2016, www.sleek-mag.com/2016/07/14/georgia-okeeffe-american-modernism-tate/.

3. George Lipsitz, *The Subcultures Reader: Cruising around the Historical Bloc* (New York: Routledge, 1997), 358.

4. Richard Lachman, "Graffiti as Career and Ideology," *America Journal of Sociology* 94, no. 2 (1988): 229–50.

5. Richard Weir, "Neighborhood Report: Long Island City; Wall Hits a Patron of Graffiti," *New York Times*, February 15, 1998, www.nytimes.com/1998/02/15/nyregion/neighborhood-report-long-island-city-wall-hits-a-patron-of-graffiti.html.

6. Alan Feuer, "Graffiti Artists Awarded $6.7 Million for Destroyed 5Pointz Murals," *New York Times*, February 12, 2018, https://www.nytimes.com/2018/02/12/nyregion/5pointz-graffiti-judgment.html.

7. Lynn Douglass, "Banksy Mural Chiseled Off Building, About to Be Sold at Auction for $700,000," *Forbes*, February 20, 2013, https://www.forbes.com/sites/lynndouglass/2013/02/20/banksy-mural-chiseled-off-building-about-to-be-sold-at-auction-for-700000/#326f4bb84b4e.

13. TECHNOLOGY

1. Thomas Kuhn, *The Structure of Scientific Revolutions* (Chicago: University of Chicago Press, 1962).

2. Mary Lindemann, *Medicine and Society in Early Modern Europe* (Cambridge: Cambridge University Press, 1999), 86.

3. Frye v. United States, 293 F. 1013 (D.C. Cir. 1923). Since *Daubert*, this test has been superseded by the Federal Rules of Evidence, allowing that the judge should be the gatekeeper when it comes to the validity of scientific evidence.

4. Although this number includes years that predate the advent of DNA fingerprinting. See Ned Walpin, "The New Speed-Up in Habeas Corpus Appeals," readings for "The Execution," *Frontline*, PBS, https://www.pbs.org/wgbh/pages/frontline/shows/execution/readings/speed.html.

5. Brandon L. Garrett, "DNA and the Boundaries of Habeas Corpus," *ACSblog*, March 7, 2011, https://www.acslaw.org/acsblog/dna-and-the-boundaries-of-habeas-corpus.

6. "Moral rights," discussed in chapter 12, are another form of intellectual property rights, but remain rare in their claims and enforcement.

7. US Const. art. I, § 8, clause 8.

8. Cornell University Library, Copyright Information Center, "Copyright Term and the Public Domain in the United States," n.d., accessed February 23, 2018, https://copyright.cornell.edu/publicdomain.

9. Rogers v. Grimaldi, 875 F.2d 994 (2d Cir. 1989).

10. Cf. Marx's "value theory" of labor.

11. Nancy Isenberg, *White Trash: The 400-Year Untold History of Class in America* (New York: Random House, 2016).

12. Notice that neither the Lockean nor the utilitarian moral bases for property rights tells us exactly how to do this balancing, because value-based and cost-benefit-based analyses could favor either side depending on circumstances.

13. Nicola Davis, "Pokémon Go Boosts Exercise Levels—but Only for a Short Period, Says Study," *Guardian*, December 13, 2016, https://www.theguardian.com/technology/2016/dec/13/pokemon-go-boosts-exercise-levels-but-only-for-a-short-period-says-study.

14. See, e.g., Rosen, *Law as Culture*.

15. Statista.com, "Number of Monthly Active Facebook Users Worldwide as of 4th Quarter 2017 (in millions)," 2018, https://www.statista.com/statistics/264810/number-of-monthly-active-facebook-users-worldwide/.

16. Statista.com, "Number of Monthly Active Twitter Users Worldwide from 1st Quarter 2010 to 4th Quarter 2017 (in millions)," 2018, https://www.statista.com/statistics/282087/number-of-monthly-active-twitter-users/.

17. Katherine Hobson, "Feeling Lonely? Too Much Time on Social Media May Be Why," NPR.org, March 6, 2017, https://www.npr.org/sections/health-shots/2017/03/06/518362255/feeling-lonely-too-much-time-on-social-media-may-be-why.

18. Adam Badawy, Emilio Ferrara, and Kristina Lerman, "Analyzing the Digital Traces of Political Manipulation: The 2016 Russian Interference Twitter Campaign," in *2018 IEEE/ACM International Conference on Advances in Social Networks Analysis and Mining (ASONAM), Barcelona, Spain, 2018* (Danvers, MA: IEEE, 2018), 258–65, https://arxiv.org/abs/1802.04291.

19. Certain titles, for instance, would have the reputation for publishing dubious information, while others of good standing might be increasing readership with a salacious story.

20. Cubby, Inc. v. CompuServe Inc., 776 F. Supp. 135 (S.D.N.Y., 1991).

21. Ibid.

22. Stratton Oakmont, Inc. v. Prodigy Services Co., 1995 WL 323710 (N.Y. Sup. Ct. 1995).

23. 47 U.S.C. § 230(c)(1).

24. Zeran v. America Online, Inc., 129 F.3d 327 (4th Cir. 1997).

25. Note that libel is the written form of defamation, whereas slander is the spoken form. There are minor procedural implications of this distinction, but culturally it is significant whether we consider Twitter statements or "tweeting" as writing rather than speech (in the verbal sense).

26. Alicia Shepard, "NPR's Giffords Mistake: Re-learning the Lesson of Checking Sources," NPR.org, January 11, 2011, https://www .npr.org/sections/ombudsman/2011/01/11/132812196/nprs-giffords-mistake-re-learning-the-lesson-of-checking-sources.

27. Fair Housing Council of San Fernando Valley v. Roommates .com, LLC, 521 F.3d 1157 (9th Cir. 2008).

28. Pound, "What Is Law?"

14. NATURE

1. Jonathan Watts, "Arctic Warming: Scientists Alarmed by 'Crazy' Temperature Rises," *Guardian*, February 27, 2018, https://www .theguardian.com/environment/2018 /feb/27/arctic-warming-scientists-alarmed-by-crazy-temperature-rises.

2. Allan Greer, *Property and Dispossession: Natives, Empires, and Land in Early Modern North America* (Cambridge: Cambridge University Press, 2018), 2.

3. Ibid., 13.

4. "Then God said, "Let Us make man in Our image, according to Our likeness; and let them rule over the fish of the sea and over the birds of the sky and over the cattle and over all the earth, and over every creeping thing that creeps on the earth" (Gen. 1:26).

5. "The fear of you and the terror of you will be on every beast of the earth and on every bird of the sky; with everything that creeps on the ground, and all the fish of the sea, into your hand they are given" (Gen. 9:2).

6. D.E. Sherkat and C.G. Ellison, "Structuring the Religion-Environment Connection: Identifying Religious Influences on Environmental Concern and Activism," *Journal for the Scientific Study of Religion* 46 (2007): 71–85; M.N Peterson and J. Liu, "Impacts of Religion on Environmental Worldviews: The Teton Valley Case," *Society and Natural Resources* 21 (2008): 704–18.

7. Jim Yardley, "Chinese Dam Projects Criticized for Their Human Costs," *New York Times*, November 19, 2007, www .nytimes.com/2007/11/19 /world/asia/19dam.html.

8. Both incidents resulted in civil liability for Exxon and British Petroleum, but these amounts never "render whole" the environment itself—partly because nature itself is still said to lack legal personhood.

9. US Environmental Protection Agency, "Husqvarna Ab and Husqvarna Consumer Outdoor Products N.A., Inc., Clean Air Act Settlement," n.d., accessed March 14, 2018, https://www .epa.gov/enforcement /husqvarna-ab-and-husqvarna-consumer-outdoor-products-na-inc-clean-air-act-settlement.

10. US Environmental Protection Agency, "History of the Clean Water Act," last updated August 8, 2017, accessed March 14, 2018, https://www.epa.gov/laws-regulations/history-clean-water-act.

11. US Environmental Protection Agency, "Deepwater Horizon—BP Gulf of Mexico Oil Spill," last updated April 19, 2017, accessed March 14, 2018, https://www.epa.gov/enforcement /deepwater-horizon-bp-gulf-mexico-oil-spill.

12. Ryan Schleeter, "As It Happened: Seattle Kayaktivists Blockade Shell's Alaska-Bound Oil Rig," Greenpeace.org, June 15, 2015, www.greenpeace.org/usa /breaking-seattle-kayaktavists-blockade-shells-alaska-bound-oil-rig/.

13. Chevron U.S.A., Inc. v. Natural Resources Defense Council, Inc., 467 U.S. 837 (1984).

14. World Wildlife Fund, "How Many Species Are We Losing?" Panda.org, n.d., accessed March 14, 2018, http://wwf.panda .org/about_our_earth/biodiversity/biodiversity/.

15. Jedediah Purdy, *After Nature: A Politics for the Anthropocene* (Cambridge, MA: Harvard University Press, 2016).

16. See, e.g., Brandon Derman, "Climate Governance, Justice, and Transnational Civil Society," *Climate Policy* 14, no. 1 (2014): 23–41.

17. European Union, "International Agreements on Climate Action," *Consilium,* n.d., accessed March 14, 2018, www.consilium .europa.eu/en/policies/climate-change/international-agreements-climate-action/.

18. Todd Cort, "The Electoral College Is Thwarting Our Ability to Battle Global Warming," *Washington Post,* December 19, 2016, https://www.washingtonpost.com/news/energy-environment /wp/2016/12/19/the-electoral-college-is-thwarting-our-ability-to-battle-global-warming/?utm_term=.cdb4f912b7e1.

19. "Trump Just Passed on the Best Deal the Planet Has Ever Seen," *Guardian,* June 2, 2017, https://www.theguardian.com /commentisfree/2017/jun/01/trump-paris-climate-deal-planet.

20. Christopher Stone, *Should Trees Have Standing? Law, Morality, and the Environment*, 3rd ed. (Oxford: Oxford University Press, 2010), 13. "The traditional way of deciding whether to issue injunctions in law suits affecting the environment, at least where communal property is involved, has been to strike some sort of balance regarding the economic hardships on human beings. . . . Why should the environment be of importance only indirectly, as lost profits to someone else? Why not throw into balance the cost to the environment?"

21. Ibid., 13.

List of Cases

Bates v. State Bar of Arizona, 433 U.S. 350 (1977).

Betts v. Brady, 316 U.S. 455 (1942).

Boumediene v. Bush, 553 U.S. 723 (2008).

Brown v. Board of Education of Topeka, 347 U.S. 483 (1954).

Burwell v. Hobby Lobby, 573 U.S. ___ (2014).

Carol Burnett v. National Enquirer, Inc., 193 Cal. Rptr. 206, July 18, 1983.

Chevron U.S.A., Inc. v. NRDC, 467 U.S. 837 (1984).

Citizens United v. Federal Election Commission, 558 U.S. 310 (2010).

Cubby, Inc. v. CompuServe Inc., 776 F. Supp. 135 (S.D.N.Y., 1991).

Dred Scott v. Sandford, 60 U.S. 393 (1857).

Employment Division v. Smith, 494 U.S. 872 (1990).

Fair Housing Council of San Fernando Valley v. Roommates. com, LLC, 521 F.3d 1157 (9th Cir. 2008).

Frye v. United States, 293 F. 1013 (D.C. Cir. 1923).

Gideon v. Wainwright, 372 U.S. 335 (1963).

Griswold v. Connecticut, 381 U.S. 479 (1965).

Hernandez v. Texas, 347 U.S. 475 (1954).

Lemon v. Kurtzman, 403 U.S. 602 (1971).

Loving v. Virginia, 388 U.S. 1 (1967).

Mendez. v. Westminster, 161 F.2d 774 (9th Cir. 1947).

Miranda v. Arizona, 384 U.S. 436 (1966).

New York Times v. Sullivan, 376 U.S. 254 (1964).

O'Keeffe v. Snyder, 83 N.J. 478 (1980), 416 A.2d 862.

Obergefell v. Hodges (U.S., 2015).

Plessy v. Ferguson, 163 U.S. 537 (1896).

Rogers v. Grimaldi, 875 F.2d 994 (2d Cir. 1989).

Roper v. Simmons, 543 U.S. 551, 578 (2005).

Stella Liebeck v. McDonald's Restaurants, P.T.S., Inc. and McDonald's International, Inc., 1995 WL 360309 (Bernalillo County, N.M. Dist. Ct. 1994).

Stratton Oakmont, Inc. v. Prodigy Services Co., 1995 WL 323710 (N.Y. Sup. Ct. 1995).

United States v. Associated Press, 52 F. Supp. 362 (S.D.N.Y. 1943).

United States v. Bhagat Singh Thind, 261 U.S. 204 (1923).

Whitney v. California, 274 U.S. 357 (1927).

Zeran v. America Online, Inc., 129 F.3d 327 (4th Cir. 1997).

Bibliography

Abraham, Kenneth. *The Forms and Functions of Tort Law*. New York: Foundation Press, 2012.

Althusser, Louis. "Ideology and Ideological State Apparatuses (Notes towards an Investigation)." In *Lenin and Philosophy and Other Essays*, 85–126. New York: Monthly Review Press, 2001.

American Bar Association. "ABA National Lawyer Population Survey 10-Year Trend in Lawyer Demographics." 2018. https://www.americanbar.org/content/dam/aba/administrative/market_research/National_Lawyer_Population_Demographics_2008–2018.pdf.

Anderson, Benedict. *Imagined Communities: Reflections on the Origin and Spread of Nationalism*. 1983. Reprint, London: Verso, 2016.

Aristotle. "The Politics—Book I: The Household and the City." In *Justice: A Reader*, edited by Michael Sandel, 264–94. Oxford: Oxford University Press, 2007.

Associated Press in El Salvador. "A Day without Murder: No One Is Killed in El Salvador for First Time in Two Years." *Guardian*, January 12, 2017.

Association of American Medical Colleges, "Diversity in the Physician Workforce Facts & Figures 2010." 2010. https://members.aamc.org/eweb/upload/Diversity%20in%20the%20Physician%20Workforce%20Facts%20and%20Figures%202010.pdf.

Badawy, Adam, Emilio Ferrara, and Kristina Lerman. "Analyzing the Digital Traces of Political Manipulation: The 2016 Russian Interference Twitter Campaign." In *2018 IEEE/ACM International Conference on Advances in Social Networks Analysis and Mining (ASONAM), Barcelona, Spain, 2018*, 258–65. Danvers, MA: IEEE, 2018. https://arxiv.org/abs/1802.04291.

Bateson, Gregory. *Naven*. 2nd ed. Stanford, CA: Stanford University Press, 1958.

Berlin, Isaiah. "Two Concepts of Liberty." In *Four Essays on Liberty*, 118–72. London: Oxford University Press, 1969.

Biagioli, Mario, Peter Jaszi, and Martha Woodmansee, eds. *Making and Unmaking Intellectual Property: Creative Production in Legal and Cultural Perspective*. Chicago: University of Chicago Press, 2011.

Blake, John. "Four Ways 9/11 Changed America's Attitude toward Religion." CNN.com, *Belief Blog*, September 3, 2011. http://religion.blogs.cnn.com/2011/09/03/four-ways-911-changed-americas-attitude-toward-religion/.

Bleich, Erik. "The Legacies of History? Colonization and Immigrant Integration in Britain and France." *Theory and Society* 34, no. 2 (2005): 171–95.

Calavita, Kitty. *Inside the State: The Bracero Program, Immigration, and the I.N.S.* New York: Quid Pro, 2010.

Calinicos, Alex. *Social Theory: A Historical Introduction*. New York: NYU Press, 1999.

Carson, Rachel. *Silent Spring*. Boston: Houghton Mifflin, 2002.

Child Welfare Information Gateway. "Intestate Inheritance Rights for Adopted Children." 2016. https://www.childwelfare.gov/topics/systemwide/laws-policies/statutes/inheritance/.

Cohen, Andrew. "Today Is the 50th Anniversary of the (Re-)Birth of the First Amendment." *Atlantic*, March 9, 2014.

Cohen, Phillip N. *The Family: Diversity, Inequality, and Social Change*. New York: Norton, 2014.

Cornell University Library. Copyright Information Center. "Copyright Term and the Public Domain in the United States." N.d., accessed February 23, 2018, https://copyright.cornell.edu/publicdomain.

Cort, Todd. "The Electoral College Is Thwarting Our Ability to Battle Global Warming." *Washington Post*, December 19, 2016. https://www.washingtonpost.com/news/energy-environment/wp/2016/12/19/the-electoral-college-is-thwarting-our-ability-to-battle-global-warming/?utm_term=.cdb4f912b7e1.

Crampon, William J., and Alex J. Norman. *Ethnic Disparities in Long Beach, California*. ReThinking Greater Long Beach, 2014. www.rethinklongbeach.org/resources/Ethnic+Disparities+in+Long+Beach.pdf.

Crusto, Mitchell. "Federalism and Civil Rights: The Meredith Case." *National Black Law Journal* 11 (1989): 233–48.

Davis, Nicola. "Pokémon Go Boosts Exercise Levels—but Only for a Short Period, Says Study." *Guardian*, December 13, 2016. https://www.theguardian.com/technology/2016/dec/13/pokemon-go-boosts-exercise-levels-but-only-for-a-short-period-says-study.

De Cruz, Peter. *Comparative Law in a Changing World*. London: Routledge Cavendish, 2008.

Delgado, Richard. 2017. *Critical Race Theory: An Introduction*. 3rd ed. New York: NYU Press.

Derman, Brandon. "Climate Governance, Justice, and Transnational Civil Society." *Climate Policy* 14, no. 1 (2014): 23–41.

Desmond, Matthew. *Evicted*. New York: Crown Books, 2016.

Douglass, Lynn. "Banksy Mural Chiseled Off Building, About to Be Sold at Auction for $700,000." *Forbes*, February 20, 2013. https://www.forbes.com/sites/lynndouglass/2013/02/20/banksy-mural-chiseled-off-building-about-to-be-sold-at-auction-for-700000/#326f4bb84b4e.

Durkheim, Emile. *The Elementary Forms of Religious Life*. Translated by Karen Fields. New York: Free Press, 1994.

Ehrenreich, Barbara. 1983. *The Hearts of Men: American Dreams and the Flight from Commitment*. New York: Knopf/Doubleday.

Ellis, Mark R. "Roscoe Pound (1870–1964)." In *Encyclopedia of the Great Plains*, edited by David A. Wisehart. Lincoln: University of Nebraska Press, 2011. http://plainshumanities.unl.edu/encyclopedia/doc/egp.law.043.

Engel, David. "The Oven Bird's Song: Insiders, Outsiders, and Personal Injuries in an American Community." In *Law and*

Community in Three American Towns, edited by Carol J. Greenhouse, Barbara Yngvesson, and David M. Engel, 27–53. Ithaca, NY: Cornell University Press, 1994.

European Union. "International Agreements on Climate Action." *Consilium*, n.d., accessed March 14, 2018. www.consilium .europa.eu/en/policies/climate-change/international-agreements-climate-action/.

Farnsworth, Ward, and Mark Grady. *Torts: Cases and Questions*. 2nd ed. Austin, TX: Aspen, 2009.

Feuer, Alan. "Graffiti Artists Awarded $6.7 Million for Destroyed 5Pointz Murals." *New York Times*, February 12, 2018. https://www.nytimes.com/2018/02/12/nyregion/5pointz-graffiti-judgment.html.

Friedman, Lawrence. "American Law in the Colonial Period." In *A History of American Law*, 29–90. New York: Simon and Schuster, 1973.

Garrett, Brandon L. "DNA and the Boundaries of Habeas Corpus." *ACSblog*, March 7, 2011. https://www.acslaw.org/acsblog /dna-and-the-boundaries-of-habeas-corpus/.

Garth, Bryant. "Crisis, Crisis Rhetoric, and Competition in Legal Education: A Sociological Perspective on the (Latest) Crisis of the Legal Profession and Legal Education." *Stanford Law and Policy Review* 24 (2013): 503–32.

Geertz, Clifford. "Local Knowledge: Fact and Law in Comparative Perspective." In *Local Knowledge: Further Essays in Interpretive Anthropology*, 3rd ed., 167–234. New York: Basic Books, 2000.

Giddens, Anthony. *Modernity and Self-Identity*. Stanford, CA: Stanford University Press, 1991.

Gilman-Opalsky, Richard. *Precarious Communism: Manifest Mutations, Manifesto Detourned* New York: Minor Compositions, 2014.

Glenn, Heidi. "Losing Our Religion: The Growth of the 'Nones.'" NPR.org, January 13, 2013. www.npr.org/sections/thetwo-way/2013/01/14/169164840/losing-our-religion-the-growth-of-the-nones.

Goffman, Erving. *Frame Analysis: An Essay on the Organization of Experience*. Boston: Northeastern University Press, 1986.

Gould, Jon B., and Scott Barclay. "Mind the Gap: The Place of Gap Studies in Sociolegal Scholarship." *Annual Review of Law and Social Science* 8 (2012): 323–35.

Grant, Tobin. "The Great Decline: 60 Years of Religion in One Graph." *Religion News Service*, January 27, 2014. http://religionnews.com/2014 /01/27/great-decline-religion-united-states-one-graph/.

Green, David. "Column: Christian Companies Can't Bow to Sinful Mandate." *USA Today*, September 12, 2012. https://usatoday30.usatoday.com/news /opinion/forum/story /2012–09–12/hhs-mandate-birth-control-sue-hobby-lobby/57759226/1.

Greenhouse, Carol J. "Separation of Church and State in the United States: Lost in Translation?" *Indiana Journal of Global Legal Studies* 13, no. 2 (2006): 493–502.

———. *Praying for Justice: Faith, Order, and Community in an American Town*. Ithaca, NY: Cornell University Press, 1986.

Greer, Allan. *Property and Dispossession: Natives, Empires, and Land in Early Modern North America*. Cambridge: Cambridge University Press, 2018.

Griffith, Mark F. "John Locke's Influence on American Government and Public Administration." *Journal of Management History* 3, no. 3 (1997): 224–37.

Gross, Ariela. *What Blood Won't Tell: A History of Race on Trial in America*. Cambridge, MA: Harvard University Press, 2009.

Gutierrez, David. *Walls and Mirrors: Mexican Americans, Mexican Immigrants, and the Politics of Ethnicity*. Berkeley: University of California Press, 1995.

Hegel, G. W. F. *Elements of the Philosophy of Right*. 1821. Reprint, Cambridge: Cambridge University Press, 1991.

———. *Lectures on the Philosophy of History*. Translated by H. B. Nisbet. New York: Cambridge University Press, 1975.

Hickey, Dave. *Air Guitar: Essays on Art and Democracy*. Los Angeles: Foundation for Advanced Critical Studies, 1997.

Hickman, Christine B. "The Devil and the One Drop Rule: Racial Categories, African Americans, and the U.S. Census." *Michigan Law Review* 95, no. 5 (March 1997): 1161–1265.

Hirschman, Charles, and Elizabeth Mogford. "Immigration and the American Industrial Revolution from 1880 to 1920." *Social Science Research* 38, no. 4 (2009): 897–920.

Hobsbawm, Eric. "Introduction: Inventing Traditions." In *The Invention of Tradition*, edited by Eric Hobsbawm and Terrence Ranger, 1–14. Cambridge: Cambridge University Press, 1983.

Hobson, Katherine. "Feeling Lonely? Too Much Time on Social Media May Be Why." NPR.org, March 6, 2017. https://www .npr.org/sections/health-shots /2017/03/06/ 518362255 /feeling-lonely-too-much-time-on-social-media-may-be-why.

Irons, Peter. "Morally Sinful by the Word of God." In *A People's History of the Supreme Court*, 3–16. New York: Viking Press, 1999.

Isacson, Adam. "Migration Patterns in 2016: A Look at the Numbers." WOLA: Advocacy for Human Rights in the Americas, November 15, 2016. https://www.wola.org /analysis/migration-patterns-2016-look-numbers/.

Isenberg, Nancy. *White Trash: The 400-Year Untold History of Class in America*. New York: Random House, 2016.

Johnson, Dirk. "Yale's Limit on Jewish Enrollment Lasted until Early 1960's, Book Says." *New York Times*, March 4, 1986. www .nytimes.com/1986/03/04/nyregion/yale-s-limit-on-jewish-enrollment-lasted-until-early-1960-s-book-says.html.

Johnson, Kevin R. "The Intersection of Race and Class In U.S. Immigration Law and Enforcement." *Law and Contemporary Problems* 72, no. 4 (2009): 1–35.

Jordan, Gwen, Aliza B. Kaplan, Valena Beety, and Keith A. Findley. "Contemporary Perspectives on Wrongful Conviction: An Introduction to the 2016 Innocence Network Conference, San Antonio, Texas." *Hofstra Law Review* 45, no. 2 (Winter 2016): 365–71.

Kelley, Robin D. G. *Race Rebels: Culture, Politics, and the Black Working Class*. New York: Free Press, 1996.

Kim, Erika. "Why Georgia O'Keeffe Is the Mother of American Modernism." *Sleek Mag*, July 14, 2016. www.sleek-mag .com/2016/07/14/georgia-okeeffe-american-modernism-tate/.

Kuhn, Thomas. *The Structure of Scientific Revolutions*. Chicago: University of Chicago Press, 1962.

Kurtzleben, Danielle. "Data Show Racial Disparity in Crack Sentencing." *US News and World Report*, August 3, 2010. https://www.usnews.com /news/articles/2010/08/03 /data-show-racial-disparity-in-crack-sentencing.

Lachmann, Richard. "Graffiti as Career and Ideology." *America Journal of Sociology* 94, no. 2 (1988): 229–50.

Lemann, Nicholas. *The Promised Land: The Great Black Migration and How It Changed America*. New York: Alfred A. Knopf, 1991.

Leonard, Devin. "Michael Jackson Is Worth More Than Ever, and the IRS Wants Its Cut." *Bloomberg Businessweek*,

February 1, 2017. https://www.bloomberg.com/news/features/2017–02–01/michael-jackson-is-worth-more-than-ever-and-the-irs-wants-a-piece-of-it.

Lewis, Anthony. *Gideon's Trumpet*. New York: Vintage Books, 1966.

Lindemann, Mary. *Medicine and Society in Early Modern Europe*. Cambridge: Cambridge University Press, 1999.

Lipsitz, George. *Dangerous Crossroads: Popular Music, Postmodernism and the Poetics of Place*. London: Verso, 1997.

———. *The Subcultures Reader: Cruising around the Historical Bloc*. New York: Routledge, 1997.

López, Gustavo. *Hispanics of Mexican Origin in the United States, 2013: Statistical Profile*. Washington, DC: Pew Research Center, 2015. www.pewhispanic.org /2015/09/15/hispanics-of-mexican-origin-in-the-united-states-2013/.

López, Ian Haney. "Race, Ethnicity, Erasure: The Salience of Race to LatCrit Theory." *California Law Review* 85 (1998): 57–125.

———. *White by Law: The Legal Construction of Race*. New York: NYU Press, 2006.

Lubet, Steven. "Reconstructing Atticus Finch," *Michigan Law Review* 97, no. 6 (May 1999): 1339–62. doi:10.2307/1290205.

Luhby, Tami. "The Truth about the Uninsured Rate in America," CNNMoney.com, March 14, 2017. http://money.cnn.com /2017/03/13/news/economy/uninsured-rate-obamacare /index.html.

Lynch, Michael, Simon A. Cole, Ruth McNally, and Kathleen Jordan. *Truth Machine: The Contentious History of DNA Fingerprinting*. Chicago: University of Chicago Press, 2010.

Marine, Gene. "The Free Speech Movement." *Nation*, December 21, 1964. https://www.thenation.com/article/free-speech-movement/.

Marx, Karl. "Economic and Philosophical Manuscripts of 1844." In *The Marx-Engels Reader*, 2nd ed., by Karl Marx and Friedrich Engels, edited by Robert Tucker,66–125. New York: Norton, 1978.

Marx, Karl, and Friedrich Engels. *The Communist Manifesto*. Sweden: Chiron, 2016.

Mattei, Ugo, Teemu Ruskola, and Antonio Gidi. *Schlesinger's Comparative Law: Cases, Text, Materials*. 7th ed. New York: Foundation Press, 2009.

Mertz, Elizabeth. *The Language of Law School: Learning to "Think Like a Lawyer."* Oxford: Oxford University Press, 2007.

———. "The Uses of History: Language, Ideology, and Law in the United States and South Africa." In *The Law and Society Reader*, edited by Richard Abel, 361–80. New York: NYU Press, 1995.

Meyer, David. "Parenthood in a Time of Transition: Tensions between Legal, Biological, and Social Conceptions of Parenthood." *American Journal of Comparative Law* 55 (2006): 2106–7.

Molloy, Antonia. "Tom Cruise Settles $50 Million Defamation Case over Claims He Abandoned Daughter Suri." *Independent*, December 23, 2013. www.independent.co.uk/arts-entertainment/films/news/tom-cruise-settles-50million-defamation-case-over-claims-he-abandoned-daughter-suri-9022484.html.

Montesquieu, Charles-Louis. *The Spirit of the Laws*. Translated by Ann M. Cohler, Basia C. Miller, and Harold Stone. 1748. Reprint, Cambridge: Cambridge University Press, 1989.

Muir, John. *My First Summer in the Sierra*. Boston: Houghton Mifflin, 1911.

Myers, John, and Henry Krause. *Family Law in a Nutshell*. 6th ed. West Academic Publishers, 2016.

Papke, David Ray. "The Impact of Popular Culture on American Perceptions of the Courts." *Indiana Law Journal* 82 (2007): 1225–34.

Peterson, M. N., and J. Liu. "Impacts of Religion on Environmental Worldviews: The Teton Valley Case." *Society and Natural Resources* 21 (2008): 704–18.

Pew Research Center. "Technology Device Ownership." October 29, 2015. www.pewinternet.org/2015/10/29/technology-device-ownership-2015.

Posner, Richard. "A Theory of Negligence." *Journal of Legal Studies* 1, no. 1 (1972): 29–36.

Pound, Roscoe. "What Is Law?" In *Social Control through Law*, 35–62. 1942. Reprint, New Brunswick, NJ: Transaction, 1997.

Purdy, Jedediah. *After Nature: A Politics for the Anthropocene*. Cambridge, MA: Harvard University Press, 2016.

Quigley, Paul. "The Birth of Thanksgiving." *New York Times*, November 28, 2013.

Quraishi-Landes, Asifa. "Five Myths about Sharia." *Washington Post*, June 24, 2016. https://www.washingtonpost.com/opinions /five-myths-about-sharia/2016/06/24/7e3efb7a-31ef-11e6– 8758-d58e76e11b12_story.html ?utm_term=.aaac8f05b65a.

Rabuy, Bernadette, and Daniel Kopf. "Prisons of Poverty: Uncovering the Pre-incarceration Incomes of the Imprisoned." Prisons Policy Initiative, July 9, 2015. https:// www.prisonpolicy.org/reports/income.html.

Raeburn, Paul. "Too Immature for the Death Penalty?" *New York Times*, October 17, 2004. www.nytimes.com/2004/10/17 /magazine/too-immature-for-the-death-penalty.html?_r=0.

Read, Piers Paul. *The Dreyfus Affair: The Story of the Most Infamous Miscarriage of Justice in French History*. London: Bloomsbury, 2012.

Rhode, Deborah. *Access to Justice*. Oxford: Oxford University Press, 2005.

Roediger, David. 2017. *Class, Race, and Marxism*. London: Verso Press.

Rosen, Lawrence. *Law as Culture: An Invitation*. Princeton, NJ: Princeton University Press, 2006.

Sampathkumar, Mythili. "Charleena Lyles: Police Officers Shoot and Kill Pregnant Black Woman after She Reports Burglary." *Independent*, June 19, 2017. www.independent.co.uk/news /world/americas/charleena-lyles-seattle-shooting-pregnant-black-mother-of-four-brettler-family-place-a7797971 .html.

Sarat, Austin, and William L. F. Felstiner. "Law and Social Relations: Vocabularies of Motive in Lawyer/Client Interaction." In *The Law and Society Reader*, edited by Richard Abel, 403– 28. New York: NYU Press, 1995.

Schleeter, Ryan. "As It Happened: Seattle Kayaktivists Blockade Shell's Alaska-Bound Oil Rig." Greenpeace.org, June 15, 2015. www.greenpeace.org/usa/breaking-seattle-kayaktivists-blockade-shells-alaska-bound-oil-rig/.

Schultz, Duane P. *A History of Modern Psychology*. 9th ed. Belmont, CA: Thomas Higher Education, 2008.

Sentencing Project. "Trends in U.S. Corrections." Fact Sheet. January 2016. https://sentencingproject.org/wp-content /uploads/2016/01/Trends-in-US-Corrections.pdf.

Shapiro, Fred R. "The Most Cited Legal Scholars." *Journal of Legal Studies* 29, no. S1 (2000): 409–26.

Shepard, Alicia. "NPR's Giffords Mistake: Re-learning the Lesson of Checking Sources." NPR.org, January 11, 2011. https://www .npr.org/sections/ombudsman/2011/01/11/132812196 /nprs-giffords-mistake-re-learning-the-lesson-of-checking-sources.

Sherkat, D. E., and C. G. Ellison. "Structuring the Religion-Environment Connection: Identifying Religious Influences on Environmental Concern and Activism." *Journal for the Scientific Study of Religion* 46 (2007): 71–85.

Smith, Adam. *An Inquiry into the Nature and Causes of the Wealth of Nations*. Indianapolis, IN: Liberty Classics, 1981.

Spencer, A. Benjamin. "The Law School Critique in Historical Perspective." *Washington and Lee Law Review* 69 (2012): 1949–2063.

Statista.com. "Number of Monthly Active Facebook Users Worldwide as of 4th Quarter 2017 (in millions)." 2018. https://www.statista.com/statistics/264810/number-of-monthly-active-facebook-users-worldwide/.

———. "Number of Monthly Active Twitter Users Worldwide from 1st Quarter 2010 to 4th Quarter 2017 (in millions)." 2018. https://www.statista.com/statistics/282087/number-of-monthly-active-twitter-users/.

———. "Value of Gross Premiums Written by General Liability Insurance Companies in the United States from 2009 to 2025 (in billion U.S. dollars)." Accessed March 12, 2018. https://www.statista.com/statistics/422059/general-liability-insurance-sector-usa/.

Stevens, Robert. "History of the Yale Law School: Provenance and Perspective." In *History of the Yale Law School: The Tercentennial Lectures*, edited by Anthony T. Kronman, 1–16. New Haven, CT: Yale University Press, 2004.

Stone, Christopher. *Should Trees Have Standing? Law, Morality, and the Environment*. 3rd Eed. Oxford: Oxford University Press, 2010.

Switek, Brian. "DNA Shows How the Sweet Potato Crossed the Sea." *Nature*, January 21, 2013. www.nature.com/news/dna-shows-how-the-sweet-potato-crossed-the-sea-1.12257.

Tamanaha, Brian. *Failing Law Schools*. Chicago: University of Chicago Press, 2012.

Taylor, Aaron. "Diversity as a Law School Survival Strategy." Saint Louis University Legal Studies Research Paper No. 2015–1. February 2015. https://ssrn.com/abstract=2569847 or http://dx.doi.org/10.2139/ssrn.2569847.

Tejani, Riaz. *Law Mart: Justice, Access, and For-Profit Law Schools*. Stanford, CA: Stanford University Press, 2017.

———. "Little Black Boxes: Legal Anthropology and the Politics of Autonomy in Tort Law." *University of New Hampshire Law Review* 11 (2013): 129–70.

———. "'A Logic of Camps': French Antiracism as Competitive Nationalism." *Political and Legal Anthropology Review* 38, no. 1 (Spring 2015). https://papers.ssrn.com/sol3/papers.cfm?abstract_id=2602830.

———. "Professional Apartheid: The Racialization of U.S. Law Schools after Global Crisis." *American Ethnologist* 44, no. 3 (2017). https://doi.org/10.1111/amet.12521.

Tocqueville, Alexis de. *Democracy in America*. Vol. 2. Edited by Francis Bowen. Translated by Henry Reeve. Cambridge, MA.: Harvard University Press, 1862.

"Trump Just Passed on the Best Deal the Planet Has Ever Seen." *Guardian*, June 2, 2017. https://www.theguardian.com/commentisfree/2017/jun/01/trump-paris-climate-deal-planet.

Tsing, Anna Lowenhaupt. *The Mushroom at the End of the World: On the Possibility of Life in Capitalist Ruins*. Princeton, NJ: Princeton University Press, 2017.

US Census Bureau. "Overview of Race and Hispanic Origin: 2010." March 2011. https://www.census.gov/content/dam/Census/library/publications/2011/dec/c2010br-02.pdf.

US Courts. "Federal Judicial Caseload Statistics 2017." 2017. www.uscourts.gov/statistics-reports/federal-judicial-caseload-statistics-2017.

US Department of Health and Human Services. "Indicators of Welfare Dependence: Annual Report to Congress, 2008." December 20, 2008. https://aspe.hhs.gov/report/ indicators-welfare-dependence-annual-report-congress-2008.

US Environmental Protection Agency. "Deepwater Horizon—BP Gulf of Mexico Oil Spill." Last updated April 19, 2017. Accessed March 14, 2018. https://www.epa.gov/enforcement/deepwater-horizon-bp-gulf-mexico-oil-spill.

———. "History of Reducing Air Pollution from Transportation in the United States (U.S.)." N.d. Accessed March 14, 2018. https://www.epa.gov/air-pollution-transportation/accomplishments-and-success-air-pollution-transportation.

———. "History of the Clean Water Act." Last updated August 8, 2017. https://www.epa.gov/laws-regulations/history-clean-water-act.

———. "Husqvarna Ab and Husqvarna Consumer Outdoor Products N.A., Inc., Clean Air Act Settlement." N.d. Accessed March 14, 2018. https://www.epa.gov/enforcement /husqvarna-ab-and-husqvarna-consumer-outdoor-products-na-inc-clean-air-act-settlement.

US Internal Revenue Service. "Entities." IRS.gov. N.d. Accessed July 31, 2017. https://www.irs.gov/help-resources/tools-faqs/faqs-for-individuals/frequently-asked-tax-questions-answers/small-business-self-employed-other-business/entities/entities-5.

Wagner, Peter, and Bernadette Rabuy. "Mass Incarceration: The Whole Pie 2017." Prison Policy Initiative, March 14, 2017. https://www.prisonpolicy.org/reports /pie2017.html.

Walpin, Ned. "The New Speed-Up in Habeas Corpus Appeals." Online readings for "The Execution," *Frontline*, PBS. https://www.pbs.org/wgbh/pages/frontline/shows/execution/readings/speed.html.

Watson, Alan. *Legal Transplants: An Approach to Comparative Law*. Athens: University of Georgia Press, 1974.

Watts, Jonathan. "Arctic Warming: Scientists Alarmed by 'Crazy' Temperature Rises." *Guardian*, February 27, 2018. https://www.theguardian.com/environment/2018 /feb/27/arctic-warming-scientists-alarmed-by-crazy-temperature-rises.

Weber, Max. "Politics as a Vocation." In *From Max Weber: Essays in Sociology*, edited by H. H. Gerth and C. Wright Mills, 77–128. New York: Oxford University Press, 1958.

———. *The Protestant Ethic and the Spirit of Capitalism*. by Max Weber, edited by Peter Baehr and Gordon Wells. New York: Penguin Classics, 2002.

———. "The Protestant Sects and the Spirit of Capitalism." In *From Max Weber: Essays in Sociology*, edited and translated by H. H. Gerth and C. Wright Mills, 302–22, 1906. Reprint, New York: Oxford University Press, 1976.

Weir, Richard. "Neighborhood Report: Long Island City; Wall Hits a Patron of Graffiti." *New York Times*, February 15, 1998. www.nytimes.com/1998/02/15/nyregion/neighborhood-report-long-island-city-wall-hits-a-patron-of-graffiti.html.

Weissmann, Jordan. "The Jobs Crisis at Our Best Law Schools Is Much, Much Worse Than You Think." *Atlantic*, April 9, 2013. https://www.theatlantic.com/business/archive/2013/04/the-jobs-crisis-at-our-best'-law-schools-is-much-much-worse-than-you-think/274795/.

Williamson, John. "What Washington Means by Policy Reform." In *Latin American Readjustment: How Much Has Happened?*, edited by John Williamson, 7–20. Washington, DC: Institute for International Economics, 1989.

World Bank. "GDP per Capita, PPP (current international $)." World Development Indicators Database, updated December 16, 2016. http://data.worldbank.org/indicator/NY.GDP.PCAP.PP.CD.

World Wildlife Fund. "How Many Species Are We Losing?" Panda.org, n.d. Accessed March 14, 2018. http://wwf.panda.org/about_our_earth/biodiversity/biodiversity/.

Yardley, Jim. "Chinese Dam Projects Criticized for Their Human Costs." *New York Times,* November 19, 2007. www.nytimes.com/2007/11/19 /world/asia/19dam.html.

Zara, Christopher. "Tom Cruise vs. the Gossip Rags: How Hard Is It to Win a Defamation Case?" *International Business Times,* October 25, 2012.

Zinn, Howard. *A People's History of the United States.* New York: Harper Collins, 2005.

Index